THE
OPTIMUM
NUTRITION
BIBLE

By the same author:

100% Health
Say No to Heart Disease
Balancing Hormones Naturally
Boost Your Immune System
The Whole Health Manual
Elemental Health
Optimum Nutrition
How To Protect Yourself from Pollution
Supernutrition for a Healthy Heart
The Better Pregnancy Diet
Say No to Arthritis
The Fatburner Diet
Living Food
Mental Health and Illness – The Nutrition Connection

THE
OPTIMUM
NUTRITION
BIBLE

PATRICK HOLFORD

THE CROSSING PRESS
FREEDOM, CALIFORNIA

This book is dedicated to you—
the promoter of your own health

For information on bulk purchases or group discounts for this and other Crossing Press titles, please contact our Special Sales Manager at 800/777-1048.
Visit our Web site on the Internet: www.crossingpress.com

The Optimum Nutrition Bible is intended solely for informational and educational purposes and not as medical advice. Please consult a medical or health professional if you have questions about your health.

While the nutritional supplements, in the doses referred to in this book, have been proven to be safe, neither the author nor the publishers accept liability should you choose to self-prescribe. All supplements, especially those containing iron, should be kept out of reach of infants and young children.

Library of Congress Cataloging-in-Publication Data on file
Holford, Patrick.

CONTENTS

PART 4: THE BENEFITS OF OPTIMUM NUTRITION

PART 5: NUTRITION FOR ALL AGES

PART 6: YOUR PERSONAL NUTRITION PROGRAM

Acne—Alcoholism—Allergies—Angina and Atherosclerosis—Arthri-tis—Asthma—Breast Cancer—Bronchitis—Burns, Cuts, and Bruises—Cancer—Candidiasis—Colds and Flu—Colitis—Constipation—Chronic Fatigue—Cystitis—Depression—Dermatitis—Diabetes—Diverticulitis—Ear Infections—Eczema—Gallstones—Gout—Hair Problems—Hang-overs—Hay Fever—Headaches and Migraines—High Blood Pressure—Indigestion—Infections—Infertility—Inflammation—Irritable Bowel Syndrome—Menopausal Symptoms—Muscle Aches and Cramps—Obesity—Osteoporosis—PMS—Prostate Problems—Psoriasis—Schiz-ophrenia—Senility—Sinusitis—Sleeping Problems—Thyroid Problems—Ulcers—Varicose Veins

Vitamins—Minerals—Semi-essential Nutrients

Which Protein Foods—Which Fats and Oils—Which Carbohydrates—How much Fiber—Balancing Acid/Alkaline

Acknowledgments

This book would not have been possible without the help and support of many people. Thanks to Kate Neil for contributing to Part 2, Antony Haynes for contributing to Chapter 24, Susan Clift and Eleanor Burton for their research, Jonathan Phillips, Chris Quayle, Rodney Paull and Dick Vine for their illustrations and charts, Heather James for coordinating all the figures, Jan Shepheard for her proofreading, and Heather Rocklin for her editorial help and advice.

Guide to abbreviations and measures

1 gram(g) = 1000 milligrams (mg) = 1,000,000 micrograms (mcg or μg).
Most vitamins are measured in milligrams or micrograms. Vitamins A, D, and E are also measured in International Units (IUs), a measurement designed to standardize the various forms of these vitamins that have different potencies.

1 mcg of retinol (mcg RE) = 3.3 IUs of vitamin A
1mcgRE of betacarotene = 6 mcg of betacarotene
100 IUs of vitamin D = 2.5 mcg
100 IUs of vitamin E = 67 mg

1 pound (lb) = 16 ounces (oz)   2.2pounds = 1 kilogram (kg)
1 pint = 0.6 liters   1.76 pints = 1 liter
In this book calories means kilocalories (kcals)

References and further sources of information

Hundreds of references from respected scientific literature have been used in writing this book. Details of specific studies referred to are listed on pp. 333–337. Other supporting research for statements made is available from the Lamberts Library at the Institute for Optimum Nutrition (ION) (see p. 338), whose members are free to visit and study there. ION also offers information services, including literature search and library search facilities, for those readers who want to access scientific literature on specific subjects. On p. 331 you will find a list of the best books to read, linked to each chapter, to enable you to dig deeper into the topics covered.

INTRODUCTION

In 1977 I met two extraordinary nutritionists, Brian and Celia Wright. They explained to me, over an enormous bowl of salad and some "soy sausages," followed by a handful of vitamin pills, how most disease was the result of sub-optimum nutrition. I found this hard to swallow, but, being an adventurous spirit, asked them to devise me a diet. There I was, a university student studying psychology, eating a wheat-free, virtually vegetarian diet with masses of fruit and vegetables, and taking a handful of supplements shipped from America since they were not available in Britain at that time. It was a far cry from the usual fish and chips and a pint of bitter! My colleagues, friends, and family thought I was crazy. But I persisted.

Within two months I lost 14 pounds in weight, which has never returned; my skin, which had resembled a lunar landscape, cleared up; my regular migraines virtually vanished; but most noticeable of all was the extra energy. I no longer needed so much sleep, my mind was much sharper and my body full of vitality. I started to investigate this "optimum nutrition." Being a psychology student, I looked up research on the greatest problem in mental health today, schizophrenia. There, in the scientific journals, was clear proof that "optimum nutrition" produced results better than drugs and psychotherapy combined. A pioneer in this field, Dr. Carl Pfeiffer, an American doctor and psychiatrist, was claiming an 80 percent remission rate. I was fascinated, and before long went to America to see for myself.

Pfeiffer, a brilliant man who spent most of his life studying the chemistry of the brain, had a massive heart attack when he was fifty. His chances of surviving were very slim—ten years at the absolute most, and only then if he had a pacemaker fitted. He decided not to, and spent his next thirty years pursuing and researching optimum nutrition. "It is my firmly held belief," he told me, "that with an adequate intake of micro-nutrients—essential substances we need to nourish us—most chronic diseases would not exist. Good nutritional therapy is the medicine of the future. We have already waited too long for it."

The optimum nutrition approach is not new: many great visionaries have embraced it. In A.D. 390 Hippocrates said, "Let food be your medicine and medicine be your food." Edison in the early twentieth century said, "The doctor of the future will give no medicine but will interest his patients in the care of the human frame, diet, and the cause and prevention of disease." In 1960 one of the geniuses of our time, twice Nobel prize winner Dr. Linus Pauling, coined the phrase "orthomolecular nutrition." By giving the body the right (ortho) molecules, he asserted, most disease would be eradicated. "Optimum nutrition," he said, "is the medicine of tomorrow."

In 1984 I founded the Institute for Optimum Nutrition in London to research and promote this idea. We extolled the virtues of healthy eating and vitamin supplements; we warned of the dangers of lead in gasoline, additives in food, pollutants in water, of fried food and free radicals; and we explained the value of antioxidant vitamins A, C, and E, and minerals such as selenium and zinc, and the link between nutrition, mental health, and behavior. It is gratifying that many of these concepts have since been taken to heart. Lead in gasoline and additives in food are on the way out, tighter controls on pollutants in water on the way in. Governments are now funding research into the optimal intake of vitamins A, C, and E to prevent cancer and heart disease. Nutrition is creeping on to the agenda for dealing with mental health problems, including criminal behavior. Optimum nutrition is, it seems, an idea whose time has come.

The purpose of this book is to show you how to achieve vibrant health and resistance to disease through optimum nutrition. Part 1 explains the principles of optimum nutrition, which necessitates a whole new definition of health, health care, and medicine. Part 2 defines the perfect diet—not easy to acquire overnight, but good to aspire to. Parts 3, 4, and 5 prove the benefits of optimum nutrition based on the latest breakthroughs in nutritional science. Part 6 shows you how to put optimum nutrition into practice with a step-by-step guide to help you improve your diet and design your own supplement program. Part 7 is an A to Z guide to specific health problems and how to heal them with optimum nutrition. Part 8 is an A to Z guide to nutrients: what they do, signs and causes of deficiency, what to eat, and what to supplement. Part 9 gives you food facts and tables to help put optimum nutrition into practice.

Twenty years have passed since I discovered optimum nutrition. In that time thousands of scientific papers have been published proving its potency, and virtually none that negate it. I am now completely convinced that the concept of optimum nutrition is the greatest step forward in medicine this century, and, if applied from an early age, is a guarantee for a long and healthy life.

1

HEALTH—WHO WANTS TO BE AVERAGE?

This book is a means to a goal—health. And that means not just an absence of disease, but an abundance of vitality. Positive health, sometimes called functional health, can be measured in three ways:

- Performance—how you perform physically and mentally
- Absence of ill-health—disease signs and symptoms
- Longevity—healthy life span

I believe the experience of a profound sense of well being can be achieved by everyone. It is characterized by a consistent, clear, high level of energy, emotional balance, a sharp mind, a desire to maintain physical fitness, and a direct awareness of what suits our bodies, what enhances our health, and what our needs are in any given moment. This state of health includes resilience to infectious diseases and protection from the major killer diseases such as heart disease and cancer. As a result the aging process is slowed down and we can live a long and healthy life. At its most profound level, health is not merely the absence of pain or tension, but a joy in living, a real appreciation of what it is to have a healthy body with which to taste the many pleasures of this world.

For me, this is not just a belief but an experience which I have had personally and have also witnessed in many other people with whom I have worked over the years since I started to pursue optimum nutrition. Health has not been a static state, but an endless journey of learning about myself from the diseases and imbalances that I have suffered, and a continuing discovery of even higher and clearer levels of energy. From these experiences, and those gained through working with thousands of people suffering from all categories of disease, I am totally convinced that, by means of optimum nutrition, exercise, living in the right environment, and being willing to change obsolete beliefs and behavior patterns that create tension and stress, virtually all disease can be eliminated without recourse to drugs or surgery.

HEALTH CARE — THE FASTEST-GROWING FAILING BUSINESS

Nothing in Western culture really teaches us to be healthy. Apart from a little wisdom imparted by our parents, most of whom spend their later years in increasing pain, we are not taught how to be healthy at elementary school, at college, or by the media. Government campaigns may advise against smoking and drinking, but there is little real guidance and few results. Each year in the U.S. alone we consume 200 million alcoholic drinks and 487 billion cigarettes.

What we call "health care" is really "disease care." Described by Dr. Emanuel Cheraskin, Emeritus Professor at the University of Alabama Medical School, as "the fastest-growing failing business," modern medicine is failing to provide true health care and making a lot of money out of it. It is, says Cheraskin, "primary prevention of health deterioration."

Take heart disease as an example. Currently, you have a 50 percent chance of acquiring heart disease during your life. It accounts for a quarter of all deaths before the age of sixty-five, and one in four men have a heart attack before they retire from work. It is well accepted that high blood pressure is the leading warning of serious cardiovascular problems. Conventional medicine recommends weight loss and drugs to lower high blood pressure, but little attention is paid to the many dietary factors also known to achieve this end. Even 1000 mg of vitamin C can significantly lower blood pressure, yet this is rarely recommended. A mere 500 mg of vitamin E reduces the risk of a heart attack in those with cardiovascular disease by 75 percent, according to a large-scale placebo-controlled trial undertaken at Cambridge University Medical School.[1]

Contrary to popular belief, the risk of death from many common types of cancer is increasing, not declining. Consider breast cancer, which accounts for one-third of all cancer diagnosed in women. If treatment was working, women with breast cancer would live longer and be at less risk of dying. We are told that, in the last thirty years, the survival rate has increased from 60 to 75 percent. However, the death rate from cancer over the same period has steadily increased. All that has happened is that people are being diagnosed earlier, and so appear to survive longer. We are losing the cancer war, not winning.

According to medical expert Dr. John Lee, breast cancer is occurring more frequently and earlier in women's lives compared to the mid-1980s. Mammograms show microcalcifications in the breasts which could never have been picked up before. The usual treatment is surgery followed by the drug Tamoxifen, yet medicated and non-medicated patients do just as well. Dr. Lee believes the major cause of breast cancer is "unopposed estrogen," (normally balanced in the body with progesterone), and there are many factors that would lead to this situation. Stress, for example, raises levels of the hormone cortisol which competes with progesterone. Xenoestrogens from the environment, found in pesticides and plastics among other common sources, can damage tissue and lead to increased cancer risk later in life. Clearly there are also nutritional elements to consider. Yet doctors continue to prescribe unopposed estrogen for women on hormone-related therapy. Dr. Bergkvists' study in Scandinavia showed that if a woman is on HRT for longer than five years she doubles her risk of breast cancer.[2] A study by Emery University School of Public Health followed 240,000 women for eight years and found that the risk of fatal ovarian cancer was 72 percent higher in women given estrogen.[3]

Taking another example, by the age of sixty, nine in every ten people have arthritis. Once the level of pain is unbearable, sufferers are recommended steroidal or non-steroidal anti-inflammatory drugs. While both classes of drugs reduce the pain and swelling, they also speed up the progression of the disease. In the US, non-steroidal anti-inflammatory drugs are a $9.5 billion industry—$5 billion for the drugs and $4.5 billion for treating the side-effects. Thousands of people die from the side effects of these drugs alone. Yet there are proven, safe nutritional alternatives that have as great an anti-inflammatory effect without the harmful side effects.

Put all these and other risks into the health equation and it is easy to understand why the average person today is destined to live a measly seventy-five years and spend the last twenty in poor health, when it is an established medical fact that a healthy human life span should be at least a hundred years. And the sad truth is that the statistics are not getting any better. For all our advances in drugs, surgical procedures, and medical technology, a forty-five year-old man today can expect to live for only two more years than the same man in 1920—until seventy-four, instead of seventy-two. Conventional approaches to health care are clearly barking up the wrong tree. Perhaps what is needed is a new tree.

THE NEW IDEA OF HEALTH

Instead of thinking of the body as a machine, and disease as a spanner in the works that must be removed or destroyed with drugs or surgery, medical scientists are now beginning to look at human beings as "complex adaptive systems," more like a self-organizing jungle than a complicated computer. Rather than trying to "control" a person's health by playing God with hi-tech medicine, a new way of looking at health has emerged that considers a

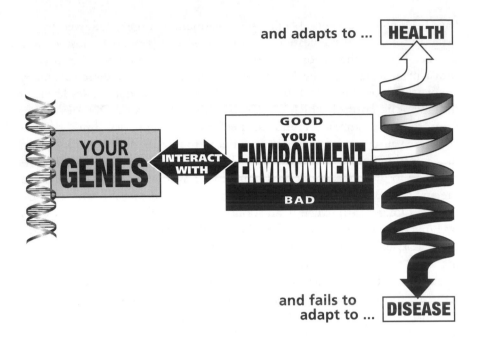

The path to health or disease

human being as a whole, with an interconnected mind and body designed to adapt to health if the circumstances are right.

Of course, this adaptive capacity is not the same for everyone. We are each born with different strengths and weaknesses and different levels of resilience—some of us have what is popularly called "good genes" or come from "good stock," and some of us do not. So, according to this new concept, our health is a result of the interaction between our inherited adaptive capacity and our circumstances. On a physical/chemical level, for example, that interaction would be between our genes and our environment. If our environment is sufficiently hostile (bad diet, pollution, exposure to viruses, allergens, etc.) we exceed our ability to adapt and get sick.

Going back to cancer, we know that the risk is higher if we smoke, regularly drink alcohol, eat meat, take certain drugs and hormones, and are exposed to exhaust fumes and other pollutants—to name a few. The risks, on the other hand, are lower if we have a high intake of certain vegetables, fiber, antioxidant vitamins such as beta-carotene, C, and E, and live in an unpolluted environment. Evidence shows that, when the pluses significantly outweigh the minuses, health can be restored.

Genes and the environment are like the chicken and the egg. Science is proving that our genes are influenced by the environment in which we have evolved. Similarly, how we interact with our environment—for example, our ability to digest certain nutrients—depends on our genetics. I believe that the future of medicine will focus primarily on genetics and on environmental medicine, of which nutrition plays a major part, as the means to influence health. Genes, however, are harder to change than diet, so it is likely that nutrition will form the major part of the new approach to health care, along with strategies to reduce "anti-nutrients"—substances, such as environmental pollutants, pesticides, and chemical food additives, which all interfere with the action of nutrients.

Remember, we are always being challenged—be it the neighbor's cold, or unavoidable exhaust fumes. What we take into our body—be it healthy food, drink, drugs, or junk—can dramatically affect our ability to stay healthy.

2

DEFINING OPTIMUM NUTRITION

Most of us are unwitting students of the Breakfast Cereal School of Nutrition. Morning after morning we stare at the cereal packet, reading, "…RDAs…one serving provides…thiamine, riboflavin, niacin," and, together with other clever advertising, this assures us that our reasonably well-balanced diet will give us everything we need. It is, however, the greatest lie in health care today—a belief based on wrong information and a complete misconception of the nature of the human body.

MAN AS MACHINE

The concept of the body as a machine is a product of the thinking of philosophers such as Newton and Descartes and of the industrial revolution, which envisioned a clockwork universe and man as a thinking machine. Until a couple of hundred years ago our ancestors had spent millions of years being hunter-gatherer's and ten thousand years being peasant farmers, only to be propelled, as many country people were, into the new towns and cities to fuel the need for labor during the industrial revolution. The diet that the new industrial workers were fed consisted of fat, sugar, and refined flour. A cookie or cake is a good example. Flour was refined so that it would not support weevils and, like refined sugar and saturated fat, did not go bad. These cheap, energy-providing foods were considered "fuel" in the same way that a car needs gasoline. Not surprisingly, health declined. By about 1900 people had started to be smaller than in earlier generations. This led to the discovery of protein—the factor in food needed for growth. Sugar for energy, protein for muscle. With this concept the Western diet of high sugar, fat, and protein was born.

Yet people were still sick and, one by one, the classic vitamin deficiency diseases such as scurvy and rickets were solved as new vitamins were discovered. The importance of minerals was also established, but all these vital nutrients were still dealt with in a very mechanical way. All each person needed was the Recommended Daily Allowance (RDA) of each nutrient—a level considered to be sufficient to protect the body against deficiency diseases. Yet, according to Dr. Jeffrey Bland, world-renowned nutritional biochemist and former professor of chemistry, "the RDAs have absolutely no relevance to individual nutritional assessment. They are standards of identity to meet the needs of practically all healthy people to prevent the known nutrition disorders beriberi, pellagra, scurvy, kwashiorkor, rickets, and marasmus. They have nothing to do with the common disorders of Western society."

FOOD, GENES, ENVIRONMENT, AND DISEASE

Your body is composed entirely from molecules derived from food. In a lifetime you will eat 100 tons of food, which is broken down by enzyme-rich secretions in the digestive tract produced at a rate of about 10 liters per day. Macronutrients (fat, protein, carbohydrate) and micronutrients (vitamins, minerals) are absorbed through the digestive tract, whose health and integrity depends fundamentally on what you eat. Your nutritional status determines, to a substantial extent, your capacity to adapt and maintain health. Biochemical imbalances resulting from sub-optimum nutrition experienced over generations are recorded and expressed genetically as strengths and weaknesses of specific body processes. Your genes express themselves in your environment (food, air, water, and so on.) If your environment is too hostile for them, you cannot adapt and disease results. If your environment is nourishing, you have a greater resistance to disease and are more likely to experience health and vitality.

WHAT DOES OPTIMUM NUTRITION MEAN?

Optimum nutrition is very simply giving yourself the best possible intake of nutrients to allow your body to be as healthy as possible and to work as well as it can. It is not a set of rules. For example, you do not have to be vegetarian or take supplements or not eat any particular food, although for some people such advice would be appropriate. Your needs are completely unique and depend on a whole host of factors, from the strengths and weaknesses that you were born with right up to the effects that your current environment has on you. You only have to look at the tremendous variation in the way we look, our talents and personalities to realize that our nutritional needs are not likely to be identical. No one diet is perfect for everyone, although there are general guidelines that apply to us all.

Your optimum nutrition is the intake of nutrients that

- promotes your optimal mental performance and emotional balance
- promotes your optimal physical performance

- is associated with the lowest incidence of ill-health
- is associated with the longest healthy life span

To date, fifty nutrients have been identified as essential for health. Your health can be promoted and maintained at the highest level by achieving your optimal intake of each nutrient every single day. Gradually your entire body, including your skeleton, is rebuilt and rejuvenated. Through optimum nutrition you can

- improve mental clarity and concentration
- increase IQ
- increase physical performance
- improve quality of sleep
- improve resistance to infections
- protect yourself from disease
- extend your healthy life span

These might sound like bold claims, yet each has been proven by proper scientific research. Recently I called two doctors who had been in general

The Fifty Essential Nutrients

Fats	Amino Acids	Minerals	Vitamins	Plus
Linoleic acid	Leucine	Calcium	A (retinol)	Carbohydrate
Linolenic acid	Lysine	Magnesium	B1 (thiamine)	Fibre
	Isoleucine	Phosphorus	B2 (riboflavin)	Light
	Threonine	Potassium	B3 (niacin)	Oxygen
	Tryptophan	Sodium	B5 (pantothenic acid)	Water
	Methionine	Sulphur	B6 (pyridoxine)	
	Valine	Iron	B12 (cyanocobalamine)	
	Phenylalanine	Zinc	Folic acid	
	Histidine	Copper	Biotin	
		Manganese	C	
		Chromium	D	
		Selenium	E	
		Cobalt	K	
		Fluorine		
		Silicon		
		Iodine		
		Molybdenum		
		?Vanadium		
		?Arsenic		
		?Nickel		
		?Tin		

Note:. Minerals preceded by a question mark are thought to be essential although studies have not yet confirmed this.

practice for many years before discovering the optimum nutrition approach. One told me, "I'm convinced that nutrition will be a major part of medicine in the foreseeable future. I'm getting substantially better results with diet and supplements than I used to with drugs." The other, a general practitioner in Dublin, said, "The evidence for nutritional therapy is becoming so strong that if the doctors of today don't become nutritionists, the nutritionists will become the doctors of tomorrow."

DISCOVER YOUR OPTIMUM NUTRITION

Old-fashioned concepts of nutrition assess your needs by analyzing what you eat and comparing it to the RDA for each nutrient. This method is very basic since RDAs do not exist for a number of key nutrients, have little relevance to what is needed for optimal health, and do not take into account individual variations in need, or lifestyle factors that alter your needs, such as exposure to pollution, level of stress, or exercise.

This book will enable you to assess your optimum nutrition using three proven methods, each of which represents a piece of the jigsaw for calculating your needs. The more methods that can be used, the more effective will be the resultant nutritional plan. In addition, nutrition consultants have access to biochemical tests to find out more precisely what a person's nutritional needs are. The three methods listed below also take into account four key principles—evolutionary dynamics, biochemical individuality, synergy, and environmental load—that are fundamental to the optimum nutrition approach and are explained in the following chapters.

Symptom analysis

This enables you to see, from clusters of signs and symptoms (such as lack of energy, mouth ulcers, muscle cramps, easy bruising, poor dream recall, etc.) which nutrients you may be lacking.

Lifestyle analysis

This helps you to identify the factors in your life that change your nutritional needs (such as your level of exercise, stress, pollution, etc.).

Dietary analysis

This compares your diet not with RDAs but with optimal levels of nutrients, and takes into account the "anti-nutrients" that you consume— substances that rob the body of nutrients.

3

FROM MONKEYS TO MAN— NUTRITION AND EVOLUTION

You are much older than you think. The human body you walk around in is the result of millions of years of evolution, the vast majority of which was spent living in an environment and eating a diet very different from those of today. Understanding the dynamics of our evolution can provide essential clues for promoting health.

TO C OR NOT TO C?

Take the case of vitamin C. Practically all animals make it in their bodies, so they do not have to eat it. The exceptions are guinea pigs, fruit-eating bats, the red-vented bulbul bird, and primates, including man. Most animals produce the equivalent of 3000 to 16,000 mg per day—a little different from the RDA of 60 mg and more consistent with the levels known to boost immunity and minimize the risk of cancer. In fact, vitamin C-producing animals are immune to some cancers and viral diseases.

Linus Pauling postulated that we used to make vitamin C but, through eating a fruit-rich diet, lost the ability because we could get enough from our food. Indeed, one characteristic shared by us and other species which have lost the ability is our previously high fruit diet. But now most humans live in a *concrete* jungle and are prone to vitamin C deficiency, as illustrated by the high incidence of infections and diseases which are associated with poorly functioning immune systems. While a gorilla can eat 3000 mg a day (66 oranges), children eat, on average, one piece of fruit a week, while the average adult intake of vitamin C is around 50 mg. This low level contradicts our evolutionary design and is simply not enough for optimal health. Since humans in all age groups are smaller than gorillas, eating 22 oranges might be more appropriate—but taking a vitamin C tablet is a lot easier!

HOMO AQUATICUS

One of the great mysteries of human evolution concerns how we became upright and developed complex brains, manual dexterity, and the ability to use language. We have a brain which is ten times larger, in relation to body mass, than almost all other animals alongside which we have evolved. While it is accepted that we share many characteristics with tree-dwelling primates, for example, the "gripping" reflex of infant chimps and humans that is good for swinging on branches, how did we develop the characteristics that make us human?

One theory which is rapidly gaining credence in scientific circles is that our early ancestors may have picked the best neighborhood as far as nutrition was concerned. According to Professor Michael Crawford and David Marsh, authors of *Nutrition and Evolution*, the environment in which a species develops is a major factor in determining its evolution. Derek Ellis, Professor of Biology at the University of Victoria in Canada, believes that for a critical period in our ancestors' evolution they exploited the nutrient-rich environment of the water's edge, eating shellfish, crustaceans, and fish, and therefore consumed the high levels of essential fats and nutrients needed to develop modern man's complex brain and nervous system which is paralleled only in aquatic mammals.[4]

This would certainly explain the one big chemical difference between human brains and those of other animals—the high concentration of complex essential fats which make up a large part of the human brain. According to Elaine Morgan and Marc Verhaegen, this may also explain why we became upright, lost our hair, and developed a layer of subcutaneous fat, making humans one of the few species prone to obesity.[5] They believe that early man may have needed to wade in water to access the food supply. In the course of time these characteristics would have allowed us to survive better in a semi-aquatic environment.

This theory can also explain the extraordinary "diving reflex" of an infant in the first six months of life. If dropped into water an infant will submerge, stop breathing, slow down its heart rate, then re-emerge, turn its head to the side, breathe, and dive again. This reflex is similar to that of aquatic mammals like dolphins—whose flippers, incidentally, contain every single bone that we have in our arms and hands. The evidence suggests that they evolved on land, then returned to the sea to stay there. Ever wondered what it is you love about being in water?

CLUES FROM THE PAST—HOPE FOR THE FUTURE

While these theories have yet to gain widespread acceptance, supporters of the "Homo aquaticus" theory, such as Professor Michael Crawford, a zoologist now specializing in brain biochemistry, have shown that, for proper mental development, infants need a very high level of the essential fats found in fish. These fats, formerly excluded from formula milk for babies, are now being added after recommendations from the World Health Organization. Other sources for these essential fats are seeds and their oils, vital for both infants and mothers. Breast-feeding mothers who are "fat-phobic" for fear of gaining weight need to eat seafood or seeds and their oils, both for their own health and to support the development of their child's brain.

OUT OF SYNC WITH NATURE

In many ways modern living goes against the grain of millions of years of evolution. For instance, if you jolt into action in the morning to the sound of the alarm clock and head on remote control for the kitchen, with neither brain nor body responding, to make a strong cup of coffee or smoke a cigarette, followed by two pieces of toast with marmalade and a glass of orange juice, you, like most people, are living out of line with your natural design. The result can be poor concentration, insomnia, fluctuating "highs" and "lows," energy drops, food cravings, uneven weight, feelings of stress and, inevitably, life-threatening illness.

Our ancestors had no alarm clocks. At dawn light enters through the eyes and translucent portions of the skull to stimulate the pineal and pituitary glands, which in turn stimulate the adrenal glands to release adrenalin into the bloodstream. As adrenalin levels rise we wake up naturally, refreshed and alert. Not so if you wake in the dark to the sound of the alarm clock. Instead of allowing the body to respond naturally we load in a stimulant like caffeine or nicotine. The effect on the body is adrenalin overload. Sure, you wake up—but the body's chemistry scrambles to produce hormones such as insulin and glucagon to restabilize soaring blood sugar levels. So let the light in and get up early if you want to experience more energy.

GRAZING OR GORGING?

Nor are we really designed to eat as soon as we wake up. Little digestion will have occurred when the body was asleep. It is better not to eat until you are totally awake, perhaps an hour after waking. Another way to encourage the body to wake up is to have a brief cold shower after a hot shower, which stimulates circulation and digestion. Even then, most people function better on easy-to-digest carbohydrate-based breakfasts such as fruit or cereal, rather than high-protein cooked breakfasts.

Breakfast—in fact all meals—should be light. We are designed to graze, not gorge. Large meals are hard to digest and can result in indigestion and sleepiness. Our ancestors ate when hungry, not at set times, nor as emotional compensation. Studies comparing the effects of eating little and often, compared to two or three large meals a day, have consistently shown that better health is the result of small, frequent meals.[6] Just as our jungle ancestors did, this means snacking on fresh fruit—three to four pieces a day between (smaller) meals. Doing this also helps to keep our blood sugar levels even, resulting in more consistent energy, moods, and concentration.

Exercise is another great appetite stabilizer. People with sedentary lifestyles tend to have poor appetite control and will actually eat more calories compared to their expenditure than those with active lifestyles. Physical activity appears to be essential to balance appetite in line with body needs.

AGAINST THE GRAIN

Modern man's pattern of eating has totally changed, and so too has the food we select. Primates are designed to run on carbohydrates and have a naturally sweet tooth. However, we have learned to cheat nature and isolate the sweetness, sugar, from foods, as well as choosing foods with concentrated sweetness such as juice, dried fruit and honey. These foods are too sweet for the body to deal with. A natural diet limits all concentrated sugars, whether called honey, malt, or sucrose, choosing whole foods with their sweetness intact, and limits dried fruit unless it is soaked or eaten in small quantities with a slow-releasing carbohydrate food, such as oats. Fruit juices, too, are best either limited or diluted with water.

Our distant ancestors ate no dairy products or grains. Grains only started to be cultivated ten thousand years ago and some scientists believe that we have not yet adapted to tolerate them, unlike ruminant animals which live off grasses and grains. This may explain why grain allergy is so widespread. Of all the grains, wheat is the number one culprit. Modern wheat is also very different from the wheat that grew in the Bronze Age. A substance called gluten, which contains an intestinal irritant called gliadin, comprises 78 percent of the total protein in modern wheat. When yeast reacts with sugar, gluten is activated to produce "a lighter loaf." Goods news for the profits of baking companies since the material costs are lower, but bad news for our intestines. Adverse reactions to bread are far more common than to pasta, which is made from "hard" wheat with a lower gluten content.

RAW OR COOKED?

Another relatively recent addition to the kitchen is heat. Mankind discovered fire four hundred thousand years ago, but even then still ate most food raw. For millions of years before then, everything was raw. Cooking changes the molecules in food and destroys many valuable nutrients and the enzymes that break food down into components that can be used by the body, so a natural diet includes a lot of food which is raw or only very lightly cooked. Raw food requires more chewing, which not only breaks down food, mixing it with digestive enzymes in the mouth, but also sends signals to the digestive tract to enable the right cocktail of digestive enzymes to be produced, depending on what is in the mouth. Most fast food is soft food that requires minimal chewing; as a result, modern man's jaw is smaller than that of his ancestors.

THE EVOLUTIONARY DIET

What you have just read are a few examples of the principle of **evolutionary dynamics**, which is fundamental to the optimum nutrition approach. They also illustrate clearly how modern man is digging his own grave with a knife and fork, choosing high-sugar, high-fat, highly processed, and synthetic food.

By investigating what our ancestors ate and how our bodies have adapted to these foods, we can pick up vital clues about the kind of nutrition that is likely to promote our health. Current theories suggest that early primate evolution took place in the jungle, which provided a carbohydrate-rich diet of fruit and other vegetation. This diet would have provided substantially larger amounts of vitamins and minerals than our modern diet does. For example, the estimated intake of vitamin A in those times, principally from beta-carotene, is around 50,000 IUs a day, which is 20 times more than today's average.

By studying evolution it also becomes clear that the environment we choose determines our diet, which alters our design and prospects for future survival. Mankind now has the ability to manipulate the environment in ways never before possible, and we can choose exactly what we eat. Will we choose to nourish ourselves in a way that does not plunder the resources of the earth? Or will we continue to pollute, overpopulate, and plunder the earth? If we choose the latter the earth and those species best adapted to the changes will continue to exist, but humanity may not. If we choose the former, what a wonderful world this could be. Good planets are, after all, hard to find.

Here are a few simple tips to help you conform with your natural design:

- Get up earlier in summer and later in winter, in line with natural sunlight hours. Don't eat late at night, or before you're fully awake.

- Eat when you are hungry, not out of habit. Graze rather than gorge. Eat little and often, with plenty of fruit as snacks in between.

- Eat a mainly vegan diet, with half your intake of food consisting of fruit, vegetables, seed sprouts, nuts, and seeds. If you do eat meat, avoid the intensively reared kind. Choose fish or organic game instead. Eat these foods only with vegetables.

- Eat food as raw and unprocessed as possible. Avoid synthetic chemicals.

- Avoid concentrated foods such as sugar and sweeteners. Dilute fruit juices. Drink plenty of water.

- Minimize your intake of dairy foods, refined wheat, and grains.

- Exercise frequently and keep active.

4

YOU ARE UNIQUE

There is nobody quite like you. There are many principles that apply to us all as members of the human race—for example, we all need vitamins; but the actual amount we need for peak performance varies from individual to individual. It depends on the evolutionary dynamics that you have inherited from your parents, together with genetically inherited strengths and weaknesses, and the interaction of your genetics with your environment right through fetal development and early infancy. The complex interaction of these factors ensures that each individual is born biochemically unique, although clearly similar to other individuals.

This principle, called **biochemical individuality**, was first succinctly proposed by Dr. Roger Williams in 1956. Dr. Williams also discovered vitamin B5 (pantothenic acid) and helped isolate pantothenic acid. He was one of the grandfathers of optimum nutrition. True to form, he was actively teaching, writing, and researching into his nineties. In his book *Biochemical Individuality* he showed how in each one of us our organs are different shapes and sizes, how we have different levels of enzymes, and different needs for protein, vitamins, and minerals. A ten-fold difference in the requirement for vitamins from one person to the next is not at all uncommon. For example, a comparison of the level of vitamin A in the blood of ninety-two individuals, most of whom were on a very similar diet, found a thirty-fold difference. Repeated testing revealed that individuals' blood level of vitamin A stayed remarkably consistent, although the levels from individual to individual varied considerably.[7] This suggests a wide range of need for vitamin A.

Some of us have difficulty digesting protein or fat, or need more of a particular vitamin than the average diet can supply. This is well illustrated by the vitamin deficiency disease pellagra, whose symptoms include mental illness, sometimes accompanied by digestive and skin problems. For most people a mere 10 mg of vitamin B3 (niacin) will prevent pellagra. That is the amount you would find in a serving of rice or a handful of peanuts. Yet Dr. Abram Hoffer, psychiatric research director for part of Canada, found that many patients diagnosed with schizophrenia got better and stayed better only when given 1000 mg or more a day.[8] These people needed a hundred times more than the average level to stay healthy.

Once again this kind of information makes a mockery of Recommended Daily Allowances (RDAs), nicknamed "Ridiculous Dietary Arbitraries" by Dr. Stephen Davies, a leading nutrition researcher in London. How do you know if these government-set averages, which vary from country to country, are the right amounts for you?

FROM THE CRADLE TO THE GRAVE

What happens during pregnancy and early childhood has a profound effect on health in later life. In fact the risk of cardiovascular disease increases substantially for those whose birth weight is low, according to research by Professor Barker at the Medical Research Council Environmental Epidemiology Unit in Southampton.[9] Professor Derek Bryce-Smith from the University of Reading found that, simply by analyzing the level of lead, cadmium, and zinc in placental tissue, he could predict with remarkable accuracy the birth weight and head circumference of a newborn baby.[10] That means that if your mother was exposed to exhaust fumes containing lead, or to cigarette smoke which contains cadmium, or was zinc-deficient, it will have taken its toll on you. Professor Bryce-Smith concluded from his research that any child born below a weight of 6.9 lbs should be investigated for sub-optimum nutrition.

ONE MAN'S FOOD...

According to the Royal College of Physicians, one in ten people suffer from allergies. In reality the figure is probably closer to one in three, with foods being the most common provokers of allergic symptoms. As Lucretius said in 50 B.C., "One man's food is another man's poison."

Most of the symptoms do not occur immediately after eating an offending food, but creep up on you over twenty-four hours, so it is easy to live for years without knowing that a particular food does not suit you. What is more, many people may never have felt truly healthy, so do not even know that how they feel is under par.

These are just a few examples that illustrate how each person's optimum nutrition is likely to be slightly different from anyone else's. This book will give you the opportunity to investigate the major lifestyle factors that shape your nutritional needs and to assess your personal nutritional needs on the basis of your symptoms, not on some arbitrary general guideline. From then on it is a matter of educated trial and error, and noticing which foods make you feel good and which take your energy away.

Symptoms Linked to Food Allergy

Anxiety	Celiac disease	Diarrhea	Insomnia
Arthritis	Colitis	Ear infections	Learning disorders
Asthma	Crohn's disease	Eczema	Multiple sclerosis
Attention deficit	Depression	Hay fever	Rhinitis
Bedwetting	Dermatitis	Headaches	Sleep disorders
Bronchitis	Diabetes	Inflammatory bowel	Tonsillitis
Chronic fatigue		disease	
syndrome			

Here are a few simple tips to help you work with your biochemical individuality:

- Notice after which meals you feel worse. Look for the common foods, eliminate for two weeks, then see how you feel.

- Just because others can tolerate a certain food does not mean that you can.

- Assess your own nutritional needs (see Part 6) and supplement the recommended nutrients until you are feeling healthy, full of energy, and symptom-free.

- Find out what lifestyle works best for you and adjust your life accordingly.

- If you have a family history of particular health problems, pay particular attention to the prevention tips in this book and adjust your nutrition accordingly.

- Listen to your body. It will tell you more than all the experts.

SYNERGY—THE WHOLE
IS GREATER

The science fiction of the 1960s envisaged a future in which mankind would simply eat pills or powder containing the finite number of nutrients proved to be essential for the human machine to function. Yet, as each decade passes, we learn more and more about the complexities of the human body and nutrition. Of the fifty currently known essential nutrients (see p. 8), all interact with other nutrients and can be said to work in **synergy**.

Knowing this, it would be unrealistic to deprive a body of one nutrient, for experimental purposes, or to prescribe one nutrient for the treatment of disease. For example, deficiencies of vitamin B6, B12, folic acid, iron, zinc, and manganese can all contribute to anemia. Indeed, in some circumstances prescribing one nutrient can exacerbate deficiency of another. Iron is, for example, a zinc antagonist. Both are frequently deficient. Prescribing excessive amounts of iron exacerbates an undiagnosed or untreated zinc deficiency. Since zinc is a critical nutrient for fetal development, this could have serious detrimental effects during pregnancy.

GREATER THAN THE SUM OF THE PARTS

Some nutrients simply will not work without their synergistic mates. Vitamin B6, pyridoxine, is useless in the body until it is converted into pyridoxal-5-phosphate, a job done by a zinc-dependent enzyme. If you are zinc-deficient and take a vitamin B6 supplement to help relieve PMS, it will not make any difference. Studies have shown that giving women both zinc and B6 relieves the symptoms of PMS much more effectively.

Yet the vast majority of research in nutrition has looked at the effects on health of a single nutrient. The results are not comparable with the effects of giving a person optimum nutrition, the right balance of all essential nutrients. For instance, there is little evidence that individual vitamins or minerals can increase IQ scores in children. However, the combination of all vitamins and minerals, even if given only at RDA levels, has consistently shown a four- to five-point increase in children's IQ scores.[11] If vitamin E

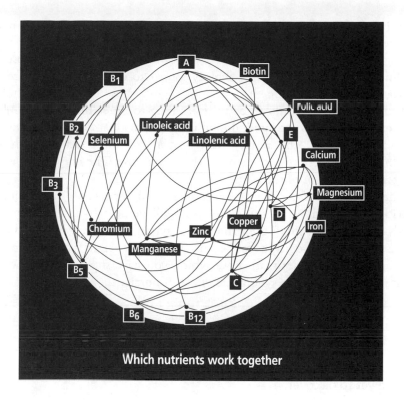

Which nutrients work together

alone can reduce the risk of a heart attack by 75 percent, as shown by Professor Morris Brown from Cambridge University Medical School,[1] what might be the results of giving those at risk optimum nutrition—the ideal diet plus supplements, including all the nutrients known to improve cardiovascular health? One ten-year study which followed 11,178 people between the ages of 67 and 105 found that those who supplemented vitamin E during that time reduced the incidence of death by 33 percent and the risk of death from a heart attack by 47 percent.[12] Those who supplemented both vitamin E and vitamin C reduced overall risk of death by 42 percent and risk of death from a heart attack by 52 per cent. Studies that have measured the effects of multinutrient programs on health consistently get better results than those which use nutrients in isolation.

In fact your need for nutrients may be substantially less if given in the right combination. Consider this experiment, carried out to test the memory-improving effects of two nutrients—choline and piracetam, a derivative of the amino acid pyroglutamate, marketed as a drug.[13] The researchers, led by Raymond Bartus, used aging rats, which are well known for their memory decline in later life.

The rats were divided into four groups, given either a placebo, choline (100 mcg/kg) or piracetam (100 mg/kg), and then placed in a box with two chambers—one lit, one dark. Rats prefer the dark chamber and normally take less than twenty seconds to enter it. This time, on arrival they were given a mild electric shock in the feet. On return to the box those on choline or piracetam took only slightly longer to enter the dark chamber, indicating slight improvement in memory, while those taking both choline and piracetam took nearly three times as long to enter the dark chamber. The experiment was repeated, doubling the individual dose of choline or piracetam, and still the results were not nearly so good as with the combination of these two nutrients at the lower dose. The combination was greater than the sum of the parts.

The principle of synergy is a fundamental aspect of the optimum nutrition approach. With this book you will be able to assess your own needs taking into account the principle of synergy. You may achieve better results by eating the right foods and taking the right combination of nutrients at lower doses than those which you have supplemented before. Such is the power of the synergistic effect of nutrients.

Here are a few tips to bear in mind:

- There is no substitute for whole foods, which contain hundreds of health-promoting substances, the importance of many of which we have yet to discover.

- Eat a varied diet, choosing from a wide range of different kinds of food.

- Do not supplement your diet with individual nutrients without also taking a good all-round multivitamin and mineral supplement.

- Do not take a large amount of an individual B vitamin without also taking a B complex or a multivitamin.

- Do not supplement your diet with a large amount of an antioxidant nutrient (e.g. vitamin C or E) without also taking a good all-round antioxidant formula.

Anti-nutrients—Avoiding the Vitamin Robbers

Optimum nutrition is not just about what you eat—what you do not eat is equally important. Since the 1950s over 3500 man-made chemicals have found their way into manufactured food, along with pesticides, antibiotics and hormone residues from staple foods such as grains and meat. Many of these chemicals are "anti-nutrients" in that they stop nutrients being absorbed and used, or promote their excretion.

Gone are the days when healthy eating meant simply getting the right balance of nutrients from your food. Now an equally important part of the equation is avoiding harmful chemicals and protecting against those that cannot be avoided. Many of today's diseases are caused just as much by an excess of anti-nutrients as by a deficiency of nutrients. Take cancer, for example. Three-quarters of all cancers are associated with an excess of anti-nutrients, be it cancer-causing chemicals or excessive free radicals as a result of smoking. Many health problems, from arthritis to chronic fatigue, can follow from an overload of anti-nutrients exceeding the body's capacity to detoxify itself. Once this threshold is exceeded, toxins such as pesticide residues accumulate in fat tissue, common drugs from alcohol to painkillers become increasingly toxic, and even the otherwise harmless by-products of the body making energy from carbohydrates start to accumulate, bringing on muscle aches and fatigue.

Nowadays in the U.S. alone we consume every year a staggering one million tons of food chemicals, 9.45 billion gallons of alcoholic drinks, 487 billion cigarettes, 36 million prescriptions for painkillers, and 275 million prescriptions for antibiotics. In addition, 50,000 chemicals are released into the environment by industry and 2.6 billion pounds of pesticides and herbicides are sprayed onto food and pastures. Together it constitutes a staggering onslaught of man-made chemicals and pollutants, with undeniable global health and environmental repercussions.

Making up the deficit

Even refined food that is free from artificial additives is not neutral. Any food you eat that requires more nutrients for the body to make use of it than the food itself provides is effectively an anti-nutrient. Living on these foods gradually robs the body of vital nutrients. In fact, two-thirds of the calories in the average person's diet in the Western world come from these foods. That leaves one-third of the diet to provide, not only enough nutrients for general health, but also enough to make up the deficit of nutrient-deficient food and to combat other anti-nutrients from car pollution to pesticides.

Exactly what extra quantities of key nutrients we need to combat these anti-nutrients is not known, but it is certainly well in excess of RDA levels. Take vitamin C, for example. How much does a smoker need to consume every day to have the same blood level of vitamin C as a non-smoker, assuming they both start with the same dietary intake equivalent to the RDA level? The answer is in excess of 200 mg, roughly quadruple the RDA, according to research by Schectman and colleagues at the Medical College of Wisconsin.[14] The same is true if you compare heavy drinkers with non-drinkers. A heavy drinker needs to take in at least 500 mg a day, six times the RDA, to have the same vitamin C blood level as a non-drinker. And what about pollution? If you live or work in an inner city, what is your need for antioxidant protection? Certainly it will be higher than the RDA and, in the case of vitamin C, which detoxifies over fifty undesirable substances including exhaust fumes, a daily intake of 1000 mg is more likely to be optimal.

CHEMICAL SELF-DEFENSE

To a large extent man-made chemicals have been allowed into the food chain as long as they were not associated with any health risks. Their "anti-nutrient" status has never been an issue. Tartrazine or E102, one of the more common food coloring agents, is a case in point. It has long been known to cause allergic reactions and hyperactivity in sensitive children, and Dr. Neil Ward and his team from the University of Surrey wanted to know why.[15] They gave two groups of children identical-looking and tasting drinks, except that one contained tartrazine. They measured the children's mineral levels before and after they consumed the drink. Those who had the drink containing tartrazine became hyperactive and exhibited a decrease in their blood levels of zinc and an increase in the amount of zinc excreted in the urine. What the researchers had found was that tartrazine robbed the children of zinc, a deficiency of which is associated with increased risk of behavioral and immune system problems.

This is the first of hundreds of food chemicals to be tested in this way and, of course, it begs the question as to what safety criterion a chemical must meet before being allowed to enter the food chain? Or are new chemicals simply innocent until proven guilty? While the legislation on "novel foods" is becoming more stringent, the concept of testing for anti-nutrient effects is not yet on the checklist.

THE PESTICIDE PROBLEM

Labeling on food does not tell you everything. Unless you only eat organic, most foods contain traces of pesticides. In fact, the amount of fruit and vegetables consumed by the average person in a year has the equivalent of up to one gallon of pesticides sprayed on it.

The first family of pesticides were organochlorines. These proved so toxic and non-biodegradable that most have been banned. They were replaced by organophosphates, of which there are about a hundred types on the market. In the U.S. alone over $2 billion a year is spent on these pesticides and herbicides. That's several pounds per person.

Like their ancestors, organophosphates are known to be carcinogenic, mutagenic, and toxic to the brain and nervous system. Forty percent of pesticides now in use have been proved to be cancer-promoting, and linked to birth defects or decreased fertility. Pesticide exposure is associated with depression, memory decline, destabilization of moods and aggressive outbursts, Parkinson's disease and, according to Professor William Rea, asthma, eczema, migraine, irritable bowel syndrome, and rhinitis. Excessive exposure is more common than we are led to believe. In 1994 a survey of carrots found that some contained residue levels twenty-five times higher than the safety limit. In 1995 10 percent of lettuces were shown to have levels in excess of the safety limits.

GENETICALLY ENGINEERED FOOD

The long-term consequences on the eco-system and on our health of genetically engineering foods is unknown. One of the main aims of the genetic engineers is to make plants such as soy resistant to particular types of pesticides. In other words the soy plant can be sprayed, all bugs will die, the plant will be contaminated, and the yield will be increased. We, the consumers, pay the price, while the farmers and agrochemical companies (who own both the patent for the new strain of soy and the pesticide to which it is resistant) profit—and we are told that this technological advance is for the benefit of humanity. Consumer groups are campaigning for clear labeling to state when a food contains genetically engineered ingredients, and sensible consumers are advised to avoid these products.

IS YOUR WATER FIT TO DRINK?

Water is not simply H_2O. Natural water provides significant quantities of minerals: a typical bottled spring water, for instance, provides about 100 mg of calcium per quart. The recommended daily intake of water is at least 1 quart a day, while for calcium it is 600 mg. So natural spring water can provide a sixth of your calcium requirements. However, not all bottled water is spring water, and artificially carbonated water actually depletes our minerals. The carbon molecules in naturally carbonated water are bound to minerals found in the rock bed and deliver them into our bodies, but the carbon in carbonated drinks is unattached and binds to minerals in us, taking them from the body. For this reason people who consume a lot of carbonated drinks tend to have less dense bones than those who do not.

Tap water in a soft water area provides as little as 30 mg of calcium a day. In addition, tap water contains significant levels of nitrates, trihalomethanes, lead, and aluminum, all anti-nutrients in their own right. More than three-quarters of all U.S. drinking water is contaminated with a significant quantity of anti-nutrients. Approximately a quarter of all British tap water contains pesticides at levels above Maximum Admissible Concentrations. Concerns over pollutants in water have led many people to switch to bottled, distilled, or filtered water. However, filtering or distilling water removes not only the impurities but also many of the naturally occurring minerals. This again pushes up the need for minerals from food.

OUT OF THE FRYING PAN

What we do to food in the kitchen can alter the balance between nutrients and anti-nutrients. Frying food in oil produces what are known as free radicals, highly reactive chemicals that destroy essential fats in food and can damage cells, increasing the risk of cancer, heart disease, and premature aging, as well as destroying the very nutrients such as vitamins A and E which protect us from these dangerous substances.

The damaging effects of frying depend on the oil, the temperature, and the length of time. Ironically it is the good polyunsaturated oils (see p. 28) that oxidize most rapidly, becoming undesirable "trans" fats. So frying with butter (saturated fat) or olive oil (monounsaturated fat) is safer. Deep frying is much worse than a two-minute sauté, followed by adding a water-based sauce and putting a lid on the pan so that the food "steam-fries" in a much lower temperature. Grilling, steaming, boiling, or baking, however, are better cooking methods than any form of frying. Finally, any form of overcooking will increasingly reduce the nutrient content of the food.

It is not just what is in your food that matters—what your food is in is also important. The mid-1990s' scare concerning phthalates, substances used to soften plastics, being found in nine brands of infant food begged the question as to how significant quantities of such hormone-disrupting chemicals are finding their way into the food chain. Inspection of an average shopping cart will tell you why. Not only is fresh produce usually wrapped in soft plastics, so too are drinks in cartons, which contain an inner plastic lining. An analysis of twenty brands of food in cans, now also lined with

What's Your Anti-nutrient Load?

Score 1 point for each "yes" answer
_____ Do you drink tap water?
_____ Is more than half the food you eat not organic?
_____ Do you spend an hour or more a day in traffic?
_____ Do you live in a city?
_____ Do you smoke, or live or work with smokers?
_____ Do you often eat fried food?
_____ Do you take more than twenty painkillers in a year?
_____ Do you take, on average, a course of antibiotics each year?
_____ Is most of the food you eat or drink in contact with plastic wrap?
_____ Do you have an alcoholic drink most days?

TOTAL [   ] *The ideal score is 0. A score of 5 or more means you are likely to be taking in a significant quantity of anti-nutrients. Any "yes" answer highlights areas in your diet and lifestyle that warrant attention.*

plastic, found significant levels of Bisphenol-A—some twenty-seven times higher than levels known to cause breast cancer cells to proliferate.

Unfortunately, plastics manufacturers are not required to state which chemicals are present in their products. Also, while the list of hormone-disrupting chemicals is growing, there is as yet no definitive list of what we should be avoiding and what is safe. For now, the best advice is to minimize the amount of food, especially wet or fatty food, which you buy in direct contact with soft plastic. This means that glass bottles are better than plastic bottles or plastic-lined cartons, and paper bags are better than plastic ones. Hard plastic is less likely to be a problem. So store cheese, for example, in a plastic container rather than wrapping it in plastic film.

MINIMIZE PHARMACEUTICAL DRUGS

Many common medicines are also anti-nutrients. In Britain alone 461 million prescriptions are written every year, at a total cost of $8.4 billion; the U.S. annual drug bill is $75 billion. In the U.S. $4.3 billion alone is spent each year on painkillers such as aspirin and acetaminophen.

Salicylic acid, the active ingredient in aspirin and other painkillers, is a gastro-intestinal irritant, increasing the permeability of the stomach wall. This in turn upsets absorption of nutrients, allowing incompletely digested foods to pass into the bloodstream, alerting the immune system and triggering allergy responses to common foods. In the long term this weakens the immune system, encourages inflammation and burns up vital vitamins and minerals needed for healthy immunity, as well as triggering intestinal bleeding.

The alternative is acetaminophen, of which 4 billion tablets are taken world-wide every year. While acetaminophen does not irritate the stomach like aspirin, it is bad news for the liver. As a result, in Britain alone thirty thousand people a year end up in the hospital. In the U.S. the figure is much higher and the treatment costs as many health-care dollars as they spend annually on the drug. According to Professor Sir David Carter of Edinburgh University, one in ten liver transplants is made necessary because of damage caused by acetaminophen overdose. While twenty acetaminophen can kill you, even one is extra work for the liver. If a person takes six a day and lacks the nutrients that help the liver to detoxify, this can reduce their ability to deal with other toxins such as alcohol. The combination of alcohol and acetaminophen is particularly dangerous; acetaminophen produces a toxic by-product which can only be broken down by the liver if the body contains sufficient stores of the amino acid glutathione. If you run out, the result is trouble.

Many common drugs have direct or indirect effects on your nutritional status. Antibiotics, for example, wipe out the healthy stomach bacteria that manufacture significant amounts of B vitamins. They also pave the way for unfriendly bacteria to multiply, increasing the risk of infection which, by stressing the immune system, again leads to nutrient deficiency. Meanwhile the U.S. National Institutes of Health estimate that, by the year 2000, a total of 50,000 tons of antibiotics will be used every year throughout the world.

In summary, the twentieth century has fundamentally changed the chemical environment of every species. Let us hope that the twenty-first century will pursue, with equal fervor, cleaning up the mess. As far as nutrition is concerned we will all need to consider what "optimum nutrition" is, in the light not only of what our bodies need to be healthy, but of what extra they need for anti-nutrient protection. There are also simple changes that we can make to our diet and lifestyle to reduce our **environmental load**, which is a fundamental principle of optimum nutrition.

Here are some tips to help decrease your environmental load:

- Invest in a good-quality, plumbed-in water filter, and replace the cartridge every six months. Jug filters are also good, if you replace the cartridge as instructed.

- Buy organic. When not possible, wash or peel fruit and vegetables.

- Never deep-fry foods, and switch to steam-frying instead of sautéing.

- Buy drinks in glass not plastic containers or cartons, and recycle them.

- Rearrange your daily schedule to minimize time spent in traffic.

- Drink alcohol very infrequently, and avoid smoky places.

- Avoid medical drugs unless they are the only viable option for treating a health problem. If you get frequent infections or aches, investigate the underlying cause rather than relying on painkillers or antibiotics.

7

THE MYTH OF THE
WELL-BALANCED DIET

A human being is made up of roughly 63 percent water, 22 percent protein, 13 percent fat and 2 percent minerals and vitamins. Every single molecule comes from the food you eat and the water you drink. Eating the highest-quality food in the right quantities helps you to achieve your highest potential for health, vitality, and freedom from disease.

Today's diet has drifted a long way off the ideal intake and balance of nutrients. The pie charts below show the percentage of calories we consume that come from fat, protein, and carbohydrate. While little overall change has occurred throughout 99 percent of humanity's history, in the last century, particularly the last two decades, we have started eating much more saturated fat and sugar and less starch (complex carbohydrates) and polyunsaturated fats. Even the government guidelines fall a long way short of our ancestors' diets or what are generally considered to be ideal dietary guidelines.

Part of the problem is propaganda. We are led to believe that as long as you eat a well-balanced diet you get all the nutrients you need. Yet survey after survey shows that even those who believe that they eat a well-balanced diet fail to get anything like the ideal intake of vitamins, minerals, essential fats and complex carbohydrates. It is not easy in today's society, in which food production is inextricably linked to profit. Refining foods makes them last, which makes them more profitable but at the same time deficient in essential nutrients. The food industry has gradually conditioned us to eat sweet foods. Sugar sells, and the more of it we eat the less room there is for less sweet carbohydrates. As our lives speed up we spend less time preparing fresh food and become ever more reliant on ready-meals from companies more concerned for their profit than our health.

Since 1985 the Institute for Optimum Nutrition has been researching what a perfect diet would be. Our conclusions to date are shown in the Top Ten Daily Diet Tips on page 33. While for many people this kind of balance

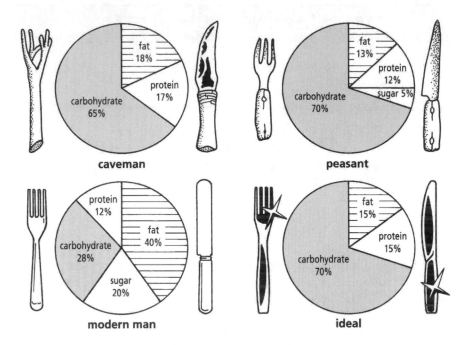

Diets ancient and modern

of foods is not going to be achievable overnight, it does give a clear indication of where your diet should be heading. The general guidelines, which are substantiated in later chapters, are as follows.

FAT

There are two basic kinds: saturated (hard) fat and unsaturated fat. It is neither essential to eat saturated fat, nor ideal to eat too much. The main sources are meat and dairy products. There are also two kinds of unsaturated fats: monounsaturated fats, of which olive oil is a rich source; and polyunsaturated fats, found in nut and seed oils and fish.

Certain polyunsaturated fats, called linoleic and linolenic acid or Omega 6 and Omega 3 oils, are vital for the brain and nervous system, immune system, cardiovascular system, and skin. A common sign of deficiency of these substances is dry skin. The optimal diet provides a balance of these two essential fats. Pumpkin and flax seeds are rich in linolenic acid (Omega 3), while sesame and sunflower seeds are rich in linoleic acid (Omega 6). Linolenic acid is converted in the body into DHA and EPA, which are also found in mackerel, herring, salmon, and tuna. These essential fats are easily destroyed by heating or exposure to oxygen, so having a fresh daily source is important.

Processed foods often contain hardened or "hydrogenated" polyunsaturated fats. These are worse for you than saturated fat and are best avoided.

Eat one tablespoon of cold-pressed seed oil (sesame, sunflower, pumpkin, flax seed, etc.) or one heaped tablespoon of ground seeds a day.
Avoid fried food, burnt or browned fat, saturated, and hydrogenated fat.

PROTEIN

The twenty-five amino acids—different forms of protein—are the building blocks of the body. As well as being vital for growth and the repair of body tissue, they are used to make hormones, enzymes, antibodies, and neurotransmitters, and help transport substances around the body. Both the quality of the protein you eat, determined by the balance of these amino acids, and the quantity you eat are important.

The government recommends that we obtain 15 percent of our total calorie intake from protein, but gives little guidance as to the kind of protein. The average breast-fed baby receives just 1 percent of its total calories from protein and manages to double its birth weight in six months. This is because the protein from breast milk is very good-quality and easily absorbed. Assuming good-quality protein, 10 percent of calorie intake, or around 35 grams of protein a day, is an optimal intake for most adults, unless pregnant, recovering from surgery, or undertaking large amounts of exercise or heavy manual work.

The best-quality protein foods in terms of amino acid balance include eggs, quinoa, soybean, meat, fish, beans, and lentils. Animal protein sources tend to contain a lot of undesirable saturated fat. Vegetable protein sources tend to contain additional beneficial complex carbohydrates and are less acid-forming (see p. 330) than meat. It is best to limit meat to three meals a week. It is difficult not to take in enough protein from any diet that includes three meals a day, whether vegan, vegetarian, or meat-eating. Many vegetables, especially "seed" foods like runner beans, peas, corn, or broccoli, contain good levels of protein and help to neutralize excess acidity which can lead to mineral losses including calcium—hence the higher risk of osteoporosis among frequent meat-eaters.

Eat two daily servings of beans, lentils, quinoa, tofu (soybean), "seed" vegetables (such as peas, broad beans) or other vegetable protein, or one small serving of meat, fish, cheese, or a free-range egg.
Avoid too much animal protein.

CARBOHYDRATE

The main fuel for the body, carbohydrate comes in two forms: "fast-releasing," as in sugar, honey, malt, sweets, and most refined foods, and "slow-releasing," as in whole grains, vegetables, and fresh fruit. The latter foods contain more complex carbohydrate and/or more fiber, both of which help to slow down the release of sugar. Fast-releasing carbohydrates tend to give a sudden burst of energy followed by a slump, while slow-releasing carbohydrates provide more sustained energy and are therefore preferable. Refined foods like sugar and white flour lack the vitamins and minerals needed for the body to use them properly and are best avoided. The perpetual use of fast-releasing carbohydrates can give rise to complex symptoms and health problems. Some fruit, like bananas, dates, and raisins, contain faster-releasing sugars and are best kept to a minimum by people with glucose-related health problems. Slow-releasing carbohydrate foods— fresh fruit, vegetables, legumes, and whole grains—should make up two-thirds of what you eat, or around 70 percent of your total calorie intake. Every day, aim to:

Eat three or more servings of dark green, leafy and root vegetables such as watercress, carrots, sweet potatoes, broccoli, brussels sprouts, spinach, green beans or peppers, raw or lightly cooked.

Eat three or more servings of fresh fruit such as apples, pears, bananas, berries, melon, or citrus fruit.

Eat four or more servings of whole grains such as rice, millet, rye, oats, whole wheat, corn, quinoa as cereal, breads, pasta or legumes.

Avoid any form of sugar, foods with added sugar, white, or refined foods.

FIBER

Rural Africans eat about 55 grams of dietary fiber a day, compared to the U.K. average intake of 22 grams, and have the lowest incidence of bowel diseases such as appendicitis, diverticulitis, colitis, and bowel cancer. The ideal intake is not less than 35 grams a day. It is easy to take in this amount of fiber—which absorbs water in the digestive tract, making the food contents bulkier and easier to pass through the body—by eating whole grains, vegetables, fruit, nuts, seeds, lentils, and beans on a daily basis. Fruit and vegetable fiber helps slow down the absorption of sugar into the blood, helping to maintain good energy levels. Cereal fiber is particularly good at preventing constipation and putrefaction of food, which are underlying causes of many digestive complaints. Refined diets that are orientated towards meat, eggs, fish, and dairy produce will undoubtedly lack fiber.

Eat whole foods—whole grains, lentils, beans, nuts, seeds, fresh fruit, and vegetables.

Avoid refined, white, and overcooked foods.

WATER

Two-thirds of the body consists of water, which is therefore our most important nutrient. The body loses over a quart of water a day through the skin, lungs, and stomach, and via the kidneys as urine, ensuring that toxic substances are eliminated from the body. We also make about a third of a quart of water a day when glucose is "burnt" for energy. Therefore our minimum water intake from food and drink needs to be more than one quart a day. The ideal daily intake is around two quarts.

Fruit and vegetables consist of around 90 percent water. They supply it in a form that is very easy for the body to use, at the same time providing the body with a high percentage of its vitamins and minerals. Four pieces of fruit and four servings of vegetables can provide a quart of water, leaving the other recommended quart to be taken as water or in the form of diluted juices or herb or fruit teas. Alcohol, tea, and coffee cause the body to lose water, so are not recommended as sources of fluid intake. They also rob the body of valuable minerals.

Drink 1 quart of water a day as water or in diluted juices, herb or fruit teas.
Minimize your intake of alcohol, coffee, and tea.

VITAMINS

Although needed in much smaller amounts than fat, protein, or carbohydrate, vitamins are no less important. They "turn on" enzymes, which in turn make all body processes happen. Vitamins are needed to balance hormones, produce energy, boost the immune system, make healthy skin, and protect the arteries; they are vital for the brain, nervous system, and just about every body process. Vitamins A, C, and E are antioxidants: they slow down the aging process and protect the body from cancer, heart disease, and pollution. B and C vitamins are vital for turning food into mental and physical energy. Vitamin D, found in milk, eggs, fish, and meat, helps control calcium balance. It can also be made in the skin in the presence of sunshine. B and C vitamins are richest in living foods—fresh fruit and vegetables. Vitamin A comes in two forms: retinol, the animal form found in meat, fish, eggs and dairy produce; and beta-carotene, found in red, yellow, and orange fruits and vegetables. Vitamin E is found in seeds, nuts, and their oils, and helps protect essential fats from going rancid.

Eat three or more servings of dark green, leafy and root vegetables, and three or more servings of fresh fruit plus some nuts or seeds, every day.
Supplement with a multivitamin containing at least the following: vitamin A 2250 mcg, vitamin D 10 mcg, vitamin E 100 mg, vitamin B1 25 mg, vitamin B2 25mg, vitamin B3 (niacin) 50mg, vitamin B5 (pantothenic acid) 50 mg, vitamin B6 50 mg, vitamin B12 5 mcg, folic acid 50 mcg, biotin 50 mcg. Also supplement with 1000 mg of vitamin C a day.

MINERALS

Like vitamins, minerals are essential for just about every body process. Calcium, magnesium, and phosphorus help make up the bones and teeth. Nerve signals, vital for the brain and muscles, depend on calcium, magnesium, sodium, and potassium. Oxygen is carried in the blood by an iron compound. Chromium helps control blood sugar levels. Zinc is vital for all body repair, renewal, and development. Selenium and zinc help boost the immune system. Brain function depends on adequate magnesium, manganese, zinc, and other essential minerals. These are but a few out of thousands of key roles that minerals play in human health.

We need large daily amounts of calcium and magnesium, which are found in vegetables such as kale, cabbage, and root vegetables. They are also abundant in nuts and seeds. Calcium alone is found in large quantities in dairy produce. Fruit and vegetables provide lots of potassium and small amounts of sodium, which is the right balance. All "seed" foods—which include seeds, nuts, lentils and dried beans, as well as peas, broad beans, runner beans, whole grains, and even broccoli (the heads are the seeds)—are good sources of iron, zinc, manganese and chromium. Selenium is abundant in nuts, seafood, seaweed, and seeds, especially sesame.

Eat one serving of mineral-rich foods such as kale, cabbage, root vegetables, low-fat dairy products such as yogurt, seeds, or nuts, as well as plenty of fresh fruit, vegetables, and whole foods such as lentils, beans, and whole grains.
Supplement with a multimineral containing at least the following: calcium 150 mg, magnesium 75 mg, iron 10 mg, zinc 10 mg, manganese 2.5 mg, chromium 50 mcg, selenium 25 mcg.

PURE FOOD

Organic, unadulterated whole foods have formed the basis of the human diet through the ages. Only in the twentieth century have we been subjected to countless man-made chemicals in food and in the environment.

One foundation for health is to eat foods that provide exactly the amount of energy required to keep the body in perfect balance. A good deal of energy is wasted in trying to disarm these alien and often toxic chemicals, some of which cannot be eliminated and accumulate in body tissue. It is now impossible to avoid all these substances, as there is nowhere on this planet that is not contaminated in some way from the by-products of our modern chemical age. Choosing organic foods whenever possible is the nearest we can get to eating a pure diet today. By supporting the movement back to these kinds of food we are helping to minimize the damage of chemical pollution, which poses a real threat to the future of humanity.

Raw, organic food is the most natural and beneficial way to take food into the body. Many foods contain enzymes that help digest them once chewed. Raw food is full of vital phytochemicals (see Chapter 14), whose effect on our health may prove as important as that of vitamins and minerals. Cooking food destroys enzymes and reduces the activity of phytochemicals.

Eat organic as much as you can. Make sure that at least half your diet consists of raw fruit, vegetables, whole grains, nuts and seeds.

Avoid processed food with additives, and cook food as little as possible.

1
One heaped tablespoon of ground seeds or one tablespoon of cold-pressed seed oil

2
Two servings of beans lentils, quinoa, tofu (soya), or "seed" vegetables

3
Three pieces of fresh fruit such as apples, pears, bananas, berries, melon, or citrus fruit

4
Four servings of whole grains such as brown rice, millet, rye, oats, wholewheat, corn, quinoa as cereal, breads, and pasta

5
Five servings of dark green, leafy and root vegetables such as watercress, carrots, sweet potatoes, broccoli, spinach, green beans, peas, and peppers

6
Six glasses of water, diluted juices, herb or fruit teas

7
Eat whole, organic, raw food as often as you can

8
Supplement your diet with a high-strength multivitamin and mineral preparation and 1000 mg of vitamin C a day

9
Avoid fried, burnt and browned food, hydrogenated fat, and excess animal fat

10
Avoid any form of sugar, also white, refined or processed food with chemical additives, and minimize your intake of alcohol, coffee, or tea—have no more than one unit of alcohol a day (e.g., a glass of wine, half a pint of beer or lager, or a spirit)

Top ten daily diet tips

8

THE PROTEIN CONTROVERSY

What words do you associate with protein? Meat, eggs, cheese, muscles, growth. You have to eat these foods to get enough protein to grow big and strong. The protein in meat is more usable than the protein in plants. If you do muscle-building exercise you need more protein.... Right or wrong? Many myths abound about protein, how much you need, and the best food sources.

The word itself is derived from *protos* a Greek word, meaning "first," since protein is the basic material of all living cells. The human body, for example contains, approximately 65 percent water and 25 percent protein. Protein is made out of nitrogen-containing molecules called amino acids. Some twenty-five types of amino acids are pieced together in varying combinations to make different kinds of protein, which form the material for our cells and organs, in much the same way that letters make words which combine to form sentences and paragraphs.

From the eight basic amino acids most of the remaining seventeen can be made. These eight are termed essential amino acids and the body cannot function without them, although others are semi-essential under certain conditions. Each of the basic eight deserves its own Recommended Daily Intake, although these have yet to be set. The balance of these eight amino acids in the protein of any given food determines its quality or usability. So how much protein do you need, and what is the best-quality protein?

PROTEIN—ARE YOU GETTING ENOUGH?

Estimates for protein requirement vary depending on who you speak to. This is not so surprising, since there may be widespread "biochemical individuality." At the low end of the scale are reports of protein sufficiency when 2.5 percent of total calorie intake comes from protein. The World Health Organization estimates we need 4.5 percent of total calories from protein, while the US National Research Council adds on a safety margin and regards 8 percent as adequate for 95 percent of the population. The

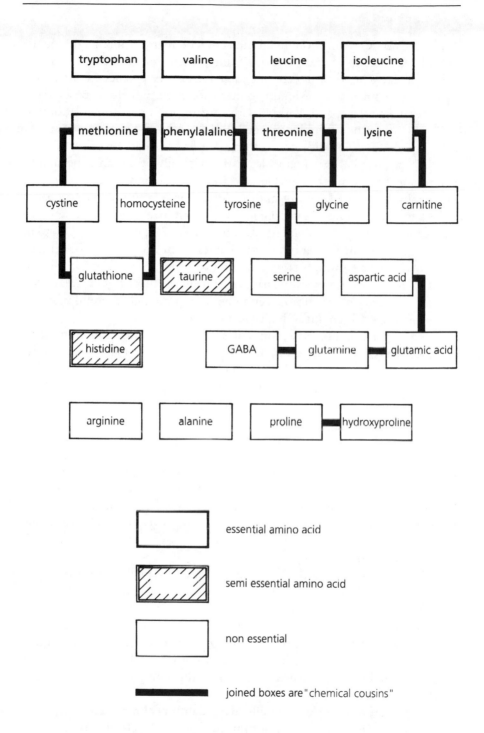

Amino acid family

World Health Organization builds in a safety margin and recommends around 10 percent of total calories from protein, or about 35 grams of protein a day. The U.S. Recommended Dietary Allowance is 50 grams protein for women and 63 grams protein for men, which is substantially higher than European and World Health Organization recommendations. If the quality of protein is high, less needs to be eaten.

So which foods provide more than 10 percent of their calories from protein? You may be surprised to learn that virtually every lentil, bean, nut, seed, and grain, and most vegetables and fruit, provide more than 10 percent protein. In soybeans 54 percent of the calories come from protein, compared to 26 percent in kidney beans. Grains vary from 16 percent for quinoa to 4 percent for corn. Nuts and seeds range from 21 percent for pumpkin seeds to 12 percent for cashews. Fruit goes from 16 percent for lemons down to 1 percent for apples. Vegetables vary from 49 percent for spinach to 11 percent for potatoes. What this means is that if you are eating enough calories you are almost certainly getting enough protein, unless—you are living off high-sugar, high-fat junk food.

This may come as a surprise, contradicting all we are taught about protein. Yet the fact of the matter is, to quote a team of Harvard scientists investigating vegetarian diets, "It is difficult to obtain a mixed vegetable diet which will produce an appreciable loss of body protein." But surely animal protein is better quality than plant protein?

ANIMAL OR VEGETABLE?

Once again, there are a few surprises. Top of the class is quinoa (pronounced keenwa), a high-protein grain from South America that was a staple food of the Incas and Aztecs. Soybean too does well. Most vegetables are relatively low in the amino acids methionine and lysine; however, beans and lentils are rich in methionine. Soybeans and quinoa are excellent sources of both lysine and methionine.

Early theories, such as those first expounded by Frances Moore Lappe in *Diet for a Small Planet* (Ballantine Books, 1975), suggested that vegetable proteins had to be carefully combined with complementary proteins in order to match the quality of animal proteins. However, we have since learned that careful combining of plant-based proteins is quite unnecessary. As Lappe says in the revised edition of her book, "With a healthy, varied diet, concern about protein complementarity is not necessary for most of us."

Even so, you can increase the effective quality of the protein you eat by combining foods from different groups so that low levels of certain amino acids in one food group are made up by high levels in another. Over a forty-eight-hour period aim to eat a varied diet across the food groups

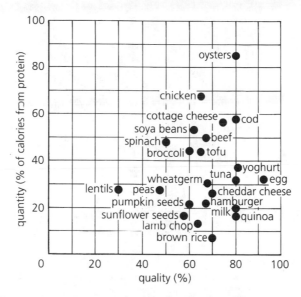

Protein quality and quantity

shown in the illustration above. The combination of rice with lentils, for example, increases the protein value by a third. This is, of course, the basis of the diet in the Indian subcontinent.

THE BEST PROTEIN FOODS

The best foods to eat for protein are not necessarily those that are highest in protein. The pros and cons of a food's other nutritional constituents have to be taken into account. A lamb chop, for example, provides 25 percent of total calories as protein and 75 percent as fat, much of which is saturated fat. Half the calories in soybeans come from protein, so it is actually a better source of protein than lamb, but its real advantage is that the rest of the calories come from desirable complex carbohydrates. It also contains no saturated fat. This makes foods made from soybean ideal, especially for vegetarians.

The easiest way to eat soybean is in the form of tofu, a curd made from beans. There are many kinds of tofu—soft, hard, marinated, smoked, braised. Soft tofu can be used to give a creamy texture to soups. Hard tofu can be cubed and used in vegetable stir-fries, stews, and casseroles. Since tofu is quite tasteless it is best to use it with well-flavored foods or sauces.

Quinoa has been grown for five thousand years and has a long-standing reputation as a source of strength for those working at high altitudes. Called the "mother grain" because of its sustaining properties, it contains

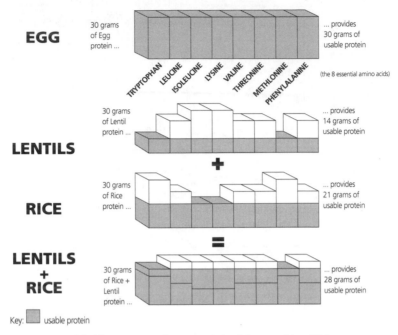

Making a complete protein (rice and lentils)

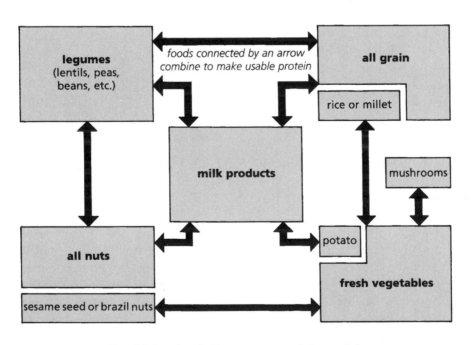

Combining foods for more complete protein

protein of a better quality than that of meat. Although known as a grain, quinoa is technically a fruit. Nutritionally it is quite unique, containing more protein than a grain and more essential fat than fruit. It is also rich in vitamins and minerals, providing almost four times as much calcium as wheat, plus extra iron, B vitamins and vitamin E. Quinoa is also low in fat: the majority of its oil is polyunsaturated, providing essential fatty acids. As such, quinoa is about as close to a perfect food as you can get.

Quinoa can be found in many health food stores and used as an alternative to rice. To cook it, add two parts water to one of quinoa and boil for fifteen minutes.

MEAT

The average person in Britain eats over 4 pounds (1800 grams) of meat a week. The traditional view is that meat is good for you, being high in protein and iron. Meat consumption is going down as more and more people are becoming vegetarian and vegan. Leaving moral considerations aside, there are a number of safety issues that give causes for genuine concern: they include the use of antibiotics, growth hormones, and pesticide dips.

Described by the microbiologist Professor Richard Lacey as "fake meat," much of what is available in supermarkets and butcher's shops contains growth hormones, sex hormones, antibiotics, and high pesticide residues.

BSE – is it a serious risk?

BSE (Borine Spongiform Encepalopathy/Mad Cow Disease) is the fatal disease that has affected cows and has been passed on to humans in the U.K. The infectious agent responsible for BSE is called a prion; it latches on to proteins in the brain, changing them and thereby triggering disease. It is now proven to pass from species to species, and into man. The altered brain proteins in the first fourteen cases of a new strain of Creutzfeldt-Jakob disease, the human equivalent of the disease, bear the same genetic markings as those in BSE. This is as close as you can get to a proven connection. Genetic research has also found a link between those first fourteen cases, highlighting those more susceptible to CJD. About 20 million people in Britain are thought to have this genetic susceptibility; however, this does not rule out the possibility that the remaining 40 million, though they may be less susceptible, are not immune.

Two key questions remain unanswered. How much infected meat is needed to trigger the disease? And how many people will be affected? In cattle as little as a teaspoon of infected meat will result in fatal BSE. In mice the amount needed is several hundred times higher in relation to body weight. How the human species reacts is, at this point, completely unknown.

Predictions regarding the scale of the likely epidemic range from hundreds to hundreds of thousands of cases. Dr James Ironside, a member of the UK CJD Surveillance Unit, whose paper was published in the *Lancet*, in 1977, believes that 'a total number of cases over the whole course of the disease will be in the hundreds, rather than thousands'. Professor Richard Lacey, advisor to the NHS, is not so optimistic. These estimates, he says, are pure guesswork. Nobody knows what the incubation period is in humans. If it is longer than fifteen years, these first few cases are from meat that was infected before the epidemic in cattle was even noticed – meaning that the epidemic in humans is in its infancy and numbers affected are more likely to run into hundreds of thousands.

In any event, this is a bad time to be eating British beef, unless it is from animals raised organically and parented by animals which were also raised organically, without any possible contact with BSE-infected livestock since the epidemic began, in the 1980s. At the time of writing, a small number of cases of BSE have also been reported in chickens.

Hormones—a growing problem

Most meat today, whether chicken, beef, pork, or lamb, has received hormone treatment of one kind or another. An animal may be slaughtered only a few days after a hormone pellet. Milk, too, is a rich source of hormones, particularly estrogen.

Some hormones used widely in the U.S. are banned in Europe, although there are commercial pressures to rescind the ban. These hormones, including synthetic estradiol and testosterone, are used to force growth rates and increase milk yields. These are the same chemicals that are at the center of the concern about "estrogen dominance," an increasingly common syndrome found in men and women with hormone-related disease. So far, breast cancer, fibroids, ovarian cancer, cervical cancer, prostate and testicular cancer, and endometriosis have all been linked to excessive estrogen levels.

Of course, it is not easy to find out what long-term effects the introduction of hormones into our food is having. Dr. Malcolm Carruthers, a specialist in male hormone-related disease, investigated a thousand cases of patients exhibiting symptoms of the "'male menopause'" over seven years. The most common symptoms are fatigue, depression, loss of libido, testicular atrophy, impotence, and breast enlargement. Of those thousand cases the highest occupational risk group was farmers, the "front-line" troops in the agrochemical arms race. According to Carruthers: "For some the causative agent appeared obvious. They had worked on farms caponizing chickens or turkeys with estrogen pellet implants, to make the birds plumper and more tender. Unfortunately, though it might be considered poetic justice, they must have taken in large amounts of estrogen which caused them to become partly caponized themselves." Farmers less directly exposed to hormones—and to pesticides, which are also known to interfere with male hormone balance—were also at high risk of "male menopause" symptoms.

Is your meat bugged?

Antibiotics are in widespread use in both humans and animals. Over 500 tons are dished out every year in Britain alone. Unlike human medicines, given for a limited period for the treatment of an infection, antibiotics are routinely added to animal feed to prevent infection and enhance growth: the aim is higher profits faster. The consumer, however, is being hit with a double-whammy. Antibiotic residues are frequently found in samples of meat, fish, and eggs. So are infectious agents that have become resistant to antibiotics—superbugs. There is growing concern about a strain of enterococci faecium, a dangerous bacteria found in chickens which is resistant to Vancomycin, one of the strongest "last resort" antibiotics. Fortunately, infection with enterococci is rare compared to salmonella or campylobacter. With 350,000 cases of salmonella and 400,000 cases of campylobacter infection from meat and eggs per year, there would be grounds for worry if these common strains of bacteria causing food poisoning were to become resistant to the available antibiotic treatment. Currently, a hundred people die each year in Britain from food poisoning. Many more are saved by antibiotics.

Is meat good for you?

Meat-eaters have a low health rating. The risk of heart disease and cancer, particularly cancer of the stomach and colon, is directly related to meat consumption. So too are other digestive diseases such as diverticulitis, colitis, and appendicitis. Even more likely to result in cardiovascular disease is a high consumption of milk and dairy products. Overall, a meat-eater is likely to visit the doctor, or be admitted to the hospital, twice as often as a vegetarian, and is likely to suffer from degenerative diseases ten years earlier than a vegetarian, according to a survey by Professors Dickerson and Davies from the University of Surrey.[16]

Most people are in more danger of eating too much protein than too little. Excess protein is a contributor to osteoporosis, over-acidity, and many other common health problems. Reducing your consumption of meat, especially of these types that contain high levels of saturated fat, and eating vegetarian foods, chicken, or fish instead, is good health advice.

The meat muscle myth

Whether you eat steak, of which 52 percent of the calories comes from protein, or spinach (the reputed source of Popeye's strength), of which 49 percent of the calories comes from protein, surely you need more to make strong muscles? But according to Sylvester Stallone's former nutritionist and adviser to many U.S. Olympic athletes, Dr. Michael Colgan, this is a myth. He points out that, with hard training, the maximum amount of extra muscle you could build in a year would be less than 8 pounds. That represents a gain of 2.5 ounces a week, or 0.3 ounces a day. Muscle is only 22 percent protein, so an increased consumption of less than a tenth of an ounce a day, equivalent to a quarter of a teaspoonful, is all that is needed to bring about the greatest possible muscle gain! So instead of loading in unnecessary protein, which taxes the body more than it helps it, follow the rules of optimum nutrition to ensure that you make proper use of the protein in your diet.

MILK

Milk and milk products are the mainstay of the American diet. It is considered an essential source of protein, iron, and calcium. So beneficial are milk products to our health, according to the National Dairy Council, that you may wonder how we ever existed without them. So why do some authorities not encourage milk-drinking, if it is such a good source of minerals?

Ignore the hype

The truth is that milk is not a very good source of many minerals. Manganese, chromium, selenium, and magnesium are all found in higher levels in fruit and vegetables. Most important is magnesium, which works alongside calcium. Relying on dairy products for calcium is likely to lead to magnesium deficiency and imbalance. Seeds, nuts, and crunchy vegetables like kale, cabbage, carrots, and cauliflower give us both these minerals and others, more in line with our needs. Milk is, after all, designed for the very young, not for adults.

Not recommended for babies

Another common myth is that a breast-feeding mother needs to drink milk in order to make milk. This, of course, is nonsense. The move away from breast-feeding led to the substitution of human milk with cow's milk. Cow's milk is designed for calves, and is very different from human milk in a number of respects, including its protein, calcium, phosphorus, iron, and essential fatty acid content. Early feeding of human babies on cow's milk is now known to increase the likelihood of developing a cow's milk allergy, which affects as many as 75 in every 1,000 babies. Common symptoms include diarrhea, vomiting, persistent colic, eczema, urticaria, catarrh, bronchitis, asthma, and sleeplessness. The American Society of Micro-biologists has suggested that some crib deaths may be attributable to cow's milk allergy. Cow's milk should not be given to infants under four months.

Allergy and its effects

Milk allergy or intolerance is very common among both children and adults. Sometimes this is the result of lactose intolerance, since many adults lose the ability to digest lactose (milk sugar). The symptoms are bloating, abdominal pain, gas, and diarrhea, which subside on giving lactase, the enzyme that breaks down lactose. Probably equally common is an allergy or intolerance to dairy products. For reasons not yet completely understood, the most common symptoms are blocked nose and excessive mucus production, respiratory complaints such as asthma, and gastro-intestinal problems. Such intolerances are more likely to occur in people who consume dairy products regularly, in large quantities. Some people who are intolerant to milk can tolerate yogurt. Some can tolerate goat's milk or sheep's milk.

Growing evidence is also linking child-onset diabetes to allergy to bovine serum albumin (BSA) in dairy products.[17] This type of diabetes tends to strike in the early teenage years and affects 2 out of 1,000 people by the age of twenty. It starts with the immune system destroying the cells in the pancreas that produce insulin. Why this occurs has long been a mystery.

While there is a genetic predisposition to insulin-dependent diabetes (IDD), this is only part of the picture. Genetically susceptible children who had been breast-fed for at least seven months or exclusively breast-fed for at least three or four months were found to have a significantly decreased incidence of IDD, which suggested another factor. Children who have not been given cow's milk until four months or older also show the same substantially reduced risk. The highest incidence of IDD is found in Finland, which has the world's highest milk product consumption.

Animal studies showed that rats bred to be susceptible to diabetes had a much higher risk of contracting the disease if their feed contained either milk or wheat gluten. In one study even the addition of 1 percent skimmed milk to their diet increased the incidence of IDD from 15 percent to 52 percent. In 1993 Dr, Hans-Michael Dosch, Professor of Immunology at Mount Sinai Hospital, New York, identified BSA as the specific factor in dairy produce that increased the risk of diabetes, and showed that it cross-reacted with the cells of the pancreas. He and his fellow researchers theorized that diabetes-susceptible babies introduced to BSA earlier than around four months, before which age the stomach wall is immature and more permeable, would develop an allergic response to BSA. As a result their immune cells would mistakenly destroy not only the BSA molecules but also pancreatic tissue. He went on to show that, of 142 newly diagnosed IDD children, 100 percent had antibodies to BSA, compared to 2 percent in normal children. Dr. Dosch believes that the presence of these anti-BSA antibodies indicated future child-onset diabetes in 80–90 percent of cases.

He believes that keeping children off dairy products for at least their first six months halves the risk. BSA can, however, pass from the mother's diet into her milk. So if breast-feeding mothers avoid beef and dairy products the risk can be completely removed in genetically susceptible children. The current opinion is that about one in four children are genetically susceptible.

MILK AND MEAT—THE VERDICT

From the current evidence, given the present state of intensive farming, neither meat, (particularly beef) nor milk, (especially for young children) is safe if you really want to pursue optimum nutrition. But this is no loss; not only is it possible to have a healthy diet without including dairy produce and meat, its almost certainly going to decrease your risk of the common killer diseases. For meat-lovers who feel they do not want to go vegetarian I recommend eating meat no more than three times a week, substituting more fresh vegetables and whole foods such as beans, lentils, and whole grains, and choosing only organic meats and free-range chicken or fish. For milk, substitute soy or rice milk, or buy organic milk. If you suspect you might be allergic, stay off all dairy products for 14 days. If it makes no difference, limit your intake of milk to one quart a week.

Here are some general guidelines for your protein intake:

- Eat two servings of beans, lentils, quinoa, tofu (soybean), "seed" vegetables or other vegetable protein, or one small serving of meat, fish, or cheese, or a free-range egg, every day.

- Reduce your intake of dairy products and avoid them altogether if you are allergic, substituting soybean or rice milk.

- Reduce other sources of animal protein, choosing lean meat or fish and eating no more than three servings a week.

- Eat organic wherever possible, to avoid possible contamination with hormones and antibiotics.

9

THE FATS OF LIFE

Fat is good for you! Eating the right kind of fat is absolutely vital for optimal health. Essential fats reduce the risk of cancer, heart disease, allergies, arthritis, eczema, depression, fatigue, infections, PMS—the list of symptoms and diseases associated with deficiency is growing every year. If you are fat-phobic you are depriving yourself of essential health-giving nutrients and increasing your risk of poor health. The same is true if the fat you eat is hard—this means fat from dairy products, meat, and most margarines.

In fact, unless you go out of your way to eat the right kind of fat-rich foods, such as seeds, nuts, and fish, the chances are that you are not getting enough good fat. Most people in the Western world eat too much saturated fat, the kind that kills, and too little of the essential fats, the kind that heal.

FAT FIGURES

It is considered optimum to consume no more than 20 percent of your total calories in the form of fat. The current average in the U.S. is above 40 percent. Inhabitants of countries which have a low incidence of fat-related diseases, like Japan, Thailand, and the Philippines, consume only about 15 percent of their total calorie intake as fat. For example, Japanese people eat on average 40 grams of fat a day, whereas Americans eat 142.

Saturated and monounsaturated fat are not nutrients: you do not need them, although they can be used by the body to make energy. But polyunsaturated fats or oils are essential.

Almost all foods that contain fat have a balance of all three. A piece of meat will contain mainly saturated and monounsaturated fat with little polyunsaturated fat. Olive oil has mainly monounsaturated fat. Sunflower seed oil has mainly polyunsaturated fat.

Most authorities now agree that no more than one-third of our total fat intake should be saturated (hard) fat, and at least one-third should be polyunsaturated oils providing the two essential fats: the linoleic acid family, known as Omega 6, and the alpha-linolenic acid family, known as Omega 3.

The ideal balance between these two is about twice as much Omega 6 as Omega 3. So an ideal "fat profile," based on fat forming no more than 20 percent of our total calorie intake, might consist of

- 4 percent Omega 6
- 3 percent Omega 3
- 7 percent monounsaturated fat
- 6 percent saturated fat

Most people are deficient in both Omega 6 and Omega 3 fats. In addition, a high intake of saturated fats and damaged polyunsaturated fats, known as "trans" fats, stops the body making good use of the small quantity of essential fats that the average person eats in a day.

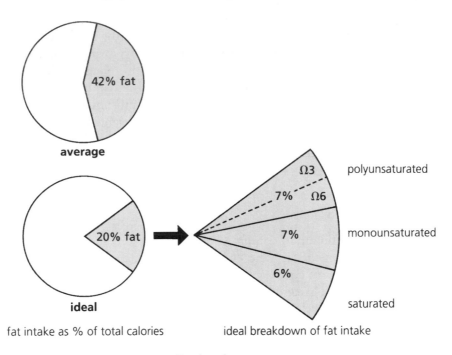

Fat intake

THE OMEGA 6 FAT FAMILY

The grandmother of the Omega 6 fat family is linoleic acid, which is converted by the body into gamma-linolenic acid (GLA). Evening primrose oil and borage oil are the richest known sources of GLA, and if you take these in supplement form you need less overall oil to obtain enough Omega 6 fats. The ideal intake is around 150 mg of GLA a day, equivalent to

Fats that Heal

Hemp
Flax
Soybeans
Walnuts
Seaweed
Sunflower seeds
Sesame seeds
Almonds
Wild birds
Filberts
Venison
Chicken
Fresh, mechanically
pressed oils in
opaque containers
Evening Primrose oil
Eggs
Butter
Lamb
Beef
Roasted nuts
and seeds
Dairy products
Pork
Refined oils
Margarines,
Shortenings

Fats that Kill

1,500mg of evening primrose oil or 750 mg of high-potency borage oil—a capsule a day.

GLA is subsequently converted into DGLA (di-homo gamma linolenic acid) and from there into prostaglandins, which are extremely active hormone-like substances. The particular kind made from these Omega 6 oils are called series 1 prostaglandins. They keep the blood thin, which prevents clots and blockages, relax blood vessels, lower blood pressure, help to maintain the water balance in the body, decrease inflammation and pain, improve nerve and immune function, and help insulin to work, which is good for blood sugar balance. And this is only the beginning. Every year more and more health-promoting functions of prostaglandins are being discovered. Prostaglandins themselves cannot be supplemented, as they are very short-lived; we rely instead on a good intake of their source, Omega 6 fats.

Omega 6 deficiency signs

☐ Do you have high blood pressure?

☐ Do you suffer from PMS or breast pain?

☐ Do you suffer from eczema or dry skin?

☐ Do you suffer from dry eyes?

☐ Do you have an inflammatory health problem, like arthritis?

☐ Do you have difficulty losing weight?

☐ Do you have a blood sugar problem or diabetes?

☐ Do you have multiple sclerosis?

☐ Do you drink alcohol every day?

☐ Do you have any mental health problems?

☐ Do you suffer from excessive thirst?

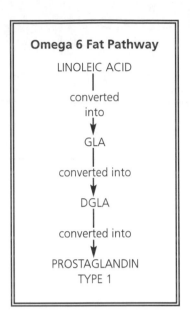

Omega 6 Fat Pathway

LINOLEIC ACID
|
converted
into
↓
GLA
|
converted into
↓
DGLA
|
converted into
↓
PROSTAGLANDIN
TYPE 1

How did you score? Five or more "yes" answers indicates that you may be deficient in Omega 6 fats. Check your diet carefully for the foods listed below.

This family of fats comes exclusively from seeds and their oils. The best are hemp, pumpkin, sunflower, safflower, sesame, corn, walnut, soybean, and wheat germ oil. About half of the fats in these oils comes from the Omega 6 family, mainly as linoleic acid. An optimal intake would be one to two tablespoons of oil a day, or two to three tablespoons of ground seeds.

THE OMEGA 3 FAT FAMILY

The modern diet is likely to be more deficient in Omega 3 fats than in Omega 6. This is because the grandmother of the Omega 3 family, alpha-linolenic acid, and her metabolically active grandchildren EPA (eicosapentaenoic acid) and DHA (docosahexaenoic acid), from which series 3 prostaglandin are made, are more unsaturated and more prone to damage in cooking and food processing. As these fats get converted in the body to more "active" substances they become more unsaturated, and generally the word used for them gets longer (for instance, oleic acid: one degree of unsaturation; linoleic: two degrees of unsaturation; linolenic: three degrees of unsaturation; eicosapentaenoic: five degrees of unsaturation).

You can observe this increasing complexity as we move up the food chain. For example plankton, the staple food of small fish, is rich in alpha-linolenic acid. Carnivorous fish, like mackerel or herring, eat the small fish which have converted some of their alpha-linolenic acid into more complex fats. The carnivorous fish continue the conversion. Seals eat them and have the highest EPA and DHA concentration. Finally Eskimos eat the seals and benefit from a ready-made meal of EPA and DHA, from which they can easily make series 3 prostaglandins.

These prostaglandins are essential for proper brain function which affects vision, learning ability, coordination, and mood. Like series 1 they reduce the stickiness of the blood, as well as controlling blood cholesterol and fat levels, improving immune function and metabolism, reducing inflammation, and maintaining water balance.

Omega 3 deficiency signs

☐ Do you have dry skin?

☐ Do you have any inflammatory health problems?

☐ Do you suffer from water retention?

☐ Do you get tingling in the arms or legs?

☐ Do you have high blood pressure or high triglycerides (the name for fat in the blood)?

☐ Are you prone to infections?

☐ Are you finding it harder to lose weight?

☐ Have your memory and learning ability declined?

☐ Do you suffer from a lack of coordination or impaired vision?

☐ If you are a child, are you small for your age or growing slowly?

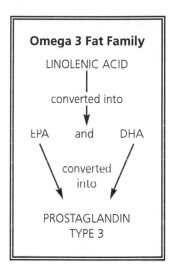

How did you score? Five or more "yes" answers indicates that you may be deficient in Omega 3 fats. Check your diet carefully for the foods listed below.

The best seed oils for Omega 3 fats are flax (also known as linseed), hemp, and pumpkin. In much the same way as evening primrose oil bypasses the first "conversion" stage of linoleic acid, if you eat carnivorous fish such as mackerel, herring, tuna, and salmon, or their oils, you can bypass the first two conversion stages of alpha-linolenic acid and go straight to EPA and DHA. This is why fish-eaters like the Japanese have three times more Omega 3 fats in their body fat than the average American. Vegans, who eat more seeds and nuts, have twice the Omega 3 fat level of the average American.

ESSENTIAL BALANCE

While borage oil or evening primrose oil may be the best source of Omega 6 and fish oil the best source of Omega 3, that does not make them the best all-rounders. The ideal source of essential fats should have high levels of both. Differing views exist about the perfect ratio. Estimated intakes of our hunter-gatherer ancestors suggest that we need equal amounts. The blood even of high fish-eaters contains about five times as much Omega 6 as Omega 3, suggesting that it is either relatively more important or that all cultures have a relatively greater deficiency of Omega 3 fats. Some researchers advise that we may need to take in twice as much Omega 6 as Omega 3 to match our relative need. Both these ratios, however, are a long way off the average Western diet, which is deficient in both—but with at least ten times more Omega 6 than Omega 3 fat.

The best source in this respect is hemp seed oil from the marijuana plant. Hemp fiber is used to make rope, while hemp butter can be produced from the seeds and the leaves are a good fertilizer. It is, however, illegal to grow the plant in many parts of the world because of its better-known uses. The seeds and fiber, though, will not make you high, and can therefore be sold legally over the counter. Hemp is now making a comeback, both as a source of nutrition and as a fabric for clothing. Hemp seed oil contains 19 percent alpha-linolenic acid (Omega 3), 57 percent linoleic acid and 2 percent GLA (both Omega 6). It is the only common seed oil that meets all known essential fatty acid needs.

Another way of meeting the needs for both Omega 3 and Omega 6 fats is to combine seeds. Sunflower and sesame are good sources of Omega 6, pumpkin provides reasonable quantities of both, while flax seed is richest in Omega 3, containing approximately 50 percent Omega 3 and 10 percent Omega 6. Put one measure each of sesame, sunflower, and pumpkin seeds and two measures of flax seeds in a sealed jar, and keep it in the fridge, away from light, heat, and the air. Grinding two tablespoons of these seeds in a coffee grinder and adding them to your daily breakfast cereal will guarantee a good intake of essential fatty acids. Alternatively, just add one tablespoon and make up the difference with a salad dressing using cold-pressed seed oils, or with some more nuts or seeds later in the day. (Cold pressing oils prevents damage to the essential fats caused by heat processing.)

Of all these, flax seed is the most unsaturated and therefore the most prone to damage. For this reason it is important to buy fresh seeds that have been properly stored away from heat, light, and the air. A small number of companies offer seed oils that are processed in such a way as to protect the oils from oxidation, thus preserving their essential fat status. I recommend buying only cold-pressed oils from organic seeds and storing them in a light-proof container, preferably flushed with nitrogen to exclude any oxygen. In this case a good daily balance of essential fatty acids could be obtained by taking one tablespoon of flax seed oil or a high-potency capsule of EPA/DHA, plus two tablespoons of ground seeds (e.g., sesame, sunflower, and pumpkin) or a high-potency evening primrose oil or borage oil capsule.

Omega 3	Omega 6
2.5–5 percent of total calories **8–17 grams a day**	**3–5 percent of total calories** **10–17 grams a day**
Hemp seed oil 1 tablespoon	Hemp seed oil 1 tablespoon
or	or
Flax seed oil 1 tablespoon	Evening primrose oil 1,000mg
or	or
Flax seeds 2 tablespoons	Borage oil 500mg
or	or
EPA/DHA 1000mg	Sunflower seeds 1 tablespoon
or	or
Pumpkin seeds 4 tablespoons	Pumpkin seeds 2 tablespoons
	or
	Sesame seeds 1.5 tablespoons

Ideally, consume one item in each column per day to achieve your optimum intake of essential fatty acids. Individual needs do vary, however, so take this only as a guideline.

THE BENEFITS OF OLIVE OIL

While olive oil contains no appreciable amounts of the essential Omega 3 and Omega 6 oils, much of it is cold-pressed and unrefined. This makes it better for you than refined vegetable oils like the sunflower oil you can buy in the supermarket. Also, while there is a strong association between a high intake of saturated fats, mainly from meat and dairy products, and cardio-vascular disease, the reverse is true for olive oil. People in Mediterranean countries, whose diet includes large quantities of olive oil, have a lower risk of cardiovascular disease. However, this may be due to a number of positive factors in their diet, including a high intake of fruit and vegetables, and relatively more fish than meat. The use of cold-pressed olive oil, which contains tiny amounts of phytochemicals, also means fewer "trans" fats.

THE DANGERS OF TRANS FATS

Refining and processing vegetable oils can change the nature of the polyunsaturated oil. An example is making margarine. To turn vegetable oil into hard fat the oil goes through a process called hydrogenation. Although the fat is still technically polyunsaturated, the body cannot make use of it. Even worse, it blocks the body's ability to use healthy polyunsaturated oils. This kind of fat is called a "trans" fat because its nature has been changed— it is like a key that fits the body's chemical locks but will not open the door. Most margarines contain these so-called "hydrogenated polyunsaturated oils" and are best avoided. So too are manufactured foods that contain hydrogenated fats, so check ingredients lists on labels carefully. (Given the bad reputation that the process of hydrogenation has attracted, some companies are using a different processing procedure known as esterification. This is also undesirable and likely to interfere with the body's ability to make use of essential fatty acids.)

Frying, as mentioned earlier, is another way to damage otherwise healthy oils. The high temperature makes the oil oxidize so that, instead of being good for you, it generates harmful "free radicals" in the body (explained fully in Chapter 13). Frying is therefore best avoided as much as possible, as is any form of burning or browning fat. If you do fry, use a tiny amount of olive oil or butter because they are less prone to oxidation than top-quality cold-pressed vegetable oils. The latter should be kept sealed in the fridge, away from heat, light, and air, and only used cold in salad dressings or instead of butter on your baked potato or peas.

The general guidelines for getting the right kind and amount of fat in your diet are:

- Eat one tablespoon of cold-pressed seed oil (sesame, sunflower, pumpkin, flax seed, etc.) or one heaped tablespoon of ground seeds a day.

- Avoid fried food, burnt or browned fat, saturated and hydrogenated fat.

- If you do fry, use olive oil or butter.

SUGAR—THE SWEET TRUTH

The human body is designed to run on carbohydrates. While we can use protein and fat for energy, the easiest and most "smoke-free" fuel is carbohydrate. Plants make carbohydrate by trapping the sun's energy in a complex of carbon, hydrogen, and oxygen. Water from the roots provides the hydrogen and oxygen (H_2O), while carbon dioxide (CO_2) from the air provides carbon and more oxygen. Vegetation consists mainly of carbohydrate. We eat the carbohydrate and, in the presence of oxygen from the air, break it down and release the stored solar energy which then provides energy for the body and mind.

When you eat complex carbohydrates like whole grains, vegetables, beans or lentils, or simpler carbohydrates such as fruit, the body does exactly what it is designed to do. It digests these foods and gradually releases their potential energy. What is more, all the nutrients that the body needs for digestion and metabolism are present in those whole foods. Such foods also contain a less digestible type of carbohydrate, classified as fiber, which helps keep the digestive system running smoothly.

While a cat likes the taste of protein humans are principally attracted to the taste of carbohydrate—sweetness. This inherent attraction towards sweetness worked well for early man because most things in nature that are sweet are not poisonous. It also worked well for plants, too. They hid their seeds in their fruit, waiting for animals to pass by, eat the fruit, and deposit the seed some distance from the original plant, along with an "organic manure" starter kit!

But we have discovered how to extract the sweetness and leave the rest—bad news for our nutrition. All forms of concentrated sugar—white sugar, brown sugar, malt, glucose, honey, and syrup—are fast-releasing, causing a rapid increase in blood sugar levels. If this sugar is not required by the body it is put into storage, eventually emerging as fat. Most concentrated forms of sugar are also devoid of vitamins and minerals, unlike the natural sources such as fruit. White sugar has around 90 per cent of its vitamins and minerals removed. Without vitamins and minerals our metabolism becomes inefficient, contributing to poor energy and poor weight control.

Fruit contains a simple sugar called fructose, which needs no digesting and can therefore enter the bloodstream quickly, like glucose or sucrose. However, unlike them it is classified as slow-releasing. This is because the body cannot use fructose as it is, since cells only run on glucose. As a result the fructose first has to be converted by the body into glucose, which effectively slows down this sugar's effect on the metabolism. Some fruits, such as grapes and dates, also contain pure glucose and are therefore faster-releasing. Apples, on the other hand, contain mainly fructose and so are slow-releasing. Bananas contain both and therefore raise blood sugar levels quite speedily.

Refined carbohydrates such as white bread, white rice, or refined cereals have a similar effect to refined sugar. The process of refining or even cooking starts to break down complex carbohydrates into simple carbohydrates, in effect predigesting them. When you eat simple carbohydrates you get a rapid increase in blood sugar level and a corresponding surge in energy. The surge, however, is followed by a drop as the body scrambles to balance your blood sugar level.

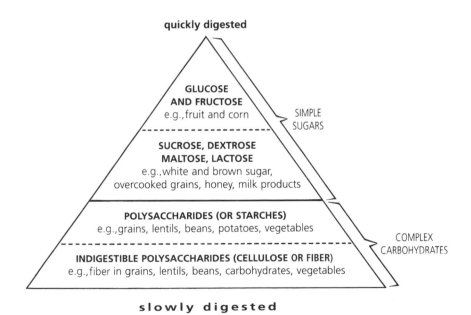

The sugar family

BALANCING YOUR BLOOD SUGAR

Keeping your blood sugar balanced is probably the most important factor in maintaining even energy levels and weight. The level of glucose in your blood largely determines your appetite. When the level drops, you feel hungry. The glucose in your bloodstream is available to your cells to make energy. When the levels are too high the body converts the excess to glycogen (a short-term fuel store mainly in the liver and muscle cells) or fat, our long-term energy reserve. When the levels are too low we experience a whole host of symptoms including fatigue, poor concentration, irritability, nervousness, depression, sweating, headaches, and digestive problems. An estimated three in every ten people have impaired ability to keep their blood sugar level even. It may go too high, and then drop too low. The result, over the years, is that they become increasingly fat and lethargic. But if you can control your blood sugar levels the result is even weight and constant energy.

Diabetes is an extreme form of blood sugar imbalance. This condition arises when the body can no longer produce sufficient insulin, a hormone which helps to carry glucose out of the blood and into cells. The result is too much glucose in the blood and not enough for the cells. The early warning signs are similar to those of mild glucose imbalance, but they rarely go away as a result of simple dietary changes. One of the tell-tale signs is a continuous raging thirst as the body tries to dilute the excess blood sugar by stimulating us to drink.

Glucose tolerance check

Answer the questions below, checking those that you answer "yes" to. If you check four or more, there is a strong possibility that your body is having difficulty keeping your blood sugar level even.

☐ Are you rarely wide awake within twenty minutes of rising?

☐ Do you need a cup of tea or coffee, a cigarette, or something sweet to get you going in the morning?

☐ Do you often feel drowsy or sleepy during the day, or after meals?

☐ Do you fall asleep in the early evening or need naps during the day?

☐ Do you avoid exercise because you do not have the energy?

☐ Do you get dizzy or irritable if you go six hours without food?

☐ Is your energy level now less than it used to be?

☐ Do you get night sweats or frequent headaches?

So what makes your blood sugar level unbalanced? The obvious answer is eating too much sugar and sweet foods. However, the kind of foods that have the greatest effect are not always what you might expect (see table below). The worst is glucose, which is the simplest form of sugar. Malt sugar, Lucozade, and Mars bars all contain glucose, as does most commercial honey. (Unheated and unprocessed honeys from private beekeepers are slower-releasing.) Fructose, the sugar in fruit, has little effect.

In the fruit category, bananas and dried fruit have the greatest effect and apples the least. It is easier to eat more dried fruit, and hence sugar,

Which Foods Raise Blood Sugar Levels?

The foods with the greatest effect on blood sugar have the highest score. Scores above 55 are considered high. Scores ranging from 0 to 54 are considered low.

	HIGH (55+) Limit	LOW (0–54) Increase		HIGH (55+) Limit	LOW (0–54) Increase
Sugars			**Cereals**		
Glucose	100		Cornflakes	80	
Maltose	100		Weetabix	69	
Lucozade	95		Shredded wheat	67	
Honey	87		Muesli	66	
Mars bar	68		Kellogg's All-Bran		52
Sucrose (ordinary			Porridge oats		49
household sugar)	59				
Fructose (fruit sugar)		20	**Legumes**		
			Baked beans		
Fruit			(no sugar)		40
Raisins	64		Butter beans		36
Bananas	62		Chick peas		36
Orange juice		46	Blackeye beans		33
Oranges		40	Haricot beans		31
Apples		39	Kidney beans		29
Grapefruit		25	Lentils		29
			Soybeans		15
Grain products					
French baguette	95		**Dairy products**		
White rice	72		Ice cream		50
White bread	69		Yogurt		36
Wholemeal bread	69		Whole milk		34
Ryvita	69		Skimmed milk		32
Brown rice	66				
Pastry	59		**Vegetables**		
Digestive biscuits	59		Cooked parsnips	97	
Sweetcorn	59		Baked potatoes	85	
Basmati rice	58		Instant potatoes	80	
Oatmeal biscuits (oatcakes)		54	New potatoes	70	
White spaghetti		50	Cooked beet	64	
Wholemeal spaghetti		42	Peas		51
Whole-grain rye bread		41	Carrots		49

because it has all the water removed. Also, the fiber in dried fruit is less effective at filling you up. A handful of raisins is the equivalent of a pound of grapes. Whole grains do not have much effect on blood sugar, unless they are refined. Commercial bread, brown or white, white rice, and white pasta all have greater effects than their whole counterparts. The best bread is a Scandinavian or German whole rye grain bread, such as pumpernickel. Oatcakes also have a small effect on blood sugar. Cornflakes came out badly for breakfast cereals, with porridge oats being the best.

The best foods of all are legumes—peas, beans, and lentils. None of these have substantial effects on blood sugar. Milk products, which contain the sugar lactose, are also good.

Vegetables, when cooked or highly processed, can have a considerable effect on blood sugar. Instant mashed potato has a stronger effect than a Mars bar. Parsnips are the sweetest vegetables—however, if eaten raw or only lightly cooked they have a much less dramatic effect.

Alcohol, which is a chemical cousin of sugar, also upsets blood sugar levels. So do stimulants such as tea, coffee, cola drinks, and cigarettes. These substances, like stress itself, stimulate the release of adrenalin and other hormones that initiate the "fight or flight" response, preparing the body for action by releasing sugar stores and raising blood sugar levels to give our muscles and brain a boost of energy. Unlike our ancestors, whose main stresses (like avoiding being eaten for dinner by a saber-toothed tiger) required a physical response such as shinning up a tree, we in the twentieth century suffer stress mainly in mental or emotional forms. The body has to cope with the excess of blood sugar by releasing yet more hormones to take the glucose out of circulation. The combination of too much sugar,

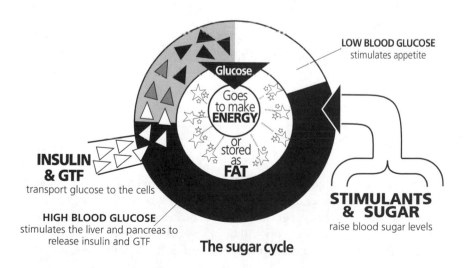

The sugar cycle

stimulants, and prolonged stress taxes the body and results in an inability to control blood sugar levels which, if severe, can develop into diabetes.

The only way out of this vicious circle is to reduce or avoid all forms of concentrated sweetness, tea, coffee, alcohol, and cigarettes, and start eating foods that help to keep your blood sugar level even. The best foods are all kinds of beans, peas, and lentils, oats, and whole grains. They are high in complex carbohydrates, and contain special factors that help release their sugar content gradually. They are also high in fiber, which helps to normalize blood sugar levels as well as assisting the digestive processes.

BREAKING THE HABIT

The taste for concentrated sweetness is often acquired in childhood. If sweet things are used as a reward or to cheer someone up, they become emotional comforters. The best way to break the habit is to avoid concentrated sweetness in the form of sugar, sweets, sweet desserts, dried fruits, and neat fruit juice. Instead, dilute fruit juice and get used to eating fruit instead of having a dessert. Sweeten breakfast cereals with fruit, and have fruit instead of sweet snacks. If you gradually reduce the sweetness in your food you will get used to the taste. Remember, we are designed to eat food that you can pick off a tree or pull out of the ground. Take a look at your average supermarket cart. Ever seen that stuff grow on trees?

SUGAR ALTERNATIVES

Alternatives to sugar, such as honey or maple syrup, are only marginally better. They both contain more minerals than refined sugar; however, most commercial honey is heated to make it more liquid so that it can be cleaned up and put into jars. The heat turns honey's natural sugar, d-levulose, into another, fast-releasing sugar more like glucose. If you like to eat honey, buy the untreated kind from small local suppliers.

Artificial sweeteners are not so great either. Some (admittedly in large quantities) have been shown to have harmful effects on health, and all perpetuate a sweet tooth.

FIBER

Not all types of carbohydrate can be digested and broken down into glucose. Indigestible carbohydrate is called fiber. This is a natural constituent of a healthy diet high in fruit, vegetables, lentils, beans, and whole grains, and by eating such a high-fiber diet you will be at less risk of bowel cancer, diabetes, and diverticular disease, and are unlikely to suffer from constipation.

Contrary to the popular image of fiber as "roughage," it can absorb water. As it does so it makes fecal matter bulkier, less dense, and easier to pass along the digestive tract. This decreases the amount of time that food waste spends inside the body and reduces the risk of infection or cell changes due to carcinogens that are produced when some foods, particularly meat, degrade. A frequent meat-eater with a low-fiber diet can increase the stomach transit time of food from 24 to 72 hours, giving time for some putrefaction to occur. So if you like meat make sure you also eat high-fiber foods.

There are many different types of fiber, some of which are proteins and not carbohydrates. Some kinds, such as that found in oats, are called "soluble fiber" and combine with sugar molecules to slow down the absorption of carbohydrates. In this way they help to keep blood sugar levels balanced. Some fibers are much more water-absorbent than others. While wheat fiber swells to ten times its original volume in water, glucomannan fiber, from the Japanese konjac plant, swells to one hundred times its volume in water. By bulking up foods and releasing sugars slowly, highly absorbent types of fiber can help to control appetite and play a part in weight maintenance.

An ideal intake of fiber is not less than 35 grams a day. Provided the right foods are eaten, this level can easily be achieved without adding extra fiber. Professor of Nutrition John Dickerson from the University of Surrey has stressed the danger of adding wheat bran to a nutrient-poor diet. The reason is that wheat bran contains high levels of phytate, an anti-nutrient which reduces the absorption of essential minerals, including zinc. Overall, it is probably best to get fiber from a mixture of sources such as oats, lentils, beans, seeds, fruits, and raw or lightly cooked vegetables. Much of the fiber in vegetables is destroyed by cooking, so they are best eaten crunchy.

To ensure that you get enough of the right kinds of carbohydrates:

- Eat whole foods—whole grains, lentils, beans, nuts, seeds, fresh fruit, and vegetables—and avoid refined, white, and overcooked foods.

- Eat five servings a day of dark green, leafy and root vegetables such as watercress, carrots, sweet potatoes, broccoli, brussels sprouts, spinach, green beans, or peppers, either raw or lightly cooked.

- Eat three or more servings a day of fresh fruit such as apples, pears, bananas, berries, melon, or citrus fruit.

- Eat four or more servings a day of whole grains such as rice, millet, rye, oats, whole wheat, corn, quinoa as cereal, breads, pasta, or legumes.

- Avoid any form of sugar, added sugar, and white, or refined foods.

- Dilute fruit juices and only eat dried fruits infrequently in small quantities, preferably soaked.

11

THE VITAMIN SCANDAL

Major surveys of eating habits in the U.S. since the 1980s have consistently and repeatedly shown that the average American diet, even among those who consider themselves to be eating a well-balanced diet, fails to achieve the Recommended Daily Allowances. But these RDAs of nutrients are set by governments to prevent deficiency diseases like scurvy; they are certainly not designed to ensure optimal health, and there is a big difference between a lack of illness and the presence of wellness. For example, the average person gets 3.5 colds a year. In a study of 1,038 doctors and their wives, those who took 410 mg of vitamin C a day had the least signs of illness and lowest incidence of colds. This intake is roughly ten times the RDA for vitamin C.

RDAs are set by panels of scientists in different countries, based on what is known to prevent classic nutrient deficiency diseases. The trouble is that the scientists cannot agree. From country to country there is often a tenfold variation in recommended levels of nutrients. Dr. Stephen Davies, a medical researcher, tested blood levels of B vitamins in thousands of people and found more than seven in every ten to be deficient.[18] The RDAs do not take into account an individual's circumstances, nor do they consider the question of what is optimal. For example, if you smoke, drink alcohol, live in a polluted city, are premenstrual, menopausal, or on the pill, exercise a lot, are fighting an infection, or stressed out, your nutrient needs can easily double.

What is more, it is very difficult to eat a diet that meets the RDA levels. What most people conceive of as a well-balanced diet fails to meet RDA requirements. The Bateman Report, published in 1985,[19] found that more than 85 percent of people who generally thought they ate a well-balanced diet failed to meet RDA levels. At the other end of the scale, 25 percent of women on income support take in smaller quantities of eight nutrients than the level known to result in serious deficiency diseases (Food Commission,

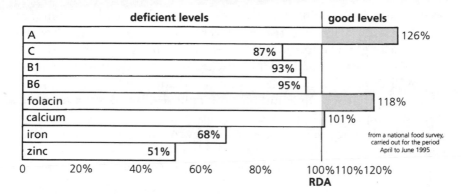

Average intake as a percentage of the EU RDA

1992). In truth, fewer than one in ten people eat a diet that meets even the RDA requirements.

EMPTY CALORIES

As much as two-thirds of the average calorie intake is from fat, sugar, and refined flours. The calories in these foods are called "empty" because they provide no nutrients, and are often hidden in processed foods and snacks which usually weigh little but satisfy our appetite instantly. For instance, two sweet cookies provide more calories than one pound of carrots and are considerably easier to eat—but they provide no vitamins or minerals. If a quarter of your diet by weight, and two-thirds by calories, consists of such dismembered foods, there is little room left to accommodate the necessary levels of the essential nutrients. Wheat, for example, has twenty-five nutrients removed in the refining process that turns it into white flour, yet only four (iron, B1, B2, and B3) are replaced. On average, 87 percent of the vital minerals zinc, chromium, and manganese are lost. Have we been short-changed? This raises three questions. What is "need"? Are the RDA levels enough? And how can we achieve the necessary intake?

WHY FEELING JUST "ALL RIGHT" IS NOT ALL RIGHT

To date the evidence is that most people are being short-changed on health, due to inadequate intakes of vitamins and minerals. Since the 1980s proper scientific studies using multinutrient supplements have shown that they boost immunity, increase IQ, reduce birth defects, improve childhood development, reduce colds, stop PMS, improve bone density, balance moods, increase energy, reduce the risk of cancer and heart disease, and basically promote a long and healthy life. Most people are putting up with "feeling all right"—accepting the odd cold, headache, mouth ulcer, muscle cramp or bout of PMS, mood fluctuations, poor concentration, and lack of energy. In 1982 the Institute for Optimum Nutrition put seventy-six volunteers on a six-month supplement program.[20] At the end of this time 79 percent reported a definite improvement in energy, 60 percent spoke of better memory and mental alertness, 66 percent felt more emotionally balanced, 57 percent had fewer colds and infections, and 55 percent had better skin.

WHAT IS OPTIMUM?

The RDAs are not enough for optimum health. Thanks to Dr. Emanuel Cheraskin and colleagues from the University of Alabama, we are one step closer to defining optimum nutrition.[21] Over a fifteen-year period they studied 13,500 people living in six regions of the U.S.. Each participant completed in-depth health questionnaires and was given physical, dental, eye, and other examinations, as well as numerous blood tests, cardiac function tests, and a detailed dietary analysis. The object was to find which nutrient intake levels were associated with the highest health ratings. The results consistently revealed that the healthiest individuals, meaning those with the fewest clinical signs and symptoms, were taking supplements and eating a diet rich in nutrients relative to calories. The researchers found that the intake of nutrients associated with optimal health was often ten or

Suggested Optimal Nutrient Allowances compared to RDAs

	RDA	Suggested Optimal Intake	
	Male/Female	Male/Female 25–50	Male/Female 51+
Vitamin A (retinol)	1,000/800 mcg	2000mcg RE	2000mcg RE
Vitamin C	60 mg	400mg	800/1000mg
Vitamin E	10/8 mg	400mg	800mg
Vitamin B1 (thiamine)	1.5/1.1 mg	7.5/7.1mg	9.2/9.0mg
Vitamin B2 (riboflavin)	1.7/1.3 mg	2.5/2mg	2.5/2mcg
Vitamin B3 (niacin)	19/15 mg	30/25mg	30/25mg
Vitamin B6 (pyridoxine)	2.0/1.6 mg	10mg	25/20mg
Vitamin B12	2.4 mcg	2μg	3/2μg
Folic Acid	400 mcg	800μg	1000μg

(RDAs are Reference Nutrient Intakes from Department of Health, 1991)

more times higher than the RDA levels. On the basis of this evidence they have established Suggested Optimal Nutrient Allowances, SONAs for short, for vitamins. These levels, shown in the table opposite, are more likely to be the kind of intake you need to maintain optimum health.

The conclusion was that SONAs are often ten times the RDA, which is confirmed by many large-scale supplement studies. For example, ninety-six healthy elderly people were given a SONA-type supplement or placebo. Those on the supplement had fewer infections and blood tests revealed a stronger immune system; in fact they were healthier overall. Of 22,000 pregnant women, some on supplements, some not, the group taking supplements gave birth to 75 percent fewer babies with birth defects. In another study, ninety schoolchildren were given SONA-type supplements, placebos, or nothing. Seven months later the IQ scores of those on supplements were 10 percent higher than those of the other two groups. A professor of medicine examined all studies looking at vitamin C versus the common cold, selecting only those where 1,000 mg or more was given, and involving a placebo group (known as double-blind testing).[22] Of these tests, thirty-seven out of thirty-eight concluded that supplementing 1,000 mg, twenty times the RDA, had a protective effect. Professor Morris Brown at Cambridge University gave two thousand patients with heart disease vitamin E or a placebo. Those taking vitamin E had 75 percent fewer heart attacks.[1]

These are just some of the hundreds of scientific studies published in respected medical journals which prove that an intake of vitamins above RDA levels enhances resistance to infection, improves intellectual performance, and reduces the risk of birth defects, cancer, and heart disease. Despite this, some "flat-earthers" continue to say that supplements are a waste of money. To quote one anti-supplement survey of people who took supplements, published in the journal *Nutrition Reviews*, "It is ironic that adults who were not overweight and whose health was good used supplements more frequently than did less healthy individuals" What a strange coincidence!

Vitamin A

This vitamin is essential for reproduction and for the maintenance of epithelial tissue found in skin, inside and out, such as the lungs, gastro-intestinal tract, uterus, and so on. Beta-carotene is the most active precursor of vitamin A, and in high doses, unlike vitamin A itself, is not toxic. Vitamin A is important in cancer prevention and treatment of pre-cancerous conditions. People with low beta-carotene intake have a 30–220 percent higher risk of developing lung cancer, for example.[23] The optimal intake of vitamin A is likely to be at least double the RDA. Even higher levels of beta-carotene may confer extra benefit.

VITAMIN B COMPLEX

This group of vitamins includes eight essential nutrients. B1 (thiamine) is unlikely to be needed at levels more than eleven times the RDA unless you are consuming a lot of refined carbohydrates. A study of 1,009 dentists and their wives found the healthiest to consume on average 9 mg of thiamine a day.

Vitamin B2 (riboflavin) is needed in greater quantities by those who exercise frequently. To date there is insufficient evidence to recommend more than double the RDA.

Vitamin B3 (niacin) is famous for its ability to help remove unwanted cholesterol but notorious for its vasodilatory or blushing effect in high doses. According to one study the healthiest people consume 115 mg a day, which is nine times the RDA.

Vitamin B6 (pyridoxine) is another B vitamin that appears to have considerable benefit at levels ten times higher than RDAs. It is essential for all protein utilization and has been helpful in a variety of conditions from PMS to carpal tunnel syndrome (a strain condition affecting nerves in the wrist) and cardiovascular disease.

Folic acid is now recognized as essential for the prevention of neural tube defects in pregnancy, and the U.S. government recommends pregnant women to take a daily 400 mcg supplement. Optimal levels, especially in the elderly, may be much higher. There is one caution, however: folic acid supplementation can mask B12 deficiency anemia. So it is best to supplement extra folic acid with vitamin B12.

VITAMIN C

This one is necessary for a strong immune system, for collagen and bone formation, for energy production, and as an antioxidant. In a study of 1,038 doctors and their wives, those with a daily intake of 410 mg of vitamin C had the fewest signs of illness or degenerative disease.[24] This intake, roughly ten times the RDA, is close to that of our primitive ancestors. A large number of studies have found a reduced risk of cancer in those with a high vitamin C intake. Vitamin C status and bone density decline from the age of thirty-five. Numerous studies have shown vitamin C to be associated with improved bone density as well as keeping the absorption of iron, giving us good reason to increase our intake as we get older.

The protective role of vitamin C against various cancers, cardiovascular disease, and the common cold only becomes significant above 400–1,000mg a day. In a large survey in the U.S., analyzed by Dr. Enstrom and Dr. Pauling, significant reductions in overall mortality and mortality from cancer and cardiovascular disease were reported in those who took vitamin E and C supplements.[25]

Since 1,000 mg of vitamin C is equivalent to twenty-two oranges, supplementation is essential. The RDA for vitamin C is only 60 mg—the equivalent of an orange a day.

VITAMIN E

One of the most essential antioxidants, vitamin E helps the body to use oxygen properly. A number of studies have found low vitamin E status to be associated with high cancer incidence. Supplementation of this vitamin has been shown to boost immunity and reduce infections in the elderly as well as halving the risk of cataracts. The RDA for vitamin E is 60 IU. The optimal intake of vitamin E is ten times this, and double that for people over fifty.

VITAMINS D AND K

These are not commonly deficient. Vitamin K is made by bacteria in the stomach, while vitamin D can be made in the skin on exposure to sunlight. Vitamin D is also found in milk, meat, and eggs. Deficiency is only likely in dark-skinned vegans who have little exposure to the sun.

THE DECLINE OF FRUIT AND VEGETABLES

The sad truth is that today's food is not what it used to be. Fruit and vegetables are only as good as the soil in which they are grown. Minerals pass from the soil to the plant, and in turn help the plant to grow and produce vitamins. The trouble is that modern farming, which relies heavily on artificial fertilizers and pesticides, robs the soil of nutrients and does not replace them. Phosphates found in fertilizers and pesticides bind to the minerals in the soil, making them less available to the plant. Through overfarming, the soil becomes nutrient-deficient anyway. However, adding fertilizer (nitrogen, phosphate, and potassium) enables plants to go on growing, but without the full complement of minerals. So the plant does not make its full complement of vitamins and we too end up deficient.

For these reasons, plus the length of time we store foods, there is a staggering range of nutrient content in fruit and vegetables. An orange may provide from 180 mg to none at all, the average being around 60 mg. Yes, some supermarket oranges contain no vitamin C! A hundred grams of wheat germ (about three cups) provides from 2.1 mg to 14 mg of vitamin E.

Variations in nutrient content in common foods

Nutrient	Variation (per 100 g of food)
Vitamin A in carrots	70 to 18,500 IU
Vitamin B₅ in whole wheat flour	0.3 to 3.3 mg
Vitamin C in oranges	0 to 116 mg
Vitamin E in wheat germ	3.2 to 21 IU
Iron in spinach	0.1 to 158 mg
Manganese in lettuce	0.1 to 16.9 mg

A large carrot can provide from 70 to 18,500 IU of vitamin A. While it's great to eat lots of fruit and vegetables, the quality is just as important as the quantity. For these reasons it is best to buy local produce in season and consume it quickly. The worst thing you can do is to buy fruit shipped in from the other side of the world, and leave it hanging around for two weeks before you eat it.

GOOD FOOD GOES BAD

Food manufacturing, more than farming practices, is the greatest cause of vitamin loss. Foods are refined so that they last longer. Flour, rice, and sugar loses more than 77 percent of their zinc, chromium, and manganese in the refining process. Other essential nutrients, such as essential fats, will not be present in processed foods because these and other nutrients (except antioxidant vitamins A, C, and E, which preserve foods) can decrease shelf-life. There is an old saying among nutritionists that "good food goes bad"— the trick is to eat it first.

WHAT ABOUT COOKING?

More than half the nutrients in the food you eat are destroyed before they reach your plate, depending on the food you choose, how you store it, and how you cook it. Every process that food goes through, whether boiling, baking, frying, or freezing, takes its toll. Think about the life of a string bean. It is picked, stored, cooked, frozen, stored in the supermarket until you buy it, partially defrosted on the way home, refrozen, boiled, and eaten. Just how much goodness is left?

The three main enemies of vitamins and minerals are heating, water, and oxidation. Vitamin C is very prone to oxidation, sacrificing itself to harmful oxides that make food go rancid. While it might protect your food, it will not protect you if there is none left by the time you eat it. The longer your food has been stored, and the more surface area is exposed to air and light, the less vitamin C there is likely to be. Orange juice, which is packed using a special process to minimize oxide exposure on packing, suffers a 33 percent loss of vitamin C in twenty-two weeks, which is a conceivable timelag between orange grove and breakfast glass. Once you open the carton oxidation occurs rapidly, especially if you fail to put it back in the fridge, which also protects it from light. Analysis of rosehip tea bags have shown negligible traces of vitamin C or none at all, even before immersing it in boiling water which is likely to kill off any remaining traces.

Nor is vitamin C the only vitamin susceptible to oxidation: the anti-oxidant vitamins A and E are also prone to damage. Being fat-soluble, they tend to be protected by being in fattier foods. Beta-carotene, the vegetable form of vitamin A, is water-soluble and highly prone to oxidation. While storing foods in cool, dark places tends to help, oxidation still occurs even in the fridge. Spinach stored in an open container will lose 10 percent of its vitamin C content every day.

On the whole, frozen foods keep their nutrient content much better. Chilled foods, kept for two weeks in the supermarket and one week in your fridge, will have lost their vitamin vitality, while there is little difference in nutrient loss between frozen peas and fresh peas, once boiled.

Any form of heating destroys nutrients. The degree of destruction depends on the cooking time, whether the container disperses the heat evenly, but most of all the temperature. On average, 20–70 percent of the nutrient content of leafy vegetables is lost in cooking.

Deep-frying produces temperatures in excess of 232°F, which oxidize fat and turn essential fatty acids into trans fats that are no good for anything. Animals fed such oils develop atherosclerosis. Refined oils, left for weeks on supermarket shelves exposed to light, are already damaged. These oils should not be used for frying as they increase the destruction of antioxidant nutrients like vitamins A, C, and E both in the food and later in the body. See p. 52 for the best way to fry food if you still want to use this cooking method.

Minerals and water-soluble vitamins leach into cooking water. The more water you use and the longer the cooking time, the more this is likely to occur. If the temperature is above 82°F cell structures begin to break down, which enables nutrients within them to be leached out. High temperatures can also destroy some of the vitamins, though not the minerals. If you boil or steam food for a short while, the temperature at the core of the food will be much lower than at the outside. Foods can therefore be protected by cooking them whole, or in large pieces. The loss of nutrients in boiled food tends to be around

20–50 percent. It is a good idea to use the mineral-rich water as stock for soups or sauces.

Microwaving water-based foods such as vegetables generates heat by vibrating the water particles in the food, and vitamin and mineral losses are minimal. However, as far as essential fats are concerned the heat generated by microwaving rapidly destroys them, so never microwave a dish with oils, nuts, or seeds in it.

Here are some guidelines for getting the most vitamins out of your food:

- Eat foods as fresh and unprocessed as possible.

- Keep fresh food cool and in the dark in the fridge in sealed containers.

- Eat more raw food. Be adventurous: try raw beet and carrot tops in salad.

- Prepare foods cold where possible (e.g., carrot soup) and heat to serve.

- Cook foods as whole as possible, slicing or blending before serving.

- Steam or boil foods with as little water as possible, and keep the water for stock.

- Fry as little food as possible and do not overcook, burn, or brown it.

- Supplement your diet to ensure optimum levels of vitamins.

12

ELEMENTAL HEALTH
FROM CALCIUM TO ZINC

More than a hundred years ago a Russian chemist called Mendelyeff noticed that all the basic constituents of matter, the elements, could be arranged in a pattern according to their chemical properties. From this he produced what is known as the periodic table. There were many gaps where elements should be, and sure enough over the years these missing elements have been discovered. All matter, including your body, is made out of these elements.

Some of these are gases, like oxygen and hydrogen; some are liquids; and some, such as iron, zinc, and chromium, are solids. Ninety-six percent of the body is made up of carbon, hydrogen, oxygen, and nitrogen, which form carbohydrate, protein, and fat, as well as vitamins. The remaining 4 percent is made from minerals.

These minerals are mainly used to regulate and balance our body chemistry, the exceptions are calcium, phosphorus, and magnesium, which are the major constituents of bone. These three, plus sodium and potassium, which control the water balance in the body, are called macro-minerals because we need relatively large amounts each day (300–3,000 mg). The remaining elements are called trace minerals because we need only traces (30 mg to 30 mcg). But all these minerals are required in tiny amounts compared to carbon, hydrogen, and oxygen. For instance, a 140-pound man needs 400 grams of carbohydrate a day but only 40 micrograms of chromium, which is less than a millionth of the amount. Yet chromium is no less important.

MINERAL DEFICIENCY IS WIDESPREAD

Minerals are extracted from the soil in the first place by plants. Like vitamins, they may be obtained directly from those plants or indirectly via meat. And, again like vitamins, they are frequently deficient in our modern diets. There are three primary reasons.

Mineral levels in natural foods are declining. This is partly because soil gradually loses its mineral content through overfarming, unless the farmer replaces the minerals by adding back mineral-rich manure. But many of the minerals that pass from plant to us are not needed to make the plant grow, so there is no incentive for the farmer to add them back. The minerals that are added back in fertilizer (nitrogen, phosphate and potassium) make the plant grow faster, and, in the case of phosphate, bind to trace minerals like zinc and make them harder for the plant to take up. Analysis of mineral levels in plants in 1939 compared to 1991 show, on average, a drop of 22 percent. (The accuracy of this data is, however, a little suspect as analytical methods have improved dramatically over this time period.)

Essential minerals are refined out of food. Refining food to make white rice, white flour, and white sugar removes up to 90 percent of the trace minerals. Foods like refined cereals must meet a legal minimum nutrient requirement and therefore have some calcium, iron, and B vitamins added back. To help sell them the packet says "enriched" or "with added vitamins and minerals." This would not be necessary if the food was not refined in the first place.

Our mineral needs are increasing. Dr. Stephen Davies from London's Biolab Medical Unit has analyzed 65,000 samples of blood, hair, and sweat over the past fifteen years.[26] Without exception, when the results are compared with the ages of the patients, levels of lead, cadmium, aluminum, and mercury are increasing, while those of magnesium, zinc, chromium, manganese, and selenium are decreasing. The first group are toxic minerals—anti-nutrients which compete with essential minerals. As we age, those toxic elements accumulate. Today we need more "good" minerals than ever to protect us from the unavoidable toxic minerals that reach us via polluted food, air, and water.

Mineral Loss Caused by Food Processing

	WHITE FLOUR	SUGAR REFINING	RICE POLISHING
Chromium	98%	95%	92%
Zinc	78%	88%	54%
Manganese	86%	89%	75%

For these reasons, and the fact that many of us choose to eat foods such as refined bread, pasta, and cereal, and avoid the mineral-rich foods such as seeds and nuts, modern man is mineral-deficient. The average dietary intake of zinc (7.5 mg) is half the RDA of 15 mg. The recommended intake for a

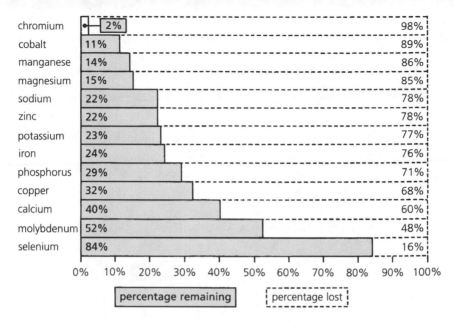

Percentage of minerals lost in refining flour

breast-feeding woman is 25 mg, more than three times the average intake, leaving breast-fed infants hopelessly deficient in a mineral that is essential for all growth processes including intellectual development.

The average intake of iron and magnesium is well below Recommended Daily Amounts. While no RDAs exist for manganese, chromium and selenium, dietary intakes are certainly below estimates of what we need for optimal health.

In animals, such a state of mineral malnutrition is a known cause of a wide range of illnesses. For this reason livestock feed is enriched with minerals. Not so with man. Is it any wonder we are not healthy?

THE MACRO-MINERALS

Those minerals that are present in the body in relatively large amounts include calcium, magnesium, phosphorus, potassium, and sodium.

Calcium—the bone-builder

Nearly 3 pounds of your body weight is calcium, and 99 percent of this is in your bones and teeth. Calcium is needed to provide the rigid structure of the skeleton. It is particularly important in childhood when bones are growing, and also in the elderly because the ability to absorb calcium becomes impaired with age. The remaining 10 or so grams of calcium are in the nerves, muscles, and blood. Working together with magnesium, it is needed to enable nerves and muscles to "fire." It also assists the blood to clot and helps maintain the right acid/alkaline balance.

The average Western diet provides marginally less than the RDA for calcium. Most of it comes from milk and cheese, which is a poor source. However, vegetables, legumes, nuts, whole grains, and water provide significant quantities of both calcium and magnesium, and it is likely that our ancestors relied on these foods for their calcium.

Calcium – How Much Is Absorbed?

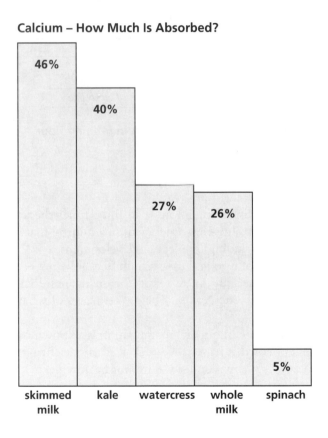

The ability to use calcium depends not only on its intake but also on its absorption. The amount absorbed depends on the food, but is normally around 20–30 percent. The calcium balance of the body is improved by adequate vitamin D intake and by weight-bearing exercise. It is made worse by vitamin D deficiency, exposure to lead, consumption of alcohol, coffee, and tea, or a lack of hydrochloric acid produced in the stomach. The presence of naturally occurring chemicals called phytates, which are found in grains and excessive phosphorus or fat in the diet, also interferes with absorption. Excessive protein consumption also causes of loss of calcium from the bones.

Symptoms of deficiency include muscle cramps, tremors or spasms, insomnia, nervousness, joint pain, osteoarthritis, tooth decay, and high blood pressure. Severe deficiency causes osteoporosis. However, this is more likely to be connected with and protein excess hormone imbalances (see Chapters 8 and 20).

Magnesium—calcium's comrade in arms

Magnesium works with calcium in maintaining both bone density and nerve and muscle impulses. The average diet is relatively high in calcium but deficient in magnesium, because milk, our major source of calcium, is not a very good source of magnesium. Both minerals are present in green leafy vegetables, nuts and seeds. Magnesium is a vital component of chlorophyll which gives plants their green color and is therefore present in all green vegetables. However, only a small proportion of the magnesium within plants is in the form of chlorophyll.

Magnesium is essential for many enzymes in the body, working together with vitamins B1 and B6. It is also involved in protein synthesis and is therefore vital for production of some hormones. It may be its role in hormone production or prostaglandin production that is responsible for its beneficial effects on pre-menstrual problems.

A lack of magnesium is strongly associated with cardiovascular disease: patients who die from this cause have abnormally low levels of the mineral in their hearts. Lack of magnesium causes muscles to go into spasm, and there is considerable evidence that some heart attacks are caused, not by obstruction of the coronary arteries but by cramping of them, resulting in the heart being deprived of oxygen.

Sodium—nerves and water balance

Eaten mainly in the form of sodium chloride, more familiarly known as salt, there are 92 g of sodium in the human body. More than half is in the fluids surrounding cells, where it plays a vital role both in nerve transmission and in the maintenance of water concentration in blood and body fluids. Deficiency is exceedingly rare, because too much is added to foods and also because its excretion is carefully controlled by the kidneys. It is present in most natural foods in small amounts and is mainly supplied in processed foods. There is no need to add it to food, and good reasons not to. Excess sodium is associated with raised blood pressure, although it appears that some people are not salt-sensitive in this way. As sodium levels in the body rise, fluids are made less concentrated by retaining more water. This gives rise to edema or fluid retention.

Potassium—Sodium's partner

This mineral works in conjunction with sodium in maintaining water balance and proper nerve and muscle impulses. Most of the potassium in the body is inside the cells. The more sodium (salt) is eaten the more potassium is required, and since the average daily intake of potassium is only 4 grams, relative deficiency is widespread. The same level of intake of these two minerals is more consistent with good health. Fruits, vegetables, and whole grains are rich in potassium.

Severe potassium deficiency may result in vomiting, abdominal bloating, muscular weakness, and loss of appetite. Potassium deficiency is more likely to occur in people taking diuretic drugs or laxatives or using corticosteroid drugs over a long period.

THE TRACE MINERALS

Iron—the oxygen carrier

Iron is a vital component of hemoglobin, which transports oxygen and carbon dioxide to and from cells. Sixty percent of the iron within us is in the form of red pigment or haem. This is the form present in meat, and is much more readily absorbed than the non-hem iron present in non-meat food sources. Non-hem iron occurs in the oxidized or ferric state in food, and not until it is reduced to the ferrous state (for example by vitamin C) during digestion can it be absorbed.

The symptoms of iron deficiency include pale skin, sore tongue, fatigue or listlessness, loss of appetite, and nausea. Anemia is clinically diagnosed by checking hemoglobin levels in the blood. However, symptoms of anemia can be caused by a lack of vitamin B12 or folic acid. Iron deficiency anemia is more likely to occur in women, especially during pregnancy. Since iron is an antagonist to zinc, increasing the requirement for zinc, supplements containing more than 30 mg of iron, over twice the RDA, should not be taken without ensuring that enough zinc is also being consumed. Although iron supplements are often given in doses above 50mg, there is little evidence that this is more effective than lower doses in raising hemoglobin levels.

Too much iron may also increase the risk of cardiovascular disease. According to a Finnish study on 1900 men, those with higher iron stores

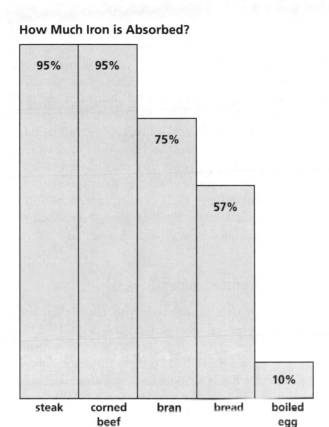

How Much Iron is Absorbed?

95% | 95% | 75% | 57% | | 10%

steak | corned beef | bran | bread | boiled egg

were more than twice as likely to have a heart attack.[27] Jerome Sullivan, a pathologist at the Veterans' Affairs Medical Center in South Carolina, found a correlation between blood ferritin levels (most iron reserves in the body are stored as ferritin), and cardiovascular risk, and thinks that this might explain why menstruating women, who lose iron each month, have a lesser risk of cardiovascular disease than men until after the menopause.[28] This theory is yet to be proven, but suggests that meat-eating men should not go overboard on iron supplements. In practice, this means limiting the dose to 10 mg a day.

Zinc—a major role player

A large part of the population is at risk of being zinc-deficient. With half the population eating less than half the RDA, few get enough from their diet. Deficiency symptoms are white marks on the nails, lack of appetite, or lack of appetite control, pallor, infertility, lack of resistance to infection, poor growth (including hair), poor skin including acne, dermatitis, and stretch marks, plus mental and emotional problems. Zinc deficiency plays a role in nearly every major disease, including diabetes and cancer. It is needed to make insulin, to boost the immune system, and make the antioxidant enzyme SOD (superoxide dismutase). It is also required to make prostaglandins from essential fatty acids. These hormone-like substances help to balance hormones and to control inflammation and the stickiness of the blood. Sucking zinc lozenges helps to shorten the life of a cold.

Zinc's main role is the protection and repair of DNA, and for this reason it is found in higher levels in animals and fish than in plants—animals have higher levels of DNA. A vegetarian diet may therefore be low in zinc. Stress, smoking, and alcohol deplete zinc, as does frequent sex, at least for men, since semen contains very high concentrations of zinc. Oysters are popularly said to be aphrodisiacs. They are also the highest dietary source of zinc, and for both men and women zinc is essential for fertility.

Manganese—the forgotten mineral

This mineral is known to be involved in no fewer than twenty enzyme systems in the body. One of the most critical is SOD which acts as an antioxidant, helping to disarm free radicals. In animals, manganese deficiency results in reduced insulin production. Since diabetics frequently have low manganese levels it is thought to be involved in maintaining blood sugar balance. It is also involved in the formation of mucopolysaccharides, a constituent of cartilage. One of the first signs associated with deficiency is joint pain.

Manganese is also required for proper brain function. Deficiency has been associated with schizophrenia, Parkinson's disease, and epilepsy. It is frequently deficient in the diet and the best sources include tropical fruits, nuts, seeds, and whole grains. Tea is also a significant source of this mineral and supplies half our daily intake. Little more than 5 percent of the manganese eaten in the diet is absorbed, though exactly why is unknown. Similarly, supplements are poorly absorbed, the best forms being manganese citrate or manganese amino acid chelate.

Copper—good and bad

Both a nutritional and a toxic element, copper is required by humans in doses as little as 2mg a day. It is rarely deficient for the simple reason that most water supplies are contaminated via copper pipes. It is needed among other things for the formation of the insulating myelin sheath around nerves. Copper and zinc are strongly antagonistic, and zinc deficiency may lead to a greater uptake of copper. Likewise, excessive zinc supplementation can induce copper deficiency.

In reality, excess is a more common problem than deficiency. If you are on a whole food diet there is no need to supplement copper, yet it is often included in multimineral tablets. Taking the birth control pill or HRT also increases your copper stores. All these factors make it relatively easy to accumulate too much copper, which is associated with schizophrenia, cardiovascular disease, and possibly rheumatoid arthritis. However, copper deficiency has also been associated with rheumatoid arthritis. Copper is a constituent of an antioxidant enzyme involved in some inflammatory reactions. This may be the reason why too much or too little can result in greater inflammation in sufferers from rheumatoid arthritis. Copper levels rise during pregnancy, and it is speculated that it plays a role in bringing on labor and, in excess, post-natal depression.

Chromium—the energy factor

This is a vital constituent of glucose tolerance factor, a compound produced in the liver which helps transport glucose from the blood to the cells. Vitamin B3 and the amino acids glycine, glutamic acid, and cystine are also required for glucose tolerance factor. Continued stress or frequent sugar consumption therefore deplete the body of chromium. A diet high in refined foods is also likely to be deficient in this mineral since it is found in whole grains, legumes, nuts, seeds, and especially in mushrooms and asparagus. Chromium supplements have been used successfully in the treatment of diabetes and glucose intolerance.

Selenium—the anti-cancer mineral

Deficiency of this mineral was first discovered in China as the cause of "Keshan disease," a type of heart disease prevalent in areas in which the soil was deficient in selenium. It has since been associated with another regional disease, this time in Russia, involving joint degeneration. Perhaps the most significant finding is selenium's association with a low risk of certain kinds of cancer.

Selenium is the vital constituent of the antioxidant enzyme glutathione peroxidase. A tenfold increase in dietary selenium causes a doubling of the quantity of this enzyme in the body. Since many oxides are cancer-producing, and since cancer cells destroy other cells by releasing oxides, it is likely to be selenium's role in glutathione peroxidase production that gives it protective properties against cancer and premature aging. It may also be essential for the thyroid gland, which controls the body's rate of metabolism.

Selenium is found predominantly in whole foods, particularly seafood and sesame seeds. If you grind the seeds the nutrients become more readily available.

The unknown minerals

As research unfolds and analytical techniques improve we will probably find that many more minerals have an important role to play. Some are already proven, although not widely known. They include boron, which helps the body use calcium and may be beneficial for arthritis sufferers; molybdenum, which helps remove undesirable free radicals, petrochemicals, and sulphites from the body and is therefore useful for city-dwellers who want protection from pollution; vanadium, proved to be essential in some animals, which may be useful for the treatment of manic depression; and germanium, which has antioxidant potential.

Since the 1970s analytical chemists have moved from being able to detect minerals in food, blood, hair, and so on at a level of one part in a million, down to one part in a quillion—that's a millionth of a million, or the equivalent of dissolving a lump of sugar in the Mediterranean and being able to detect the difference. It is highly likely that we have much more to learn about the magic of minerals.

13

ANTIOXIDANTS—THE POWER OF PREVENTION

Since the 1980s more and more research has confirmed that many of the twentieth century's most common diseases are associated with a shortage of antioxidant nutrients, and helped by their supplementation. So important is the role of antioxidants that medical science is beginning to consider the presence of any one of the diseases listed below a sign of probable antioxidant deficiency, in the same way that scurvy is a sign of vitamin C deficiency. In the future we may be tested for blood levels of antioxidant nutrients alongside levels of blood sugar and cholesterol and blood pressure. Capable of predicting your biological age and expected life span, your antioxidant nutrient status may prove to be your most vital statistic.

Probable Antioxidant Deficiency Diseases

Alzheimer's disease
Cancer
Cardiovascular disease
Cataracts
Diabetes
Hypertension
Infertility
Macular (eye lens) degeneration
Measles
Mental illness
Periodontal (tooth) disease
Respiratory tract infections
Rheumatoid arthritis

The common denominator in the process of aging and its associated diseased is called oxidative damage. This has put the spotlight on the use of antioxidants—nutrients that help protect the body from this damage by preventing and treating disease. So far, over a hundred antioxidant nutrients have been discovered and hundreds, if not thousands, of research papers have extolled their benefits. The main players are vitamins A, C, and E, plus beta-carotene, the precursor of vitamin A that is found in fruit and vegetables. Their presence in your diet and levels in your blood may prove to be the best indicator yet of your power to delay death and prevent disease.

WHAT IS AN ANTIOXIDANT?

Oxygen is the basis of all plant and animal life. It is our most important nutrient, needed by every cell every second of every day. Without it we cannot release the energy in food which drives all body processes. But oxygen is chemically reactive and highly dangerous: in normal biochemical reactions oxygen can become unstable and capable of "oxidizing" neighboring molecules. This can lead to cellular damage which triggers cancer, inflammation, arterial damage, and aging. Known as free oxidizing radicals, this bodily equivalent of nuclear waste must be disarmed to remove the danger. Free radicals are made in all combustion processes including smoking, the burning of gasoline to create exhaust fumes, radiation, frying or

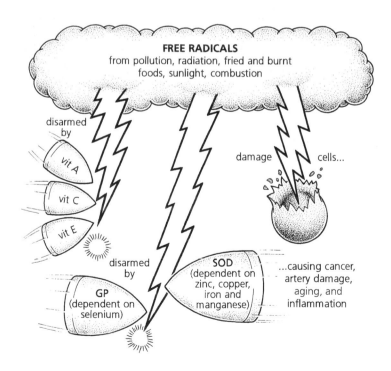

Anti-oxidant nutrients and sources of free oxidizing radicals

GP is the antioxidant enzyme Glutathione Peroxidase; SOD is the antioxidant enzyme Superoxide Dismutase.

barbecuing food and normal body processes. Chemicals capable of disarming free radicals are called antioxidants. Some are known essential nutrients, like vitamin A and beta-carotene, and vitamins C and E. Others, like bioflavonoids, anthocyanidins, pycnogenol, and over a hundred other recently identified protectors found in common foods, are not.

The balance between your intake of antioxidants and exposure to free radicals may literally be the balance between life and death. You can tip the scales in your favor by simple changes to diet and antioxidant supplementation.

ANTIOXIDANTS IN HEALTH AND DISEASE

Slowing down the aging process is no longer a mystery. The best results in research studies have consistently been achieved by giving animals low-calorie diets high in antioxidant nutrients—in other words, exactly what they need and no more. This reduces "oxidative stress" and ensures maximum antioxidant protection. Animals fed in this way not only live up to 40 percent longer, but are also more active during their lives.[29] Although long-term studies have yet to be completed, there is every reason to assume that the same principles apply to humans. Already, large-scale surveys show that the risk of death is substantially reduced in those with either high levels of antioxidants in their blood or high dietary intakes.

Conversely, a lower level of vitamin A and vitamin E is associated with Alzheimer's disease. The blood levels of vitamin E and beta-carotene in sufferers are half those of elderly people who do not have Alzheimer's.[30] Elderly people with low levels of vitamin C in their blood have eleven times the risk of developing cataracts compared to those with high levels.[31] Similarly, those with low vitamin E blood levels have almost double the risk, while people consuming 400 IUs of vitamin E a day have half the risk of developing cataracts.[32]

Levels of vitamin A are consistently found to be low in people with lung cancer. In fact, having a low vitamin A level doubles the risk of lung cancer.[33] Similarly, a high intake of beta-carotene from raw fruit and vegetables reduces the risk of lung cancer in non-smoking men and women.[34] In one study, giving a 30 mg per day supplement of beta-carotene resulted in 71 percent of patients with oral pre-cancer (leukoplakia) improving, while 57 percent of patients given 200,000 IU of vitamin A a day had complete remission.[35]

Supplementing vitamins E and C effectively halves the risk of ever having a heart attack while, in a massive study on nurses, those who consumed 15–20 mg of beta-carotene per day had 40 percent lower risk of a stroke and 22 percent lower risk of a heart attack compared to those consuming only 6 mg per day.[36] Those with high dietary intakes of beta-carotene had half the risk of death from cardiovascular disease. Supplementing 1,000 mg of vitamin C also reduces blood pressure.[37]

Antioxidants also help boost your immune system and increase your resistance to infection. In children, regular supplementation of vitamin A significantly reduces respiratory tract infections. Antioxidants have been shown to reduce the symptoms of AIDS, and, in a small number of cases, to reverse the condition. They increase fertility, reduce inflammation in arthritis, and have key roles to play in many conditions including colds and chronic fatigue syndrome. (For more information on specific diseases see Part 7.)

TESTING YOUR ANTIOXIDANT POTENTIAL

Your ability to stay free of these diseases depends on the balance between your intake of harmful free radicals and your intake of protective antioxidants. As the scales start to tip away from health, early warning signs start to develop like frequent infections, difficulty shaking an infection, easy bruising, slow healing, thinner skin, or excessive wrinkles for your age.

Another sign of impaired antioxidant status is a reduced ability to detoxify the body after an onslaught of free radicals. So, for example, if you feel groggy or achy after a burst of exercise, or after exposure to pollution such as being stuck in a traffic jam or a room full of cigarette smoke, your antioxidant potential may need a boost.

A more accurate way to determine your antioxidant status is to have a biochemical antioxidant profile done. This blood test measures the levels of beta-carotene, C, and E in your blood and determines how well your antioxidant enzyme systems are functioning. Most nutritional laboratories offer this kind of test. A less expensive and extensive TRAP test (total reactive antioxidant potential) is also available. But while this will indicate if there is an antioxidant problem, it does not define which nutrients are missing. Ask your doctor or nutritionist about these tests, as they are rarely available directly to the public.

ANTIOXIDANTS—THE BEST FOODS

Every year more and more antioxidants are found in nature, including substances in berries, grapes, tomatoes, mustard, and broccoli and in herbs such as turmeric and ginkgo biloba. These substances, such as bioflavonoids, lycopene, and anthocyanidins, are not essential nutrients but are highly beneficial. They are classified as phytochemicals and will be discussed fully in Chapter 14.

The main essential antioxidant vitamins are A, C, and E and the precursor of vitamin A, beta-carotene. Beta-carotene is found in red/orange/yellow vegetables and fruits. Vitamin C is also abundant in vegetables and fruits

Your Personal Antioxidant Profile

Test your powers of prevention and score 1 point for each "yes" answer.

Symptom Analysis
- Do you frequently suffer from infections (coughs, colds)?   YES / NO
- Do you find it hard to shake an infection?   YES / NO
- Do you have a recurrent infection (cystitis, thrush, earache, etc.)?   YES / NO
- Do you bruise easily?   YES / NO
- Have you ever suffered from any of the conditions listed on page 79?   YES / NO
- Have your parents collectively suffered from two or more of these conditions?   YES / NO
- Do you easily get exhausted after physical exertion?   YES / NO
- Does your skin take a long time to heal?   YES / NO
- Do you suffer from acne, dry skin, or excessive wrinkles for your age?   YES / NO
- Are you overweight?   YES / NO

☐ YOUR SCORE

Lifestyle Analysis
- Have you smoked for more than five years of your life, less than five years ago?   YES / NO
- Do you smoke now?   YES / NO
- Do you smoke more than ten cigarettes a day?   YES / NO
- Do you spend time most days in a smoky atmosphere?   YES / NO
- Do you have an alcoholic drink each day?   YES / NO
- Do you live in a polluted city, or by a busy road?   YES / NO
- Do you spend more than two hours in traffic each day?   YES / NO
- Are you quite often exposed to strong sunlight?   YES / NO
- Do you consider yourself unfit?   YES / NO
- Do you exercise excessively and get easily "burnt out"?   YES / NO

☐ YOUR SCORE

Diet Analysis
- Do you eat fried food most days?   YES / NO
- Do you eat less than a serving of fresh fruit and raw vegetables each day?   YES / NO
- Do you eat less than two pieces of fresh fruit a day?   YES / NO
- Do you rarely eat nuts, seeds, or whole grains each day?   YES / NO
- Do you eat smoked or barbecued food or grill cheese on your food?   YES / NO
- Do you supplement less than 500 mg of vitamin C each day?   YES / NO
- Do you supplement less than 100 IU of vitamin E each day?   YES / NO
- Do you supplement less than 10,000 IU of vitamin A or beta-carotene each day?   YES / NO

☐ YOUR SCORE

☐ YOUR TOTAL SCORE:

0–10   *This is an ideal score, indicating that your health, diet and lifestyle are consistent with a high level of antioxidant protection. Keep up the good work!*

11–15   *This is a reasonable score, although you can increase your power of prevention by converting "yes" answers into "no."*

16–20   *This is a poor score, indicating plenty of room for improvement. See a nutritionist to upgrade your diet and lifestyle for increased antioxidant protection.*

20+   *This is a bad score, putting you in the high risk group for rapid aging. See a nutritionist and ask for an antioxidant profile blood test. You will need to make changes to your diet and lifestyle, plus supplementing antioxidants, to reverse or slow down the aging process.*

eaten raw, but heat rapidly destroys it. Vitamin E is found in "seed" foods, including nuts, seeds, and their oils, vegetables like peas, broad beans, corn, and whole grains—all of which are classified as seed foods. The best all-round foods are shown in the table below. Eating sweet potatoes, carrots, watercress, peas, and broccoli frequently is a great way to increase your antioxidant potential—provided, of course that you do not fry them.

Antioxidants—the Best Foods

The best all-round antioxidant foods have the highest numbers of stars. Foods are listed in order of their star rating. Make sure these foods form a large part of your diet.

Food	Rich Source of A	C	E
Sweet potatoes	★★★	★	★★★
Carrots	★★★	★★★	
Watercress	★★★	★★★	
Peas	★	★★	★★
Broccoli	★★	★★★	
Cauliflower	★	★★★	
Lemons	★	★★★	
Mangoes	★★	★★	
Meat	★★		★★
Melon	★★	★★	
Peppers	★	★★★	
Pumpkin	★★	★★	
Strawberries	★	★★★	
Tomatoes	★★	★★	
Cabbage	★★★		
Grapefruit	★	★★	
Kiwi fruit	★	★★	
Oranges	★	★★	
Seeds and nuts			★★★
Squash	★★★		
Tuna, mackerel, salmon			★★★
Wheat germ			★★★
Apricots	★★		
Beans			★★

Another great food is watermelon. The flesh is high in beta-carotene and vitamin C, while the seeds are high in vitamin E and in the antioxidant minerals zinc and selenium. You can make a great antioxidant cocktail by blending the flesh and seeds into a great-tasting drink. Seeds and seafood are the best all-round dietary sources of selenium and zinc.

The amino acids cysteine and glutathione also act as antioxidants. They help make one of the body's key antioxidant enzymes, glutathione peroxidase, which is itself dependent on selenium. This enzyme helps to detoxify the body, protecting us against car exhaust fumes, carcinogens, infections, too much alcohol, and toxic metals. Cysteine and glutathione are particularly high in white meat, tuna, lentils, beans, nuts, seeds, onions, and garlic, and have been shown to boost the immune system as well as to increase antioxidant power.

SUPPLEMENTARY BENEFIT

Given the unquestionable value of increasing your antioxidant status, it is wise to make sure that your daily supplement program contains significant quantities of antioxidants, especially if you are middle-aged or older, live in a polluted city, or suffer any other unavoidable exposure to free radicals. The easiest way to do this is to take a comprehensive antioxidant supplement. Most reputable supplement companies produce formulas containing a combination of the following nutrients: vitamin A, beta-carotene, vitamin E, vitamin C, zinc, selenium, glutathione and cysteine, plus plant-based antioxidants like bilberry or pycnogenol. The kind of total supplementary intake to aim for is shown below.

Vitamin A

The Suggested Optimal Nutrient Allowance per day for vitamin A and beta-carotene is 800–1000 mcg RE (retinol equivalent) for children and 800–2,000 mcg RE for adults for maximum antioxidant protection. Take between 2000 mcg (6,600 IU) and 3,000 mcg (10,000 IU) per day of retinol and the same again for beta-carotene.

Vitamin C

The Suggested Optimal Nutrient Allowance per day is 150 mg for children and 400–1000 mg for adults. For maximum antioxidant protection take 1,000–3,000 mg per day.

Vitamin E

The Suggested Optimal Nutrient Allowance per day is 70 mg for children and 90–800 mg/IUs for adults. For maximum antioxidant protection take 400–800 mg/IUs per day.

Selenium

The Suggested Optimal Nutrient Allowance per day is 50 mcg for children and 100 mcg for adults. For maximum antioxidant protection take 100–200 mcg per day.

Zinc

The Suggested Optimal Nutrient Allowance per day is 7 mg for children and 15–20 mg for adults. For maximum antioxidant protection take 10–20 mg per day.

Here are some simple tips for improving your antioxidant potential and boosting your power of prevention:

- Eat lots of fresh fruit.
- Eat lots of vegetables, especially sweet potatoes, carrots, peas, watercress, and broccoli.
- Take a good antioxidant supplement daily.
- Do your best to avoid pollution, smoky places, direct exposure to strong sunlight, and fried foods.
- Don't over-exercise or exercise beyond your aerobic potential.

14

LIVING FOOD—THE PHYTOCHEMICAL REVOLUTION

So far, over 100 antioxidant nutrients have been discovered and hundreds, if not thousands of research papers have extolled their benefits. The main players are vitamins A, C, and E, plus beta-carotene. However, no less important are the presence of non-essential antioxidants found in most fruits and vegetables. These include:

Anthocyanidins and proanthocyanidins   Particularly rich in berries and grapes. These are types of bioflavonoids (see below), reputedly good against gout and certain types of arthritis.

Bioflavonoids   A group of antioxidants found especially in citrus fruit.

Curcumin   A powerful antioxidant found in mustard, turmeric, corn, and yellow peppers.

Lycopene   A powerful antioxidant with anti-cancer properties found in tomatoes.

Lutein   A powerful antioxidant found in many fruits and vegetables. It is remarkably heat-stable and can survive cooking.

Zeanxanthin   Gives corn its yellow color. It is also found in spinach, cabbage, broccoli, and peas.

PHYTOCHEMICALS—NATURE'S PHARMACY

These substances are called phytochemicals (*phyto* means "plant" in Greek) and have a major impact on our body systems, helping to promote health and prevent disease. Phytochemicals are biologically active compounds in food; they are not classified as nutrients, in that our lives do not depend on them as they do for vitamins. However, they do play a vital role in the body's biochemistry in ways that affect our health as significantly as vitamins and minerals. In this sense they are best thought of as semi-essential nutrients. As they are not stored in the body it is best to eat foods rich in phytochemicals on a regular basis. Over a hundred phytochemicals have been identified, many having a regulating effect on the immune and endocrine system. Listed below are those with proven health benefits.

Phytochemicals Found in Common Foods

Allium compounds
Anthocyanidins
Bioflavonoids
Capsaicin
Carotenoids
Chlorophyll
Coumarins
Chlorogenic acid
Curcumin
Dithiolthiones
Ellagic acid
Genistein
Glucosinolates
Indoles
Isothiocyanates
Lentinans
Lignans
Phenols
Phytoestrogens
Plant sterols
Saponins
Sulforaphane

Now let's take a look at how some of these phytochemicals can support your health.

Allium compounds   Members of the *Allium* family include garlic, onions, leeks, chives, and shallots. Garlic has long been renowned as a health food, with many benefits attributed to it. Though it is rich in many vitamins and minerals, the main active ingredients seem to be sulphur compounds. These include allicin, allixin, diallyl disulphide, and diallyl trisulphide. Many animal studies have shown that garlic has a beneficial effect on the immune system and is cancer-protective.

Bioflavonoids   These have a number of beneficial roles. They act as potent antioxidants; they can bind to toxic metals and escort them out of the body; they have a synergistic effect on vitamin C, stabilizing it in human tissue, they have a bacteriostatic and/or antibiotic effect, which accounts for their anti-infection properties; and they are also anti-carcinogenic. They are used to deal with capillary fragility, bleeding gums, varicose veins, hemorrhoids, bruises, strain injuries, and thrombosis. Bioflavonoids include rutin (lots in buckwheat) and hesperidin, found particularly in citrus fruits. The best food sources are rosehips, buckwheat leaves, citrus fruit, berries, broccoli, cherries, grapes, papaya, cantaloupe, plums, tea, red wine, and tomatoes. There are also special bioflavonoids in cucumbers which stop cancer-causing hormones from binding to cells.

Capsaicin   Abundant in hot peppers, it helps protects DNA from damage.

Chlorophyll   This is the substance that makes green plants green. Chlorophyll-rich foods like wheat grass, algae, seaweeds, and green vegetables help to "build" the blood. Vitamins C, B12, B6, A, K, and folic acid are among the nutrients needed to keep blood healthy. Research has shown that components of chlorophyll found in foods, when fed in very small purified amounts, may stimulate the production of red blood cells in the bone marrow. Chlorophyll has been shown to help protect against cancer and certain forms of radiation, to kill germs, and to act as a powerful wound-healer.

Coumarins and chlorogenic acid   These substances prevent the formation of cancer-causing nitrosamines and are found in a wide variety of fruit and vegetables including tomatoes, green peppers, pineapple, strawberries, and carrots.

Ellagic acid   Present in strawberries, grapes, and raspberries, ellagic acid, neutralizes carcinogens before they can damage DNA.

Genistein   Abundant in soybeans, this substance, a type of phytoestrogen (see below), prevents breast, prostate, and other lumps from growing and spreading.

Isothiocyanates (ITCs) and indoles   These are plentiful in what are known as the cruciferous vegetables, which include broccoli, brussels sprouts, cabbage, cauliflower, cress, horseradish, kale, kohlrabi, mustard, radishes, and turnips. Eating vegetables rich in ITCs is now linked to a lower incidence of cancer, particularly of the colon. Research has shown that if you eat cabbage more than once a week, you are only one-third as likely to develop colon cancer as someone who never eats cabbage.[38] This means that one serving of cabbage a week could cut your chances of colon cancer by 60 percent. Both broccoli and brussels sprouts also show a dose-dependent protective response against cancer. While it is best to eat organic, these protective effects are not limited to eating organically grown vegetables.

Phytoestrogens　　These substances play a protective role by binding excess estrogens made in the body, or taken in from the environment via pesticides, plastics, and other sources of estrogen-like chemicals, to a protein made in the blood. This action reduces the amount of estrogens available to estrogen-sensitive tissues. Foods rich in phytoestrogens include soybeans, particularly in the forms of tofu and miso, other legumes, citrus fruits, wheat, licorice, alfalfa, fennel, and celery. A high intake of phytoestrogens is associated with a low risk for breast and prostate cancer, menopausal symptoms, fibroids, and other hormone-related diseases.

Sulforaphane　　Found in broccoli, cauliflower, brussels sprouts, turnips, and kale, this one lessens incidence of breast cancer in animals.

ENZYMES—THE KEYS OF LIFE

We are what we eat, runs the familiar saying. Well, not quite—we are what we can digest and absorb. The food we eat cannot nourish us unless it is first prepared for absorption into the body. This is done by enzymes, chemical compounds which digest it and break down large food particles into smaller units. Protein is broken down into amino acids; complex carbohydrate into simple sugars; and fat into fatty acids and glycerol. Every day about 10 quarts of digestive juices, mainly produced by the pancreas, liver, stomach, and intestinal wall, pour into the digestive tract.

For the body to make these enzymes it needs nutrients. If you become nutrient-deficient, enzyme deficiency soon follows (which means your body will be less able to make use of the nutrients it does take in, which make you become even more enzyme-deficient—and so the cycle continues). For example, zinc is needed to make both stomach acid and protein-splitting enzymes called proteases. A zinc-deficient person soon stops breaking down protein efficiently. This makes large food molecules end up where they should not, in the small intestine. If the intestinal wall is not 100 percent intact—a common defect in zinc deficiency—these undigested food particles can get inside the body where they are seen as invaders and attacked. This is the basis of most food allergy.

Once a food becomes the subject of an allergy, every time it is eaten the reaction in the stomach leads to inflammation. This reaction disturbs the normal balance of beneficial bacteria and other micro-organisms in the stomach. Food allergy triggered by digestive enzyme deficiency is always a possible cause if you are suffering from indigestion, bloating, flatulence, digestive pain, colitis, irritable bowel syndrome, Crohn's disease, or candidiasis.

The main families of digestive enzymes are amylases, which digest carbohydrate; proteases, which digest protein; and lipases, which digest fat. As an aid to digestion, many nutritional supplements contain these enzymes. Freeze-dried plant enzymes are often used for this purpose. The most common of them are bromelain from pineapples and papain from papaya, which is chemically similar to pepsin, a powerful protein-digesting enzyme capable of digesting between 35 and 100 times its own weight in protein.

Enzymes from raw food

A good way of boosting your enzyme potential is to eat foods raw, because in this state they contain significant amounts of enzymes. The cooking process tends to destroy enzymes. Professor Artturi Virtanen, Helsinki biochemist and Nobel prize winner, showed that enzymes are released in the mouth when raw vegetables are chewed: they come into contact with the food and start the act of digestion. These food enzymes are not denatured by stomach acid, as some researchers have suggested, but remain active throughout the digestive tract. Extensive tests by Kaspar Tropp in Würzburg, Germany, have shown that the human body has a way of protecting enzymes that pass through the stomach so that more than half reach the colon intact. There they alter the intestinal flora by binding free oxygen, reducing the potential for fermentation and putrefaction in the intestines, a factor linked to cancer of the colon. In so doing they also help to create conditions in which lactic acid-forming beneficial bacteria can grow.

Some foods, unfortunately contain enzyme blockers. For example, lentils, beans and chickpeas contain trypsin-inhibitors, preventing protein from being completely digested. However, this anti-enzyme factor is destroyed either by sprouting these legumes or by cooking them. So bean sprouts or cooked beans are OK. The same is true for grains rich in phytates, which can bind to beneficial minerals.

The two main digestive enzymes, amylase and protease, are found in many foods. For centuries man has put these food enzymes to work by pre-digesting foods before eating them. Fermented and aged foods are examples of this. However, raw foods too contain these enzymes, which become active when we chew them. These foods need to be chewed properly, which helps to liberate and activate the enzymes they contain. Some foods, like apples, grapes, and mangoes, also contain the antioxidant enzymes peroxidase and catalase, which help to disarm free radicals. The chart below shows those foods which have so far been found to contain significant levels of health-promoting enzymes; many foods have still not been investigated.

Enzymes Naturally Present in Raw Foods

	AMYLASE (digests sugars)	PROTEASE (digests protein)	LIPASE (digests fat)	PEROXIDASE and CATALASE (disarm free radicals)
Apples				★
Bananas	★			
Cabbage	★			
Eggs (uncooked)	★	★	★	★
Grapes				★
Honey (raw/unpasteurized)	★			★
Kidney beans	★	★		
Mangoes				★
Milk (raw/unpasteurized)	★			★
Mushrooms	★	★		★
Pineapple	★	★		
Rice	★			
Soybeans		★		
Sweet corn	★			★
Sweet potatoes	★			
Wheat	★	★		

LIVING FOOD IN ACTION

Every time you eat a combination of fresh, living foods, such as fruit and vegetables, you are giving yourself a cocktail of essential vitamins, minerals, amino acids, antioxidants, enzymes, and phytochemicals that work together synergistically to promote your health. The idea of separating each ingredient out and then treating it like a drug to cure a specific illness is not just impractical but nonsensical.

The moral of this story is to eat foods that you can pick out of the ground or pluck from a tree.

Here is a simple checklist of good habits to develop to ensure that living foods, and the nutrients they contain, form a regular part of your diet.

- Eat at least three pieces of fresh fruit a day.

- Have a salad as a major part of one meal each day.

- Eat frequently the many foods rich in antioxidants and phytochemicals such as sweet potatoes, broccoli, watercress, peas, carrots, and berries.

- Eat a multi-colored variety of foods, as each natural color contains different health-promoting phytochemicals.

- Eat whole foods, rather than refined or processed food full of artificial chemicals.

- Eat as much raw food as possible. For hot dishes such as soup, prepare them raw and heat just before serving. Steam food often and fry as little as possible.

- Wherever possible, buy organic food. If not possible, peel or throw away outer leaves and wash to reduce pesticide residues.

- Buy fresh foods little and often. Keeping them destroys their nutrients.

- Supplement your diet with a synergistic collection of vitamins, minerals, antioxidants, and other phytochemicals (see Part 6).

15

FOOD COMBINING—FACTS AND FALLACIES

Many people find that certain types or combinations of food do not suit them. Based on this observation and on his research into health and nutrition, in the 1930s Dr. Howard Hay devised a diet plan popularly known as "food combining," which has helped millions of people towards better health. He recommended eating a healthy diet consistent with the optimum nutrition approach, and formulated rules about which foods you can eat together. The key elements in Dr. Hay's original theory were to eat "alkaline-forming foods," to avoid refined and heavily processed foods, to eat fruit on its own, and not to mix protein-rich and carbohydrate-rich foods.

Protein and carbohydrate are digested differently. That is a fact. Carbohydrate digestion starts in the mouth when the digestive enzyme amylase, which is present in saliva, starts to act on the food you chew. Once you swallow food and it enters the relatively acid environment of the stomach, amylase stops working. Only when the food leaves the stomach, where the digestive environment becomes more alkaline, can the next wave of amylase enzymes, this time secreted into the small intestines from the pancreas, continue and complete the digestion of carbohydrate.

Protein, on the other hand, is not digested in the mouth at all. It needs the acid environment of the stomach and may hang out there for three hours until all the complex proteins are broken down into smaller collections of amino acids known as peptides. This only happens in the stomach because it contains the high levels of hydrochloric acid needed to activate the protein-digesting enzyme pepsin. Once peptides leave the stomach they meet peptidase enzymes, again from the pancreas, which break them down into individual amino acids, ready for absorption.

THE MYTH OF THE BEAN

The simplistic view of food combining is that carbohydrate and protein foods should be separated because they are digested differently. The fact that eating certain kinds of beans produces flatulence is often quoted as a negative effect, because beans contain both protein and carbohydrate. However, it is now known that this is not the reason for beans' boisterous reputation. Some beans contain proteins such as lectin which cannot be digested by the enzymes in our digestive system, even when eaten alone. These proteins can, however, be digested by the bacteria that live in the large intestine. So when you eat beans you feed not only yourself but also these bacteria. After a good meal of lectin these bacteria produce gas, hence the flatulence. It has got nothing to do with food combining. Many healthy cultures throughout the world have evolved to eat a diet in which beans or lentils are a staple food—but they suffer no digestive problems.

PROTEIN AND CARBOHYDRATE—FOODS THAT FIGHT?

Of course, since items of food do not consist exclusively of either carbohydrate or protein, in practical terms separating them means not combining *concentrated* protein foods with *concentrated* starch foods. Meat is 50 percent protein and 0 percent carbohydrate. Potatoes are 8 percent protein and 90 percent carbohydrate. In between are beans, lentils, rice, wheat, and quinoa. So where exactly do you draw the line, if a line should be drawn at all?

A brief excursion into our primitive past may solve the puzzle. The general consensus is that the human race has been eating a predominantly vegetarian diet for millions of years, with the occasional meal of meat or fish. Monkeys can be divided into two types: those which have a ruminant-like digestive tract and slowly digest even the most indigestible fibrous foods, much like a cow; and those which have a much speedier and technologically advanced digestive system that produces a whole series of different enzyme secretions. We fit into the second category. The system is more efficient but can only handle foods that are easier to digest—fruit, young leaves, certain vegetables. No stalks for us! Evolutionary theorists believe that this digestive system did two things: firstly, it gave us the motive to improve our mental and sensory processing so that we would know when and where to find the food we needed, and secondly, it gave us the nutrients to develop a more advanced brain and nervous system.

Did monkeys eat meat and two vegetables?

I believe the human body has three basic programs for digestion. The first is for digesting concentrated protein, which means meat, fish, and eggs. To digest these foods we have to produce vast amounts of stomach acid and protein-digesting enzymes. After all, when our early ancestors had hunted down and killed an animal do you think they then went off to hand-pick a few tasty morsels of vegetation to create that "balanced meal"? I doubt it. I imagine they ate their catch, organs and all, as fast as possible before it went bad and other predators moved in. They might have had a couple of days living on nothing but concentrated animal protein. Fresh, raw, organic meat is, after all, highly nutritious.

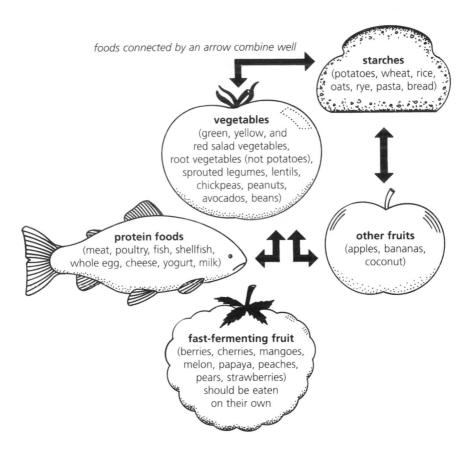

Food combinations – do's and don'ts

Fruit—the Lone Ranger

At certain times of year early man would have had access to certain fruits. No doubt we were not the only fruit-eating creatures. Since fruit is the best fuel for instant energy, requiring very little digestion, our second program produces the enzymes and hormones necessary to process the simple carbohydrates in fruit. Again, my guess is that we mainly ate fruit on its own. After all, once you have chomped three bananas there would be little reason to go digging up a few roots.

Many kinds of soft fruits ferment rapidly once ripe. They will do the same if you put them in a warm, acidic environment, which is what the stomach is. That is what happens if you eat a slice of melon followed by a steak. So Dr. Hay's advice to eat fruit separately makes a lot of sense. Since fruit takes around thirty minutes to pass through the stomach, whole concentrated protein takes two to three hours, this means that the best time to eat fruit is as a snack more than 30 minutes before a meal, or not less than two hours after a meal—possibly more if you eat a lot of concentrated protein. The only exception to this advice is combining fruits that do not readily ferment, like bananas, apples, or coconut, with complex carbohydrate-rich foods such as oats or millet. So a chopped apple on your porridge or a whole rye banana sandwich would be fine.

However, for most of the time our ancestors seem to have eaten a varied vegan diet. That means leaf vegetables, root vegetables, nuts, seeds, legumes, and sprouts. This, I propose, is the third and most common digestive program—a mixture of foods containing a mixture of carbohydrate and protein, but never as protein-dense as meat. I see no problem in combining rice, lentils, beans, vegetables, nuts, and seeds.

80 PERCENT ALKALINE

One of Dr. Hay's greatest observations was that people with more acidic blood were more likely to be ill. He identified a range of acidity, a pH of 7.4 to 7.5, which is slightly alkaline and associated with good health. A pH of 7 or below is increasingly acid, while a pH above 7 is increasingly alkaline.

Many factors affect the acid/alkaline balance of the blood. When foods are metabolized, acids are produced which are neutralized by the alkaline salts (carbonates) of calcium, magnesium, potassium, and sodium. So our intake of these mineral salts affects our acid/alkaline balance, as does the type of food we eat. Foods containing large amounts of chlorine, phosphorus, sulphur, and nitrogen (for example, most animal products) tend to be acid-forming. Those rich in calcium, potassium, magnesium, and sodium (for example, most vegetables) tend to be alkaline-forming. Exercise too has an effect—it makes the blood more acidic. Deep breathing makes the blood more alkaline.

In her book *The Wright Diet*, Celia Wright describes the over-acidic person as being grouchy, sensitive, and exhausted, inclined to aches and pains, headaches, problems with sleeping, and acidity of the stomach. Smokers have been found to have a high acid level in their urine. Cravings appear to reduce on a more alkaline diet.

Nearly all fresh fruit, vegetables, and legumes are alkaline-forming. Exceptions include butter beans and broad beans, asparagus, olives, and mustard and cress. Meat, fish, eggs, and butter are acid-forming, while skimmed milk and whole milk are mildly alkaline-forming. A few grains are acidic, including oatmeal, wholemeal flour, sago, and tapioca. Walnuts and hazelnuts are acidic, but other nuts are alkaline. (For a comprehensive list of acid and alkaline foods see the chart on p. 330.)

No doubt part of the success of Dr. Hay's approach was his emphasis on alkaline-forming foods. This, as you can see, means eating plenty of fruit and vegetables which are naturally high in many vital nutrients.

REFINED CARBOHYDRATES ARE OUT

Refining food or cooking it, Dr. Hay did not recommend either. As explained earlier, the more refined, processed, or cooked a food is, the less nutrition it will provide. The obvious advice is to eat raw or lightly cooked whole foods instead of overcooked and overprocessed junk foods. Refined high sugar foods are a new invention as far as your digestive system is concerned. Very few naturally occurring foods contain the kind of concentrations of fast-releasing sugars that modern food can provide. The body is simply not adapted to deal with a flood of fast-releasing sugars which not only make your blood sugar levels rocket, requiring all sort of hormones to swing into emergency action to restore the balance, but also feed potentially undesirable micro-organisms that can occur in the stomach.

IMPROVE YOUR DIGESTION

In a nutshell, food combining can be condensed into five simple steps as shown in the illustration on p. 96. If you still have problems digesting these food combinations you may have a digestive enzyme deficiency, a food intolerance, or a stomach infestation of candida or unfriendly bacteria, and should see a nutritionist. Vegans only have one rule to follow, which is to eat certain fruits separately. Easy, isn't it?

Here are five quick guidelines to help improve your digestion:

- Eat 80 percent alkaline-forming foods, 20 percent acid-forming foods. This means eating large quantities of vegetables and fruit, and less concentrated protein foods like beans, lentils, and whole grains instead of meat, fish, cheese, and eggs.

- Eat fast-fermenting and acid fruits on their own as snacks. Most soft fruits, including peaches, plums, mangoes, papayas, strawberries, and melons, ferment quickly. High acid fruits (although alkaline-forming) may also inhibit digestion of carbohydrate; they include oranges, lemons, grapefruit, and pineapple. All these fruits require little digestion, releasing their natural fructose content quickly. Eat them on their own as a snack when you need an energy boost.

- Eat animal protein on its own or with vegetables. Concentrated protein like meat, fish, hard cheese, and eggs requires lots of stomach acid and a stay of about three hours in the stomach to be digested. So do not combine fast-releasing or refined carbohydrates or food that ferments with animal protein.

- Avoid all refined carbohydrates. Eat unrefined, fast-releasing carbohydrates with unrefined slow-releasing carbohydrates. Fruits that do not readily ferment, such as bananas, apples, and coconut, can be combined with slow-releasing carbohydrate cereals like oats and millet.

- Do not eat until your body is wide awake. Do not expect to digest food when your body is asleep. In the morning, leave at least an hour between waking up and eating. If you exercise in the morning, eat afterwards. Never start your day with a stimulant (tea, coffee, or a cigarette), because the "stress" state inhibits digestion. For breakfast, eat only carbohydrate-based foods such as cereal and fruit, just fruit, or whole-grain rye toast. In the evening, leave at least two hours between finishing dinner and going to sleep.

16

YOU ARE WHAT YOU EAT

Nothing created by man compares to the magnificent design of the human body. As you read this book 2.5 million red blood cells are being made every second within your bone marrow, in order to keep your body cells supplied with oxygen. Meanwhile your digestive system is producing its daily 10 quarts of digestive juices to break down the food you eat and enable it to pass through your "inside skin," the gastro-intestinal wall, a 30-foot-long tract with a surface area of about 22 yards which effectively replaces itself every four days. The health of your gastro-intestinal tract is maintained by a team of some three hundred different strains of bacteria and other micro-organisms as unique to you as your fingerprint, which exceed the total number of cells in your entire body. Meanwhile, your immune system replaces its entire army every week, and, when under viral attack, has the capacity to produce two hundred thousand new immune cells every minute. Even your outside skin is effectively replaced every month, while most of your body is renewed over a seven-year period. Your brain, a mere three pounds of mainly fat and water, is processing information of immense complexity through its trillion nerve cells, each connected to a hundred thousand others in a network whose connections are formed as our life, and the meaning we attach to it, unfolds.

The energy produced from a small amount of food powers all these unseen processes, with plenty left over to keep us warm and allow us to undertake a wide range of physical activity. The by-products are water and carbon dioxide, both of which are essential for plants which in turn produce carbohydrate, our fuel, and oxygen, the spark that lights our cellular fires. It is estimated that we use only a quarter of a percent of our brain's capacity and, in many cases, half the potential life span of our bodies. The design, the capacity and the resilience of the human body are truly awesome.

Yet, unlike a new car, we arrive without a maintenance manual and rely on instructions developed by those who have made their livelihood from a study of the human body. These instructions are in their infancy, a fact which is obvious when you consider how much of medicine is based on giving drugs which poison the body, radiation which burns it, and surgery which removes defective parts. Most of us only begin to think about body maintenance when something goes wrong. Yet, due to the body's incredible resilience, most serious diseases like cancer and cardiovascular disease take twenty to thirty years to develop. By the time we notice the symptoms it may be too late.

LEARNING FROM EXPERIENCE

Once you realize that your body is a collection of highly organized cells, designed by the forces of nature, adapting to the changing environment over millions of years, it becomes natural to give that body what it needs, with the tangible benefit of health. Experience is, of course, the greatest motivator. If something you eat makes you feel good you are likely to continue eating it, while if something makes you feel bad you are likely to stop—unless you have become addicted. But in order to learn from experience we must first understand something called the general adaptation syndrome. It was first described in 1956 by Professor Hans Selye, who proposed three basic stages of reaction to any event. This can be applied to a cigarette, a food, a stress, or a physical activity.

Stage 1: the initial response Your first response to any event or substance is the best indicator of whether or not it suits you. Remember your first cigarette, your first alcoholic drink, or your first cup of coffee? You are unlikely to remember your first taste of sugar, meat, or milk, or other foods introduced when you were very young.

Stage 2: adaptation Very quickly your body learns to adapt. Gone is the pounding heart after a cup of coffee, or coughing after a cigarette. An example of this stage is the rise and subsequent fall to normal levels of the blood pressure of country dwellers, not normally exposed to air pollution, who move to a city. The cells in the lungs of a smoker change form to protect themselves from smoke. Plaque develops in the arteries to repair damaged tissue. What is going on behind the scene in all these cases? The body is trying to protect itself, and in so doing is in an unseen state of stress.

Stage 3: exhaustion Continue the insult for long enough and one day you are sick. Your energy is gone, your digestive system is not functioning properly, your blood pressure is raised, and you develop anything from chest infections to cancer. The body cannot cope, it cannot adapt any more. This is the stage at which most people seek help from a health practitioner.

We could add two further stages to this process.

Stage 4: recovery To enable the body to recover, it is usually necessary to avoid or greatly restrict the initial insult and other undesirable substances. This means being as puritanical as possible for a period during which you may have to wean yourself off all sorts of things to which you have become addicted or allergic. Generally these are the substances of which you would say, "I can give up anything but not my...." This is the nature of addiction. To help the body recover, much larger amounts of vitamins and minerals are needed than would normally be required just to maintain good health.

Stage 5: hypersensitivity Once you have recovered and your body is basically healthy, which can take years, you are effectively back to stage one. But this time, because your diet and lifestyle are much improved, you may seem to be hypersensitive and react to all sorts of things that you never reacted to before: certain wines which contain additives, ordinary foods like wheat or milk, fumes, and so on. This is healthy because, just as in an initial reaction, your body is telling you what suits you. The more you follow this guidance the healthier you will become. In due course, as your reserve strength builds up, you can tolerate the odd insult without such hypersensitivity, but by then it is to be hoped that you will have learned (or suffered) enough not to indulge those old bad habits!

Once you understand this cycle and why it is that you can sometimes apparently abuse the body without noticeable ill-effects, and at other times react strongly to small insults, it is easier to interpret what happens to you, and alter your diet or lifestyle accordingly. Think about the substances that you have suspected may not suit you. What do they have in common? Perhaps there are subtle signs which you have chosen to ignore. Here is a list of the most common suspects that my clients have found they react to:

Foods That Commonly Cause Reactions

Wheat and other grains	Yeast-based alcohols (beer and
Milk and dairy produce	wine, but not champagne)
Chocolate	Additives in alcohol
Sugar	Cigarettes
Coffee, including de-caffeinated	Fumes
Tea	Vehicle exhaust
Food additives	Gas fires
Alcohol	Grass pollens

It is interesting that our ancestors, who until relatively recently in evolutionary terms were not cultivating grains, nor milking animals, were not exposed to any of these substances.

THE DELAYED EFFECT

Another noteworthy phenomenon is the delayed effect. The General Adaptation Syndrome describes a long-term delayed effect, but with many foods there is a short-term delay of up to twenty-four hours before you notice their effect on you. For example, if you eat something very sweet you may feel fine as your blood sugar level rises. But when it plummets four hours later you may fall asleep. And alcohol has its worst effects many hours later. This is largely because, once the liver's ability to detoxify alcohol is exceeded, the remaining alcohol is changed into a toxic by-product which is what induces headaches and nausea. Most substances that are not good for you show an initial reaction within twenty-four hours.

A HAIRY BAG OF SALTY SOUP

Scientists believe that we, like all other mammals, evolved from the sea. We carry our "sea" around inside us, and it has many of the same constituents as the oceans from which we came. We are 66 percent water, 25 percent protein and 8 percent fat, the rest being carbohydrate plus minerals and vitamins. Saddam Hussein, Tony Blair, Madonna, you, and I are all just 66 percent water. "Hairy bags of salty soup," said Dr. Michael Colgan, a British-born scientist who has pioneered the optimum nutrition approach. Yet if you were to throw all these compounds together you would not end up with a human being. So what is it that makes life happen?

The answer, of course, as explained in Chapter 15, is enzymes. They turn the food we eat into fuel for every single cell, be it a muscle cell, a brain cell, an immune cell, or a blood cell. Further enzymes within these cells turn the fuel into usable energy which makes our heart beat, our nerves fire, and all other bodily functions take place. Everything in this universe is part of a vast on-going chemical reaction. Our part, as temporary living organisms, is to provide ourselves and others with the best possible components to allow this process to continue in such a way that we all have a good, long, enjoyable life. And what makes our life-giving enzymes function at their peak? The answer is vitamins and minerals. Nearly all the thousands of enzymes in the body depend directly or indirectly on the presence of vitamins and minerals.

Once you understand that the body, and health itself, depend on this vast and complex interacting network you will appreciate that there is little point in taking extra quantities of a single vitamin. That would be like replacing only one dirty spark plug and expecting your car to run smoothly. Yet most medical research into nutrition has done just that, by taking one nutrient and measuring its effect on one aspect of health. As you will see, the research that has produced the most astonishing results in improving energy, mental performance, longevity, fertility, and resistance to disease has involved a multinutrient approach which recognizes the fact that nutrients interact. Parts 4 and 5 of this book explain the kind of results that can be achieved and the conditions helped by applying the optimum nutrition approach.

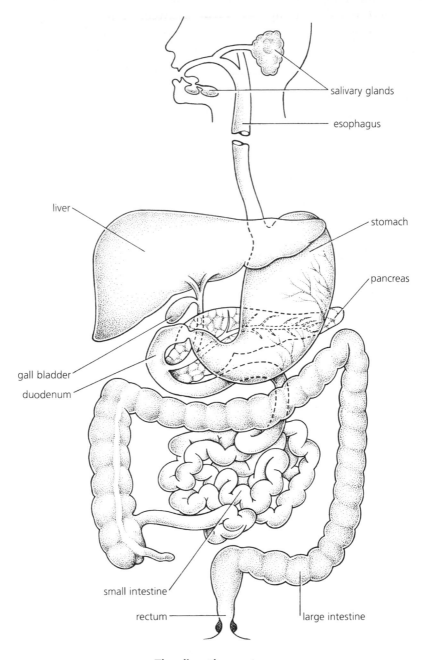

The digestive system

17

IMPROVING YOUR DIGESTION

Like all other animals, we spend our physical lives processing organic matter for waste. How good we are at it determines our energy level, longevity and state of body and mind. A lack of nutrients and the wrong kind of food can mean faulty digestion, faulty absorption, abnormal stomach reactions including bloating and inflammation, stomach infections, and poor elimination. The knock-on effects disrupt every body system—immunity, the brain and nervous system, hormonal balance, and our ability to detoxify.

STOMACH ACID—THE RIGHT BALANCE

Digestion starts in the senses. The sight and smell of food initiate chemical reactions that get us ready to assimilate and digest food. Chewing is particularly important because messages are sent to the digestive tract to prepare different enzyme secretions according to what is in the mouth.

Food then passes into the stomach, where large proteins are broken down into smaller groups of amino acids. The first step in protein digestion is carried out by hydrochloric acid released from the stomach wall, which is dependent on zinc. Hydrochloric acid production often declines in old age, as do zinc levels. The consequence is indigestion, particularly noticeable after high-protein meals, and the likelihood of developing food allergies because undigested large food molecules are more likely to stimulate allergic reactions in the small intestine.

The nutritional solution for too little stomach acid is to take a digestive supplement containing betaine hydrochloride, plus at least 15 mg of zinc in an easily absorbable form such as zinc citrate. Some people, however, produce too much stomach acid, a possible cause of "acid stomach," experienced as indigestion and a burning sensation. This is usually rectified by avoiding acid-forming and irritating foods and drinks; alcohol, coffee, tea, and aspirin all irritate the stomach wall. Meat, fish, eggs, and other concentrated proteins stimulate acid production and can aggravate over–acidity. The minerals calcium and magnesium are particularly alkaline and tend to have a calming effect on people suffering from excess acidity.

DIGESTIVE ENZYMES

The stomach also produces a range of enzymes, collectively called proteases, to break down protein. Protein digestion continues in the first part of the small intestine, the duodenum, into which flow digestive enzymes produced in the pancreas and liver. The pancreas is the primary organ of digestion, and

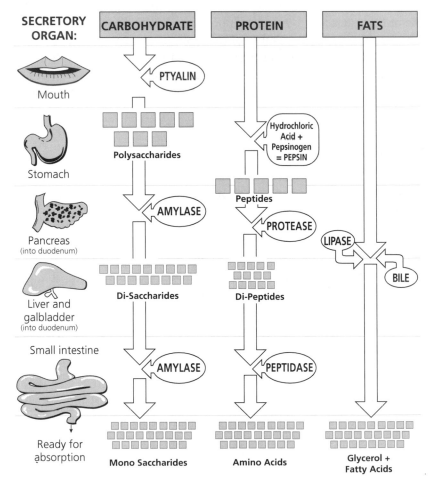

Digestive enzymes

special cells in it produce enzymes for breaking down carbohydrates, fats, and proteins. These enzymes are called amylase, lipase and, once again, proteases. Again, there are many different kinds.

The production of digestive enzymes depends on many micronutrients, especially vitamin B6. Sub-optimum nutrition often results in sub-optimum digestion, which in turn creates sub-optimum absorption so that nutritional intake gets worse and worse. The consequence is undigested food in the small intestine, which encourages the proliferation of the wrong kind of bacteria and other micro-organisms; symptoms can include flatulence, abdominal pain, and bloating.

The easiest way to correct this kind of problem is to take a broad-spectrum digestive enzyme supplement with each meal. This can make an immediate difference. You can test the effects of these enzyme supplements by crushing them and stirring them into a thick porridge made from oats and water. If the product is good, the porridge will become liquid in thirty minutes. While there is no harm in taking digestive enzymes on an on-going basis, correcting their levels with supplements paves the way for increasing nutrient levels in the body. Once this is achieved the digestion often improves of its own accord and the supplements may no longer be necessary.

Before being digested, fat has to be specially prepared. This is achieved by a substance called bile, produced by the liver and stored in the gall bladder. Bile contains lecithin, which helps to emulsify large fat particles and turn them into tiny particles with a greater surface area for the fat-splitting lipase enzyme to work on. Supplementing lecithin as granules or capsules improves emulsification and can help people with poor tolerance of fat—for instance, anyone who has had their gall bladder removed and cannot therefore store bile.

STOMACH REACTIONS

While indigestion can be caused by a lack or excess of stomach acid, or a lack of digestive enzymes, these are not the only possibilities. Many of the foods we eat irritate and damage our very sensitive and vitally important interface with the inside world. One such food is wheat, in which a protein called gluten contains gliadin, a known intestinal irritant. A small amount may be tolerated, but most people consume wheat in the form of bread, cereals, cakes, pastry, and pasta at least three times a day. Modern wheat is very high in gluten, and baking increases its ability to react with the stomach wall. In cases of severe gluten sensitivity the villi, the tiny protrusions that make up the small intestine, get completely worn away. For those with gluten sensitivity, all foods containing gluten must be avoided. Rice, corn, quinoa, and buckwheat are fine as all are gluten-free.

Stomach infections

The best way to get a stomach infection is to eat plenty of sugar, suffer from indigestion, and have regular courses of antibiotics. There are around three hundred different strains of bacteria in the stomach, most of which are essential. They protect us from harmful bacteria, viruses, and other dangerous organisms. Antibiotics wipe out all the bacteria in the body, good as well as bad, and are best not taken unless absolutely necessary. If the stomach contains the wrong kind of bacteria, or perhaps an overgrowth of a yeast-like organism called candida albicans, a high-sugar diet, including fruit, can exacerbate the problem. Feelings of intoxication, drowsiness, and bloating after consuming sugar are good indicators of a potential imbalance. In the same way that yeast ferments sugar to alcohol, it is possible to check for the presence of yeast-like organisms by testing the blood, eating sugar, and then testing the blood again for the presence of alcohol.

A number of powerful natural remedies have been proven to help with stomach infections. Caprylic acid, extracted from coconuts, is anti-fungal. Grapefruit seed extract, taken as drops in water, is anti-fungal, anti-viral, and anti-bacterial but does not destroy all the essential strains of bacteria. Even so, it is best not taken with meals. Another strategy, called probiotics, aims to improve the strength of the beneficial bacteria in the stomach. This is easily achieved by short (one month) courses of supplements. Since bacteria are fragile it is best to choose a high-quality product containing acidophilus and bifidus bacteria. Some probiotic supplements are cultivated from strains that occur in the stomach, such as acidophilus salivarius and bifidus infantis.

Preventing flatulence and constipation

Indigestion is a cause of flatulence, as is eating foods which contain indigestible carbohydrates. These carbohydrates are found particularly in beans and vegetables. The enzyme alpha-galactosidase breaks down these indigestible carbohydrates and reduces flatulence, and is available as a supplement.

Constipation has many causes, the most common of which is hard fecal matter. Natural foods stay soft in the digestive tract because they contain fibers which absorb water and expand. Fruit and vegetables naturally contain a lot of water. Provided they are prepared properly, whole grains such as oats and rice absorb water and provide soft moist bulk for the digestive tract. Meats, cheese, eggs, refined grains, and wheat (because of its gluten content) are all constipating. While it should not be necessary to add fiber, oat fiber has particular benefits in that it has been shown to help eliminate excess cholesterol and slow-down carbohydrate uptake, as well as preventing constipation. It is naturally present in oats, which are best soaked and eaten cold.

Some foods and nutrients exert a mild laxative effect. These include linseed, which can be ground and sprinkled on food, prunes, and vitamin C in doses of several grams. But most laxatives, even natural ones, are gastro-intestinal irritants and, while they work, they do not solve the underlying issue. A new kind of laxative, fructo oligosaccharides, supplied in powder form, is a complex carbohydrate that helps keep moisture in the stomach and stimulates production of healthy lactic acid bacteria. While the results are not quite so rapid, this is a far preferable way of dealing with constipation. Eating plenty of fruit, vegetables, and whole grains, plus drinking lots of water, is essential as well.

For some people long-term constipation can result in physical blockages and distension of the bowel. Dietary changes help but are not always enough to clean out the intestinal tract. A combination of particular fibers, such as psyllium husks, beet fiber, oat fiber and herbs, will assist in loosening up old fecal material. These are available via colon cleansing formulas, consisting of powders and capsules to be taken over a one- to three-month period. Another helpful treatment is colonic therapy: water is passed into the bowel by enema under pressure and this, together with abdominal massage, helps to release and remove old fecal material. Exercise that stimulates the abdominal area also helps to improve digestion, as do breathing exercises that relax the abdomen. It is a natural reflex of the body to stop digesting in times of stress.

Improving digestion is the cornerstone to good health. Energy levels improve, the skin becomes softer and clearer, body odor reduces and the immune system is strengthened. The trick is to work from the top down, first ensuring good digestion, then good absorption, and finally good elimination. If you have any specific digestive difficulties the best person to see is a nutrition consultant. With current testing methods and recent advances in natural treatments most digestive problems can be solved with relative ease, little expense, and no need for invasive tests or treatment.

18

Secrets for a Healthy Heart

You have a 50 percent chance of dying from heart or artery disease. That is the bad news. The good news is that heart disease is, in most cases, completely preventable. Yet so widespread is this epidemic that we almost take it for granted. We fail to protect ourselves from a disease more life-threatening than AIDS, a disease whose cause for the most part is known and whose cure is already proven.

There is nothing natural about dying from heart disease. Many cultures do not experience a high incidence of strokes or heart attacks. By contrast, in the U.S. over a million people die prematurely from cardiovascular disease. Autopsies performed on the mummified remains of Egyptians who died about 3000 B.C. showed signs of deposits in the arteries but no actual blockages that would result in a stroke or heart attack. Despite the obvious signs of a heart attack (severe chest pain, cold sweats, nausea, fall in blood pressure, and weak pulse), in the 1930s it was so rare that it took a specialist to make the diagnosis. According to American health records, the incidence of heart attack per 100,000 people was none in 1890 and had risen to 340 by 1970. Although deaths did occur from other forms of heart disease, including calcified valves, rheumatic heart, and other congenital defects, the incidence of actual blockages in the arteries causing a stroke or heart attack was minimal. Even more worrying is the fact that heart disease is occurring earlier and earlier. Autopsies performed in Vietnam showed that one in two soldiers killed in action, with an average age of twenty-two, already had atherosclerosis (see below). Nowadays most teenagers can be expected to show signs of atherosclerosis, heralding the beginning of heart disease. Obviously something about our lifestyle, diet, or environment has changed radically in the last sixty years to bring on this modern epidemic.

What is Heart Disease?

The cardiovascular system consists of blood vessels that carry oxygen, fuel (glucose), building materials (amino acids), vitamins, and minerals to every single cell in your body. The blood is oxygenated when tiny blood vessels, called capillaries, absorb oxygen from the lungs and in turn discharge carbon dioxide, which we then exhale. These blood vessels feed into the heart, which pumps the oxygenated blood to all cells. At the cells the blood vessels once more become a network of extremely thin capillaries which give off oxygen plus other nutrients and in return receive waste products. Oxygen plus glucose is needed to make energy within every cell of the body; the waste products are carbon dioxide and water.

The blood vessels that supply cells with nutrients and oxygen are called arteries, while the blood vessels which carry away waste products and carbon dioxide are called veins. Arterial blood is redder because oxygen is carried on a complex called hemoglobin, which contains iron. The pressure in the arteries is also greater than in the veins. As well as returning to the heart after it has visited the cells, all blood passes through the kidneys. Here, waste products are removed, and formed into urine which stores in the bladder.

Heart disease is wrongly named. The main life-threatening diseases are diseases of the arteries. Over a number of years a deposit can start to form in the artery wall. This is called arterial plaque or atheroma, from the Greek word for porridge, because of the porridge-like consistency of these deposits. The presence of arterial deposits is called atherosclerosis, and it only occurs in certain parts of the body. Atherosclerosis, coupled with thicker than normal blood containing clots, can lead to a blockage in the artery, which stops the flow of blood. If this occurs in the arteries feeding the heart, the part of the heart fed by these blood vessels will die from lack of oxygen. This is called a myocardial infarction or heart attack. Before this occurs many people are diagnosed as having angina, a condition in which there is a limited supply of oxygen to the heart due to partial blockage of coronary arteries which feed oxygen + glucose to the heart muscle, causing chest pain, most classically on exertion or when under stress.

If a blockage occurs in the brain, part of the brain may die. This is called a stroke. The arteries in the brain are especially fragile and sometimes a stroke occurs not as a result of a blockage but because an artery ruptures. This is called a cerebral hemorrhage. If a blockage occurs in the legs it can result in leg pain, which is a form of thrombosis (a thrombus is a blood clot). When peripheral arteries get blocked this can result in poor peripheral circulation, for example in the hands and feet.

Reversing high blood pressure

So two main factors are responsible for so-called heart disease: atherosclerosis (the formation of deposits) and the presence of blood clots (thick blood). However, there is a third problem that can and usually does occur along with atherosclerosis. That is arteriosclerosis, the hardening of the arteries. Arteries are elastic and, whether or not atherosclerosis is present, tend to lose their

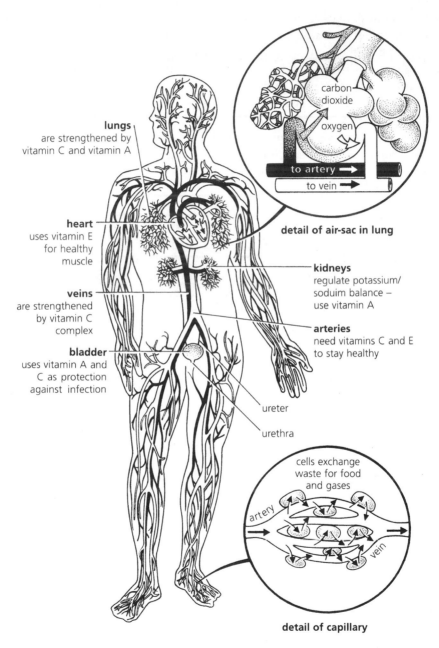

lungs
are strengthened by
vitamin C and vitamin A

carbon
dioxide

oxygen

to artery ➡

to vein ➡

detail of air-sac in lung

heart
uses vitamin E
for healthy
muscle

kidneys
regulate potassium/
soduim balance –
use vitamin A

veins
are strengthened
by vitamin C
complex

arteries
need vitamins C and E
to stay healthy

bladder
uses vitamin A and
C as protection
against infection

ureter

urethra

cells exchange
waste for food
and gases

artery

vein

detail of capillary

The respiratory and cardiovascular system

elasticity and harden with age. One reason is a lack of vitamin C which is needed to make collagen, the intercellular "glue" that keeps skin and arteries supple. Arteriosclerosis, atherosclerosis, and thick blood can all raise blood pressure, putting you at greater risk of thrombosis, angina, a heart attack, or a stroke.

In the same way that the pressure in a hosepipe increases and decreases as the tap is turned on and off, the pressure in the arteries increases when the heart beats and decreases in the lull before the next beat. These are called your systolic and diastolic blood pressure respectively, and a normal reading should be 120/80 irrespective of age. However, if the arteries are blocked, or if the blood is too thick, the pressure increases. Given that blood pressure increases with age in most people, conventional medical wisdom is that a systolic blood pressure of 100 plus your age (say 150 for a fifty-year-old) means that you are in "normal" health. Yet, these are the very same normal people who drop dead unexpectedly from heart attacks. These guidelines are certainly not ideal.

There are four ways to lower blood pressure. The arteries are surrounded by a layer of muscle and an excess of sodium, or a lack of calcium, magnesium, or potassium, can increase the muscular pressure. Increasing your intake of these minerals, while avoiding added salt (sodium chloride), can make a substantial difference to blood pressure in a month. Of these, magnesium is the most important. There is a strong association between magnesium deficiency and heart attack risk. A pronounced magnesium deficiency can cause a heart attack by cramping a coronary artery even in the absence of an atherosclerotic blockage. So checking your magnesium level is essential.

Another way to change blood pressure is to thin the blood. Conventionally aspirin is used, and reduces the risk of a heart attack by 20 percent. Vitamin E, however, is four times as effective, according to Professor Morris Brown whose double-blind controlled trial of vitamin E at Cambridge University Medical School showed a 75 percent reduction in risk.[1] These results are consistent with two recent studies, both published in 1993. In one, whose findings were published in the *New England Journal of Medicine*, 87,200 nurses were given 100 IU of vitamin E daily for more than two years. A 40 percent drop in fatal and non-fatal heart attacks was reported compared to those not taking vitamin E supplements.[39] In the other study 39,000 male health professionals were given 100 IU of vitamin E for the same length of time and achieved a 39 percent reduction in heart attacks.[40] These results confirm the first reports of vitamin E's protective effect, made by Dr. Evan Shute in the 1950s. The Omega 3 fish oils EPA and DHA also thin the blood and, in combination with vitamin E, are much more effective and considerably safer than aspirin.

However, the major risk associated with high blood pressure is narrowing arteries caused by atherosclerosis. A number of nutritional strategies have been shown to stop and even reverse this process. The main results have been produced by supplements of antioxidants, fish oil, and a combination of vitamin C and lysine. Vitamin C also helps to stop arterial tissue from hardening, another cause of high blood pressure. Supplementing a combination of these nutrients is more effective in the long term than drugs designed to lower blood pressure—they deal with the cause of the problem, rather than the symptom.

A three-month trial on thirty-four people with high blood pressure at the Institute for Optimum Nutrition achieved an average eight-point drop in systolic and diastolic blood pressure, with the greatest decreases in those with the highest initial blood pressure.[41] Dr Michael Colgan found that, irrespective of age, people placed on comprehensive nutritional supplement programs showed gradual decreases in blood pressure from an average of slightly above 140/90 to below 120/80. The optimal range is a systolic blood pressure no higher than 125 and a diastolic blood pressure no higher than 85, irrespective of age. Certainly blood pressure above 140/90 is cause for concern.

Dr. Colgan also found that pulse rate, which is more a measure of heart strength and is therefore lower in fitter people, decreased from 76 to an average of 65 over a period of five years on nutritional supplements. Again, an ideal pulse rate is probably below 65 beats per minute.

WHAT CAUSES HEART DISEASE?

To understand how nutritional supplementation, plus dietary changes, makes all the difference we need to examine the underlying cause of arterial disease. Back in 1913 a Russian scientist, Dr. Anitschkov, thought he had got the answer. He found that feeding cholesterol (an animal fat) to rabbits induced heart disease. What he failed to realize was that rabbits, being vegetarians, have no means of dealing with this animal fat. Since the fatty deposits in the arteries of people with heart disease had also been found to be high in cholesterol, it was soon thought that these deposits were the result of excess cholesterol in the blood, possibly caused by excess cholesterol in the diet. Such a simple theory had its attractions, and many doctors still advocate a low-cholesterol diet as the answer to heart disease—despite a consistent lack of results.

The cholesterol myth

In 1975 a research team headed by Dr. Alfin-Slater from the University of California decided to test the cholesterol theory.[42] They selected fifty healthy people with normal blood cholesterol levels. Half of them were given two eggs per day (in addition to the other cholesterol-rich foods they were already eating as part of their normal diet) for eight weeks. The other half were given one extra egg per day for four weeks, then two extra eggs per day for the next four weeks. The results showed no change in blood cholesterol. Later Dr. Alfin-Slater commented, "Our findings surprised us as much as ever…"

Many other studies have also found no rise in blood cholesterol levels caused by eating eggs. In fact, as long ago as 1974 a British advisory panel set up by the government to look at "medical aspects of food policy on diet related to cardio-vascular disease" issued this statement: "Most of the dietary cholesterol in Western communities is derived from eggs, but we have found no evidence which relates the number of eggs consumed to heart disease."

Since high blood cholesterol levels are associated with a high risk of coronary artery disease, it is assumed that having a low cholesterol level is good news. Not so, according to three independent research groups. One, in Japan, found that, while high levels are associated with cardiovascular disease, which is low in Japan, low levels are associated with strokes. As cholesterol levels dropped below 190 mg% in the blood, in this group of 6500 Japanese men, incidence of strokes increased. Meanwhile, a Finnish researcher, Jykri Penttinen, has found a higher rate of depression, suicide, and death from violent causes.[43] These findings were confirmed by David Freedman of the Centers for Disease Control in Atlanta—he found that people with anti-social personality disorders had lower cholesterol levels. Freedman believes that very low levels of cholesterol lead to aggression.

While there is no doubt that high blood cholesterol represents a risk factor for arterial disease, eating a diet containing moderate amounts of cholesterol, for example in eggs, is not associated with an increased risk of heart disease. So what is ideal? According to a survey carried out by medical researcher Dr. Cheraskin, comparing overall health with cholesterol levels, there is a very narrow band that represents a "healthy" cholesterol level in the blood.[44] This is between 190 mg% and 210 mg%. Variations either side correlate with increasing rates of disease.

Ideal Test Scores for Cardiovascular Health

	Sick	'Normal'	Healthy
Cholesterol	<120–>330mg%	120–330mg%	190–210mg%
Cholesterol/HDL	>8:1	>5:1	<3.5:1
Blood Pressure	>140/90	<140/90	<125/85
Pulse	>85	<85	<70

> = more than
< = less than

Good cholesterol

Of course, the nail in the coffin of the dietary cholesterol hypothesis was hammered in by the Eskimos. Although they have one of the highest cholesterol diets in the world they also have one of the lowest incidences of cardiovascular disease. We now know that there is "good" and "bad" cholesterol.

When cholesterol, which is a component of bile, is reabsorbed into the bloodstream it is carried to the arteries by a lipoprotein (fat/protein complex) called LDL (short for low-density lipoprotein). If a large proportion of a person's cholesterol is combined with LDL it is more likely to be deposited in the artery walls. Another lipoprotein called HDL (short for high-density lipoprotein) can take cholesterol out of the arteries and back to the liver. Not surprisingly, it has been popularized as "good" cholesterol, the higher a person's HDL cholesterol compared to their LDL cholesterol, the lower the risk. The ideal ratio is one part HDL cholesterol to three parts of total cholesterol.

Once again, multivitamin and mineral programs are highly effective at achieving this ideal cholesterol balance. Dr. Michael Colgan has demon-strated that, by putting people on a supplement program for six months, then taking them off for three months, and doing this repeatedly over two years, he could consistently lower blood cholesterol and increase the ratio of HDL to LDL.[45] Vitamin B3 (niacin) is also highly effective at increasing HDL levels, although you need to supplement 500–1000 mg a day. Because niacin can produce an unfortunate blushing effect, many people take niacin inositolate or "no-flush niacin." Another effective way to raise HDL and lower LDL and total cholesterol is by consuming significant quantities of Omega 3 oils.[46] In practical terms this means taking an EPA fish oil supplement or eating a lot of oily fish. This is what is understood to have protected the Eskimos.

Another important point about cholesterol is that, like any fat, it can be damaged by oxidation. Cigarette smoking, for instance, increases the oxidation of fats. Once damaged, cholesterol becomes more difficult to clear from the arteries. Oxidation can also injure the cells that line the artery wall, causing them to get clogged up. Antioxidant nutrients are protective, and low dietary and blood levels of beta-carotene, vitamin A, C, and E have repeatedly been shown to increase the risk of heart disease. By increasing intake of antioxidants and decreasing your exposure to free radicals (see Chapter 13) you can reduce your risk.

The Mediterranean Diet

People who live in the mediterranean have a much lower risk of cardiovascular disease. While their diet traditionally contains lots of fruit, vegetables, and fish, their lowered incidence of heart disease has been correlated with their high intake of olive oil, a source of monounsaturated fat. Using olive oil on your foods will help to reduce "bad" LDL cholesterol and increase "good" HDL cholesterol, as well as keep your arteries fluid and supple. Another good reason to use olive oil is that it contains a myriad of minor components that have major health benefits. These include phytosterols, chlorophyll, magnesium, vitamin E, and carotenes. Vitamin E and magnesium in particular are vital for good cardiovascular health. One thing to remember however is that you must buy extra virgin (unrefined) olive oil to obtain these health advantages.

Another source of monounsaturated oil is canola oil, from rape seed, which also contains various properties beneficial to cardiovascular health. However, in its highly refined form as sold in supermarkets it is actually detrimental to health. It is also often hydrogenated to make margarine, a process which damages the beneficial polyunsaturated fats rendering them useless and in fact harmful to your body. If you want to use canola oil, buy it as nature intended, cold-pressed and unrefined.

New theory on heart disease

According to Dr. Linus Pauling and Matthias Rath, even these factors may be but a small part of the underlying cause of atherosclerosis.[47] On the understanding that our ancestors lost the ability to make vitamin C when living in a tropical environment, they wondered how we survived through repeated ice ages without dying from scurvy which used to decimate ship's crews. The first sign of scurvy is vascular bleeding, as blood vessels start to leak—nowhere else in the body is membrane under such pressure.

According to Pauling and Rath, we may have developed the ability to deposit lipoproteins (fat-protein complexes) along the artery wall in order to increase our chances of surviving during vitamin C-deficient times. Two groups of proteins that normally accumulate at injury sites to carry out repairs are fibrinogen and apoprotein. Apoproteins have a natural affinity with fat (lipids) and become lipoprotein A (LpA), which can repair damaged or leaky blood vessels. However, it also increases the risk of heart disease by building up deposits on the artery wall. In fact, of all the factors that can be measured, a person's level of lipoprotein A is the best indicator of risk.

Genetic research is now strongly suggesting that the development of lipoprotein A was most likely a genetic response to a species threatened with extinction through leaky blood vessels. Could this have been nature's way of dealing with life-threatening scurvy? The estimated dates for the development of lipoprotein A in monkeys correlate with the period in which primates are thought to have lost the ability to produce vitamin C.

How well does the theory of vitamin C deficiency as a root cause for cardiovascular disease fit with the facts? Vitamin C deficiency raises cholesterol, triglycerides (fats in the blood), bad LDLs, apoprotein, and lipoprotein A, and lowers the beneficial HDLs. Conversely, increasing vitamin C intake lowers a high-cholesterol, triglyceride, LDL, or LpA level and raises HDLs.

The significance of all these beneficial effects for our ancestors could have been that, during the summer when they could take in enough vitamin C, the increased HDL production would remove excess cholesterol. Vitamin C also inhibits excessive cholesterol production and helps convert cholesterol to bile. All this would lead to a decrease in unnecessary atherosclerotic deposits. In one study it was shown that a daily 500 mg of vitamin C can lead to a reduction in atherosclerotic deposits within two to six months. "This concept also explains why heart attacks and strokes occur today with a much higher frequency in winter than during spring and summer, the seasons with increased ascorbate intake," says Pauling.

If vitamin C deficiency does prove to be the common cause of human cardiovascular disease, then vitamin C supplementation is destined to become the universal treatment for this disease. Pauling and Rath recommend somewhere between 3 and 10 grams a day, and, for those with cardiovascular disease, the addition of the amino acid lysine at around 3 grams a day. The combination of these two nutrients appears to reverse atherosclerosis.

Homocysteine—The Heart Attacker

While vitamin C weakens the very matrix of the artery wall, making it more prone to damage, there is another, more insidious factor produced by the body that is at least as dangerous as having high cholesterol—homocysteine.

The homocysteine theory was first proposed by Dr. Kilmer McCully, a pathologist at the VA Medical Center in Providence, Rhode Island in 1969. Homocysteine is made from protein in the diet. The amino acid methionine is converted into homocysteine in the body, and provided you have enough vitamin B6, B12, and folic acid, the body will convert it into cystanthionine. We now know that homcysteine is very toxic and can cause the initial damage to the artery wall that starts the whole process of cardiovascular disease.

In 1992 a study of 14,000 male doctors found that those in the top 5 percent of homocysteine levels had three times the heart-attack risk, compared to those in the bottom 5 percent (Newsweek, August 11, 1997). This increased risk was confirmed by the Massachusetts-based Framingham Heart Study in 1995 which found that having more than 11.4 micromoles per liter of homocysteine in the blood increased the risk (Selhub J et al.

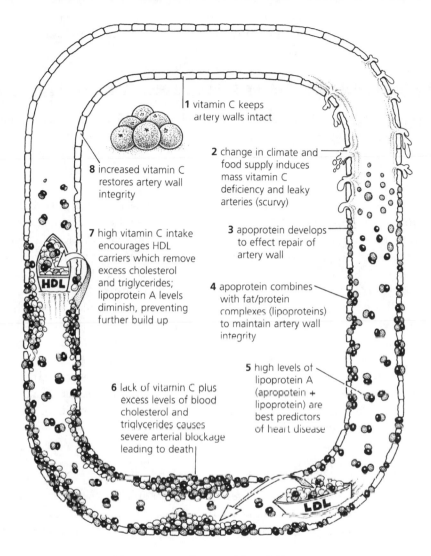

1 vitamin C keeps artery walls intact

2 change in climate and food supply induces mass vitamin C deficiency and leaky arteries (scurvy)

3 apoprotein develops to effect repair of artery wall

4 apoprotein combines with fat/protein complexes (lipoproteins) to maintain artery wall integrity

5 high levels of lipoprotein A (apropotein + lipoprotein) are best predictors of heart disease

6 lack of vitamin C plus excess levels of blood cholesterol and triglycerides causes severe arterial blockage leading to death

7 high vitamin C intake encourages HDL carriers which remove excess cholesterol and triglycerides; lipoprotein A levels diminish, preventing further build up

8 increased vitamin C restores artery wall integrity

HDL

LDL

The cause and cure of heart disease

Association between plasma homocysteine concentrations and extracranial carotid artery stenosis. New England Journal of Medicine 1995; 332(5): 286-291). Another study at the University of Washington found that having high homocysteine doubles the risk of heart attack in young women.

The real clincher was a study carried out by the European Concerted Action Group, a consortium of doctors and researchers from nineteen medical centers in nine European countries (Graham I et al. Plasma homocysteine as a risk factor for vascular disease, JAMA 1997; 277 (22): 1775-1781). They studied 750 people under the age of 60 with atherosclerosis, compared to 800 people without such cardiovascular disease. They found that having a high level of homcysteine in the blood was as great a risk factor for cardiovascular disease as smoking or having a high blood cholesterol level. Those in the top fifth of homocysteine levels had double the risk of cardiovascular disease because of high homocysteine levels.

They also found that those taking vitamin supplements reduced their risk to a third of those not taking supplements. When they compared blood levels of vitamin B6, B12 and folic acid they found that there was a direct relationship between increasing homocysteine levels with decreasing levels of folic acid and vitamin B6, with vitamin B6 being the strongest association.

Those most at risk are high protein (meat) eaters with a poor dietary status of vitamin B6, B12, and folic acid. While meat is considered a reasonable source of vitamin B6 one survey found that you need to eat at least five hamburgers a day to achieve the basic RDA of vitamin B6 which is 2 mg. A hamburger diet is therefore high in protein, high in saturated fat, and cholesterol and clearly deficient in both vitamin B6 and folic acid. Better foods for B6 and folic acid are green leafy vegetables, nuts, whole grains, wheat germ, fish, and free-range chicken.

However, researchers are recommending higher levels of these vitamins than can easily be gained from diet alone, namely at least 10 to 50 mg of vitamin B6 and 400 to 1,000 mcg of folic acid, plus 10 mcg of B12. As *Newsweek* reported in August 1997 "It may turn out that we can accommodate more with nickel-and-dime vitamin supplements than with drugs that cost hundreds of times more."

SUPERNUTRITION FOR A HEALTHY HEART

Much is known about the causes of cardiovascular disease and how to prevent it, and no doubt more is yet to be discovered. However, few if any general practitioners are applying what is already known to prevent and reverse heart disease.

The following guidelines apply to us all as a means of eliminating risk and adding at least ten healthy years to our life span:

- Avoid fried food and limit your intake of meat and foods high in saturated fat. Oily fish such as mackerel, herring, salmon, and tuna are better.

- Eat plenty of fresh fruit and vegetables, which are high in calcium, magnesium, and potassium.

- Do not add salt when cooking, or on your plate, and restrict your consumption of foods with added salt.

- Keep fit, not fat.

- No smoking.

- Avoid prolonged stress.

- Know your blood pressure and have your blood lipid level checked every five years.

- Take a supplement of B vitamins and antioxidant nutrients, including at least 10 mg of B6, 400 mcg of folic acid, 400 mg of vitamin E, and 2 grams of vitamin C.

If you have cardiovascular disease or high blood pressure the following also apply:

- See a nutritionist and have your blood lipid levels measured.

- If you have low HDL, take 1 gram of "no flush" niacin a day.

- If you have high cholesterol or triglycerides, take an EPA fish oil supplement.

- If you have high lipoprotein A, take a supplement of at least 5 grams of vitamin C and 3 grams of lysine.

- If you have high blood pressure, take a magnesium supplement.

- Do all you can to improve your diet and lifestyle.

19

BOOSTING YOUR IMMUNE SYSTEM

Louis Pasteur, who discovered in the nineteenth century that micro-organisms were responsible for infections, realized late in his life that strengthening the body, rather than conquering the invading organism, might prove a more effective strategy. Yet for the last hundred years medicine has focused on drugs designed to destroy the invader—antibiotics, anti-viral agents, chemotherapy. By their very nature these drugs are poison to the body. AZT, the first prescribable anti-HIV drug, is potentially harmful and proving less effective than vitamin C.[48] Although initially antibiotics fight bacterial infection, in the long term they may do more harm than good as they encourage the evolution of new drug-resistant strains of bacteria.[49] Chemotherapy depletes the immune system and, even in the best situations, wins a victory at a cost.

Only recently, with the seemingly endless onslaught of new infectious agents, has attention turned within—towards strengthening our immunity. The immune system is one of the most remarkable and complex systems within the human body. When you realize that it has the ability to produce a million specific "straitjackets" (called antibodies) within a minute and to recognize and disarm a billion different invaders (called antigens), the strategy of boosting immune power makes a lot of sense. The ability to react rapidly to a new invader makes all the difference between a minor twenty-four-hour cold or stomach bug and a week in bed with flu or food poisoning. It may also be the difference between a non-malignant lump and breast cancer, or symptom-free HIV infection and full-blown AIDS.

IMMUNE POWER

How do you boost your immune power? Exercise, your state of mind, and your diet all play a part. Overtraining or vigorous exercise actually suppress the immune system, while the Chinese art of Tai-chi has been shown to increase the count of T-cells (one of the body's types of immune cell) by 40 percent. More calming, less stressful forms of exercise are probably best for immunity. This may be because corticosteroids, substances produced by the adrenal glands as a response to stress (and also taken as the drug cortisone), suppress the immune system. This too may be a key explanation for numerous studies which have found that low psychological states such as stress, depression, and grief depress the immune system. Learning how to cope with stress, deal with psychological issues, and relax is an important part of boosting the immune system. Meditation, for example, has been shown to increase T-cell counts and improve the T-helper/suppressor ratio (see p. 124).[50]

UNDERSTANDING IMMUNITY

The purpose of the immune system is to identify the body's enemies and destroy them. They includes defective body cells as well as foreign agents such as bacteria and viruses. The main "gates" into the body are the digestive tract, which lets in food, and the lungs, which let in air. Within the digestive tract is the "stomach-associated immune system," which is programmed to allow completely digested food particles, such as amino acids, fatty acids, and simple sugars, to pass unhindered through the stomach wall into the body. Incompletely digested food can result in immune reactions and eventually allergies, especially if large food molecules pass into the bloodstream. The nasal passages help to prevent unwanted agents from entering the lungs. Healthy, strong mucous membranes in the respiratory and digestive tract are the first line of defense against invaders.

THE IMMUNE ARMY

Once inside the body, the immune system has an army of special cells to deal with invaders. These defenders differ in their function and territory. For example, some cells operate in the blood, keeping an eye out for invaders, and whistling up other troops which can destroy specific invaders. The three main types of immune cells found in the blood, collectively called white cells, are B-cells, T-cells, and macrophages.

B-cells or B-lymphocytes are produced in an antibody for each specific invader or antigen. When a B-cell comes into contact with an antigen it grows larger and divides into several cells which secrete specific antibodies that latch on to the invader. Antibodies cannot destroy bacteria and viruses, but they do give them a hard time. They stop bacteria producing toxins, and they prevent viruses from entering body cells. Since a virus cannot reproduce unless it enters a body cell and takes over the cell's control center, reprogramming it to produce more viruses, antibodies are a major nuisance for viruses. Antibodies also whistle up other, more belligerent members of the immune army, such as T-cells.

THE ARMY

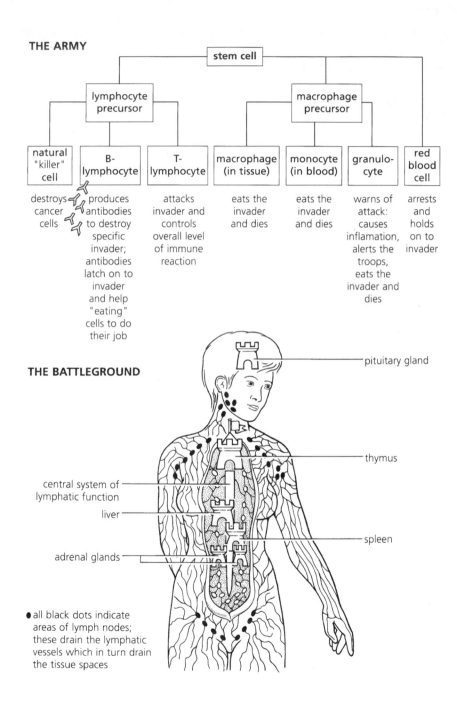

natural "killer" cell	B-lymphocyte	T-lymphocyte	macrophage (in tissue)	monocyte (in blood)	granulo-cyte	red blood cell
destroys cancer cells	produces antibodies to destroy specific invader; antibodies latch on to invader and help "eating" cells to do their job	attacks invader and controls overall level of immune reaction	eats the invader and dies	eats the invader and dies	warns of attack: causes inflamation, alerts the troops, eats the invader and dies	arrests and holds on to invader

THE BATTLEGROUND

pituitary gland

thymus

central system of lymphatic function

liver

adrenal glands

spleen

● all black dots indicate areas of lymph nodes; these drain the lymphatic vessels which in turn drain the tissue spaces

The immune army and battleground

T-cells or T-lymphocytes are derived from the thymus gland at the top of the chest. There are three kinds: T-helpers, T-suppressors, and NK (natural killers), NK cells produce toxins that can destroy the invader. T-helpers help to activate B-cells to product antigens, while T-suppressors turn off the reactions once the battle is won. Normally, there are roughly twice as many T-helpers as T-suppressors. In AIDS the HIV virus selectively destroys T-helpers, resulting in too many T-suppressors which depress the immune system, leaving the sufferer susceptible to other infections.

Macrophages finish off the battle by completely engulfing and digesting the invader that has been identified by B- and T-cells. This action is called phagocytosis. Phagocytic cells that operate in the blood are called mono-cytes, while those that operate in other tissues are called macrophages.

THE IMMUNE BATTLEGROUND

At any time there are a small number of immune cells roaming the body. Many of them have only a short life: T-cells, for example, live for about four days. When an invader is identified, new troops are produced in the bone marrow and thymus and posted to forts such as lymph nodes, the tonsils, appendix, spleen, and Peyer's patches. Lymphatic vessels drain into these forts, bringing in invaders to be destroyed. That is why lymph nodes (for example, in the neck, armpits and groin) become inflamed during an infection. This means they are doing their job. Since the lymphatic system doesn't have a pump, lymphatic fluid is moved along by muscle movement— so physical exercise is important for lymphatic drainage.

IMMUNE-BOOSTING NUTRIENTS

Your immune strength is totally dependent on an optimal intake of vitamins and minerals. Deficiency of vitamins A, B1, B2, B6, B12, folic acid, C, and E suppress immunity, as do deficiencies of iron, zinc, magnesium, and selenium.

Vitamins B1, B2, and B5 have mild immune-boosting effects compared with B6. The production of antibodies, so critical in any infection, depends upon B6, as does T-cell function. The ideal daily intake is probably 50–100 mg. B12 and folic acid also both appear essential for proper B-cell and T-cell function. B6, zinc, and folic acid are all needed for the rapid production of new immune cells to engage an enemy.

Since no nutrients work in isolation, it is a good idea to take a good high-strength multivitamin and mineral supplement. The combination of nutrients at even modest levels can boost immunity very effectively. Dr. Chandra and colleagues, in a research study published in the *Lancet*, took a group of ninety-six healthy elderly people and gave some a supplement of this kind, and others a placebo.[51] Those on the supplement suffered fewer infections, had a stronger immune system as measured by blood test determination of immune factors, and were generally healthier than those given the placebo.

ANTIOXIDANT POWER

The nutrients worth adding in larger amounts to fight off infection are the antioxidants and particularly vitamin C. Most invaders produce the dangerous oxidizing chemicals known as free radicals to fight off the troops of your immune system. Antioxidant nutrients such as vitamins A, C, and E, zinc, and selenium disarm these free radicals, weakening the invader. Vitamin A also helps to maintain the integrity of the digestive tract, lungs, and all cell membranes, preventing foreign agents from entering the body and viruses from entering cells. In addition, vitamin A and beta-carotene are potent antioxidants. Many foreign agents produce free oxidizing radicals as part of their defense system. Even our own immune cells produce free radicals to destroy invaders. Therefore a high intake of antioxidant nutrients helps to protect your immune cells from these harmful weapons of war. The ideal intake of beta-carotene is 10,000 to 50,000 IUs per day.

Vitamin E, another important all-rounder, improves B- and T-cell function. Its immune-boosting properties increase when given in conjunction with selenium. The ideal daily intake is between 100 and 1000 IUs.

Selenium, iron, manganese, copper and zinc are all involved in anti-oxidation and have been shown to affect immune power positively. Of these, selenium and zinc are probably the most important. While zinc is critical for immune cell production and proper functioning of B- and T-cells, excess zinc can suppress the ability of macrophages to destroy bacteria. The ideal daily intake is 15–25 mg. While zinc may be a beneficial supplement during a viral infection, it may not be a good idea to do so during a bacterial infection. The same is true for iron. While iron deficiency suppresses immune function, too much iron interferes with the ability of macrophages to destroy bacteria. When an infection is present, the body initiates a series of defense mechanisms designed to stop the invader absorbing iron, so supplementing iron is not recommended during a bacterial infection.

HOW MUCH C?

Vitamin C is unquestionably the master immune-boosting nutrient. To date more than a dozen roles of this kind have been identified for it. It helps immune cells to mature, improves the performance of antibodies and macrophages, and is itself anti-viral and anti-bacterial, as well as being able to destroy toxins produced by bacteria. In addition, it is a natural anti-histamine, calming down inflammation, and stimulates another part of the immune defense system to produce interferon which boosts immunity. Excessive levels of the stress hormone cortisol, a potent immune suppressor, are controlled by sufficient vitamin C. However, the dosage of vitamin C is crucial. Professor Harry Hemilia examined all studies that tested the effects of vitamin C or a placebo on the common cold, selecting only those that gave 1 gram daily or more. Thirty-seven out of 38 concluded that supplementing 1 gram, twenty times the RDA, had a protective effect. Studies using less than this amount tend not to be conclusive.

THE IMMUNE POWER DIET

The ideal immune-boosting diet is, in essence, no different from the ideal diet for anyone. Since immune cells are produced rapidly during an infection, sufficient protein is essential. However, too much suppresses immunity, probably by using up available B6. Diets high in saturated or hydrogenated fat suppress immunity and clog up the lymphatic vessels; but essential fats, found in cold-pressed seed oils, boost immunity. Therefore a well-balanced protein, low-fat diet, with fats obtained from essential sources such as seeds and nuts, together with plenty of fresh fruit and vegetables rich in vitamins and minerals, is the way to eat for maximum immunity. During a viral infection that increases mucus production, it is best to avoid meat, dairy products, and eggs, and also any foods that you suspect you might be allergic to. Great foods are all vegetables, especially carrots, beets and their tops, sweet potatoes, tomatoes, and bean sprouts. Fruit is particularly beneficial, especially watermelon, oranges, and kiwi fruit, plus ground seeds, lentils, beans, whole grains such as brown rice, and fish. All foods should be eaten as raw as possible, avoiding frying, which introduces free radicals.

Here are some typical items in an immune power diet.

Watermelon juice

Blend the flesh and the seeds in an electric blender. The husks will sink to the bottom, leaving the seeds, which are rich in protein, zinc, selenium, vitamin E, and essential fats, in the juice. Drink a pint for breakfast and another pint during the day.

Carrot soup

Blend three organic carrots, two tomatoes, a bunch of watercress, a third of a packet of tofu, half a cup of rice milk or soy milk, a teaspoon of vegetable stock (Bouillon or Vecon), and (optional) some ground almonds or seeds. Eat cold or heat to serve, accompanied by oatcakes or rice cakes.

A large salad

Include a selection of "seed" vegetables like broad beans, broccoli, grated carrot, beet, zucchini, watercress, lettuce, tomatoes, and avocados, adding seeds or marinated tofu pieces—organic if possible. Serve with a dressing of cold-pressed oil containing some crushed garlic.

Useful supplements

These supplements help to fight infections naturally:

- A good, high-strength multivitamin and mineral

- A good, high-strength antioxidant formula giving at least 20,000 IUs (6,600 mcg) of vitamin A, 300 IUs of vitamin E, 100 mg of B6, 20 mg of zinc, and 100 mcg of selenium

- Vitamin C, 3 grams every four hours including last thing at night and immediately on rising. (It may have a laxative effect. If so, reduce the dose accordingly.)

- Cat's Claw tea with ginger four times a day

- Echinacea, ten drops three times a day

- Grapefruit seed extract, ten drops three times a day

20

BALANCING HORMONES NATURALLY

Some of the most powerful chemicals in the body are hormones. These are biochemicals produced in special glands and, when present in the bloodstream, give instructions to body cells. Insulin, for example, tells the cells to take up glucose from the blood. Thyroxine, from the thyroid gland, speeds up the metabolism of cells, generating energy and burning fat. Estrogen and progesterone, from the ovaries, control a sequence of changes that maintain fertility and the menstrual cycle. Hormone imbalances can wreak havoc on your health.

Hormones are either fat-like, called steroid hormones, or protein-like, such as insulin. They are made from components of your food, and diet can play a crucial part in keeping your hormone levels in balance. Most hormones work on feedback loops, with the pituitary gland as the conductor of the orchestra. For example, the pituitary releases thyroid-stimulating hormone (TSH), which tells the thyroid gland to release thyroxine, which speeds up the metabolism of the cells in the body. When the blood level of thyroxine reaches a certain point, the pituitary stops producing TSH.

THE THYROID GLAND AND METABOLISM

The thyroid hormone thyroxine is made from the amino acid tyrosine. The enzyme that converts one into the other is dependent on iodine and selenium. A lack of either tyrosine or iodine can reduce thyroxine levels, although deficiency of either is quite rare. However, an underactive thyroid, which can cause symptoms such as weight gain, mental and physical lethargy, constipation, and thickening skin, is quite common. Many people suspected of having thyroid problems have borderline "normal" thyroxine levels on testing, but experience amazing health transformations after taking a low dose of thyroxine.

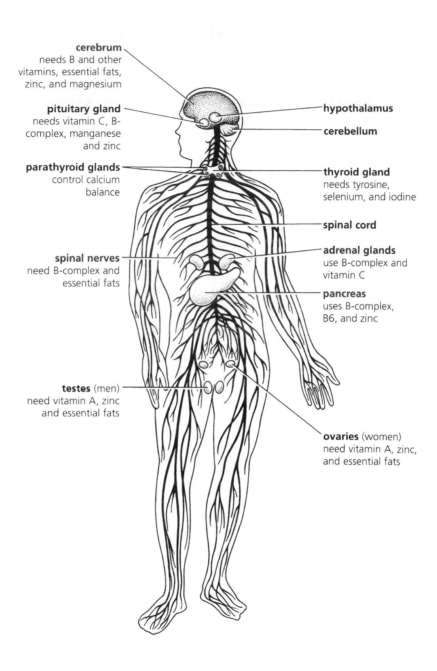

cerebrum
needs B and other
vitamins, essential fats,
zinc, and magnesium

pituitary gland
needs vitamin C, B-
complex, manganese
and zinc

parathyroid glands
control calcium
balance

spinal nerves
need B-complex and
essential fats

testes (men)
need vitamin A, zinc
and essential fats

hypothalamus

cerebellum

thyroid gland
needs tyrosine,
selenium, and iodine

spinal cord

adrenal glands
use B-complex and
vitamin C

pancreas
uses B-complex,
B6, and zinc

ovaries (women)
need vitamin A, zinc,
and essential fats

The endocrine glands and hormones

MAINTAINING CALCIUM BALANCE

The thyroid gland also produces a hormone responsible for maintaining calcium balance in the body. Calcitonin from the thyroid works in balance with parathormone (or PTH) from the parathyroid glands, four tiny glands attached to the thyroid. PTH converts vitamin D into an active hormone that helps to increase available calcium. While most of the body's calcium is in the bones, a small amount is in the blood and cells because every single nerve and muscle reaction uses calcium. PTH stimulates the bones to give up calcium, while calcitonin puts calcium back into the bones.

STRESS AND THE ADRENALS

The adrenal glands sit on top of the kidneys and produce hormones that, among other things, help us adapt to stress. The hormones adrenalin, cortisol and DHEA help us respond to an emergency by channeling the body's energy towards being able to "fight or take flight," improving oxygen and glucose supply to the muscles, and generating mental and physical energy. It is a design that helped our remote ancestors cope with truly life-threatening situations. During a stress reaction the blood thickens to help wounds to heal. In modern life all this happens when you open your bank statement to find you are overdrawn, get stuck in a traffic jam, or have a fight with your spouse. Tea, coffee, chocolate, and cigarettes have the same effect as they contain caffeine, theobromine, theophylline, or nicotine, which stimulate the release of adrenalin.

But this instant energy has a downside. The body slows down digestion, repair, and maintenance to channel energy into dealing with stress. As a consequence prolonged stress is associated with speeding up the aging process, a number of the diseases of the digestion and hormone balance.

By living off stimulants such as coffee and cigarettes, high-sugar diets, or stress itself you increase your risk of upsetting your thyroid balance (which means your metabolism will slow down and you will gain weight) or calcium balance (resulting in arthritis), or of getting problems associated with sex hormone imbalances. These are the long-term side effects of prolonged stress, because any body system that is over-stimulated will eventually under-function.

The stress hormones rely on certain nutrients for their production. For adrenalin you need enough of vitamins B3 (niacin), B12, and C. Cortisol, which is also a natural anti-inflammatory substance, cannot be produced without enough vitamin B5. Your need for all these nutrients, along with those needed for energy production such as vitamins B and C, goes up with prolonged stress.

Levels of DHEA, a vital adrenal hormone, fall as a result of prolonged stress. This hormone, which can be bought over the counter, can be supplemented in small amounts to restore stress resistance. A new kind of test can tell you where you are on the stress cycle. Saliva taken at five specific times of the day is analyzed to determine its levels of cortisol and DHEA.

DHEA can also be used to make the sex hormones testosterone (in men), progesterone and estrogen (in women), and is considered "anti-aging." However, too much can also over-stimulate the adrenal glands and, for example, induce insomnia. So it is best not to take it unless you need it, as revealed by an adrenal stress test.

Sex hormones

In women the balance between progesterone and estrogen is critical. A relative excess of estrogen, called estrogen dominance, is associated with an increased risk of breast cancer, fibroids, ovarian cysts, endometriosis, and PMS. The early warning symptoms of estrogen dominance include PMS, depression, loss of sex drive, sweet cravings, heavy periods, weight gain, breast swelling, and water retention.

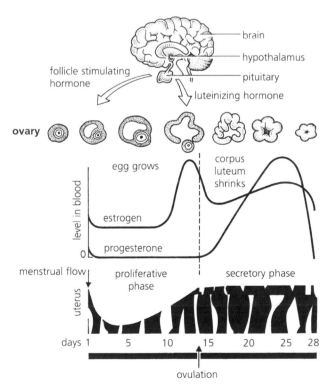

Hormones in the menstrual cycle

Estrogen dominance can be due to excess exposure to estrogenic substances, or a lack of progesterone, or a combination of both. Estrogenic compounds are found in meat, much of which is hormone-fed, in dairy products, in many pesticides, and in soft plastics, some of which leach into food when used for wrapping. Estrogen is also contained in most birth control pills and HRT.

If a woman does not ovulate, which ironically can be because of a slight lack of estrogen, no progesterone is produced. This is because progesterone is produced in the sac that contains the ovum, once the ovum is released. If no progesterone is produced, there is a relative estrogen dominance. Stress raises levels of the adrenal hormone cortisol, which competes with progesterone and lowers DHEA levels, the precursor of progesterone.

DHEA is also a precursor of testosterone, and evidence is accumulating to suggest that men too can suffer from estrogen dominance and testosterone deficiency. While men produce very little estrogen, they are exposed to this hormone in their diet and in the environment. Some, such as breakdown-products of the pesticide DDT, and Vincloxaline, used to spray lettuces, are known to interfere with the body's testosterone, creating a deficiency. This may explain the increase in the incidence of genital defects and undescended testes in male infants, and the rise in infertility as well as prostate and testicular cancer. In later life some men have the equivalent of a "male menopause." The symptoms, according to male hormone expert Dr Malcolm Carruthers, include fatigue, depression, decreased sexual performance, redistribution and gain in weight, including excessive breast tissue.

Prostaglandins, made from essential fatty acids, sensitize cells to hormones. There is considerable interaction between prostaglandins and hormones, especially sex hormones. Deficiency in essential fats, which is endemic in the Western world, or deficiency in the nutrients needed to convert essential fats into prostaglandins (vitamins B3, B6, and C, biotin, magnesium, and zinc), can also create the equivalent of hormonal imbalances.

These nutrients, plus essential fats, have proved very helpful in relieving PMS and menopausal symptoms. Also helpful for menopausal symptoms is vitamin E. One possible explanation is that vitamin E protects essential fats and prostaglandins from oxidation.

The following guidelines will help you keep your hormones in balance. However, if you are suffering from a major hormone imbalance such as estrogen dominance it may be necessary also to take small amounts of natural progesterone. This is very different from synthetic progestins, which are included in some birth control pills and HRT, often in massive amounts in comparison to what the body naturally produces. Natural progesterone, and, for men, testosterone is available on prescription from doctors only.

To keep your hormones in balance:

- Keep animal fats very low in your diet.

- Choose organic vegetables and meat wherever possible to reduce pesticide and hormone exposure.

- Do what you can to reduce the exposure of soft, acid, or fatty foods to soft plastics. For example, do not wrap cheese in plastic wrap. Buy drinks in bottles rather than in cartons lined in soft plastic.

- Use stimulants such as coffee, tea, chocolate, sugar, and cigarettes infrequently, if at all. If you are addicted to any of these, break the habit.

- Do not let stress become a habit in your life. Identify sources of stress and make some positive changes to your circumstances and the way you react to them.

- Make sure you are getting enough essential fats from seeds, their oils or supplements of evening primrose or borage oil (Omega 6) or flax oil (Omega 3).

- Make sure your supplement program includes optimal levels of vitamins B3 and B6, biotin, magnesium, and zinc.

21

BONE HEALTH—A SKELETON IN THE CUPBOARD

Not many people think about nourishing their skeleton. There is almost a belief that once your bones are formed they are there for good—until they start to break down, as in arthritis or osteoporosis. Yet the bones, like every other part of the body, are continually being rebuilt. They are a structure of protein and collagen (a kind of intercellular glue) which collects mainly calcium, plus phosphorus and magnesium. We even store heavy metals like lead in our bones when our body cannot get rid of them.

There are two kinds of bone cells: osteoblasts build new bone, while osteoclasts break down and get rid off old bone. The bone ends are made of cartilage, which is softer so that joints can work smoothly. While bones use calcium, phosphorus, and magnesium as building materials, the ability to absorb calcium into bones depends on vitamin D and is assisted by the trace mineral boron. Vitamin C makes collagen, and zinc helps make new bone cells. This orchestra of nutrients is often found in "bone-friendly" supplements.

OSTEOPOROSIS

The epidemic of osteoporosis has made many women think seriously about the health of their bones. It is the silent thief that robs up to 25 percent of your skeleton by the time you reach fifty. Particularly prevalent in women after the menopause, it increases the risk of bone fractures which occur in one in three women and one in twelve men by the age of seventy.

The conventional explanation is that once a woman stops menstruating she produces little of the estrogen which helps keep calcium in her bones, hence the recommendation for women to have hormone replacement therapy (HRT). But this is far from the truth. Firstly, analysis of skeletal remains of our ancestors, and across cultures, show that post-menopausal women do not routinely suffer from decreased bone density. It is a more recent phenomenon, particularly of Western society. Secondly, estrogen, which stimulates osteoclast cells, does not help build new bone but only stops the loss of old bone. Progesterone, on the other hand, stimulates osteoblasts which do build new bone. Taking natural progesterone increases bone density four times better than estrogen.

In the time leading up to the menopause, and afterward, a woman stops ovulating. If no ovum is released no progesterone is produced, even though the body continues to produce small amounts of estrogen. Scientists are now coming round to thinking that it is the relative excess of estrogen to progesterone, which is in effect progesterone deficiency, that is precipitating osteoporosis, not deficiency in estrogen.

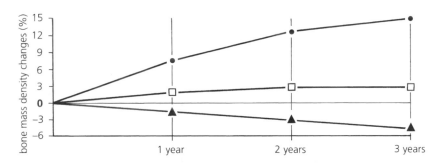

Typical bone mass density changes with natural progesterone ●, estrogen □, or no hormone supplement ▲

Of course, this is not the only factor. Changes in diet are strongly related to increased risk of osteoporosis and may explain why many cultural groups have no osteoporosis at all. But while people with very low calcium intakes may benefit from taking more, there is no strong association between osteoporosis and calcium levels. The Bantu tribes of Africa, for example, have an average calcium intake of 400 mg a day, well below the recommended intake for post-menopausal women, yet virtually no osteoporosis. In contrast Eskimos, who consume vast amounts of calcium, have an exceptionally high incidence of osteoporosis. Why the difference? What have countries and cultures with a high incidence of osteoporosis got in common? The answer may be too much dietary protein.

Protein-rich foods are acid-forming. The body cannot tolerate substantial changes in acid level in the blood and neutralizes this effect through two main alkaline agents—sodium and calcium. When the body's reserves of sodium are used up, calcium is taken from the bones. Therefore the more protein you eat, the more calcium you need. The difference between the Bantus and the Eskimos is their level of protein consumption.

The idea that high-protein diets lead to calcium deficiency is nothing new. But what research is beginning to show is that if you eat a high-protein diet no amount of calcium will correct the imbalance. In one piece of research published in the *American Journal of Clinical Nutrition*, the group of people studied were given either a moderately high protein diet (80 g protein a day) or a very high protein diet (240 g protein) plus 1,400 mg of calcium.[52] The overall loss of calcium was 37 mg per day on the 80 g protein diet and 137mg per day on the 240 g protein diet. The authors concluded that "high calcium diets are unlikely to prevent probable bone loss induced by high protein diets." In another study a protein intake of 95 grams a day (bacon and eggs for breakfast supplies 55 grams), resulted in an average calcium loss of 58 mg per day, which means a loss of 2 percent of total skeletal calcium per year, or 20 percent each decade.[53] The negative effects of too much protein have been clearly demonstrated in patients with osteoporosis. Some medical scientists now believe that a lifelong consumption of a high-protein, acid-forming diet may be a primary cause of osteoporosis.

SAY NO TO ARTHRITIS

According to Dr. Robert Bingham, a specialist in the treatment of arthritis, "No person who is in good nutritional health develops rheumatoid or osteoarthritis." Yet by the age of sixty, nine in every ten people have it. For some it is a living hell which can even be life-threatening. For all of them, arthritis means living with pain and stiffness. Arthritis is not, however, an inevitable consequence of aging and can be prevented, provided the underlying causes are eliminated.

In the search for the cause of arthritis many things have been considered, including diet, physical exercise, posture, climate, hormones, infections, genetics, old age, and stress. Most of these factors have proved relevant to some arthritis suffers. I believe the occurrence of the symptoms of arthritis, or any arthritic type of disease, is the result of an accumulation of stresses that eventually cause joint, bone, and muscle degeneration.

The likely factors that lead to the development of this painful condition are:

Poor lubrication of the joints   In between joints is a substance called synovial fluid. Good nutrition is needed to make sure that the synovial fluid stays fluid and able to lubricate. Cartilage and synovial fluid contain mucopolysaccharides, which can be provided by certain foods.

Hormonal imbalance   Hormones control the calcium balance in the

---

How Arthritis Develops

1 A healthy joint consists of strong bones, which are essentially minerals in a collagen (protein) matrix. Cartilage on the edge of bones is protected from the opposing bone and cartilage by a sac containing synovial fluid, which effectively lubricates the joint.

2 Overuse and dietary imbalances can lead to a breakdown of cartilage. Synovial fluid becomes less lubricating. Loss of cartilage also leads to breakdown of collagen components in both cartilage and bone. Bone ends become uneven and osteophytes (large bone spurs) form. Inflammation restricts movement.

3 Loss of calcium balance can lead to calcium being dumped in soft tissues, causing muscle pain. In rheumatoid arthritis (ringed) bone ends can become fused together.

---

body. If the calcium balance is out of control the bones and joints can become porous and subject to wear and tear, and calcium can be deposited in the wrong place, resulting in arthritic "spurs." The fault is not so much calcium intake, but the loss of calcium balance in the body. A lack of exercise, too much tea, coffee, alcohol, or chocolate, exposure to toxic metals like lead, excessive stress, or underlying blood sugar or thyroid imbalances can all upset calcium control. While calcium control can be worse after the menopause, probably due to the loss of estrogen, too much estrogen also makes arthritis worse. It is all a question of balance. Another hormone, insulin, stimulates the synthesis of the mucopolysaccharides from which cartilage is made. People with underactive thyroid glands are more likely to suffer from arthritis.

Allergies and sensitivities   Almost everyone who suffers from rheumatoid arthritis and many people who have osteoarthritis have food and chemical allergies or sensitivities that make their symptoms flare up. The most common food allergies are to wheat and dairy produce. Chemical and environmental sensitivities can include gas and exhaust fumes. These are well worth strictly avoiding for one month to see whether they contribute to the problem.

Free radicals   In all inflamed joints a battle is taking place, with the body trying to deal with the damage. One of the key weapons of war in the body are free radicals (see p. 126). If the immune system is not working properly, as in rheumatoid arthritis, it will produce too many free radicals, which can damage tissue around the joint. A low intake of antioxidant nutrients can make arthritis worse.

Infections   Any infection, be it viral or bacterial, weakens the immune system which controls inflammation. But some viruses and bacteria particularly affect the joints by lodging in them and recurring when immune defenses are low. Often the immune system can harm surrounding tissue in an attempt to fight an infection, like an army which obliterates its own country in trying to get rid of an invader. Building up your immune defenses through optimum nutrition is the natural solution.

Bone strain and deformities   Any damage or strain, so often caused by bad posture, increases the risk of developing arthritis. A yearly check-up with an osteopath or chiropractor, plus regular exercise that helps to increase joint suppleness and strength, is the best prevention. Once arthritis has set in, special exercises help to reduce pain and stiffness.

State of mind   Research at the Arthritis and Rheumatism Foundation and at the University of Southern California Medical School has shown a link between arthritis and emotional stress. "Hidden anger, fear, or worry often accompanies the beginning of arthritis," says Dr Austin from USC.

Poor diet   Most arthritics have a history of poor diet, which paves the way for many of the above risk factors. Too much refined sugar, too many stimulants, too much fat, and too much protein are all strongly associated with arthritic problems. A lack of any of a large number of vital vitamins, minerals and essential fatty acids could, in itself, precipitate joint problems.

In summary, if you want to keep your bones and joints in good health:

- Keep fit and supple and see an osteopath or chiropractor once a year.

- Reduce your meat consumption to avoid excessive protein.

- Get out of the "stress cycle" and keep stimulants to a minimum.

- Make sure your diet is rich in minerals from seeds, nut,s and root vegetables.

- If you have arthritis, check out possible food allergies.

- If you have osteoporosis, consider natural progesterone (as a cream, not as HRT).

- If you have joint inflammation, take a daily supplement of 300 g of GLA (Omega 6 essential oil) and flax seed oil or 1,000 mg of EPA/DHA fish oil.

22

SKIN HEALTH—EAT YOURSELF BEAUTIFUL

Skin. Where would we be without it? Not only does it keep our insides in, it protects us from infection, radiation and dehydration, keeps us warm, and makes us look good. While we are most aware of our "outside skin," the "inside skin" of the lungs and digestive tract cover a much larger area. This entire surface is replaced every twenty days, and its condition depends largely on what you eat.

Problems such as eczema, dermatitis, psoriasis, acne, and excessively oily, dry, or wrinkly skin are a good indication that you are either not eating optimally or are exposing your skin to something it does not like. Before examining these conditions and their prevention, here are a few facts that are worth knowing.

The skin has two layers, the inner or lower of which is called the dermis. It contains dermal cells, from which all skin cells originate, plus a network of blood vessels, glands, and nerve endings. The outer layer of the skin, the epidermis, consists of dermal cells which lose moisture as they move towards the surface of the skin, becoming flatter and harder and more concentrated in a protein called keratin. The skin's surface is an overlapping mesh of these dead epidermal cells which flake off and are continually replaced. They are a major constituent of household dust!

The dermis consists largely of collagen, which gives the skin its strength and structure. Woven within it are elastin fibers which give the skin its elasticity. Collagen makes up 70 percent of the skin and 20 percent of the entire body.

Nutrition is fundamentally involved at every stage of skin development. Starting with the dermis, collagen is made when vitamin C converts the amino acid proline into hydroxyproline. No vitamin C, no collagen. The flexibility of collagen and elastin fibers reduces in time due to damage caused by free radicals. This damage is limited by antioxidants such as vitamins A, C, and E, selenium, and many others. Vitamin A helps to control the rate of keratin accumulation in the skin. A lack of this vitamin can therefore result in dry, rough skin. The membranes of skin cells are made

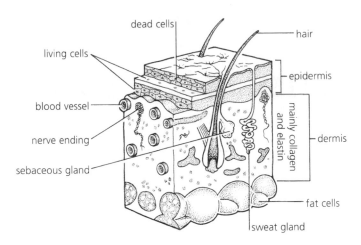

Cross-section through the skin

from essential fats. A lack of essential fats makes these cells dry out too quickly, resulting in dry skin and excessive need of moisturizers. The health of skin cells depends on sufficient zinc, which is needed for accurate production of new generations of skin cells. Lack of zinc leads to stretch marks and poor healing and is associated with a wide variety of skin problems from acne to eczema. Skin cells also produce a chemical which, in the presence of sunlight, is converted into vitamin D which is needed to maintain the calcium balance of the body. So in many ways what you eat today you wear tomorrow.

The following good dietary guidelines are especially important for people with skin problems. Limit alcohol, coffee, tea, sugar, and saturated fat (as in meat and dairy products), and increase your intake of fresh fruit, vegetables, water, herb teas, and diluted juices. It is also well worth taking a good all-round multivitamin and mineral supplement, plus at least 1,000 mg of vitamin C a day.

A TO Z OF SKIN PROBLEMS AND NUTRITIONAL SOLUTIONS

Acne

Factors to consider   Excess fat blocks the skin pores. High histamine types (see p. 200) produce more sebum, an oily secretion in the skin. Vitamin A deficiency produces skin congestion through over-keratinization of skin cells. Vitamin A and zinc deficiency leads to lowered ability to fight infection, as does lack of beneficial bacteria (often through over-use of antibiotics).

Diet Low-fat, low-sugar, high water, fresh fruit, vegetables (high water-content foods), and regular cleansing diets/fasts.

Supplements Vitamin A, zinc, vitamin C, all antioxidants, niacin for skin flushing, vitamin E for wound healing.

Cellulite

Factors to consider Excess saturated fat or fat-based toxins render fat cells immobile. If you strictly avoid dietary sources of saturated fat and eat only sources of essential oils, fat cells decongest and become softer. The body takes in many toxins, for example pesticide residues, which are hard to get rid of. These are dumped in fat cells to keep them away from vital organs. Hard fat and fat-based toxins can be eliminated by improving the circulation. Circulation to and from fat cells is stimulated by high water content while, lymphatic drainage is achieved by massage, movement, exercise, and skin brushing.

Diet A strict no-saturated-fat diet, which means no meat or dairy products. Essential fatty acids can be acquired from seeds. Drink lots of water and eat plenty of high water-content foods such as fruit and vegetables, all organic. Apples are particularly good at eliminating cellulite. The pectin found in apples, carrots, and other fruit and vegetables is an important phytochemical which strengthens the immune and detoxification systems of the body. Consider a three-day apple fast or eat only organic apples one day a week.

Supplements Lecithin granules, hydroxycitric acid, high-dose vitamin C, and niacin.

Dermatitis

Factors to consider Dermatitis literally means skin inflammation, and is similar to eczema. The term is used when the primary cause appears to be a contact allergy. Consider all possibilities such as metals in jewelry, watches, etc.; perfumes or cosmetics; detergents in washing up liquid, soaps, shampoos, or washing powders. Where there is a contact allergy there is often a food allergy too: common culprits are dairy products and wheat. Sometimes a combination of eating an allergy-provoking food and contact with an external allergen is needed for symptoms to develop. Another factor that makes dermatitis more likely is a lack of essential fatty acids from seeds and their oils, which turn into anti-inflammatory prostaglandins in the body. Their formation is blocked if you eat too much saturated fat or fried food, or lack certain key vitamins and minerals. The skin is also a route that the body can use to get rid of toxins. One kind of dermatitis, called acrodermatitis, is primarily caused by zinc deficiency and responds exceptionally well to zinc supplementation.

Diet   Keep it low in saturated fat, eat sufficient essential fats, and very little meat or dairy produce—stay mainly vegan, although fish is all right. Test for dairy or wheat allergy, if suspected, by avoiding these foods for a couple of weeks and seeing if there is any improvement. Consider a cleansing diet.

Supplements   Essential oils such as flax and evening primrose or borage oil; vitamin B6, biotin, zinc, and magnesium, plus antioxidant vitamins A, C, and E.

Dry skin

Factors to consider   Possible disturbed water balance due to essential fatty acid deficiency, poor intake of water or lack of vitamin A.

Diet   Should be low in saturated fat, high in essential fatty acids (from seeds and their oils). Drink at least one quart of water a day and eat plenty of water-rich foods such as (fruit and vegetables). Alcohol and stimulants such as coffee and tea should be limited.

Supplements   Essential oils such as flax, borage, and evening primrose oil, vitamin A, vitamin E.

Eczema

Factors to consider   As for dermatitis. Most common contributory factors are the combination of a food allergy (most often wheat or dairy) and a lack of essential fatty acids from seeds and their cold-pressed oils, which have powerful anti-inflammatory effects.

Diet   Low in saturated fat, sufficient essential fats from seeds and their cold-pressed oils, low meat and dairy, mainly vegan. Fish is all right. Test for dairy and wheat allergy, if suspected, by avoiding these foods for a set period. Consider a cleansing diet.

Supplements   Essential oils such as flax and evening primrose or borage oil; vitamin B6, biotin, zinc, and magnesium, plus antioxidant vitamins A, C, and E.

Facial puffiness and water retention

Factors to consider Food allergy, lack of essential fatty acids, hormonal imbalance such as progesterone deficiency or estrogen dominance.

Diet Test for food allergy (wheat and dairy the most common). Ensure a high intake of seeds and their oils, plenty of water, and water-rich foods (fruit and vegetables).

Supplements Essential oils such as flax and evening primrose or borage oil; vitamin B6, biotin, zinc, and magnesium.

Oily skin

Factors to consider Excess fat in the diet, high histamine type (see page 200) and excessive adrenal stimulation due to stress, all of which increase sebum production.

Diet Low in fat, ensure sufficient essential oils from seeds and their cold-pressed oils, low in alcohol, sugar, and stimulants.

Supplements Vitamin C, pantothenic acid (if you are stressed).

Psoriasis

Factors to consider Psoriasis is a completely different kind of skin condition from eczema or dermatitis and does not generally respond as well to nutritional intervention. It can occur when the body is "toxic"—perhaps due to an overgrowth of the organism candida albicans, to digestive problems leading to intoxication, or to poor liver detoxification. Otherwise consider the same factors as for eczema and dermatitis.

Diet Start with a cleansing diet followed by one low in saturated fat but with sufficient essential fats, low in meat and dairy products, and with a high vegan content. Fish is all right. Test for dairy and wheat allergy, if suspected, by avoiding these foods for a certain time.

Supplements Essential oils such as flax and evening primrose or borage oil; vitamin B6, biotin, zinc, and magnesium, plus antioxidant vitamins A, C, and E.

Rashes

Factors to consider Possible over-inflammation due to lack of essential fatty acids, or food or contact allergy, or a stress reaction due to adrenal overload, or (for example, in shingles) a viral, fungal, or bacterial infection.

Diet Low in saturated fat but with sufficient essential fats, low in meat and dairy products, high vegan content. Fish is all right. Test for dairy and wheat allergy, if suspected, by avoiding these foods for a certain time.

Supplements Essential oils such as flax and evening primrose or borage oil; vitamin B6, biotin, zinc, and magnesium, plus antioxidant vitamins A, C, and E.

Rough skin

Factors to consider Lack of vitamin A, dehydration, lack of essential fatty acids.

Diet Should be high in fruit and vegetables (especially yellow/orange/red ones which are high in beta-carotene, with lots of water and essential fatty acids from seeds and their oil.

Supplements Vitamin A, all antioxidants (vitamins A, C, and E, zinc, and selenium), gamma-linolenic acid (GLA) from borage or evening primrose oil.

THE WAY TO PERFECT SKIN

Many common nutritional factors are involved in a wide variety of skin problems. To prevent these problems and keep your skin healthy here are some key diet and supplement guidelines:

Diet

- Limit alcohol, caffeine, chemical additives, salt, saturated fat, sugar and smoking.
- Eat plenty of fresh fruit and vegetables, preferably organic.
- Eat some seeds, nuts, or their cold-pressed oil every day. Take either a heaped tablespoon of ground seeds, or a tablespoon of a blended

seed oil containing cold-pressed flax, pumpkin, sesame, and sunflower oil.

■ Drink at least a quart of water a day, either neat or in herb teas or added to juice.

Supplements

■ Take a good, all-round vitamin and mineral supplement plus extra antioxidant nutrients—vitamins A, C, and E. An ideal daily intake is 7,500 IU of vitamin A, 2,000 mg of vitamin C, and 400 IU of vitamin E.

■ If you are prone to dry skin or skin inflammation supplement borage oil or evening primrose oil to give the equivalent of 200 mg of gamma-linolenic acid (GLA).

Skin creams

■ Use a cream containing significant amounts of vitamins A, C, and E in forms that can penetrate the epidermis (such as ascorbyl palmitate, and retinyl palmitate of vitamin E acetate).

Other recommendations

■ Avoid strong sunlight and use a sunblock.

■ Wash your skin with a gentle oil-based cleanser, not soap.

23

IMPROVING INTELLIGENCE AND MEMORY

Most people believe that intelligence is something you are born with and there is nothing you can do to change it. While there is clearly an inherent component to intelligence, psychologists tell us that we use less than 1 percent of our intellectual capacity and that every day we think thousands of thoughts, the vast majority of which are repeats! Imagine what would happen if we could focus all our mental energy on the task at hand and tap into our full potential.

The brain and nervous system, our mental "hardware," consists of a network of neurons, special cells that are each capable of forming tens of thousands of connections with others. Thinking is believed to represent a pattern of activity across this network. The activity, or signals, involve neurotransmitters, chemical messengers in the brain. When we learn we actually change the wiring of the brain. When we think we change the activity of neurotransmitters. Both brain and neurotransmitters are derived from nutrients and are therefore affected by what you eat and drink.

In 1986 we at the Institute of Optimum Nutrition decided to investigate whether giving an optimal intake of nutrients used by the brain and nervous system would improve intellectual performance. We knew already that a person's nutrient status was associated with his or her intelligence. For instance, in 1960 a study by Kabula and colleagues had shown that increased vitamin C status was associated with increased intelligence.[54] He divided 351 students into high and low vitamin C groups, depending on the levels in their blood. The students' IQ was then measured and found to average 113 for those with high levels and 109 for those with low levels. (Intelligence Quotient (IQ) is an accepted measure of intelligence, with a score of 100, originally by definition, being average. About 5 percent score above 125, and less than 10 percent score below 80, which is considered to be educationally sub-normal.)

The converse was also true: high levels of anti-nutrients correlated with poor intelligence. Researchers at the Massachusetts Institute of Technology had found that the higher the proportion of refined carbohydrates—such as sugar, commercial cereals, white bread and sweets—in the diet, the lower the IQ score.[55] The difference between the scores of the high and the low sugar eaters in their study was almost 25 points. Professor Needleman devised an ingenious plan to test the effect of the anti-nutrient lead on behavior and intelligence.[56] He collected the baby teeth of thousands of schoolchildren, analyzed their lead level, and had their teachers assess their behavior. The higher the lead, the worse the behavior and the lower the IQ, a result since confirmed by many researchers, which led to legislation to stop lead being added to gasoline in the U.S. Of the thousands of children he has tested, no child with high lead has yet been found to have an IQ above 125. Normally, 5 percent of the population fall above this measurement. In the 1980s, a high percentage of children in the U.S. had lead levels high enough actually to impair intelligence. Since the advent of lead-free gasoline, blood lead levels are fortunately dropping.

To test the overall effects of vitamins and minerals on mental performance, Gwillym Roberts, a schoolteacher and nutritionist from the Institute of Optimum Nutrition, and David Benton, a psychologist from University College Swansea, put sixty schoolchildren on to a special multivitamin and mineral supplement designed to ensure an optimal intake of key nutrients.[57] Without their knowledge, half these children were placed on a placebo. On analyzing the diets of these schoolchildren, a significant minority were found to be getting less than the RDA of at least one nutrient. After eight months on the supplements the non-verbal IQs in those taking the supplements had risen by over 10 points! No changes were seen in those on the placebos, or in a control group who had not taken any supplements or placebos. Professor Schoenthaler, from the U.S., proposed that perhaps a small percentage of schoolchildren were having substantial IQ increases and that, provided the sample size was large enough, the mean IQ difference would be significant.

It was clear from all this research that supplements had an effect, but a number of questions were raised by it. Who benefits? And why? Which nutrients are important? At which levels? And how long does it take to get an effect? To answer some of these questions, 615 schoolchildren in California were assigned to either a placebo group or one of three "supplement" groups given approximately 50 percent, 100 percent or 200 percent of the U.S. RDAs for vitamins and minerals.[58] After one month, only the 200 percent RDA group had significantly higher IQ scores than the placebo group. After three months, all the supplement groups had higher IQ scores than the placebo group, with the 100 percent RDA group having the highest, and statistically significant, increase. Of this group 45 percent had an increase in IQ of 15 or more points, compared to the average increase of 4.4 points. Other researchers have repeated this study and achieved the same results. So it is clear that adding small amounts of nutrients increases intelligence by 4 to 5 IQ points.

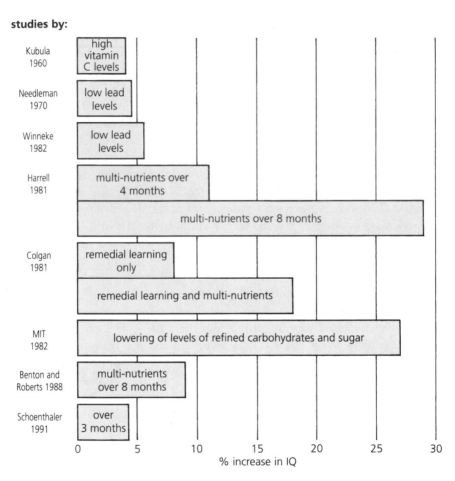

studies by:

Kubula 1960	high vitamin C levels
Needleman 1970	low lead levels
Winneke 1982	low lead levels
Harrell 1981	multi-nutrients over 4 months
	multi-nutrients over 8 months
Colgan 1981	remedial learning only
	remedial learning and multi-nutrients
MIT 1982	lowering of levels of refined carbohydrates and sugar
Benton and Roberts 1988	multi-nutrients over 8 months
Schoenthaler 1991	over 3 months

0   5   10   15   20   25   30
% increase in IQ

Effects of optimum nutrition on intelligence

IMPROVING LEARNING DIFFICULTIES

Even more convincing is the evidence of the power of optimum nutrition on those with learning difficulties (currently about one in every ten children) including children with Down's syndrome, the result of a genetic defect. When researcher Dr. Ruth Harrell heard of a case in which the IQ of a Down's syndrome child rose from 20 to 90 points after nutritional intervention, she decided to explore the idea that many mentally retarded children might have been born with increased needs for certain vitamins and minerals.[59] In her first study she took twenty-two mentally retarded children and divided them into two groups. One group received vitamin and mineral supplements, the other placebos. After four months, the IQ in the group taking the supplements had increased by between 5 and 9.6 points; those on placebos showed no change. For the next four months, both groups of children were given the supplements and the average improvement rose to 10.2 points. Six of the children showed improvements of between 10 and 25 IQ points. While not all researchers have been able to replicate these results, there have now been a substantial number of well-documented cases of Down's syndrome children having IQ shifts of 10 to 40 points.

Great improvement in intelligence has also been shown by autistic children and those with learning difficulties. In a study by Dr. Colgan on sixteen children with learning and behavioral difficulties, each child had his or her individual nutrient needs determined. Half the children were then given supplements. Each child attended a remedial reading course designed to improve his or her reading age by one year. Over the next twenty-two weeks teachers carefully monitored the reading age, IQ and behavior of the children. Those not taking supplements showed an average increase in IQ of 8.4 points and in reading age of 1.1 years. However, the group on supplements had an improvement in IQ of 17.9 points and their reading age went up by 1.8 years.

Particularly important for brain development are the essential fatty acids and phospholipids which form part of the structure of brain cell membranes. Low levels of essential fatty acids are also associated with lower levels of intelligence. This is thought to be the reason why, by the age of seven, children who were breast-fed as babies have been shown to have higher IQ scores. Breast milk contains DHA, an essential fatty acid essential for brain development. The richest dietary source of DHA is fish, which is also full of phospholipids.

A 5 percent shift in IQ score would get a substantial number of children currently classified as educationally subnormal back into regular school, saving millions of dollars currently spent on special education. Isn't it time children were given free vitamins at a fraction of this cost?

Mommy i shrank your brain

The brain and nervous system of a fetus use up more than half the available nutrients supplied during development in the womb and around a quarter this during adult life. The brain is very dependent on glucose, with almost half of all the available glucose powering it, and on essential fats and phospholipids. Recent evidence from research at the Royal Postgraduate Medical School in London shows that women's brains shrink during pregnancy. It seems to be the size of the cells, not the number, that changes, and one possible explanation is that the fetus takes supplies of essential fats and phospholipids from the mother if there is not enough to go round. If this proves to be so, it highlights the importance of getting a sufficient quantity of these vital brain nutrients.

Probably the most important phospholipid is phosphatidyl choline, which also supplies the brain nutrient choline; the latter is needed to make acetylcholine, a vital neurotransmitter for memory, control of sensory input signals, and muscular control. Acetylcholine deficiency results in poor memory, lethargy, decreased dreaming, and a dry mouth. This is thought to be one of the major causes of senile dementia, which affects one in every seven people over the age of seventy-five.

Acetylcholine—the memory molecule

This substance is made by the action of an enzyme, dependent on vitamin B5, on choline. The combination of B5 and choline has proved effective in enhancing memory and mental performance. The best supplemental source of choline is lecithin, which also supplies phospholipids. Lecithin is an emulsifier that is also used in some foods. All health food stores stock it, either as capsules or as granules which can easily be sprinkled on food. However, not all lecithin is the same. Look at the label before you buy, and make sure the product contains more than 30 percent phosphatidyl choline.

However, one problem with supplementing any form of choline is that it does not readily enter brain cells. This is why large quantities—around a tablespoon of lecithin granules a day—are needed to have an effect. Another nutrient found in fish, particularly in anchovies and sardines, is DMAE (dimethylaminoethanol), which does pass easily into the brain and can be converted into choline to make acetylcholine. DMAE has been shown to elevate mood, improve memory, increase intelligence and physical energy, and extend the life of laboratory animals. One of the pioneers of DMAE therapy, Dr. Carl Pfeiffer, found it to be an excellent slow-acting stimulant—an alternative to anti-depressants. It is now prescribed, often under the name Deaner or Deanol, for learning problems, hyperactivity, reading and speech difficulties, and behavioral problems in children, and it is currently being researched for its effects on extending life span. As one person on DMAE said, "I am more awake when I'm awake, and more sound asleep when I'm asleep. Not only does my memory improve, but I have an easier time daydreaming when I want to, and concentrating on real-world tasks when I want to."

SMART NUTRIENTS

The buzz word in brain enhancement is nootropics—substances derived from an amino acid called pyroglutamate which is found in fruit and vegetables. The discovery that the brain and cerebro-spinal fluid contain large amounts of pyroglutamate led to its investigation as an essential brain nutrient. Doctors prescribe nootropics to millions of people every year for memory deficit problems. Their basic effect is to improve learning, memory consolidation and memory retrieval, all without toxicity or side effects. One extraordinary finding was that nootropics promote the flow of information between the right and left hemispheres of the brain. The left brain is associated with analytical, logical thinking, and the right brain with creative relational thinking. This is thought to be a possible reason why nootropics have proved helpful in the treatment of dyslexia. A study published in 1988 by Dr. Pilch and colleagues suggests that nootropics may increase the number of acetylcholine receptors in the brain thereby improving the brain's efficiency.[60] Older mice were given piracetam, a pyroglutamate derivative, for two weeks. The researchers found that these mice subsequently had 30–40 percent higher density of receptors. This suggests that pyroglutamate-like molecules not only maximize mental performance but may also have a regenerative effect on the nervous system.

THE SYNERGY FACTOR

The effects of enhancing mental performance through supplementation of "smart nutrients" such as phosphatidyl choline, pantothenic acid, DMAE and pyroglutamate are likely to be far greater when taken in combination than individually. In one study in 1981, a team of researchers led by Raymond Bartus gave choline and piracetam to elderly laboratory rats, which are noted for age-related memory decline.[61] They found that "rats given the piracetam/choline combination exhibited (memory) retention scores several times better than those with piracetam alone." Only half the dose was needed when piracetam and choline were combined.

THE BRAIN DRAIN

While "good" chemicals and nutrients, can improve mental function, "bad" chemicals can and do reduce your intelligence. Alcohol is a prime example. Coffee, while commonly thought to improve concentration, actually diminishes it. A number of studies have shown that the ability to remember lists of words is made worse by caffeine. According to one researcher, Dr. Erikson, "Caffeine may have a deleterious effect on the rapid processing of ambiguous or confusing stimuli," which sounds like a description of modern living! The combination of caffeine and alcohol slows reaction time and, in one study, made subjects more drunk than alcohol alone. Caffeine is present in coffee, tea, chocolate, Lucozade, cola drinks, and the herb guarana. A diet high in sugar and refined carbohydrates, as discussed earlier, is another factor that reduces intelligence ratings.

Heavy metals such as lead, cadmium, and aluminum accumulate in the brain and have been clearly demonstrated to reduce intelligence, concentration, memory and impulse control. Therefore keeping pollution to a minimum, which includes not smoking, is another prerequisite to boosting your brain power.

Here are some simple guidelines for improving your memory and mental performance:

- Reduce your intake of stimulants such as coffee, tea, chocolate, and cola, and of sugar and refined foods.

- Minimize your exposure to pollution and cigarettes.

- Make sure you are "well oiled" with regular seeds, their oils, or essential fat supplements.

- Ensure optimum nutrition through your diet and by taking a high dose multivitamin and mineral supplement.

- Take the following daily supplements of smart nutrients: pantothenic acid 100–500 mg; choline 500–1,000 mg (or as one heaped teaspoon of high phosphatidyl choline lecithin granules); DMAE 100–500 mg; pyroglutamate 250–750 mg.

24

INCREASING YOUR ENERGY AND RESISTANCE TO STRESS

In my practice as a nutrition consultant the two most common complaints I hear from my clients are a lack of energy and too much stress. The net result is tiredness, exhaustion, lethargy, apathy, poor concentration, lack of motivation—whatever word you use, the feeling is the same. Many people turn to sugary food, coffee, or cigarettes, or become "adrenalin junkies" with high-powered jobs or exhilarating pastimes, to regain this feeling of energy. Yet often these attempted solutions only generate more stress, and soon you feel out of control and stressed out on the roller-coaster of life. Stress is one of the most common health problems, associated with a wide variety of illnesses and accounting for the loss of around 200 million working days a year in the U.S. But what has it got to do with nutrition?

One surprising result which emerged from a survey of patients seen at the ION Clinic was that, before consulting a nutritionist, 54 percent of them scored high on a questionnaire concerning their ability to cope with stress, yet within six months of starting their optimum nutrition regimes only 28 percent still had a high stress rating. For the rest, whatever happened during those six months improved their ability to cope.

THE CHEMISTRY OF STRESS

Your body chemistry changes fundamentally every time you react stressfully. Stress starts in the mind. We perceive a situation as requiring our immediate attention—a young child stepping into the road, a car driving too close to us, a hostile reaction from a colleague, a financial crisis, an impossible deadline. Rapid signals stimulate the adrenal glands to produce adrenalin. Within seconds your heart is pounding, your breathing changes, stores of glucose are released into the blood, the muscles tense, the eyes dilate, even the blood thickens. You are ready for fight or flight—the average adrenalin rush of a commuter stuck in a traffic jam is enough to keep him or her running for a mile. That represents how much glucose is released, mainly by breaking down glycogen held in muscles and the liver.

To get the fuel into body cells such as muscles, the pancreas releases two hormones, insulin and glucagon. Insulin, aided by a substance released from the liver, glucose tolerance factor, helps to carry the fuel out of the blood; glucagon tops up the blood sugar if its levels get too low. All this happens as a result of a stressful thought. Where, you might wonder, does all this extra energy and increased alertness come from? The answer is by diverting energy from the body's normal repair and maintenance jobs such as digesting, cleansing, and rejuvenating. So every moment you spend in a state of stress speeds up the aging process in your body. It is stressful just thinking about it! But the effects of prolonged stress are even more insidious than that. Imagine your pituitary, adrenals, pancreas, and liver perpetually pumping out hormones to control blood sugar that you do not even need. Like a car driven too fast, the body goes out of balance and parts start to wear out. Levels of the anti-aging adrenal hormone start to fall, as do those of cortisol, and before long your body simply cannot respond to stress as it used to.

The blood sugar blues

As a consequence your energy level drops, you lose concentration, get confused, suffer from bouts of brain lapse, fall asleep after meals, get irritable, freak out, cannot sleep, cannot wake up, sweat too much, get headaches…sounds familiar? In an attempt to regain control, most people turn to stimulants. Legal stimulants include coffee (containing theobromine, theophylline, and caffeine), tea (containing caffeine), cola drinks (containing caffeine), chocolate (containing theophylline), cigarettes (containing nicotine), and psychological stimulants such as horror movies or bungee-jumping—something to put you on the edge. Illegal stimulants include amphetamines and "uppers," cocaine, crack, and crime. Naturally it becomes increasingly difficult to relax while living on stimulants, so most people learn to use relaxants such as alcohol, sleeping pills, tranquilizers, marijuana, and so on.

Addicted to stress

Of course, you cannot live like this forever, so most people burn out and have to head for the beach to recover. Yet as they wait in the airport, what better way to relax than reading a paperback thriller? The cover promises "murder, mystery, greed, lust, gripping suspense." Sounds good. Backed up by a cup of coffee, a glass of wine, and a stressful journey, they arrive ready for the beach. Then, after two blissful hours engrossed in raunchy pulp fiction on the beach, it is time for some excitement—windsurfing, water skiing, something exhilarating. The point is that most people become addicted to stress, because without it they come crashing down, revealing their true state of adrenal exhaustion. This is why people feel exhausted or get ill when they take time off.

Test Your Stress—Symptoms Linked with Adrenal Imbalance

____ **Hard to get up in the morning**	____ **Mood swings**	____ **Feeling cold all the time**
____ **Tired all the time**	____ **Restlessness**	____ **Apathy**
____ **Craving certain foods**	____ **Energy slump during the day**	____ **Depression**
____ **Anger, irritability, aggressiveness**	____ **Regular feelings of weakness**	____ Headaches
____ Muscle and joint aches	____ Allergies	____ Hyperactivity
____ Spotty skin	____ Hair loss	____ Frequent sore throats
____ Poor concentration	____ Yeast overgrowth	____ Poor wound healing
____ Poor sleep patterns	____ Hard-to-shift fat around waist	____ Water retention
____ Rapid or pounding heartbeat	____ Hungry all the time	____ PMT
____ Prone to catching flu or colds	____ Difficulty in making decisions	____ Watery or itchy eyes
	____ Poor memory	____ Excessive sweating
		____ Bloated feeling
		____ Faintness

*If you have three or more of the symptoms printed in **bold** type you may have an adrenal hormonal imbalance. If you also have five or more of the other symptoms, this warrants investigation by a nutritionist.*

Energy consumers

Yet in a very real sense all stressors and stimulants consume our energy. The "high" is literally energy leaving the system, like a wave that breaks and seems for a few seconds to be full of energy. Yet a few seconds later there is no wave at all—likewise the energy is gone. In an article on drug abuse (*The Arican*, vol. 2, no. 2, Spring 1990), psychologist and philosopher, Oscar Ichazo says, "Drugs (all of them) can be characterized as 'energy consumers,' consuming energy at a rate much greater than our natural ability to replace it. As drugs burn all our accumulated vitality in short periods of time, the brief exaltation is inevitably followed by depletion of vital energy, felt as the 'down,' the depressant effect of drugs. Nothing can replace a natural, clean body capable of producing natural and clean vital energy." He rates the drugs most damaging to our vital energy, in descending order of harmfulness as alcohol, heroin, and opiates, tobacco, cocaine, barbiturates, anti-depressants, amphetamines, marijuana, and caffeine.

But what does it mean to "consume energy"? It means that body cells are starved of fuel nutrients like glucose, and catalyst nutrients like B vitamins, which drive the enzyme systems necessary to release energy from fuel nutrients. The nutrients necessary to make messenger molecules like neurotransmitters, or carrier molecules like insulin, are also depleted. So every moment you spend in a stressful state you are using up valuable nutrients. Consider this. Have you ever had a massage, after which you felt as if a whole load of muscular tension had gone? Every single muscle cell that you hold in tension, often for decades, even when you are asleep, is consuming energy, B vitamins, vitamin C, calcium, and magnesium—to name but a few—just to stay in that state of tension. If you could relax all the muscles in your body, think how much you would save in nutritional supplements! Conservative estimates suggest that you double your need for vitamins when you are in a stress state.

THE ENERGY EQUATION

If you want to maximize your available energy for life, and to retain that energy rather than burning out, the nutritional message is simple:

- Eat slow-releasing carbohydrates that release their "fuel" slowly.

- Ensure you have optimal intakes of all essential nutrients—vitamins, minerals, and others.

- Avoid stimulants and depressants.

The resultant increase in energy will help you to cope with the stresses and strains of life. The optimum nutrition approach is both a way of breaking energy-consuming patterns that keep depleting us, and a way of regenerating energy for breaking the mental habits that initiate a stress response in the first place. So let's examine what stress-busting optimum nutrition actually means.

THE ANTI-STRESS DIET

Fast-releasing sugars create a state of stress in the body, stimulating the release of cortisol. So avoid eating white bread, sweets, and breakfast cereals, or other foods with added sugar. Slow-releasing carbohydrates, on the other hand, provide an "even keel" of consistent energy. Scientists have investigated exactly what effect different sources of carbohydrates have on blood sugar, energy, and mood. In general these are fruit, whole grains, beans, lentils, nuts, and seeds; a complete list of these foods is given in Chapter 10. Contrary to the rules of classic food combining, recent research has found that eating some protein with carbohydrate provides additional adrenal support by reducing the stimulation of cortisol. So if you are stressed out eat your fruit with some nuts, or brown rice with fish. Nuts, seeds, beans, and lentils already contain both protein and carbohydrate and are therefore good anti-stress foods.

THE ENERGY NUTRIENTS

Energy nutrients include vitamin B6 and zinc, which help insulin to work; vitamin B3 and chromium, which are part of the glucose tolerance factor and now available as a complex called chromium polynicotinate; and a whole host of nutrients required to turn glucose within cells into energy. These include vitamins B1, B2, B3, B5, co-enzyme Q, vitamin C, iron, copper, and magnesium. Vitamin B12 is required to make adrenalin, while B5 (pantothenic acid) is required to make another class of adrenal hormones called glucocorticoids. Muscle and nerve transmission, the end result of turning fuel into energy, requires yet more B5 and large amounts of the semi-essential nutrient choline, plus the minerals calcium and magnesium. Choline is also needed to produce stress hormones. Amino acids, the building blocks of protein, are also the building blocks of stress hormones and neurotransmitters. Methionine, an amino acid that is commonly deficient, is required to make adrenal hormones. Insulin is a complex of fifty-one amino acids and zinc. Adrenalin is synthesized from the amino acids phenylalanine or tyrosine.

The ideal quantity to take in supplement form to provide top-level support for stressed people, and to maximize energy, depends very much on individual circumstances. Optimal daily requirements, however, are likely to be in the ranges shown in the following table.

Daily Supplement to Deal with Stress

B1 (thiamine)	25–100 mg
B2 (riboflavin)	25–100 mg
B3 (niacin)	50–150 mg
B5 (pantothenic acid)	50–300 mg
B6 (pyridoxine)	50–250 mg
B12 (cyanocobalamin)	5–100 mcg
Folic acid	50–400 mcg
Choline	100–500 mg
Co-enzyme Q	10–50 mg
Vitamin C	1,000–5,000 mg
Calcium	150–600 mg
Magnesium	250–450 mg
Iron	10–20 mg
Zinc	10–25 mg
Chromium	50–200 mcg

STIMULANTS AND THEIR ALTERNATIVES

Consumption of coffee, tea, sugar, and chocolate are all associated with an increased risk of diabetes. In the short term they may give a boost, but in the long term high stimulant consumption can kill you prematurely. Try this simple experiment. Give up all these stimulants for one month, and notice what happens. The more damage these stimulants are doing to you, the greater the withdrawal effect such as headaches, lack of concentration, fatigue, and nausea. (Fortunately, by eating slow-releasing carbohydrates and taking energy nutrients as supplements you can minimize the withdrawal symptoms, which usually last no more than four days.) Then start again and notice what happens with your first cup of tea or coffee, your first spoonful of sugar, or bite of chocolate. You will experience what stress expert Dr. Hans Selye called the "initial response"—in other words a true response to these powerful chemicals (a pounding head, hyperactive mind, fast heartbeat, and insomnia, followed by extreme drowsiness). Keep on the stimulants and you will adapt (phase 2). Keep doing this long enough and eventually you hit exhaustion (phase 3). This happens to everybody. The only variation is how long it will take you to get to the exhaustion phase.

Recovery is not only possible, it is usually rapid. Most people experience substantially more energy and ability to cope with stress within thirty days of cutting out stimulants and simultaneously taking nutritional support. Coffee, tea, and chocolate are best omitted from your diet altogether—decaffeinated coffee and tea still contain stimulants. Nowadays there are plenty of coffee alternatives and herb and fruit teas. Health food stores also have sugar-free "sweets" and bars. Check the label for hidden sugar.

It is best to reduce the sugar content of your diet slowly. Gradually get used to less sweetness. For example, sweeten breakfast cereal with fruit. Dilute fruit juices 50:50 with water. Avoid foods with added sugar. Limit your intake of dried fruit. Eat fruits like bananas that contain fast-releasing sugars with slow-releasing carbohydrates such as oats.

THE EXERCISE FACTOR

Exercise plays a vital role in both energy and stress resistance, but it has to be the right kind. Becoming muscle-bound doesn't necessarily enable vital energy to flow easily in the body; nor does an unfit body, nor a body full of tension. This tension literally eats up our energy—after all, it takes a lot of energy to keep muscle cells in tension. Conversely, being unfit and overweight places a strain on the body, again depleting vital energy.

Strength, suppleness and stamina

Somewhere in the middle there is an optimal balance where the body is relaxed but strong, supple, with good posture, and sufficiently fit to have the stamina necessary for physical tasks. Remember the three S's—strength, suppleness, and stamina.

The body produces energy when carbohydrate foods react with oxygen from the air we breathe. Oxygen is the most vital nutrient of all, yet most of us breathe shallowly and use only a third of our lung capacity. Deeper breathing not only energizes the body, it also clears the mind. Mastering the right way to breathe is the first step in most forms of meditation, yoga and Tai-chi. Most types of exercise ignore this, so you get out of breath. The resultant oxygen deficiency allows toxic substances to build up, generating tension in the body. If you feel exhausted or stiff after exercising, something is unbalanced in your exercise program.

If you could develop stamina, suppleness, strength, and a beautiful body by spending fifteen minutes a day on an exercise system that anyone can do anywhere, that leaves you feeling physically energized, emotionally balanced, and mentally clear, would you do it? Such an exercise system exists. It is called Psychocalisthenics, and was developed by Oscar Ichazo of the Arica Institute in New York. The word means strength (*sthenia*) and beauty (*cali*) through the breath (*psyche*), and involves a unique series of twenty-two exercises which develop the three S's and oxygenate the whole body. Psychocalisthenics is suitable for anyone, young or old, and takes only a day to learn. Classes take place all over the U.S. (for details see Useful Addresses on p. 339), or you can do it by yourself accompanied by a tape or video.

Too much exercise can elevate levels of the stress hormone cortisol and is not recommended if you are stressed out. On the other hand, Psychocalisthenics, yoga, Tai-Chi, walking for half an hour, or meditation can help to rebalance stress hormones.

Meditation is as important to the mind as food is to the body. My meditation teacher says, "Food makes the body, thoughts make the mind." For maximum energy, eat pure food and have pure thoughts. Meditation is a time you set aside to sit in silence, focusing on something simple (the breath, a mantra, a prayer) and letting go of your endless stream of thoughts and tapping into the source of energy within every human being, from which come creativity, joy, natural humor, and lightness.

I like to start each day with fifteen minutes' meditation, followed by fifteen minutes' Psychocalisthenics, followed by Get Up and Go, my special breakfast made from high energy whole foods plus energy nutrients. (Get Up and Go is available from health food stores.) The result is a consistent level of energy and resistance to stress.

ACTION PLAN FOR HIGH ENERGY LIVING

Before breakfast

- Meditation (fifteen minutes), then Psychocalisthenics, yoga, Tai Chi (fifteen minutes).

Breakfast (never miss it)

- Get Up and Go drink, mixed with banana and rice or soy milk, or oat flakes with fruit and ground seeds.

- One high-strength multivitamin and mineral, one antioxidant formula, 1,000 mg vitamin C.

Mid-morning snack

- Fresh organic fruit plus some almonds or seeds.

Lunch

- Lots of raw or lightly cooked vegetables with rice, beans, lentils, quinoa, tofu, buckwheat noodles, or fish.

- One high-strength multivitamin and mineral, one antioxidant formula, 1,000 mg vitamin C.

Afternoon snack

- Fresh organic fruit plus some almonds or seeds.

After work, every other day

- Thirty minutes' exercise (walking, jogging, swimming, cycling, aerobics).

Dinner (eat early, at least two hours before bedtime)

- Vegetable steam-fry: select from carrots, broccoli, cauliflower, broad beans, water chestnuts, soaked almonds, organic or shiitake mushrooms, bamboo shoots, green peppers, zucchini, tofu, and braised tofu. Cut into pieces, wash, put in a pan, cover with a tight lid and steam for five minutes maximum. Add one of the following four sauces. Chinese: soy sauce, water, lemon juice, ginger, fresh coriander, and garlic. Thai: coconut milk and Thai spices. Mexican: watered down Mexican spice sauce, (versions are available in supermarkets, but check chemical additives). Mediterranean: tomato sauce with peppers, mushrooms, and herbs. Serve with brown rice, quinoa, or buckwheat noodles. Alternatively, use other combinations of raw or lightly cooked vegetables with rice, beans, lentils, quinoa, tofu, buckwheat noodles, or fish.

- One high-strength multivitamin and mineral, one antioxidant formula, 1,000 mg vitamin C.

25

ACHIEVING PEAK PHYSICAL PERFORMANCE

No top-class athlete can afford to ignore optimum nutrition. Capable of increasing speed, endurance, and strength, the right diet and supplements can mean the difference between winning and losing.

My first experience of the power of optimum nutrition in the context of sport was with Mick Ballard, a veteran cyclist who, after changing his diet and starting to take supplements, broke the record for the ten-mile time trial by an astonishing thirty-seven seconds. "I'm convinced that my tremendous improvement in times and recovery are due to my special vitamin program," said Ballard. Then, at the insistence of her coach, I advised Susan Devoy, rated amongst the top ten women squash players of her day. She did not think it would make any difference. It did. She became the best in the U.K. and the world for much of the next ten years. Athletes on optimum nutrition programs consistently report increased endurance and more rapid recovery.

These findings confirm those of Dr. Michael Colgan, who advises many U.S. Olympic athletes including U.S. mile record-holder Steve Scott, twice world triathlon champion Julie Moss, and Howard Doerffling of the U.S. cycle team. Colgan also found substantial time improvements in controlled trials on long-distance runners.

MUSCLE POWER

Optimum nutrition has been shown to increase not only endurance, but also sheer muscle power, as Hollywood actor Sylvester Stallone will testify. An ardent follower of optimum nutrition, he takes handfuls of supplements every day and watches his diet carefully. The ability to increase strength is best illustrated in a study by Dr. Colgan in which two experienced weightlifters were given a special supplement program, and another two placebos.[62] After three months, those on supplements had increased the maximum weight they could lift by about 50 percent. The others, on dummy tablets, had only a 10–20 percent increase. During the following three months the supplements and the placebos were swapped around. Those previously on placebos caught up with the other weightlifters.

THE RIGHT FUEL

Maximizing physical performance depends on giving the body the right fuel. During sustained less strenuous "aerobic" exercise (jogging, tennis, swimming, walking, for example) carbohydrates yield twice as much energy as fat. During short bursts of strenuous or "anaerobic" exercise (sprinting, for example) the body can only really use carbohydrate, making carbohydrate yield five times more energy than fat. Carbohydrates, not fat, are the premier fuel for performance. Also, carbohydrates can be stored as glycogen, while fat cannot. Glycogen is a short-term store of energy, held in muscles and the liver, that can be called on during extended physical performance. That is why endurance athletes eat rice or pasta or other complex carbohydrates some hours before an event to increase their glycogen stores.

Contrary to popular opinion, increasing protein intake does not improve athletic performance. Even body-builders who are going for maximum muscle gain need little more than the recommended 15 percent of total intake of calories in the form of protein. Consider this equation: to gain 9 pounds of muscle in a year requires less than 1,000 g of protein, since muscle is 22 percent protein. Divide that by 365 days and all you need is 2.4 grams of protein a day. That is less than a teaspoonful, or the amount provided by a few almonds or a teaspoon of tuna. Difficulty in building muscle is rarely due to a lack of protein and often the result of not taking in enough muscle-building vitamins and minerals such as zinc and vitamin B6, which help to digest and use dietary protein.

While fat is not the best fuel for the body, sources of essential fats have many important benefits for athletes. They help transport oxygen and keep red blood cells, the oxygen carriers, healthy. They are vital for the immune system, which is often taxed in people who take a great deal of exercise. They are a back-up source of energy and, according to Dr. Udo Erasmus, an expert on fat, actually increase metabolic rate. So nuts, seeds, and their oils form an important part of a high-performance diet.

WATER—THE FORGOTTEN NUTRIENT

Probably the most important item in the diet of sportsmen and women is water. Muscles are 75 percent water. A loss of only 3 percent of this water causes a 10 percent drop in strength and an 8 percent loss of speed. During athletic performance thirst sensors are inhibited, so it is easy for athletes to become dehydrated. This leads to an increase in body temperature, and energy is diverted away from muscles to cool the body down. During endurance sports it is best to drink water to allow the body to sweat and cool down this way. However, it is even more important to hydrate the body in advance by drinking a glass of water every fifteen minutes for one to four hours before the event, depending on its length.

Eating plenty of carbohydrate also helps to store water because each unit of carbohydrate, stored as glycogen, is bound with nine units of water. As the glycogen is liberated to provide energy for muscles, so too is the water.

SUPPLEMENTARY BENEFIT

A considerable body of research has produced results which support the benefits of nutrient supplementation in sport. While studies testing single nutrients have often shown little or no effect, multinutrient studies using optimal, rather than RDA, levels of nutrients consistently show improvement in athletic performance. As well as vitamins and minerals, semi-essential nutrients such as co-enzyme Q are an important part of a winning formula; ideal levels are 60–100 mg a day. The ideal amount of each nutrient to take varies from person to person and is likely to be in the same range as those given on p. 159 for maximizing energy.

However, if you do regular endurance exercise such as running or cycling it is important to increase your intake of antioxidant nutrients such as vitamins A, C, and E. These help the body to use oxygen and detoxify the by-products of making energy, which reduces the stress of endurance sports.

General dietary guidelines for a sportsman or woman are:

- Eat plenty of complex carbohydrates such as whole grains, fruit, vegetables, beans, and lentils, and "load up" before a long event.

- Have some protein with your carbohydrate foods, e.g., nuts with fruit, fish with rice.

- Avoid eating too much protein.

- Drink plenty of water before and, where possible, during events.

- Take a personalized supplement program on an ongoing basis, perhaps with extra co-enzyme Q 10.

26

Turning Back the Clock

The quest for immortality or, at least, extended life span is nothing new. Since the beginning of history, myths and legends about magic potions and immensely long-lived people have abounded. But now, as we approach the twenty-first century, many scientists and gerontologists (gerontology is the study of aging) are predicting that a life span of 110 years will soon be commonplace.

To date, the oldest known living person is Madame Jeanne Calmant, who celebrated her 121st birthday on 21 February 1996, breaking the record of a Japanese fisherman named Izumi who died at the age of 120, having been essentially healthy and active until he was 113. When asked about her future, Madame Calmant replied, "Short." A bit of a rogue as far as healthy living is concerned, she is not a health fanatic, gave up smoking at the age of 117, and, until recently, drank two glasses of port every day. With most of her relatives and family living to ripe old ages, scientists think she is genetically strong and has maintained a good mental attitude, resisting stress and depression.

However, the most significant factor in increasing your chances for a long and healthy life is what you eat—or do not eat.

Preventing premature death

The vast majority of people die from preventable diseases. The U.S. Surgeon General states that "of the 2.2 million Americans who die each year 1.8 die from diet-related diseases." Three-quarters of all deaths are caused by cancer, heart disease, bronchial infections, or accidents. Eradicate these and you instantly extend your probable healthy life span by ten to twenty-five years, the key words being "healthy life span." By preventing these diseases, and all the degenerative changes that lead up to them, through optimum nutrition, you effectively turn back the clock and slow down the aging process.

However, the challenge that has occupied gerontologists is not how to prevent the diseases responsible for premature aging and death, but to discover what determines the maximum possible life span. Why, for example, can an elephant live a hundred years or more, while insects have a life span of days? The big question, of course, is how we can extend the maximum possible life span.

EXTENDING YOUR MAXIMUM LIFE SPAN

While the likely maximum life span of a human being is in the region of 110 to 120 years or more, you may be surprised to know that a proven method already exists for extending this length of time. It is, at least, proven in all animal species so far tested, and it is achieved by restricting calorie intake while providing optimum nutrition. Pioneered by Dr. Roy Walford, calorie restriction has been shown to promote health, reduce disease and extend life span from 10 to 300 percent. Studies with fish have achieved a remarkable 300 percent extension, while with rats the maximum increase has been 60 percent.[63] Although this effect has been proved in many species by U.S. government-backed research groups it is too soon to complete human trials, but there is little doubt that the same approach will produce results. The unknown factor is: how much calorie restriction, and at what level, is required to produce a result? Even a 10 percent extension means increasing maximum life span to 130 years—a concept now accepted by many gerontologists, although considered fantasy twenty years ago.

Ongoing research is aimed at discovering why optimum nutrition with calorie restriction is so effective, and the answer to this question, once found, will probably shed light on the process of aging. Current theories focus on the energy factories within cells, called mitochondria. The mitochondria are responsible for the rate of metabolism or energy production. The harder they work, the more free oxidizing radicals are produced (see Chapter 13), which in turn age the mitochondria and have the potential to damage the cell's DNA, the blueprint for new cells. Ron Hart from the National Institute of Health has demonstrated that the aging of species is also linked to the ability to repair DNA. According to Professor Denham Harman, from the University of Nebraska Medical School, the "chances are 99 percent that free radicals are the basis for aging." There is growing consensus that the process of aging hinges on declining ability to repair the damage caused by free radicals.

This also means that the key to longevity lies in reducing our exposure to free radicals and increasing the body's protection against them by increasing our intake of antioxidants. When animals are given very high-quality, low-calorie diets this is exactly what is achieved. They receive exactly what they need in the way of fuel, so there is no wasted "burning" by the body— this process is the major generator of free radicals, the toxic by-product of energy metabolism. By being provided with optimum nutrition, especially a high intake of antioxidant nutrients, the animals have both maximum protection from free radicals and all the co-factor nutrients necessary to make sure that energy metabolism takes place as efficiently as possible.

But can we apply this theory to humans? To date, the circumstantial evidence is remarkably consistent across a wide variety of species and there is no reason to believe that mankind will be any different. Longevity, or the risk of mortality, correlates very well with blood levels, or dietary intakes of vitamin C, vitamin E, vitamin A, and beta-carotene. For example, in a recent study published in the *American Journal of Clinical Nutrition*, which followed 11,178 people between the ages of 67 and 105 over ten years, the overall risk of death was reduced by 42 percent for those who took supplements of both vitamin C and vitamin E.[64] This is a remarkable finding that confirms earlier studies. What is not known, however, is how much of the reduction is due to the prevention of premature death from disease and how much is due to the extension of the maximum life span.

In practical terms there is only one way to maximize your life span, having reduced the risk of dying prematurely from disease. Restrict calories and nourish yourself optimally, especially where antioxidants are concerned.

EAT LESS, LIVE LONGER

It is more than likely that the leaner you are the longer you will live. Calorie restriction, however, is not the same as malnutrition. It is about giving the body exactly what it needs and no more. Many foods in today's diet provide "empty" calories—sugar or saturated fat, but none of the micronutrients needed to process them. These foods are out if you want to extend your life span. Nutrient-dense foods such as organic carrots, apples, nuts, and seeds provide as many nutrients as calories plus, in the case of fresh fruit and vegetables, plenty of essential and calorie-free water.

One way to restrict calories is simply to eat less. Another is to fast or have a modified fast one day a week. This may mean, for example, just eating fruit. I keep my overall calorie intake low by eating a substantial breakfast and dinner but a small lunch (sometimes no lunch at all and snacking on fruit throughout the day). Life insurance companies are well aware of the correlation between weight and longevity. Weight charts give an ideal weight range for your height; generally, the ideal weight for increased life expectancy is at the low end of this range. What really counts is keeping down the percentage of your body weight that consists of fat.

EXERCISE KEEPS YOU YOUNG

Regular exercise can add seven years to your life span, concludes Dr. Rose and Dr. Cohen of the Veterans' Administration Hospital in Boston. But the exercise must be continued late into life and must be aerobic—that is, your heart rate must reach 80 percent of its maximum for at least twenty minutes. Cycling, swimming, and running are good; weightlifting and strengthening exercises, on the other hand, do little to extend your life. Aerobic exercise reduces blood cholesterol levels, pulse rate, and blood pressure, promoting better cardiovascular health as well as increasing mental function. It also helps you to maintain proper blood sugar control and is therefore especially helpful for diabetics.

KEEPING COOL

One method of extending life span in animals has yet to prove practical or popular: it involves lowering the body temperature. Certain drugs have the ability to do this, but have undesirable side effects.

Keeping cool in terms of avoiding stress, however, may prove to be an important life extension factor. Prolonged stress causes depletion of the adrenal hormone DHEA. Low DHEA levels are associated with an increased risk of many killers including Alzheimer's, cancer, and heart disease, and of aging in general. It also helps the body to burn fat and stay lean. DHEA levels, if low, can be restored by supplementation. Nutrition consultants can determine your DHEA status through analysis of saliva samples. Although available in the U.S., DHEA is not available over the counter in other countries like the U.K., where it is classified as a medicine.

In summary, if you want to maximize your healthy life span:

- Follow all the advice in this book for preventing killer diseases.

- Ensure optimum nutrition through diet plus supplements.

- Stay away from avoidable sources of free radicals—fried or browned food, exhaust fumes, smoke, strong sunlight, etc.

- Take extra antioxidant nutrients vitamins A, C, and E, selenium, and zinc.

- Reduce your calorie intake to exactly what you need to stay fit and healthy.

- Keep fit with a moderate (not excessive) amount of aerobic exercise.

- Avoid stress.

- Have your DHEA levels checked.

27

Conquering Cancer

Cancer is the second greatest cause of death in the Western world. In the U.S. one in three people are diagnosed with cancer during their life and one in four currently die from it. Cancer occurs when cells start to behave differently, growing, multiplying, and spreading. It is like a revolution in the body, where a group of cells stop working for the good of the whole and run riot. The odd revolutionary cell is a common occurrence and the body's immune system isolates and destroys such offenders. However, in cancer the immune system is overcome and the damage spreads.

Conventional treatments see cancer very much as the enemy and cut it out, burn it out through radiation, or drug it out with chemotherapy. All these treatments weaken the body. Advances in these treatments only concern less damaging ways of applying them and cannot be considered a breakthrough. And although survival rates have slightly improved, this is a result of more advanced methods of detection rather than more successful treatment.

What causes cancer?

Where considerable advances have been made, however, is in understanding the underlying causes and risks for many types of cancer. At least 75 percent of cancers are associated with lifestyle factors including diet, smoking, and drinking alcohol. Other risk factors include hormonal imbalance exposure to radiation or ultra-violet light, pollution, food additives, drugs, and infections.

Of all risk factors diet is the greatest, a fact which is backed up by the great progress being made in both the treatment and prevention of cancer with nutritional therapy. This is because an underlying cause in many types of cancer seems to be free radical damage to the DNA of cells, triggering their altered behavior. Risk factors such as smoking and radiation encourage free radical activity, while a good intake of antioxidant nutrients provides a measure of protection.

At least 75% of cancers are associated with the following factors:

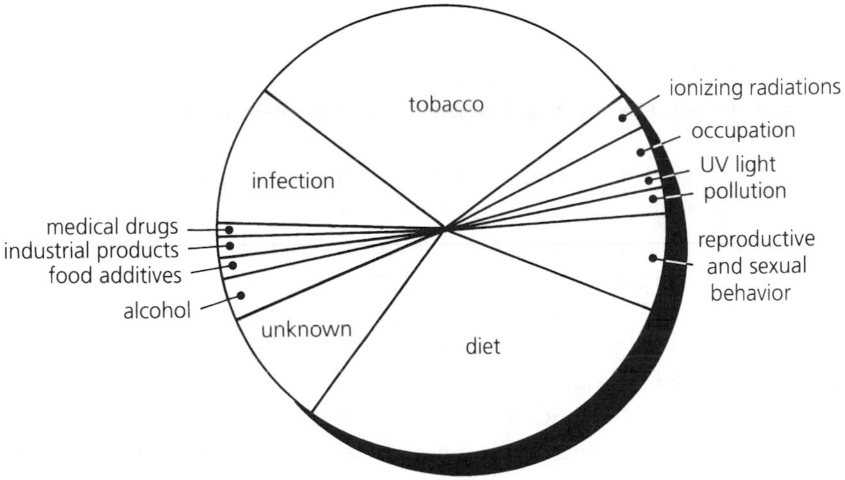

What causes cancer ?

ANTIOXIDANT PROTECTION

While there was already substantial evidence a decade ago of the protective effect of antioxidant nutrients vitamin A, beta-carotene, C and E vitamins, and selenium against certain types of cancer in animals, as every year unfolds we are now seeing data from long-term human trials that supports the role of nutritional therapy. We have also learned how nutrients work in synergy in protecting against cancer.

High levels of vitamin A (retinol) in the blood have long been associated with reduced risk. Recent research has shown that two metabolites of retinol, 13-cis-retinoic acid and trans-retinoic acid, are powerful anti-cancer agents. A study by Dr. Huang found that trans-retinoic acid puts acute myeloid leukemia into complete remission.[65] Another study, by Dr. Hong and Dr. Lippman, found that 13-cis-retinoic acid suppressed carcinomas of the neck and head.[66] They gave forty-nine patients 13-cis-retinoic acid, and after a year only 4 percent had developed another tumor, compared to 24 percent of fifty-one patients on a placebo.

Beta-carotene, which can be converted into vitamin A, is also anti-cancerous. A Japanese study on 265,000 people found a significant correlation between low beta-carotene intake and the incidence of lung cancer.[67] In fact, the risk of lung cancer is the same for those who smoke and have good antioxidant levels as it is for non-smokers with low antioxidant levels.

However, not all reported studies have been positive. One study by the National Cancer Institute gave smokers beta-carotene and reported a 28 percent increased incidence in lung cancer.[68] Confusing, isn't it? Perhaps that is the intention. A closer look at the figures shows that this "trend" represented the difference between five cases of cancer in a thousand people and six in a thousand people—people who had smoked for years and probably had undetected cancer before starting the trial. Hidden in the figures was an unreported finding. Among those who gave up smoking during the trial and took beta-carotene there were 20 percent fewer cases of lung cancer. Does this mean that beta-carotene has moral powers and gives smokers cancer but protects those who give up? Or that both results are, as the statistics state, a matter of chance, a minor variable, and that a little pill of synthetic beta-carotene (missing all the other antioxidants found in natural source beta-carotene) cannot have any effect after a lifetime of smoking? We may never know: having cost $64.8 million, the trial was abandoned. With two hundred studies already showing both the safety and efficacy of beta-carotene, how could the National Cancer Institute ever have allowed such a poor study to be started, and then abandoned?

CANCER PATIENTS LIVE FOUR TIMES LONGER ON VITAMIN C

Nobel laureate Dr. Linus Pauling and cancer expert Dr. Ewan Cameron first demonstrated vitamin C's amazing anti-cancer properties in the 1960s. They gave terminally ill cancer patients 10 grams a day and showed that they lived four times longer than patients not on vitamin C.[69] Many studies have since been performed. A review of vitamin C research concluded that "evidence of a protective effect of vitamin C for non-hormone cancers is very strong. Of the 46 studies in which a dietary vitamin C index was calculated, 33 found statistically significant protection."

As well as being an antioxidant and able to disarm free radicals, vitamin C can also disarm a number of other carcinogens (cancer-causing agents), such as nitrosamines. These can occur when chemicals called nitrates combine with amines. Nitrate levels are high in vegetables grown with nitrate-based fertilizers, as well as in water, due to soil residues leaching into water sources. Nitrates are also added to some cured meats such as ham, sausages, and bacon. Seventy percent of our intake comes from vegetables grown with artificial fertilizers, 21 percent from water, and 6 percent from meat.

THE SYNERGY OF VITAMINS C AND E AND SELENIUM

A ten-year study on over eleven thousand people, completed in 1996, found that those who supplemented both the antioxidants vitamin C and vitamin

E halved their overall risk of death from all cancers and heart disease.[70] Vitamin C is water-soluble, while vitamin E is fat-soluble. Together they can protect the tissues and fluids in the body. What is more, when vitamin C has disarmed a carcinogen it can be reloaded by vitamin E, and vice versa, so their combined presence in diet and the body has a synergistic effect.

Vitamin E is a powerful anti-cancer agent, especially in combination with selenium. While high blood levels of vitamin E alone are associated with a significant reduction in cancer risk, studies in Finland by Dr. Salonen found that combined low levels of vitamin E and selenium increase cancer risk more than ten times.[71]

The mineral selenium has long been known to protect against cancer. Studies in the region of Quidong in China, where liver cancer rates are among the highest in the world, have found a strong correlation between low selenium intake and cancer risk, with other risk factors being hepatitis-B infection, exposure to the dietary carcinogen aflatoxin, and a genetic predisposition.[72] The researchers then began a large-scale selenium study in which an entire village of twenty thousand people took a selenium supplement, which was added to their salt. In the following years there was

Which Nutrient for Which Type of Cancer?

The following antioxidant vitamins and minerals have so far been proved effective in medical research against the types of cancer indicated.

Type	Vitamin A	Beta-carotene	Vitamin C	Vitamin E	Selenium
Bladder		★			★
Breast		★	★	★	★
Cervix	★		★	★	★
Colon	★	★	★		★
Head and neck	★	★			
HIV-related			★		
Kidney			★		
Leukemia			★		★
Liver					★
Lung	★	★	★	★	
Lymphoma	★				
Oesophagus			★		★
Oral	★	★	★		★
Pancreas			★		
Prostate	★				★
Skin	★		★		★
Stomach	★		★	★	★

a significant drop in the incidence of both hepatitis-B and liver cancer. Professor Gerhard Schrauzer, an expert on selenium and cancer, recommends a supplement of 200–300 mcg of selenium for those who want optimal protection.

HORMONE-RELATED CANCERS

While antioxidant nutrients have a protective effect in many cancers, free radical damage is unlikely to be the major cause in all of them. Evidence is accumulating that the high incidence of cancer of the breast, cervix, and ovaries in women, and of the prostate and testes in men, may be related to disturbed hormone balance. All of these body tissues are sensitive to hormones, and excess estrogen, a hormone that stimulates cell growth, may play a key role in these cancers.

The research of Dr. Chang, de Lignieres and colleagues showed that, if estrogen levels are increased, the proliferation rate of breast cells increases by over 200 percent, more than twice the normal rate.[73] On the other hand, if progesterone is given and the level in breast tissue is raised to normal levels the rate of cell multiplication falls to 15 percent of that in untreated women. This study, undertaken on healthy, pre-menopausal women, shows that estrogen will promote the proliferation of breast cancers, while progesterone is protective. This may explain why the risk of breast cancer doubles for women who take estrogen HRT for five or more years and why the risk of ovarian cancer is 72 percent higher in women given estrogen HRT, according to a 1995 study by the Emery University School of Public Health, which followed 240,000 women over eight years.

However, the increased incidence of hormone-related cancers cannot be attributed solely to estrogen dominance due to HRT, especially in men, for whom prostate cancer is the fifth largest cause of death, affecting one in ten men. Hormone expert Dr. John Lee believes that many factors are contributing to estrogen dominance and progesterone deficiency, which he believes is the major cause of these cancers. "Stress, for example, raises cortisol which competes with progesterone. Xenestrogens from the environment have the ability to damage tissue and this leads to increased cancer in later life. There are also nutritional and genetic factors to consider." He recommends a plant-based diet, excluding sources of estrogen such as meat and milk, high consumption of which is associated with increased cancer incidence, particularly of the colon.

Xenestrogens from the environment come from pesticide residues, industrial residues and plastics, which contaminate water and get into the food chain. Research has shown that the combination of tiny amounts of these hormone-disrupting chemicals, equivalent to the levels found in human blood, are carcinogenic and trigger breast cells to proliferate.

Lee recommends conducting tests for estrogen dominance on people with a risk for hormone-related cancer, for and giving natural progesterone to restore the balance, plus antioxidant supplements. As far as diet is concerned, the advice is to avoid fried, browned, and burnt foods, which are sources of free radicals; to cut down on meat and milk, which are sources of natural estrogen; and to eat organic.

CANCER-FIGHTING FOODS

Eating certain kinds of foods is also associated with a decreased risk of cancer. While the evidence accumulates, adding the following foods to your diet cannot hurt, and is likely to help.

- Fruit and vegetables are top of the anti-cancer foods. These are good sources of vitamin A and C. A study in Japan on 265,000 people found that those with a low intake of beta-carotene which is found in fruit and vegetables, had a high risk of lung cancer.[74] Other studies have produced the same result for colon, stomach, prostate, and cervical cancer. Beta-carotene is found in particularly large amounts in carrots, broccoli, sweet potatoes, cantaloupe, and apricots. There is lots of vitamin C in fresh vegetables and fruit.

- Garlic, used liberally, keeps away not only others but cancer too! A National Cancer Institute study carried out in China in 1989 discovered that provinces which used garlic liberally in their cooking had the lowest rate of stomach cancer.[75] Garlic contains sulphur compounds that help deal with toxins and free radicals.

- Soybeans have been associated with a lower risk of breast cancer. In Japan and China, women who get most of their protein from soybean foods—tofu, soybeans themselves and soy milk have lower rates of breast cancer. These results have been confirmed in animal studies.

- Yogurt may protect against colon cancer. The bacterium lactobacillus acidophilus, found in many live yogurts, slows down the development of colon tumors, and yogurt eaters have a lower incidence of colon cancer as do those whose calcium intake is high.[76] Abnormal cell divisions in the colon also slowed right down when calcium intake was increased to 2000 mg a day.

- Sesame and sunflower seeds are rich in selenium, vitamin E, calcium, and zinc. Eat a spoonful every day to keep your antioxidant army in top condition.

28

FIGHTING INFECTIONS NATURALLY

Prevention is better than cure and, as Louis Pasteur said on his deathbed, the host is more important than the invader. Medical scientists are increasingly finding that we only succumb to bugs when we are run down, so your best line of defense is to keep your immune system strong so that it is ready to attack when an invader comes along (read Chapter 19 on boosting the immune system). Invaders come in many shapes and sizes: there are bacteria, viruses, and fungi, as well as parasites. It is important to know which you are dealing with, as each requires slightly different treatment. A cold, flu, herpes, and measles are all viruses. Most ear infections, stomach aches, chest, and sinus infections (usually a follow-on to a cold) are bacterial. Thrush or athlete's foot are fungal infections.

Immune-boosting nutrients are good all year-round, especially if you are run down or exposed to people with infections. During an infection both the invader and our own immune army produce free radicals to destroy each other. We can mine-sweep these dangerous chemicals with antioxidant nutrients, which are good for everybody at any time. Anti-viral, anti-bacterial, and anti-fungal agents are best increased when dealing with a specific invader.

Judging by the results of research on vitamin C, it would be wrong to believe that immune-healthy people get no infections. They just have "pre-colds" that are all over in twenty-four hours, where less healthy people end up horizontal for a week. So the aim is to boost your immune system by giving it the right food and the right environment, so that it can adapt quickly to attempted invasions.

While vitamin C's main strength is against viruses, grapefruit seed extract, for example, is anti-bacterial or "antibiotic." The table below shows which natural remedies work best against different kinds of invaders (see also the A to Z of Infection Fighters on p. 180).

GET IN FAST

The best form of defense is attack, and the quicker you get in there the more chance you have of restoring your health before an infection sets in. All

Which Invaders, Which Natural Remedy?

Nutrients	Antioxidants	Immune Boosters	Anti-viral	Anti-bacterial
Vitamin A	★	★	★	
Beta-carotene	★	★	★	
Vitamin C	★	★	★	★
Vitamin E	★	★		
Selenium	★	★		
Zinc	★	★	★	
Iron	★	★		
Manganese	★			
Copper	★			
B vitamins	★	★		
L cysteine	★			
N A cysteine	★			
Glutathione	★			
Lysine			★	
Aloe vera		★	★	★
Astragalus	★	★		
"Power" mushrooms		★	★	
Echinacea		★	★	
St John's Wort		★		★
Garlic	★	★	★	★
Grapefruit seed			★	★
Silver			★	★
Tea tree				★
Artemisia				★
Bee pollen				★
Cat's claw	★	★	★	
Goldenseal				★

invaders produce toxins as part of their weapons of war. If you wake up feeling more tired than usual, perhaps with bloodshot eyes, a slight headache, itchy throat, slightly blocked nose, or foggy brain—and you haven't been drinking the night before—you are probably under attack! As with alcohol, these are signs that your body is trying to eliminate an undesirable agent.

If the war is raging, turn up the heat. The immune system works better in a warm environment, which is why the body creates a fever to turn up the temperature. So keep yourself warm and get plenty of rest. One day taking it easy can make all the difference, especially if you boost your immune army with natural remedies. Lack of sleep depletes your energy reserves. Also avoid all the other ways in which we habitually dissipate energy: alcohol, smoky atmospheres, strong sunlight, over-eating, stress, arguments, over-exertion, sex, and antibiotics. You can tilt the balance in your favor by reducing these energy-robbers.

There is some truth in the old wives' tale: "Starve a fever, feed a cold" During an infection listen to your body. It is fine not to eat for a day, but if an infection goes on for a long time your immune system does need a number of nutrients, plus protein, to replenish the troops. It is best to eat lightly—small meals made from high-energy natural foods, raw or lightly cooked. During an infection the body fights hard to eliminate the waste products of war, so drink plenty of water or herb tea to help your body detoxify and reduce mucus. Avoid salt and mucus-forming and fatty foods, such as meat, eggs, and dairy products.

HOW TO KILL A COLD

While a gram of vitamin C a day helps to reduce the severity and incidence of colds, achieving "tissue saturation" has even greater results. In order to take hold, a cold virus, must get inside cells and reprogram them to make more cold viruses, which then infect other cells. However, if the body's tissues are high in vitamin C the virus cannot survive. Tissue saturation is more likely to be achieved by taking in around 10–15 grams a day, or 3 grams every four hours, which is 375 times the RDA! Fortunately, vitamin C is one of the least toxic substances known to man. A daily intake of 2–5 grams may be sufficient to maintain a high level of immune protection.

Viruses get into body cells by puncturing their walls with tiny spikes made of a substance called hemagglutinin. According to research by virologist Madeleine Mumcuoglu, working with Dr. Jean Linderman, who discovered interferon, an extract of elderberry disarms these spikes by binding to them and preventing them penetrating the cell membrane.[77] "This was the first discovery," says Mumcuoglu. "Later I found evidence that elderberry also fights flu virus in other ways. Viral spikes are covered with an enzyme called neuraminidase, which helps break down the cell wall. The elderberry inhibits the action of that enzyme. My guess is that we'll find elderberry acts against viruses in other ways as well."

In a double-blind controlled trial she tested the effects of the elderberry extract, called Sambucol, in people diagnosed with any one of a number of strains of flu virus. Their results, published in 1995, showed a significant improvement in symptoms—fever, cough, muscle pain—in 20 percent of patients within twenty-four hours, and in a further 73 percent of patients within forty-eight hours. After three days 90 percent had complete relief of their symptoms compared to another group on a placebo, who took at least six days to recover. While this is the first published trial of elderberry extract, I have heard many success stories from my clients who have successfully speeded up recovery from colds and flu by taking Sambucol.

IMMUNE-BOOSTING HERBS

More and more immune-boosting herbs are being discovered to help fight infections. Four excellent ones, covered in greater detail in the list below, are cat's claw, echinacea, garlic, and grapefruit seed extract. Cat's claw tea tastes good with added black currant and apple concentrate, and one cup a day helps maintain immune power. If you have a sore throat or stomach upset, add four slices of root ginger. Echinacea is the original American Indian snakeroot, which later became known as snake oil. The great advantage of grapefruit seed extract is that it has a similar effect to antibiotics but without damaging beneficial stomach bacteria as conventional antibiotics do. Even so, if you are taking probiotics like acidophlus it is best to take them separately from grapefruit seed extract.

In summary, the following steps will help you to fight an infection (for more specific information on dosages see the list below):

- Eat lightly, making sure you get enough protein, which is needed to build immune cells, and keep warm. If you have a mucus-related infection, avoid dairy products.

- Increase your intake of vitamin C to 3 grams every four hours.

- Drink cat's claw tea and consider adding ginger, echinacea drops and taking garlic capsules or cloves.

- If you have a cold, take one dessertspoon of Sambucol four times a day.

- If you have a bacterial, fungal, or parasitical infection take ten drops grapefruit seed extract (Citricidal) two or three times a day.

- Find out what your infection is, and, if necessary see your doctor, especially if you are not better within five days.

- Consider other remedies in the A to Z of Natural Infection Fighters below.

A TO Z OF NATURAL INFECTION FIGHTERS

Two doses are given: the first for pulling out the plug when under attack, the second for general maintenance. Once an invasion is over, wait forty-eight hours before going on to the maintenance dose. Some natural remedies have no maintenance dose and are only recommended to fight an infection.

Vitamin A

Vitamin A is one of the key immune-boosting nutrients. It helps to strengthen the skin, inside and out, and therefore acts as a first line of defense, keeping the lungs, digestive tract, and skin intact. By strengthening cell walls it keep viruses out. Vitamin A can be toxic in large doses, so levels above 10,000 IUs are recommended only on a short-term basis.

FIGHTING INFECTIONS   10,000–25,000 IUs (one week only) a day.
MAINTENANCE   7,500 IUs a day.

Aloe vera

Has immune-boosting, anti-viral, and antiseptic properties. It is a good all-round tonic, as well as a booster during any infection. Daily dose as instructed on the bottle.

Antioxidants

Substances that detoxify free radicals. These include vitamins A, C, E, and beta-carotene, zinc, selenium, and many other non-essential substances including silymarin (milk thistle), pycnogenol, lipoic acid, bioflavonoids, and bilberry extract. It is best to take an all-round antioxidant supplement during any infection.

Artemisia

A natural anti-fungal, anti-parasitical and anti-bacterial agent, often used alongside caprylic acid for the treatment of candidiasis or thrush.

FIGHTING INFECTIONS   100–1,000 mg a day.

Astragulus

A Chinese herb renowned for all-round immunity-boosting and high in beneficial mucopolysaccharides.

FIGHTING INFECTIONS   1–3 grams a day.
MAINTENANCE   200 mg a day.

Beta-carotene

The vegetable source of vitamin A and an antioxidant in its own right. Red, orange, and yellow foods and fresh vegetables are the best sources. Carrot or watermelon juice is a great way to drink this all-round infection fighter.

FIGHTING INFECTIONS   10,000–25,000 IUs a day.
MAINTENANCE   7,500 IUs a day.

Vitamin C

Vitamin C is an incredible anti-viral agent. Viruses cannot survive in a vitamin C-rich environment. To achieve this you need to take 3 grams of vitamin C immediately and then 2 grams every four hours. Alternatively, mix 6–10 grams of vitamin C powder in fruit juice diluted with water and drink throughout the day. Vitamin C is non-toxic but too much can cause loose bowels. Decrease the dose if this becomes unacceptable.

FIGHTING INFECTIONS   6–10 grams a day.
MAINTENANCE   1–3 grams a day.

Bee pollen

A natural antibiotic. It is probably better as a general tonic rather than a specific treatment. Be careful if you are pollen-sensitive.

FIGHTING INFECTIONS   1–2 dessertspoons a day.
MAINTENANCE   1 teaspoon a day.

Caprylic acid

An anti-fungal agent derived from coconuts, primarily used for eliminating the candida albicans organism responsible for thrush. Anti-candida programs are best carried out under the supervision of a qualified nutrition consultant.

FIGHTING INFECTIONS   1–3 grams a day.

Cat's claw

A powerful anti-viral, antioxidant, and immune-boosting agent from the Peruvian rainforest plant *Uncaria tomentosa*. It contains chemicals called alkaloids, one of which is isopteridin, which has been proved to boost immune function. It is available as a tea or in supplements.

FIGHTING INFECTIONS   2–6 grams a day.
MAINTENANCE   2 grams a day.

Cysteine

See Glutathione and cysteine.

Vitamin E

Vitamin E is the most important fat-soluble antioxidant. You will find it in nuts, seeds, wheat germ, and their cold-pressed oil, but make sure they are fresh. Vitamin E is best supplemented every day during an infection.

FIGHTING INFECTIONS　500–1,000 IUs a day.

Echinacea

A great all-rounder with anti-viral and anti-bacterial properties. The active ingredients are thought to be specific mucopolysaccharides. It comes in capsules and in extracts, taken as drops.

FIGHTING INFECTIONS　2 to 3 grams a day (or 15 drops of concentrated extract three times a day).
MAINTENANCE　1 gram a day.

Elderberry extract (also called Sambucol)

Reduces the duration of colds and flu by preventing the virus from taking hold.

FIGHTING INFECTIONS　1 tablespoon three times a day.

Garlic

Contains allicin, a substance which is anti-viral, anti-fungal, and anti-bacterial. It also acts as an antioxidant, being rich in sulphur-containing amino acids. There is no doubt it is an important ally in fighting infections, and a wise inclusion in your diet as garlic eaters have the lowest incidence of cancer. Consider a clove or capsule equivalent for an easy guide to your daily dose.

FIGHTING INFECTIONS　2–6 cloves a day.
MAINTENANCE　1 clove a day.

Ginger

Particularly good for sore throats and stomach upsets. Put six slices of fresh root ginger in a thermos with a stick of cinnamon and fill up with boiling water. Five minutes later you have a delicious, throat-soothing ginger and cinnamon tea. You can add a little lemon and honey for taste.

Glutathione and cysteine

These are both powerful antioxidant amino acids. You will find them in many all-round antioxidant supplements. During a prolonged viral infection they get depleted and it may be worth taking a supplement. The most usable forms are reduced glutathione or N–Acetyl–Cysteine.

FIGHTING INFECTIONS   2 to 3 grams a day.
MAINTENANCE   1 gram a day.

Goldenseal

A natural anti-bacterial agent containing specific alkaloids which are particularly helpful for mucus membrane problems. Can be used in douches, or in gargles as an antiseptic, and be taken internally for a healthy digestive system.

FIGHTING INFECTIONS   200–500 mg a day.

Grapefruit seed extract (also called Citricidal)

A powerful natural antibiotic, anti-fungal and anti-viral agent. It comes in drops and can be swallowed, gargled with, or used as nose drops or ear drops, depending on the site of infection.

FIGHTING INFECTIONS   20–30 drops a day.
MAINTENANCE   5 drops a day.

Lysine

An amino acid that helps get rid of the herpes virus. During an infection it is best to limit arginine-rich foods such as beans, lentils, nuts, and chocolate.

FIGHTING INFECTIONS   1–3 grams a day.
MAINTENANCE   1 gram a day.

Mushrooms

Shiitake, maiitake, reishi, ganoderma, and other mushrooms were traditionally believed by Chinese Taoists to confer immortality. All have been shown to contain immune-boosting polysaccharides. You will find them added to some immune-boosting supplements and tonics, or you can buy shiitake fresh in the supermarket or dried in health food stores.

Probiotics

Unlike antibiotics, these are beneficial bacteria that promote health. It is best to supplement them during an bacterial infection and after a course of antibiotics. Specific strains found in the human digestive tract, called human strain bacteria, are now available. Watch out for ABCDophilus, a combination of three strains beneficial for infants and children. These have been shown to halve the recovery time from a bout of diarrhea. Lactobacillus salivarius is a good strain for adults.

DOSAGE   Follow instructions on the supplement you choose.

St John's wort (hypericum)

Particularly good for anything that penetrates the skin, such as a wound or skin infection. It is a good general tonic for the immune system.

FIGHTING INFECTIONS   50–500 mg a day.

Selenium

An immune-enhancing mineral that also acts as an antioxidant. It is abundant in seafood and seeds, especially sesame, and is included in most antioxidant supplements.

FIGHTING INFECTIONS   200 to 300 mcg a day.
MAINTENANCE   100 mcg a day.

Tea tree oil

An Australian remedy with antiseptic properties. Great for rubbing on the chest, in the bath, or steam inhaling, and also helps keep mosquitoes away.

DOSAGE   Take as instructed on the bottle. Lozenges are also available.

Zinc

The most important immune-boosting mineral, well worth upping during any infection. There is no doubt that it helps fight infections. Zinc lozenges are available for sore throats. You will also find it included in most antioxidant supplements.

FIGHTING INFECTIONS   25–50 mg a day.
MAINTENANCE   15 mg a day.

29

BREAKING THE FAT BARRIER

At least one-sixth of women are trying to lose weight at any one time, reports market research company Mintel. Government health figures show that 32.6 million Americans are overweight. Women in the age of 25 to 30 are 10 pounds heavier today than they were a decade ago and one in five are trying to lose weight, all of which is good news for the $33 billion a year weight loss food industry that has quadrupled since 1988. Diet books still top the best-seller lists and newspapers continue to promote seven-day Wonder Diets, and sales still go up when they do as millions hunt for new ways to fight the flab. But how much of what we are told is fact and how much is fiction?

Consider this experiment. Two groups of women are given a milk shake to drink. One group is told it is very low in calories, the other that it is high. All the milk shakes are in fact identical. Then each participant is given an enormous bowl of chocolate ice cream. Which group eats the most? The group who thought the milk shake was high in calories. After all, if you have already broken your diet why not go the whole hog?

Successful dieting is not just about what works if you stick to it. It is about what you can stick to that works. Short-term results are easy—just stop eating. But how long will you stick to that? Meal replacement diets are also an easy option. But can you imagine spending your life drinking "diet" milk shakes—and, if you do, what will the consequences be? A good diet should:

- produce weight loss
- be good for your health
- educate you towards a lifetime diet that maintains a healthy weight and promotes your general health
- be relatively easy to follow in that it does not leave you starving or exhausted

FAT FACTS

Since fat is what you want to lose it helps to understand what it is. A visit to the local butcher will help. Ask him to show you a pound of fat. It is the size of a small brick. The idea that the body can lose 7 pounds of actual fat in a week is ludicrous. The maximum fat loss is more like 2 pounds a week, although 1 pound is more realistic. Any further weight loss will be water and is likely to come back quickly. When the intake of glucose-like molecules from carbohydrate or fat foods exceeds your needs, the excess is stored as glycogen in your muscles and the liver. If your glycogen stores are full the excess gets converted to fat and laid down in fat cells. If you eat less than your body needs, glycogen will be broken down. With each unit of glycogen that is used up, nine units of water are lost. As your glycogen stores get depleted, fat is converted into glycogen. So most diets, especially very low-calorie ones, cause an initial weight loss that consists mainly of water. As you start eating enough for your body needs, your glycogen stores replenish themselves together with water. This is one reason why some diets cause a rapid weight loss in the first week, and a rapid weight gain when you stop them.

Most diets say that what you eat, less what you "burn off" through normal activity and exercise, ends up as a wad of fat around your middle. So if you want to lose weight all you have to do is eat less or exercise more. Simple, right? In theory, but not in practice. Firstly, this approach does not embrace the reasons why we overeat (or under-exercise), and secondly, it does not work. Consider this example. An apple contains approximately 100 calories, so if you eat an apple less every day for a year you would lose 36,500 calories. A pound of body fat is equivalent to around 4,000 calories. That means you would lose 10 pounds in the first year, would have lost 49 pounds by the fifth year, 98 pounds after ten years and vanish completely after fifteen years! All by eating one less apple a day.

Your weight is a burning issue

The reason why calorie theory does not add up is the key to what is missing from most calorie-controlled diets. The missing link is metabolism—the process of turning the fuel in food into energy that the body can use. People vary considerably in their ability to turn food into energy. Those who do not do it well have a slow metabolism and consequently turn more food into fat. Most obese people have slower rates of metabolism than slim people. One of the big problems with crash diets of below 1,000 calories a day is that the body sees this reduction in food as a threat and slows down the metabolic rate by as much as 45 percent. In the short term you can lose around 7 pounds of body fluid and, if you are lucky, an absolute maximum of 2 pounds of body fat a week, which together could account for as much as 10 pounds in two or three weeks. But the minute you go back to what you were eating before, the fluid returns—and so will the fat, because your metabolic rate has slowed down, meaning that you now need less food to maintain a stable weight. Of course, this rebound effect is good business for food replacement programs, whose customers try crash dieting on average three times a year.

Consider the story of Michelle and Caroline, two volunteers for the *Sunday Times* Tried and Tested diet feature. Michelle was put on the Cambridge Diet, a 330 calorie-a-day food replacement diet. Caroline was put on the Fatburner Diet, a 1,500 calorie-a-day diet used by the Institute for Optimum Nutrition and based on influencing your metabolism rather than just reducing calories. According to Michelle,

> The first three days were torture but from then on it got worse. Walking down the road required serious will: I was constantly exhausted and couldn't concentrate, so that my work suffered badly. Weight loss came slowly—I'd expected miracles after reading the publicity boasts—but in the final week it finally plummeted. My face acquired the desired gaunt look . . . but, unfortunately, my bust rapidly followed suit. I blew up like a balloon when I resumed eating, and seemed to retain gallons of water; conversely, "loose" skin has appeared, creating an under-arm bat-wing effect. When I first stopped the diet, irresistible binging took over, but after six weeks, with the exercise of limbs and discipline, I've managed to limit the damage to a gain of 5 pounds.

Michelle lost 10 pounds in a month and gained 5. Caroline too lost 10 pounds in a month and had put on 2 pounds after the diet while on vacation. When asked about her diet, she commented, "One of the hardest—but best—things about it was the insistence on giving up coffee and stimulants. I had caffeine withdrawal headaches for the first few days, but began to feel wonderful after that—alert and fit and thoroughly detoxified, with no more puffy eyes staring back from the bathroom mirror. I regained 2 pounds while on vacation but will whittle it off by eating sensibly." Caroline ate more than four times the calories and yet lost almost double the weight. Factors that affect metabolism are critical to weight control. So what is the secret of getting your metabolism working for you rather than against you?

FOOD FOR FUEL

It is not just how much food that makes a difference, but the kind of food you eat. The human body is designed to run on complex—in other words slow-releasing—carbohydrates, which means whole grains, beans, lentils, vegetables, and fruit. Modern diets are at last emphasizing foods that release their sugar content slowly. Slow release produces a more consistent energy level and longer relief from hunger, and gives the body a better chance to use up the food rather than turning it into fat.

An estimated eight in ten overweight people have an underlying blood sugar imbalance. For these people, following a low-stimulant, high complex carbohydrate diet (as explained in Chapter 10) is essential. Yet many diet programs add stimulants, rather than taking them away. They include diet drugs and diets that include coffee or guarana, both of which are concentrated sources of caffeine, an adrenal stimulant. In the short term these stimulants may induce weight loss by speeding up metabolic processes, but in the long term they are more of a hindrance than a help.

FAT PHOBIA

The average diet derives 42 percent of its calories from fat, 15 percent from protein and the remaining 43 percent mainly from refined carbohydrates and sugar. The ideal diet should derive no more than 30 percent of its calories from fat, 15 percent from protein, and the remaining 55 percent or more from complex carbohydrates. Since fat is the most energy-dense, or calorific, food, many diets are based on restricting fat intake. Since most of the fat that the average person eats comes from meat, dairy products, margarine, and high-fat processed or "fast" foods, a low-fat diet must inevitably approach a vegan diet. Studies have shown that on a vegan diet, weight is lost and then more easily maintained. One study that tested the effects of a vegan diet on arthritis found a 9 percent reduction in body weight over three months. This was despite the fact that the diet in question was high in both nutrients and calories, largely due to a relatively high fat content from the intake of nuts, seeds, and their oil, included in sauces and salad dressings. One possible explanation is that a vegan diet contains less "bioavailable" food due to its high fiber content. Alternatively, the higher nutrient content may have had a stimulating effect on the metabolism.

While there is no need to include any saturated fat in the human diet, certain polyunsaturated fats, as found in fatty fish, nuts, seeds, and their oils, are essential. Udo Erasmus, author of *Fats and Oils*, claims that these essential fats actually help to burn fat. Cutting down radically on saturated fat and not excluding nuts, seeds, and fish achieves the best balance between a low-fat diet and optimum nutrition. In practical terms this means no more fried foods. Instead, bake, boil, or steam-fry by adding water, stock, soy sauce, lemon juice, or any made-up fat-free flavor to the food in the frying pan and put a lid on it. Eating fried or fatty foods with sauces is just a habit. Once it is broken, most people are just as happy without.

THE FIBER FACTOR

Back in the 1980s Audrey Eyton was quick to realize the major problem with low-calorie diets. You get hungry! So she devised the F-Plan Diet, which allowed dieters 1,000 calories a day and included high-fiber foods. These help to reduce your appetite as well as having other health benefits. Most people think of bran when they think of fiber, but wheat bran is one of the least effective forms of fiber—the fiber in vegetables, oats, lentils, and beans is much more effective. As well as making food more bulky and therefore making you feel full, fiber also helps to control blood sugar levels.

The extraordinary glucomannan fiber is unparalleled in this respect. Derived from the Japanese konjac plant, it absorbs more than ten times as much water as wheat bran and is therefore a better bulking agent. More importantly, it controls blood sugar levels so effectively that it is used in Japan for the treatment of diabetes. A mere 3 grams, compared to the 30 grams of fiber we are recommended to eat every day, has been shown in proper controlled trials to induce a weight loss of 2–5 pounds a month, without any apparent change in diet or increased exercise.[78]

THE SUPPLEMENT FACTOR

Your ability to burn fat does not depend just on the kind of food you eat—the fuel. It also depends on the presence of vitamins and minerals that help to control the careful breakdown of glucose, which in turn releases energy to body cells. Any lack of these vital nutrients will result in less energy and consequently a greater predisposition to laying down fat. Transporting glucose from the blood into the cells depends on the presence of vitamins B3 (niacin) and B6, chromium ,and zinc. The actual breakdown of glucose into energy depends on vitamins B1, B2, B3, B5, and C, iron, and co-enzyme Q. Ensuring that you have an adequate supply of these nutrients is another way to increase the effectiveness of any weight loss program.

Although all these nutrients are important, chromium is being dubbed the "metabolism mineral" due to studies that suggest taking chromium supplements may enhance fat burning. The form of chromium compound may also be important. Positive results have been achieved with chromium picolinate. Chromium bound with vitamin B3, known as chromium polynicotinate, may prove a highly usable form of this elusive mineral. The amount needed to guarantee that your metabolism is as efficient as possible—around 200 mcg per day—is higher than that found in even the best-balanced diet. Therefore the only way to guarantee these optimal levels is through taking a supplement. While it is not yet clearly proven that supplementation does cause weight loss in itself, clinical evidence suggests that it evens out appetite, reduces binges and enhances energy levels—all of which, of course, are related and essential to long-term weight control.

HYDROXYCITRIC ACID

Another useful fat-burning supplement is hydroxycitric acid, or HCA for short. Originally developed by the drug manufacturer Hoffman-LaRoche, it slows down the production of fat and reduces appetite. HCA is a weak acid much like citric acid, with no apparent toxicity or safety concerns. It is extracted from the rind of the tamarind fruit (*Garcinia cambogia*), which has been used as a spice in the East for hundreds of years and is thought to be the richest source of HCA.

HCA works by inhibiting the enzyme that converts sugar into fat. When the carbohydrate in a meal has been variously converted into fuel or glycogen, any excess is converted to fat by the enzyme ATP-citrate lyase. HCA blocks this enzyme and so increases the amount of glucose available, which sends signals to the brain to reduce the appetite.

Evidence of its fat-burning properties has been accumulating since 1965. Three studies by Dr. Sullivan in the 1970s found that when test animals that had deliberately been made obese were given HCA, their fat levels were reduced with no loss of body protein.[78] A decade later, the results of an investigation of HCA in obese men were published in the *Annals of the New York Academy of Sciences*.[78] The study showed an average 3.5-pound weight loss in a week when a 220-pound person was given 800 mg per day.[78] Since then a number of controlled studies have been carried out on HCA, sometimes in combination with chromium picolinate, and have consistently proved effective. For example, an eight-week double-blind trial by Dr. Conte reported an average weight loss of 11.1 pounds per person, compared to 4.2 pounds on placebo, with both groups following the same diet and exercise regime.[78]

There is also evidence that HCA may enhance the burning of calories and increase energy levels. The recommended intake is 250 mg three times a day.

MAGIC PILLS

While HCA and chromium have their merits as part of a total approach to weight loss, their benefit is often exaggerated on the bandwagon of people who market "magic pills" without recommending any change to your diet or exercise level. Other magic pills have included "starch blockers," which stop you digesting sugar, alcohol, and carbohydrates, and "fat magnets," which stop you digesting fat. The former proved ineffective and had the unpleasant side effect of producing a lot of flatulence. The latter are potentially very dangerous since, if they work, they will block the ability to absorb essential fats, which are already deficient in most weight loss diets. Avoid all these magic pills.

FAT-BURNING EXERCISES

The good news about exercise is that you really do not have to be fanatically fit to lose weight. And the reason why, once again, is not calories but metabolism. According to calorie theory, exercise does little to promote weight loss. After all, running a mile only burns up 300 calories—equivalent to two slices of toast or a piece of apple pie. But this argument misses a number of key points.

The first is that the effects of exercise are cumulative. Running a mile may only burn up 300 calories, but if you do that three days a week for a year, that makes 22,000 calories, equivalent to a weight loss of 11 pounds! Also, the amount of calories you burn up depends on how fat or fit you are to start with. The more fat and unfit you are, the more benefit you will derive from small amounts of exercise.

Contrary to popular belief, moderate exercise also decreases your appetite. It appears that a degree of physical activity is necessary for appetite mechanisms to work properly. People who take no exercise have exaggerated appetites, so the pounds pile on.

The most important reason why exercise is a key to weight loss is its effect on your metabolic rate. According to Professor McArdle, exercise physiologist at City University, New York, "Most people can generate metabolic rates that are eight to ten times above their resting value during sustained cycling, running, or swimming. Complementing this increased metabolic rate is the observation that vigorous exercise will raise metabolic rate for up to 15 hours after exercise." Surveys do show that leaner people tend to exercise more.

WEIGHT-WATCHING SUPPORT

Weight-watching clubs offer a motivating factor—support. But just how important is this? One study compared the effects of the Fatburner Diet, a 1,500 calorie-a-day diet designed to balance blood sugar in combination with a metabolism-boosting supplement program, with Unislim, a weight-watching club with a regime of sensible diet plus exercise and weekly support. However, despite the lack of support the Fatburner dieters lost, on average, 14 pounds over three months, compared to only 2 pounds on the Unislim diet.

So this, in brief, is how to lose weight without suffering:

- Follow a low- to medium-calorie diet (1,000–1,500 calories), high in fiber, low in fat, and balanced for fat, protein, and carbohydrate.

- Avoid sugar, sweetened foods, coffee, tea, cigarettes, and alcohol, or at least reduce your intake of them as much as possible.

- Exercise aerobically at least twice a week—running, swimming, brisk walking, low-impact aerobics, dance classes, etc.

- Supplement your diet with vitamins and minerals. Most important are the B vitamins, vitamin C, and the minerals zinc and chromium. Also consider taking a daily 750 mg of HCA, often found in supplements together with chromium.

- Consider supplementing your diet with a daily 3 grams of glucomannan or 5 grams of konjac fiber.

30

SOLVING THE RIDDLE OF EATING DISORDERS

For many people, especially teenagers, the problem is not gaining weight but losing it. Eating disorders including anorexia nervosa and anorexia bulimia, in which the sufferer binges and then makes herself sick, affect thousands of people, and are very much on the increase.

Anorexia was first identified by Dr. William Gull in 1874. He advocated that "The patient should be fed at regular intervals, and surrounded by persons who could have moral control over them, relations and friends being generally the worst attendants." Today the approach is often essentially the same, summed up as "drug them, feed them, and let them get on with their lives" in a *Guardian* article describing treatment in "leading hospitals." The "modern" approach includes "behavior therapy"—in other words, rewards and privileges—and drugs to induce compliance. The latter include tranquilizers such as chlorpromazine, sedatives, and anti-depressants. The diet is high-carbohydrate, sometimes as much as 5,000 calories a day, with little regard to quality.

THE GERM OF AN IDEA

In 1973 two zinc researchers, Hambidge and Silverman, concluded that, "whenever there is appetite loss in children zinc deficiency should be suspected." In 1979 Bakan, a Canadian health researcher, noticed that the symptoms of anorexia and zinc deficiency were similar in a number of respects and proposed that clinical trials should be undertaken to test its effectiveness in treatment. Meanwhile David Horrobin, most renowned for his research into evening primrose oil, proposed that "anorexia nervosa is due to a combined deficiency of zinc and EFAs."

ZINC HYPOTHESIS CONFIRMED

In 1980 the first trial started, at the University of Kentucky.[79] The researchers discovered that 10 out of 13 patients admitted with anorexia and 8 out of 14

Symptoms of Anorexia and Zinc Deficiency

Anorexia	Zinc Deficiency
Symptoms	*Symptoms*
Weight loss	Weight loss
Loss of appetite	Loss of appetite
Amenorrhoea (loss of periods)	Amenorrhoea (loss of periods)
Impotence in males	Impotence in males
Nausea	Nausea
Skin lesions	Skin lesions
Malabsorption of nutrients	Malabsorption of nutrients
Misperceptions (confused thoughts)	Misperceptions (confused thoughts)
Depression	Depression
Anxiety	Anxiety
Risk factors	*Risk factors*
Female under 25	Female under 25
Stress	Stress
Puberty	Puberty

patients with bulimia were zinc-deficient. After vigorous feeding they became even more zinc-deficient. Since zinc is required to digest and utilize protein, from which body tissue is made, the researchers recommended that extra zinc, above the amount required to correct deficiency, should be given as anorexics start to eat and gain weight.

In 1984 the penny dropped with two important research findings and the first case of an anorexic treated with zinc. The first study showed that animals deprived of zinc very rapidly developed loss of appetite, and that if these animals were force-fed a zinc-deficient diet in order to gain weight they became seriously ill. The second study revealed that zinc deficiency damages the intestinal wall and therefore the absorption of nutrients, including zinc, potentially leading to a vicious spiral of deficiency.

Then in 1984 Professor Bryce-Smith, renowned for his exposure of the dangers of lead, and Dr Simpson, a Reading general practitioner, reported the first case of anorexia treated with zinc. The patient was a thirteen-year-old girl, tearful and depressed, who weighed 80 pounds. She was referred to a consultant psychiatrist, but, despite counseling, three months later her weight was down under 70 pounds. Within two months of zinc supplementation at a level of 45 mg per day her weight had risen to almost 98 pounds, she was cheerful again, and tests for zinc deficiency produced normal results.

Scientists all over the world now started to test the effects of zinc on anorexia. Two Swedish doctors at the University of Gothenburg reported that "our initial patient is currently maintained on zinc supplementation (45 mg per day). She is doing very well: her weight as well as her menstruations are normalized."[80] Meanwhile, the first double-blind trial with fifteen anorexics was being carried out at the University of California.[81] In 1987 the researchers reported their findings: "Zinc supplementation was followed by a decrease in depression and anxiety. Our data suggest that individuals with anorexia nervosa may be at risk for zinc deficiency and may respond favorably after zinc supplementation." By 1990 many researchers had found that over half the anorexic patients studied showed clear biochemical evidence of zinc deficiency. In 1994 Dr. Birmingham and colleagues carried out a double-blind controlled trial in which one group was given 100 mg of zinc gluconate.[82] They concluded that "the rate of increase of body mass of the zinc supplemented group was twice that of the placebo group and this difference was statistically significant." Sadly, many treatment centers still fail to give zinc supplements to those suffering from anorexia.

MIND OR BODY?

The fact that high levels of zinc supplementation help to treat anorexia does not mean that the root cause of anorexia is zinc deficiency. Psychological issues may, and probably do, bring about a change in the eating habits of susceptible people. By avoiding eating, a young girl can suppress the signs of growing up. Menstruation stops, her breast size decreases, and the body stays small. Starvation induces a kind of "high" by stimulating changes in important brain chemicals that may help to block out difficult feelings and issues that are too hard to face. But once the route of not eating is chosen and becomes established, zinc deficiency is almost inevitable, due to both poor intake and poor absorption. With it comes a further loss of appetite and even more depression, misperceptions, and the inability to cope with the stresses that face many adolescents growing up in the late twentieth century.

The optimum nutrition approach to help someone with anorexia or bulimia is best carried out alongside work with a skilled psychotherapist. It emphasizes quality of food rather than quantity, including supplements to ensure that the patient takes in enough vitamins and minerals, and of course 45 mg of zinc per day. The dose can be halved once weight gain has been achieved and is being maintained.

31

MENTAL HEALTH—THE NUTRITION CONNECTION

One definition of insanity is to keep doing the same things and expect different results. That is exactly what has been happening in the conventional treatment of pronounced mental illness such as schizophrenia. The treatment hinges on drugs, perhaps backed up with counseling. Neither has an impressive success rate. Even the definition of "success" from the use of drugs like chlorpromazine warrants examination. When normal people are put on to a fraction of the dose used for those with pronounced mental illness, their "normality" disappears. Bill Mandel, a journalist on the *San Francisco Examiner*, tried 50 mg of Thorazine and reported, "It made me stupid. Because Thorazine and related drugs are called a 'liquid lobotomy' in the mental health business I'd expected a grey cloud to descend over my faculties. There was no grey cloud, just small, unsettling patches of fog. My mental gears slipped. I had no intellectual traction. It was difficult to remember simple words."

According to Dr. Abram Hoffer, former Director of Psychiatric Research for part of Canada, tranquilizers never cure mental illness because they merely replace one psychosis with another. After forty years' experience as a psychiatrist he recommends them only as a last, and temporary, resort. Instead he favors nutritional intervention which, he says, cures 80 percent of acute schizophrenia, a claim backed up by his own and independent double-blind controlled studies.[83] His definition of "cure" is threefold: free from symptoms, able to socialize with family and community, and paying income tax! The latter, meaning gainful employment, is a rare event for people on tranquilizers.

So here we are, forty years on from the introduction of the first tranquilizer, chlorpromazine, with a few more drug variations, concerns about long-term side effects confirmed, and ever-increasing prescriptions for drugs that cannot cure. This, in my opinion, is insanity.

THE NUTRITION CONNECTION

If there was no better treatment there might be grounds to keep doing the same thing, but there is a better treatment that has been tried, tested, and proven over forty years—the same span of time that chemical intervention has been in vogue. Nutrition intervention is nothing new. In fact, the very first double-blind controlled trials in the history of psychiatry tested the effects of niacin (vitamin B3) on the treatment of acute schizophrenia. These tests were carried out by Dr. Hoffer and Dr. Osmond in 1953. The results showed that niacin therapy doubled the recovery rate, and were later confirmed by the research of Dr. Wittenberg from Rutgers University, New Jersey.[84] However, in the meantime repeat trials using chronic patients, most of whom had been in hospital for many years, failed to produce the same result; soon interest in niacin therapy was forgotten in the wake of the chemical revolution.

The combination of other nutrients, plus eliminating food sensitivities, has pushed up the success rate of nutrition intervention to 80 percent. Over the next thirty years a comprehensive model of nutritional assessment and treatment of schizophrenia, depression, anxiety, addictions, learning difficulties, eating disorders, and other such conditions evolved, fueled by an increasing number of consistently encouraging reports from practitioners who have applied these methods. Some of the results have been so remarkable that psychiatrists have viewed them with disbelief against the yardstick of conventional therapy. In the 1960s Dr. Henry Turkel, from Michigan, reported on a Down's syndrome girl whose IQ score went over five years from 44 to 85, classifying her as no longer educationally subnormal; the result was verified by an independent psychologist.[85] Dr. Alfred Libby, from California, reported on a mega-nutrient approach to drug addiction which effectively eliminated withdrawal symptoms and cravings within forty-eight hours.[86]

Seeing is believing. It was not until 1980, when I went to the Brain Bio Center in Princeton, New Jersey, founded by Dr. Carl Pfeiffer, then the leading light in the new nutrition approach, that I became convinced that a major breakthrough had been made. More than fifteen years on, my experiences with people suffering from a wide range of mental health problems have strengthened this conviction.

THE WHOLE PICTURE

Generally speaking, the best results have been achieved, not by a "magic bullet" such as niacin, folic acid, or zinc, but by the careful assessment of a person's biochemical status and a tailor-made diet, plus supplements to help bring them back into balance. Niacin (B3) on its own dramatically lessens symptoms and improves recovery. So too does zinc, according to the research of Pfeiffer and others. So too does folic acid, as confirmed in a recent double-blind study at King's College Hospital in London, which reported significant improvements in both schizophrenic and depressed patients.[87] In the light of these findings it should not really be any surprise that a shotgun approach of ensuring optimal intakes of all nutrients would produce even better results.

However, while multinutrient approaches do produce better results than single nutrients alone, there are some assumptions that need questioning. Do all people with certain types of mental illness need extra nutrients? If so, do they need the same nutrients? And why? Among scientific circles there is little doubt that biochemical imbalances, often linked to genetic differences, are involved in many forms of mental illness. Yet, despite this, conventional clinical assessment includes neither biochemical assessment nor genetic consideration.

Pfeiffer and his colleagues were successful in showing that a proportion of schizophrenics and depressives produced excess histamine, a chemical involved in both brain function and immune reactions, and developed both the test and the treatment—a combination of calcium and the amino acid methionine. They reported that producing too much histamine results in a fast metabolism, excessive thoughts, and a tendency to compulsive and obsessive behavior and deep depressions. High histamine types, with their fast metabolism, soon became deficient in other nutrients too, which also need to be replaced.

This research team also unravelled the mystery of "mauve" factor, a substance found in the urine of about half those diagnosed with schizophrenia. They identified it as the chemical kryptopyrrole, and showed that taking extra zinc and vitamin B6 would eradicate the production of this abnormality and improve the symptoms of schizophrenia. These are two examples of biochemical traits, both probably involving a genetic predisposition plus a dietary lack, that result in sufficient biochemical imbalance to cause mental health problems.

Advances like these are allowing nutrition consultants to test for biochemical imbalances and, if present, to correct them using diet plus nutritional supplements. Of course, not everyone who is mentally unwell got there through genetic predisposition or sub-optimum nutrition. That is why testing can help to determine who is most likely to respond well to nutritional intervention. Also, the illness of those who exhibit no obvious nutritional/biochemical imbalance may have a primarily psychological cause. If so, nutrition is not going to help. However, if there is indeed an underlying nutritional/biochemical imbalance counseling may also prove less effective, according to research. Among young offenders, for example, once nutrition is improved so does their response to counseling.

The modern classification of mental illness

We now know that there are many biochemical ways to develop mental illness, the majority of which can be successfully prevented or reversed with nutritional intervention. These can and should be tested in patients before considering potentially harmful therapies such as the long-term use of tranquilizers.

From a nutritional perspective this boils down to five main factors which are always worthy of investigation.

Pyroluria—the stress factor

Some people produce excessive amounts of kryptopyrroles (see above), which can be detected in the urine. The formation of this biochemical robs the body of zinc and vitamin B6, effectively creating a deficiency and need far in excess of what is generally considered necessary for optimal health. This condition, called pyroluria, is found in about 10 percent of the general population and about 50 percent of those with mental illness. A period of stress, which depletes zinc, can tip a person with this biochemical tendency over the edge. The result may well be symptoms such as depression, confusion, disturbed thinking, and social withdrawal.

Pyroluria is easily detected with a simple urine test and corrected by improved nutrition together with supplements of zinc and vitamin B6. Since zinc competes with manganese, this element is usually supplemented as well.

Are You Pyroluric?

Do you have misperceptions (confused thoughts) and some of the following?

____ Intolerance to some protein foods, alcohol, or drugs

____ Definite breath and body odor

____ Morning nausea and constipation

____ Difficulty remembering your dreams

____ Crowded upper front teeth

____ White spots on your fingernails

____ Pale skin which does not tolerate sunlight

____ Frequent upper abdominal pain

____ Frequent head colds and infections

____ Stretch marks in the skin

____ Irregular menstrual cycle or impotence

____ Any of the above when stressed

____ You belong to an all-girl family with look-alike sisters

If a majority of the above apply, you may benefit from:

- Vitamin B6 100 mg, morning and evening—enough for nightly dream recall (do not exceed 1,000 mg)
- Zinc 30 mg, morning and evening
- Manganese 10 mg, morning and evening
- Plus a basic supplement program

PSYCHOANALYSIS OR NEUROANALYSIS?

Brain and nerve cells communicate with each other by releasing neuro-transmitter chemicals, which allow for the exchange of information. The basis of the way anti-depressant and tranquilizing drugs work is by altering neurotransmitter balance. In the not-too-distant future psychiatric screening may involve testing for neurotransmitter imbalances and giving tailor-made treatment accordingly. One neurotransmitter that can be tested for, and corrected using nutritional intervention, is histamine—the same chemical responsible for allergic and inflammatory reactions. Those born with the tendency to produce excess histamine are fast metabolizers and fast thinkers. Pfeiffer described them as "built for the 21st century, complete with self-destruct," because fast metabolism often leads to nutrient depletion and, as a result, high-histamine individuals become very depressed. However, too little can cause problems too, and is associated with hallucinations and paranoia.

Are you Histadelic?

Do you:

____ Sneeze in bright sunlight?

____ Feel you were shy and over-sensitive as a teenager?

____ Cry, salivate, and feel nauseous easily?

____ Hear your pulse in your head on the pillow at night?

____ Get itches elsewhere when you scratch your leg?

____ Have frequent back aches, stomach aches, and muscle cramps?

____ Have easy orgasm with sex?

____ Have regular headaches and seasonal allergies?

____ Have inner tension and occasional depression?

____ Have abnormal fears, compulsions, or rituals?

____ Think you are a light sleeper?

____ Burn up foods rapidly?

____ Sometimes have suicidal thoughts?

____ Tolerate a lot of alcohol and other "downers"?

____ Have little body hair and a lean build?

____ Have large ears and long fingers and toes?

____ Belong to an all-boy family?

If a majority of the above apply, you may benefit from:

- A low-protein, high complex carbohydrate diet
- Calcium 500 mg, morning and evening, with…
- Methionine 500 mg, morning and evening
- Plus a basic supplement program (see p. 253)
- But avoid folic acid and multivitamins which contain folic acid, because these can raise histamine levels

Histamine excess or deficiency is detected by a blood test. High histamine levels can be corrected by supplementing calcium and methionine, while low-histamine people respond well to extra folic acid and vitamin B12.

NUTRIENT DEFICIENCY OR ANTI-NUTRIENT EXCESS?

Some people need much more of certain nutrients than others do. This has been well demonstrated by the apparent dependency on large amounts of niacin (vitamin B3) or folic acid in some mental health patients. Current thinking is that there may be genetic imbalances that are somehow corrected by keeping the intake of these nutrients high.

Niacin and folic acid deficiency can be tested by blood tests; however, normal levels do not necessarily mean that you will not respond to supplementation. Remember to go for "no-flush niacin" to avoid the associated blushing effect. It is really best to embark on this therapy with expert guidance.

Also testable by hair, blood, or sweat analysis are excessive levels of toxic elements like lead, cadmium, or mercury. This is a simple factor well worth checking for in a person with mental health problems.

WIll Niacin Therapy Help You?

Do you have any of the following characteristics?

_____ A recent diagnosis of mental illness

_____ Visual or auditory hallucinations or illusions

_____ Anxiety or paranoia

_____ Loose bowels or skin problems when the illness started

_____ Mental confusion and inability to think straight

_____ Depression

_____ Personality deterioration

If the majority of the above apply, you may benefit from:

- Niacin, 'no-flush' niacin or niacinamide 1,000mg (1 gram) twice a day
- Vitamin C 1 gram after each meal
- Plus a basic supplement program (see p. 253)

Balancing your blood sugar

The brain runs on glucose, the end result of breaking down dietary carbohydrates, and the balance of circulating levels of glucose in the blood determines the balance of the mind. Shortfalls bring on confusion, mental exhaustion, misperceptions and, as a result, irritability, stress, and aggression. Blood sugar levels can be disrupted by eating too much refined sugar or using stimulants including tea, coffee, cola drinks, and cigarettes. Also, the ability to use glucose depends on the presence of a whole host of micronutrients, especially vitamins B3 and B6, chromium, zinc, and manganese.

Blood sugar balance can be determined by a blood test called (glycosylated haemoglobin) or five-hour glucose tolerance tests, although symptoms are a good indicator of a likely problem. Supplementing the above nutrients and eating a whole food diet helps correct an imbalance in blood sugar levels.

Are You Glucose-intolerant?

Do you have misperceptions (confused thoughts) and . . .

_____ Weakness, fatigue, faintness and dizziness

_____ Nervousness, irritability, trembling and anxiety

_____ Depression, forgetfulness, confusion, and difficulty concentrating

_____ Palpitations or blackouts

If a majority of the above apply, you may benefit from:

- Avoidance of junk foods, sugar, alcohol, and white bread
- Regular exercise
- Manganese 10 mg morning and evening
- Zinc 15 mg morning and evening
- Chromium 200 mcg a day
- Plus a basic supplement program (see p. 253)

Food or chemical sensitivity

Some people get depressed or become manic simply because they unwittingly eat a substance to which they are sensitive. While the mechanism for these "brain allergies" is not clearly understood, the phenomenon has been well researched and is thought to apply to perhaps as many as one in four people with mental health problems. While different people react to different foods, the most common food allergens are wheat gluten, other gluten-containing grains (oats, rye, barley), and dairy products.

There are numerous options for allergy tests, and laboratories are becoming increasingly accurate at pinpointing sensitivities. I favor quantitative IgG ELISA tests which look at various foods. Once sensitivities are identified, the foods in question need to be avoided for at least three months. In that time you should correct any digestive problems which can bring on allergies due to foods being improperly digested or absorbed.

Mental illness is a complex affair and the best results are always achieved

Do You Have Cerebral (Brain) Allergies?

Do you have misperceptions (confused thoughts) and . . .

____ A history of infantile colic

____ A history of infantile eczema

____ A history of coeliac disease (malabsorption of nutrients)

____ A history of asthma, rashes, or hay fever

____ Favorite daily foods

____ Excessive daily mood swings

____ Frequent rapid colds

____ Seasonal allergies

____ Relief of symptoms with fasting

____ Intolerance to foods such as wheat or milk

If a majority of the above apply, you may benefit from:

- Methionine 500 mg morning and evening
- Calcium 500 mg morning and evening
- Zinc 15 mg morning and evening
- Manganese 10 mg morning and evening
- B6 adequate for dream recall (no more than 1,000 mg a day)
- Vitamin C 1,000–2,000 mg morning and evening
- Plus a basic supplement program (see p. 253)
- As well as testing for, and avoiding, allergens

by working with a nutrition consultant trained in this area. He or she can advise you on which tests are appropriate for you and devise a therapeutic diet and supplement program to bring your body chemistry back into balance.

32

BIRTHRIGHTS AND WRONGS

We are all older than we like to think. From a health perspective, the nine months spent in the womb and the months prior to conception are the most critical period of our life. Scientists are increasingly discovering that a mother's health and nutrition during pre-conception and pregnancy have a profound effect on the health of the infant, and that patterns of disease in adulthood can be traced to infant nutrition. Optimum nutrition increases fertility, the health of a pregnancy, and the chances of having a healthy baby with strong resilience to disease.

MAXIMIZING FERTILITY

One in every four couples suffer from some degree of infertility. For some, this means having fewer children than they want; for most, it means no children at all. And even for couples who are fertile, getting pregnant is not the easy matter that it is commonly thought to be. The average length of time taken to get pregnant is six months, although eighteen months is not uncommon. But unless fertility tests show otherwise, failure to conceive within eighteen months does not necessarily mean that you are completely infertile.

Fertility and the speed of conception depend on many factors, some psychological, some physical and some nutritional. Conception rate is very high during holiday periods, for example, since stress—a major factor in infertility—is reduced. Knowing how to time intercourse to coincide with ovulation (the release of the female egg to be fertilized by the sperm) greatly increases the chances of conception. Also, your nutrition and especially your vitamin status play a crucial role.

Vitamins for fertility

The male partner is responsible in about a third of infertility cases. (It should be stressed that infertility has nothing to do with sexual virility, which is usually not affected.) The usual test for infertility in a man involves a sperm count—the higher the sperm count, the greater the fertility. One study has shown that extra vitamin C increased sperm count as well as sperm mobility, but exactly why this is so is not yet known.[88] Likewise, vitamin E or essential fat deficiency has been found to induce sterility in both sexes by causing damage to the reproductive tissues. Unfortunately, however, simply taking vitamin E will not reverse the condition if you are sterile.

The high rate of infertility among diabetics may provide us with a clue. Diabetics are frequently low in vitamin A, which is essential for making the male sex hormones. Vitamin A is dependent on zinc being released from the liver. Of all the nutrients known to affect male fertility, zinc is perhaps the best researched. Signs of zinc deficiency include late sexual maturation, small sex organs, and infertility. With adequate supplements of zinc these problems can be corrected. Dr. Carl Pfeiffer also found a high degree of impotence and infertility in male patients who suffer from zinc deficiency. "With adequate dosage of vitamin B6 and zinc," he wrote, "the sexual ability of the male should return in one or two months' time." In view of the fact that the average dietary intake of zinc is half the RDA, the effects of zinc on fertility may be quite substantial and widespread. Zinc is found in high concentrations in male sex glands and in the sperm itself, where it is needed to make the outer layer and the tail.

PRE-CONCEPTUAL CARE

The best odds for a healthy offspring are achieved when both partners prepare for pregnancy. It takes three months for sperm to mature, while the egg or ovum takes a month. If, during these pre-conceptual months, each partner pursues optimum nutrition, minimizes his or her intake of anti-nutrients, especially alcohol, and stays healthy, the chances of a healthy conception are high, especially if the couple abstain from sex during the non-fertile phases of the month.

One in three conceptions are spontaneously aborted during the first three months of pregnancy. This risk is reduced when both partners are optimally nourished and healthy. A common cause of miscarriage is a lack of progesterone, which is needed to maintain the pregnancy in the early weeks. This can be a result of estrogen dominance (see Chapters 20 and 34).

VITAMINS FOR A HEALTHY PREGNANCY

Optimum nutrition can greatly improve your chances of having a healthy pregnancy. Even the slightest deficiencies during pregnancy can have serious effects on the health of the offspring, and the idea that birth defects are often cased by nutritional imbalances in the mother is rapidly gaining wider acceptance. So far, slight deficiencies of vitamins B1, B2, and B6, folic acid, zinc, iron, calcium, and magnesium have all been linked to birth abnormalities. So too have excesses of toxic metals, especially lead, cadmium, and copper. Severe deficiencies of any vitamin will cause birth abnormalities, since a vitamin is by definition necessary for maintaining normal growth. A healthy pregnancy will of course depend on a greater supply than normal of all these nutrients, since accommodating the needs of a growing fetus as well as her own put extra demands on the expectant mother.

As many as 5 percent of births show some developmental defect, many of which affect the central nervous system. Spina bifida, a condition in which the spinal chord does not develop properly, has been strongly linked to a lack of folic acid and probably of other nutrients too in the mother's diet. A survey of 23,000 women found that those who supplemented their diet during the first six weeks of pregnancy had a 75 percent lower incidence of neural tube defects than those who did not.[89] The incidence of this condition is far higher when mothers have had a nutritionally poor diet for the first three months of pregnancy. One study found that dietary counseling alone lowered the rate of spina bifida in those mothers at risk, but that the administration of extra folic acid, on its own or in a multivitamin, resulted in a much lower number of babies with neural tube defects. Since the recommended folic acid intake is 400 mcg per day and the average intake is between 109 and 203 mcg per day, a supplement of at least 300 mcg per day is recommended for women intending to become pregnant.

During the first three months of pregnancy all the organs of the baby's body are completely formed, so during this period optimum nutrition is extremely important. Yet many women experience continual sickness and do not feel like eating healthily. Misnamed "morning sickness," this condition has been accepted as normal during the first three months of pregnancy and is probably due to increases in a hormone called HCG. Women with poor diets are particularly at risk. During pregnancy the need for vitamins B6 and B12, folic acid, iron, and zinc all increase; supplements of these usually stop even the worst cases of pregnancy sickness. Eating small, frequent amounts of fruit or complex carbohydrates like nuts, seeds, or whole grains often helps. However, the best approach is to ensure optimum nutrition well before pregnancy. At ION we followed up four women on optimum programs before and during pregnancy—the average number of days on which nausea or sickness was reported was two. Yet for some women nausea continues throughout pregnancy!

Another common complication of pregnancy is pre-eclamptic toxemia, consisting of an increase in blood pressure, edema (swelling), and excessive protein in the urine. Many theories abound as to why this occurs, but once more optimum nutrition is a vital factor. One of my clients who had had pre-eclamptic toxemia during her first pregnancy improved her diet and added nutritional supplements: her second pregnancy was entirely healthy.

For the mother, optimum nutrition before and during pregnancy ensures a healthier pregnancy with fewer complications, resulting in a healthier and heavier baby. Your supplement program should include 200 mcg of folic acid, 20 mcg of vitamin B12, 200 mg of Vitamin B6, 15 mg of zinc, 500 mg of calcium, 250 mg of magnesium and 12 mg of iron. Do not take more than 10,000 IU of vitamin A, and have a hair mineral analysis carried out to check for excesses of copper, lead, or cadmium. My book *The Better Pregnancy Diet* goes into this subject in much more detail.

BOOSTERS AFTER BIRTH

Optimum nutrition is doubly important after birth, when the mother has to continue nourishing herself and her child. The stress of motherhood and sleepless nights, coupled with extra nutritional needs, often makes the first few months hard work. This is the time when an ideal diet plus supplements really pays off. Make sure you have good support and a good supply of easy-to-prepare nutritious foods, especially during the first few weeks.

Post-natal depression

It is not uncommon for mothers to experience depression immediately after the birth. No doubt there is a psychological component to consider: now you have a baby—a big responsibility. However, many researchers believe that this post-natal depression is brought on by hormonal and chemical changes which can be stopped with good nutrition.

One possibility is an excess of copper. The levels of copper tend to rise during pregnancy, while zinc levels tend to fall because the baby requires more. In most women the zinc content in breast milk declines rapidly as the infant uses up the mother's reserves. With a World Health Organization estimated requirement of 25 mg a day, and an average intake of 7.5 mg a day, yet no medical advice to increase zinc-rich foods or take supplements, zinc deficiency in mothers after giving birth is commonplace. Depression is a classic symptom, which can be corrected by supplementation with zinc and B6. According to Dr. Carl Pfeiffer, who helped establish the importance of zinc for brain function, "We have never seen post-natal depression or psychosis in any of our patients treated with zinc and B6."

THE IMPORTANCE OF BREAST-FEEDING

While breast-feeding does not guarantee optimum nutrition for the baby there is little doubt that breast is best, especially when the mother is optimally nourished. The balance of nutrients in breast milk in an optimally nourished woman is far superior to those in formula milks. One key factor is the high levels of essential fatty acids necessary for intellectual development. In fact, the discovery that breast-fed babies later achieved better intellectual performance than bottle-fed babies led to the realization of the importance of giving infants high levels of essential fatty acids.

One other great disadvantage of bottle-feeding is the milk itself. The consumption of cow's milk is strongly discouraged in infants before they are at least six months old. This is because their digestive and immune systems are too immature to deal with this complex protein—the result is often allergy. The recent discovery that insulin-dependent child-onset diabetes results from the immune system becoming allergic to a protein in cow's milk and beef, and then cross-reacting with a virtually identical protein in the pancreas, resulting in the destruction of pancreatic tissue, has led many pediatricians not only to caution against giving infants cow's milk before the age of six months, but also to advise mothers to keep off beef and milk for as long as they are breast-feeding. If this finding proves correct, a simple sacrifice could eliminate child-onset diabetes (see Chapter 8 for a fuller discussion).

Weaning—when and what?

Once a child can no longer sleep through the night without a feed, or is developing teeth, this is a good sign to wean them on to solid foods—usually when they are around six months old. Chewing on a piece of cucumber or carrot also helps to encourage other teeth to come through. Since the longest time between meals should be dinner to breakfast, introducing some solid food for dinner may help the child to sleep through the night.

Healthy babies, like healthy adults, need food that is fresh, unprocessed, additive-free, sugar-free (which includes sucrose, glucose, dextrose, maltose, and fructose), salt-free, and low in fat. In other words, they should be given food that is close to how it is found in nature. The baby will eventually be eating the food that you eat (which is, of course, completely healthy if you are following the recommendations in this book) and so will need to get used to eating this way right from the start. Below are a number of suggestions on how to eat healthily without using lots of packaged baby foods. To be fair, packaged baby foods are improving all the time; they no longer contain artificial additives, and some are sugar-free. However, the idea that a baby needs fiber or should not have sugar on his pureed roast beef dinner has not yet filtered through to all baby food manufacturers. As with adult food, if you are going to use the occasional prepared food read the label. If it contains cereal it should be wholemeal and unrefined; it should not contain any of the sugars listed above, modified starch, hydrogenated fat, hydrolyzed vegetable protein or any ingredient that you do not understand.

FIBER FOR BABIES

Some mothers will not give their baby a high-fiber diet as it "goes straight through them." What they often mean is they are getting three dirty diapers a day and cannot be bothered to change them that often. Frankly I would rather change three dirty diapers a day for a year or two than nurse an older person through the horrors of bowel cancer when your "baby" is grown up. As with an adult, a healthy infant bowel should be emptying itself two to three times a day. Much of the food will come out as recognizable lentils or grape skins, due to the fact that a baby cannot chew foods properly.

PREVENTING ALLERGIES

At the start of weaning, give your baby food that is very easily digested and unlikely to cause an allergic reaction. Cooked, pureed vegetables and fruit are a good start. If a fruit or vegetable can be given raw leave it like that— for example, bananas, avocados, very ripe William pears, or paw-paws. The later you introduce a food, the less likelihood there is of producing an allergic reaction. So if you suspect that your child may react allergically (if there is, for instance, a family history of allergy) or you just want to be absolutely certain that your child does not have any allergies, introduce potential allergens as late as you can. Below is a list of foods and food groups in increasing order of being likely to give an allergic reaction. So start by giving the foods at the top and, as each one is cleared, move down the list.

- Vegetables
- Fruit (except oranges)
- Nuts and seeds
- Legumes and beans
- Rice
- Meat
- Oats, barley, and rye
- Oranges
- Wheat
- Milk products
- Eggs

Introduce one or two foods on each day and make a note of which ones you have given and any possible reaction, which may be anything from mild to severe eczema, excessive sleepiness, a runny nose, colic, ear infection, excessive thirst, over-activity or asthmatic breathing. If you notice a reaction, withdraw that food and carry on with new foods once the reaction has died down. You can double-check your observations a few months later: the reaction may disappear as the digestive system matures. The last four foods should not be introduced until your baby is nine or ten months old; this also applies to any foods that either parent is known to have a reaction to.

BABY FOOD PUREES

Your newly weaned baby will still be getting plenty of nourishment from breast milk, and you may well find that you are breast-feeding as much as before. This is quite all right—in fact mothers should be encouraged to breast-feed a lot right up until the baby is a year old. Assuming your baby is getting most of his or her protein, fat, and carbohydrate from breast milk, you would do best to feed plenty of vitamin- and mineral-rich vegetables and fruit. Simply cook a combination of vegetables or fruit (there is no need to add sugar) and puree them. Here are some good combinations:

- Carrots alone
- Cauliflower and turnip
- Carrots, spinach, and cauliflower
- Broad beans and cauliflower or carrot, plus a very little celery
- Jerusalem artichokes and carrot
- Peeled zucchini (the skins can be bitter) and fennel
- Leek and potato
- Rutabaga, turnip, and potato

But do experiment. To save time and effort, not to mention disappointment when your baby rejects your lovingly prepared purees, you can freeze these mixtures. Start by using ice-cube trays for the tiniest amounts (you can also express breast milk and freeze it in sterilized ice-cube trays to mix with purees and make them taste more like what your baby is used to) and progress to small jars with lids.

You can slowly add other ingredients to these purees. Try red split lentils, cooked bean sprouts, well-cooked brown rice, black-eyed beans, and other legumes, milk, cheese, yogurt, or soy milk.

Breakfast can consist of more pureed vegetables—babies do not have to have sweet breakfast cereals or fruit, which only encourages a sweet tooth. As you introduce cereals into the diet more, you can cook brown rice flour as you would semolina and add pureed fruit for a lovely breakfast. An easier alternative is to pour some boiling water on to three teaspoons of fine oatmeal and leave it to stand for a few minutes. Pureed fruit, mashed banana, yogurt, or expressed breast or rice milk may be added. Millet flakes, which can be bought in health food shops, can be prepared in the same way as oatmeal. As the child gets older, porridge oats may be used in place of oatmeal, and the banana can be sliced instead of mashed.

33

SUPERKIDS—NOURISHING THE NEXT GENERATION

What you feed your child to a large extent determines their health and dietary habits for life. As a parent, the time spent nourishing your child properly may be the greatest contribution you can make to their development. In today's snack culture, in which children and adults are bombarded with advertisements for junk food, you have to be strong to help your child develop good eating habits. But it is worth it.

DEVELOPING GOOD HABITS

The taste for sugar is acquired through eating sweeter and sweeter foods. It can also be lost, usually with some resistance, by gradually reducing the level of sweetness in foods and drinks. This means replacing sweetened drinks with fruit juice, diluted half and half with water. Among the fruit juices apple contains the slowest-releasing sugars, while grape juice contains the fastest releasing ones. So apple juice is preferable. Few children drink enough water. You can encourage your child to drink water by putting it on the table at mealtimes, and when they are thirsty give them water for the first glass and diluted juice for the second.

Do not give sweets, sweetened foods, cola, and other sweetened drinks as treats. If you do, these drinks become associated with something good. Later in life your offspring may choose to treat themselves all the time. Instead give fresh orange or pineapple juice, diluted with fizzy water. Cola drinks are especially bad because most contain caffeine, an addictive drug. It is quite amazing, given that you have to be an adult to smoke and drink alcohol, that caffeine can be freely added to drinks advertised to children who cannot even read.

Very few breakfast cereals are truly sugar-free. Food manufacturers help children to develop a sweet tooth at an early age: most processed cereals contain fast-releasing sugars and have added sugar. Instead, give your children a choice of oats, sugar-free cornflakes or millet flakes, and encourage them to sweeten their cereal with fruit such as a sliced banana, apple or pear, some berries, or perhaps a few raisins.

The best snacks are fruit, so make sure you always have a mountain of fresh, appealing fruit for them to nibble on at their discretion. Send them to school with fruit rather than money to buy sweets.

Sure, when they are older and have pocket money they will buy sweets and get them at parties. But if sweets, sweetened drinks and foods are not part of their day-to-day diet they are unlikely to crave sweets or develop an addiction.

Another good habit to develop in your children is eating vegetables with each meal and offering something raw. The trick here is to find ways of preparing vegetables so that they taste good. Too many vegetables are cooked to death and taste bland. Raw organic carrots, peas, parsnip chips (made by steam-frying in diluted soy sauce), mashed, and baked potatoes are naturally quite sweet and favorites with children. Serving something raw with each meal, even if it is just a few leaves of watercress, grated red cabbage, tomato, or carrot, develops the taste for salad foods.

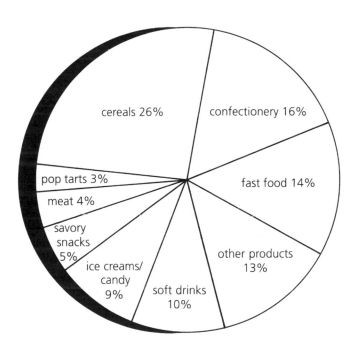

**Sugar and spice and all things nice—
that's what children's diets are made of**

While there are many ways of making healthy desserts, if a child always ends a meal this way they acquire a habit for life. Instead, restrict healthy desserts as a treat and give the child as much of the main course as he or she wants. If my children are still hungry they help themselves to fruit.

ALLERGIES START YOUNG

Children are like the canaries once used to check whether coal mines were safe from poisonous gases: they are very sensitive and react readily to substances. This is the first stage of the stress response (see p. 156). By paying attention you can find out what does not suit your child. Many children react adversely to food additives, sugar, dairy products, peanuts, wheat, detergents, dust, or exhaust fumes. Some react to eggs, oranges, and other gluten grains like oats. Watch out for the following symptoms:

Face: Rings around the eyes, "black" eyes, facial puffiness, constant sniffling, frequent colds, excessive mucus production, frequent earache, tonsillitis
Skin: Itches, rashes, eczema, puffiness, or water retention
Digestive: Colic, vomiting, diarrhea, stomach ache, flatulence
Mental: Hyperactivity, poor concentration, being over-emotional, sleeplessness, bed-wetting
Respiratory: Coughing, frequent sore throats, swollen tongue or throat, asthma, respiratory infections

All these are the classic signs of allergy. The good news is that children rapidly respond once the offending substances are removed. Try removing suspected foods or environmental allergens for ten days and see if the child improves. If the allergic reactions are severe it is best to carry out what is known as an elimination/challenge investigation under the supervision of a qualified health professional. Also make sure that the child's diet is not becoming too restrictive.

Optimum nutrition, plus judicious use of supplements, can greatly decrease potential to allergies provided the offending items are removed. Often, after a couple of months, a child can tolerate a food that previously offended, perhaps eating it only every four days to prevent the body from "remembering" the food and learning to react allergically again.

FOOD FOR THOUGHT

There is no question that optimum nutrition improves your child's ability to learn and perform at school. All properly designed studies have shown that mental performance increases when children are given multivitamin and mineral supplements (see Chapter 23). Also vital for intellectual development are essential fatty acids. Research by Professor Crawford and colleagues has shown that essential fatty acid levels in infants correlates with their intellectual performance as children. Essential fats not only make prostaglandins, hormone-like substances that affect brain function, but are also vital for the membranes of nerve cells. Following the successful results of trials in which essential fats were given to children with dyslexia and attention deficit disorder, a theory is emerging that children prone to these problems may have slightly defective membranes due to a combination of heredity and essential fatty acid deficiency.

There is no harm in giving children plenty of food sources of essential fats, such as seeds, nuts, and their oils. The best are sesame, sunflower, pumpkin, and flax seeds, almonds, walnuts, and pecans. (Peanuts and olive oil are not a source of essential fats.) Unfortunately, many weight-conscious adults leave these foods out of meal planning at the expense of their children. The best way to increase your children's intake of essential fats is to put ground seeds on cereals and in soups, to use a cold-pressed oil or oil blend instead of butter on vegetables and baked potatoes, and to encourage them to snack on nuts and sunflower seeds. Seeds can also be added to home-made cakes, bread, and rolls, but on the whole they are best eaten raw as the heat of cooking damages the essential fats.

CHILDREN WITH PROBLEMS

More and more children are being diagnosed with dyslexia, attention deficit disorder or hyperactivity, and delinquency. In some the problems are mild, but most schools have a few children with major problems who disrupt the learning environment for others. More often than not, the children in question have one of more of the following nutritional imbalances:

• sugar imbalance
• deficiency of vitamins or minerals, often zinc and B6 or niacin
• deficiency of essential fatty acids
• allergies

Once these factors have been identified and corrected, most children become manageable. But if these factors are not corrected, the hyperactive six-year-old might grow up to become a delinquent sixteen-year-old. The girl whose handwriting is shown on the next page had been in care since the age of ten, and had a history of assault, burglary, severe depression and solvent abuse. Within three weeks of going on a low-sugar diet plus supplements she had freed herself of drugs, was no longer depressed, was enjoying increased energy, and said she had never felt so relaxed.

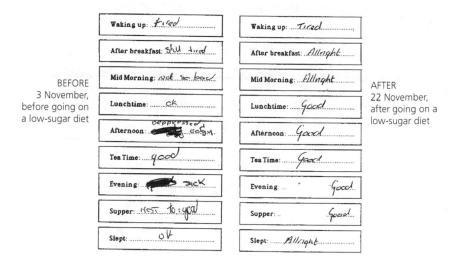

Handwriting and mood—before and after sugar

Sadly, many hyperactive children are not treated nutritionally but are put on drugs such as Ritalin. In a survey of the results of treatment, Professor Bernard Rimland from California found that one child in two got worse on Ritalin, while eighteen children in every nineteen treated got better with nutritional treatment.

SUPPLEMENTS FOR CHILDREN

Once a child is off the breast and on to food it is time to supplement his or her diet. The best way to do this is to find a good chewable multivitamin and mineral formula designed for children. Check that it is not sweetened with sugar, using fruit extracts or a small amount of fructose to disguise the taste of the vitamins. Children need all the nutrients that adults do, especially vitamin A to build up strong membranes capable of resisting infection; vitamin D to aid calcium absorption; vitamins B and C for brain development; zinc to assist growth; plus chromium, selenium, magnesium, and manganese. Check that these are all present in reasonable amounts, especially zinc. Zinc can also be given as drops, or supplemented, together with calcium, magnesium, and essential fats, by adding ground seeds to your child's diet. The table below gives optimal supplemental intakes of vitamins and minerals, assuming a reasonable diet.

Optimum Nutrient Amounts to Supplement from the Age of One to Thirteen

Vitamins	Less than 1	Age 1	2	3–4	5–6	7–8	9–11	12–13	
A (retinol and beta-carotene)	2,500	2,800	3,200	3,600	4,000	4,400	4,800	5,500	IUs
(in mcgRE)	750	840	970	1,080	1,200	1,320	1,440	1,650	mcg
D	200	200	200	200	200	200	200	300	IUs
E	10	15	20	30	40	50	60	70	IUs
C	100	175	250	325	400	475	550	625	mg
B1 (thiamine)	3	4	5	6	8	12	16	20	mg
B2 (riboflavin)	3	4	5	6	8	12	16	20	mg
B3 (niacin)	7	8	9	10	15	20	25	35	mg
B5 (pantothenic acid)	7	8	9	10	15	20	25	35	mg
B6 (pyridoxine)	7	8	9	10	15	20	25	35	mg
B12	3	4	5	6	7	8	9	10	mcg
Folic acid	50	55	60	65	70	80	90	100	mcg
Biotin	20	25	30	35	40	45	50	55	mcg
Minerals									
Calcium	150	150	150	150	150	150	150	150	mg
Magnesium	25	35	45	55	65	75	85	95	mg
Iron	2	2	3	4	5	6	7	8	mg
Zinc	3	4	5	6	7	8	10	12	mg
Manganese	0.7	1	1.3	1.5	1.7	1.8	1.9	2	mg
Chromium	10	12.5	15	17.5	20	22.5	25	30	mcg
Selenium	7	8	10	12	14	16	18	20	mcg

Reproduced with the kind permission of Natural Justice

Data is sparse on children's optimal requirements, so if you achieve within 20 percent of these values for your child this is likely to be sufficient. Few supplements provide enough calcium and magnesium. These are abundant in seeds (best ground for young children), which are also a source of essential fatty acids.

For very young children chewing is difficult or dangerous, so crush their chewable vitamins and sprinkle them on their food. My favorite chewables are those designed so that the child takes one for every two years of life. Assuming that they like the taste (and there are some great-tasting multivitamins), this can set a child up until he or she is twelve, when it is time to switch to adult supplements that require swallowing.

34

PUBERTY, PMS, AND MENOPAUSE

The transition from child to adult is no less easy biologically than psychologically. At puberty the body undergoes rapid changes focused on sexual development that require optimal nutrition to avoid "side effects." These include acne and obesity, eating, mental, and behavioral problems. These are common indications that the person is not adapting as well as possible to the changes.

Both girls and boys need relatively more vitamins A, D, and B6, biotin, zinc, calcium, magnesium, and essential fatty acids during puberty. In assessing nutritional needs (p. 216) these nutrients are upped between the ages of fourteen and sixteen. Once a child reaches fourteen his or her nutritional needs are essentially the same as those of adults, with a greater emphasis on these nutrients, plus an ongoing need for adequate protein because adolescents are still growing.

Of these nutrients, zinc and magnesium are most often found to be lacking. Zinc is needed for sexual maturation by both sexes but boys need more. The relative decline in the growth rate of boys during adolescence is probably partly due to sub-optimal intake of zinc—what zinc they do have is taken for sexual maturation in preference to growth. Growth problems, "growing pains" and acne are all possible indications of a lack of zinc.

Teenage years are also associated with increasing "food freedom" and it is important that teenagers learn to nourish themselves. If they are not given nutrition education from school or their parents they opt for food that tastes good, rather than food which does them good. The link between food, good skin, and physical and mental strength needs to be emphasized, since these are all desired qualities. The key habits to encourage are:

- eating seeds, perhaps a tablespoon of ground seeds on cereal. These are very rich in zinc, magnesium, and essential fatty acids.

- eating fruit in preference to sweets and fatty, sugary snacks

- always having some vegetables with a meal. Most schools have no idea how to make vegetables enticing and teenagers often develop an aversion to them during their school years

- eating real meals rather than refueling on the move

BEATING PMS THROUGH DIET

Pre-menstrual problems were, until relatively recently, accepted as a woman's lot. Yet these symptoms—which include depression, tension, headaches, breast tenderness, water retention, bloating, low energy, and irritability—are in most cases avoidable. Classically, they occur in the week preceding menstruation, though a small percentage of women have the symptoms from the middle of the cycle, coinciding with ovulation. Since pre-menstrual problems are a result of hormonal changes, hormone treatment has been used to correct them. But the use of such drug treatment must be seriously questioned, as it disrupts the body's chemistry and has been associated with increased risk of cancer.

The effectiveness of vitamin B6 has been proved in some studies to help 70 percent of pre-menstrual sufferers.[90] But researchers soon found that B6 with zinc, which is needed to convert B6 into its active form, was more effective. Dr. Guy Abrahams then discovered that magnesium was especially effective at reducing the symptom of breast tenderness and swelling.[91] More recently, research has focused on the role of GLA (gamma linolenic acid), an essential fatty acid found in evening primrose and borage oils. GLA's 60 percent success rate is almost certainly due to its role in making prostaglandins.[92] We now know that vitamin B6, zinc, and magnesium are also required to make prostaglandins and, perhaps for this reason, have been shown to help PMT sufferers.

These nutrients alone can easily halve symptoms, as we found out in a trial at ION. In this trial of PMT sufferers, in which both clients and their doctors rated their improvement, for each pre-menstrual health problem there was a substantial improvement of 55–85 percent. On average, within three months a woman on a supplement program of this kind could expect a 66 percent improvement in each problem.

In some kinds of PMS, hormonal changes disturb blood sugar control and bring on sugar and stimulant changes, as well as symptoms of tiredness and irritation. Following a strict no-sugar, no-stimulant diet, while eating complex carbohydrates or fruit, little and often, can make all the difference. Diet, coupled with supplements, can often relieve symptoms of PMS all together.

In a small percentage of women, PMS indicates a more pronounced hormonal imbalance that cannot be corrected by diet and supplements alone. Such an imbalance is usually due to estrogen dominance (see p. 132) and a relative lack of progesterone. This condition can be brought on by a period of time on the birth control pill and needs testing and correcting by a qualified nutrition consultant or doctor.

THE PROS AND CONS OF CONTRACEPTION

As a source of contraception, the pill has too many health drawbacks. In my opinion the best method of contraception for any couple is knowing when ovulation occurs through observing temperature and vaginal mucus changes (for more details read the book *Natural Family Planning*[93]). Once a woman is in tune with her cycle she will very often have feelings and sensations that mark ovulation, and test kits can also now be bought. Once the time of ovulation is known, there is no chance of conception from three days after ovulation until seven days before the next ovulation. That is half the cycle dealt with. At other times non–invasive barrier methods such as condoms or caps, or even abstinence, can be practiced.

The Chinese say that too much sex depletes vital energy, particularly in a man. We know that a man can lose up to 3 mg of zinc per ejaculation. With an average daily intake of only 7.5 mg, a man having sex three times a day has certainly blown it as far as zinc is concerned.

The only trouble with using ovulation times as a means of contraception is that sub–optimum nutrition often leads to irregular periods. Also, if there is an underlying hormone imbalance such as estrogen dominance, it may take a while to establish a regular, healthy cycle. In such cases it is especially important to avoid synthetic hormones, which are more often than not the cause of the imbalance in the first place.

BEATING MENOPAUSE

The menopause is a natural transition from the child-bearing phase of life for a woman. It occurs most often between the ages of forty-five and fifty, sometimes without any unpleasant symptoms and sometimes with a whole host of them, the most common being hot flushes, night sweats, vaginal dryness, tiredness, headaches, irritability, depression, and joint pains. These may occur for just a few months or for as long as eighteen months. More insidious is the increased risk of brittle bones or of osteoporosis.

There is increasing evidence that optimum nutrition can alleviate many of these symptoms and shorten their duration. Factors that have been shown to help are correcting underlying blood sugar imbalances or allergies, and supplementation with vitamin E, B complex, calcium, magnesium, and zinc. Essential fatty acids such as evening primrose oil may also be of help. One study at ION found that the addition of vitamin E relieved symptoms.[94] A later trial found even better results using a combination of calcium, magnesium, and vitamins D and E.[95] In this study there was a 62.7 percent reduction in reported symptoms in a group of nineteen women over a twelve-week period. While improved diet may help, diet plus supplements seems to be most effective.

Synthetic or natural HRT?

The conventional view is that menopausal symptoms are brought about by a lack of estrogen. There is little doubt that the cessation of menstruation is due to declining levels of estrogen, which are needed to trigger ovulation. For this reason estrogen HRT is given. However, as soon as a woman starts having cycles without ovulation, often many years before her periods stop, no progesterone is produced (this is because the progesterone is produced in the sac that is left after the ovum is released). While oestrogen levels decline—they do not stop—progesterone production drops to zero. The continued relative excess of estrogen to progesterone, coupled with progesterone deficiency, may prove to be the major cause of menopausal symptoms.

Both estrogen HRT and natural progesterone augmentation (given as a small amount of skin cream twice a day) can stop symptoms. However, conventional HRT suits few women and 70 percent stop within a year of starting it, usually due to unpleasant symptoms or a lack of results. While estrogen or synthetic progestin HRT are associated with an increased risk of breast cancer, natural progesterone is anti-cancer (see p. 174) and four times more effective at reversing osteoporosis (see p. 135). It is best to get professional advice, including tests, to correct hormone imbalances. However, the combination of diet, supplements, and, when needed, small amounts of natural progesterone can transform a woman's experience of the menopause.

THE MALE MENOPAUSE

Men too can suffer from menopausal symptoms later in life. The symptoms of the male menopause, known as the andropause, are very similar to those of the female menopause—fatigue, depression, irritability, rapid aging, aches and pains, sweating, flushing, and decreased sexual performance.

Having successfully treated thousands of ailing men, Dr. Malcolm Carruthers is convinced that the andropause is real and connected to decreasing levels of free testosterone, the male sex hormone (see p. 133). Exactly why free testosterone levels decline is a bit of a mystery; however, a number of contributors may be involved. These include stress, too much alcohol, and overheating of the testes. More insidious, however, are the effects of increasing xeno-estrogens, chemicals in the environment with actions similar to those of the female hormone estrogen, which have recently been found to be anti-androgenic, blocking the action of testosterone.

Xeno-estrogens are found in everything from pesticides to plastic. "Perhaps future generations of archaeologists," says Carruthers, "will come across a thick strata of plastic bags, marking the demise of *homo plasticus* or 'plastic bag man' who was neutered by the by-products of the consumer society." According to recent research the pesticide DDT breaks down into a substance (DDE) which has little estrogenic activity, but fifteen times the anti-androgen effect of DDT. Residues of these chemicals, long since banned, are still found in the food chain. To what extent the average intake of pesticide residues is contributing to decreasing levels of testosterone is unknown.

Testosterone is made in the body from cholesterol. Very low-cholesterol diets can lower testosterone levels, but antioxidant nutrients such as vitamin E help to protect valuable cholesterol from being damaged. Testosterone can also be made from DHEA, a natural hormone produced by the adrenal glands, which is available over the counter in the U.S. For those suspected of suffering from the andropause, I recommend following the general optimum nutrition principles in this book, testing for testosterone deficiency and only then, if necessary, correcting with testosterone implants or creams.

35

PREVENTING THE PROBLEMS OF OLD AGE

The best way to stay healthy in old age is to prevent disease before it starts. Many animals, after all, stay healthy throughout their lives. In the Western world it is not even legal to die of old age: death certificates require a cause, a disease. I firmly believe that it is possible to lead an active life without years of poor health and unnecessary suffering. Certainly three of the "grand-fathers" of optimum nutrition, Linus Pauling, Roger Williams, and Carl Pfeiffer, all lived to a ripe old age.

The trick, of course, is to prevent cancer and heart disease by following the advice in Chapters 18 and 27. Both Pauling and Pfeiffer were convinced that, through optimum nutrition, you could add at least ten years of healthy living. Williams said, "Well-rounded nutrition, including generous amounts of vitamins C and E, can contribute materially to extending life span of those who are already middle-aged. The greatest hope of increasing life span can be offered if nutrition—from the time of prenatal development to old age—is continuously of the highest quality." Pfeiffer took 10 grams of vitamin C a day towards the end of his life, while Pauling took 16 grams. There is certainly a good case for taking a gram of vitamin C (1,000 mg) and 100 IUs of vitamin E (67 mg) for every decade of life. So an eighty-year-old may benefit most from 8 grams of vitamin C and 800 IUs of vitamin E.

While optimum nutrition is most critical in old age, this is the time when deficiency of nutrients is most common. Research by Dr. Jacob Selhub at the USDA Human Nutrition Center at Tufts University found 60% of seniors were deficient in folic acid (Selhub J. et al. JAMA. 1993; 270: 2693-2726). A survey of geriatric hospital patients found 44 percent deficient in vitamins B1, B2, and B6 (Morgan A. Int J Vit Nut Re. 1975, 4:448-62), 57% had low levels of vitamin D (New England Journal of Medicine 1998, 338; 777-83) and up to a third of elderly people may be deficient in B12—possibly due to an inability to absorb B12 as opposed to a deficient diet (Jnl of the Am Ger Soc 1997; 45). One reason for B12 deficiency is a poor production of stomach acid, needed for its absorption.

IMPROVING DIGESTION AND ABSORPTION

The production of stomach acid and enzymes often declines with age. Stomach acid production depends on zinc, so it is important to ensure that your zinc intake is important. A lack of zinc also reduces people's sense of taste and smell, leading to a liking for salt, sauces, and strong-tasting food like cheese and meat. Zinc-deficient people often go off fruit and vegetables. Improving zinc nutrition, rather than overcooking vegetables and adding lots of strongly flavored sauces, can improve your health considerably, including relieving constipation.

The lack of stomach acid and enzymes also leads to poor absorption of nutrients from food into the body. If you have digestive problems or are sixty-plus, to assist nutrient absorption it is worth trying a digestive enzyme supplement containing a small amount of betaine hydrochloride (stomach acid). This can improve the effectiveness of vitamin and mineral supplements. It is also worth paying a little extra for the most easily absorbed mineral formulas (see Chapter 40).

COMBATING ARTHRITIS, ACHES, AND PAINS

One of the greatest causes of suffering in old age is aching joints and arthritis. One is often led to believe there is nothing that can be done except to take painkillers, which more often than not speed up the progression of the disease. This is completely untrue. There are many proven ways to reduce pain and inflammation without drugs, outlined in Chapter 21 and discussed fully in my book *Say No to Arthritis*, even when degeneration is severe. One of my clients in her eighties had no more leg pain and a 50 percent reduction in back pain after six weeks on optimum nutrition.

Key strategies for reducing pain and inflammation are:

- identifying and avoiding allergens
- supplementing essential fatty acids (e.g. 300 mg a day of GLA plus fish oils)
- supplementing niacin (up to 500 mg a day) and pantothenic acid (500 mg a day)
- supplementing antioxidants, including curcumin, a natural anti-inflammatory agent found in turmeric and mustard
- supplementing and/or applying as a cream boswellia, another anti-inflammatory agent without side-effects
- good, all round optimum nutrition

Sometimes aches and pains occur in the muscles and not the joints. This is not arthritis and may be due to one of two conditions. The first is fibromyalgia, which is characterized by a number of tender points in specific muscles. This is now thought to be due to a problem in the energy metabolism of the muscle cells, and not inflammation. Anti-inflammatory agents may therefore not help, although painkillers can suppress the symptoms. A particular form of magnesium, magnesium malate, is proving very effective at relieving fibromyalgia, together with a supportive diet plus supplements. Stress, which uses up magnesium, makes this condition worse.

Polymyalgia, characterized by early morning stiffness, often in the shoulders and hips, is more often brought on when the body's detoxification systems are overloaded. This means that the liver, kidneys, brain, and all the cells, including muscle cells, cannot deal with the garbage produced by digestion and daily living. Different systems of the body can be affected. Some people experience chronic fatigue, others body aches as in polymyalgia. Yet others find that their nervous system is affected, bringing on premature senility or multiple sclerosis type symptoms, or else the immune system starts misbehaving, resulting in infections, allergies, inflammation, and auto-immune diseases like rheumatoid arthritis. Polymyalgia, being an inflammatory condition,

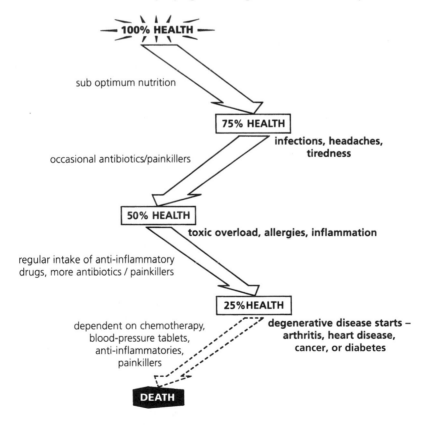

The drug dilemma

usually responds to antioxidant supplementation and liver detoxification. The conventional treatment is the drug prednisolone.

AVOIDING THE DRUG CYCLE

Most people in this scenario end up on the drug cycle, perhaps starting with painkillers or steroids, then moving on to antibiotics when infections set in. The drugs treat the symptom but not the cause—in fact they usually aggravate the cause by irritating the stomach and making the intestinal wall more leaky, which is what non-steroidal anti-inflammatory drugs and antibiotics do. This means that more garbage gets into the body, further overloading detoxification pathways. Many drugs, such as paracetamol, are toxins in their own right and severely tax the liver. The result is ever-increasing overload on body systems, attracting more serious diseases and infections.

PREVENTING PREMATURE SENILITY AND ALZHEIMER'S

I am convinced that toxic overload is often one of the underlying causes of premature senility and perhaps Alzheimer's too, as the brain and nervous system cannot detoxify and start to accumulate toxins. Low levels of antioxidants and high levels of heavy metals, especially aluminum, are associated with premature senility. So too are blockages in the blood vessels that supply the brain with fuel and food. Antioxidants such as vitamins C and E help the body to use oxygen, as well as helping to prevent and reverse arterial blockage.

TREAT THE CAUSE AND NOT THE SYMPTOM

The way out is to treat the cause and not the symptom, as well as ensuring optimum brain nutrition including the smart nutrients discussed in Chapter 23 which help to maximize memory.

A combination of poor diet, alcohol, drugs, and infections often leads to problems in later life. Thanks to recent biochemical advances it is now possible, through simple urine tests, to discover whether the sensitive balance of beneficial bacteria in the stomach has been disrupted (known as dysbiosis), also to what extent the stomach wall has become permeable, which is a primary underlying cause of toxic overload, and in addition exactly which pathways in the liver are overloaded. Each pathway depends on a sequence of enzymes, themselves dependent on nutrients. A nutrition consultant can then devise a specific diet and supplement program using specific vitamins, minerals, amino acids, and fatty acids designed to decrease the toxic load on the body and restore the body's detoxification potential. The results are often spectacular.

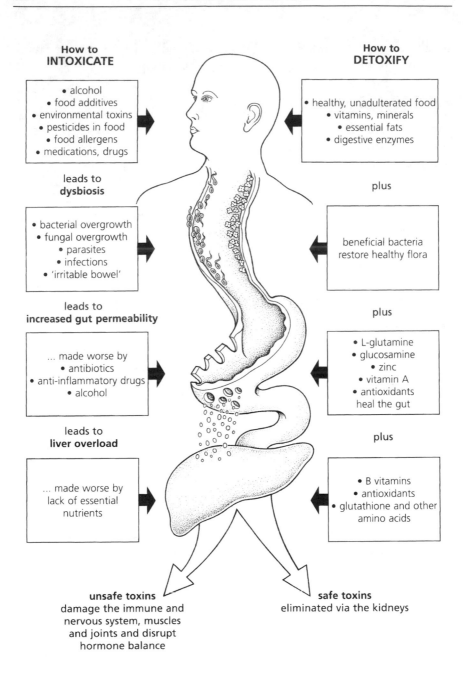

How to
INTOXICATE

- alcohol
- food additives
- environmental toxins
- pesticides in food
- food allergens
- medications, drugs

leads to
dysbiosis

- bacterial overgrowth
- fungal overgrowth
- parasites
- infections
- 'irritable bowel'

leads to
increased gut permeability

... made worse by
- antibiotics
- anti-inflammatory drugs
- alcohol

leads to
liver overload

... made worse by
lack of essential
nutrients

How to
DETOXIFY

- healthy, unadulterated food
- vitamins, minerals
- essential fats
- digestive enzymes

plus

beneficial bacteria
restore healthy flora

plus

- L-glutamine
- glucosamine
- zinc
- vitamin A
- antioxidants
heal the gut

plus

- B vitamins
- antioxidants
- glutathione and other
amino acids

unsafe toxins
damage the immune and
nervous system, muscles
and joints and disrupt
hormone balance

safe toxins
eliminated via the kidneys

How to intoxicate and detoxify the body

36

WORKING OUT YOUR OPTIMUM NUTRITION

How healthy do you want to be? If you want to realize your full potential, mentally and physically, finding out your optimum nutritional requirements is essential. But if your needs are unique, how do you find these out? Since 1980 I have been developing and refining a precise system for analyzing people's nutrient needs, based on assessing the major factors that influence individual requirements. This system is now used by qualified nutritionists all over the world.

More than twenty thousand people have benefited from this system, so I know what sort of results to expect. They include

- greater mental alertness
- improved memory
- more physical energy
- better weight control
- reduced risk of degenerative disease.

Although many people with diagnosed illnesses have been helped while on a personal health program, it is not designed to treat illness so much as to prevent it. **If you suffer from a recognized medical condition, please check that this program is compatible with any treatment you may already be receiving.**

Chapters 36 and 37 present a simplified version of that system, based on the Optimum Nutrition Questionnaire. It provides a useful assessment of what you need for optimum health and is a good place to start. It is not, however, the same as having a personal assessment of your nutritional needs carried out by a nutrition consultant. This is, of course, highly preferable— and essential for anyone who is currently unwell or suffering from a diagnosed disease. Details of how to find a qualified nutrition consultant are given under Useful Addresses on p. 339.

FACTORS THAT AFFECT YOUR NUTRITIONAL NEEDS

At least eight factors affect your optimum nutritional requirements. Age, sex, and amount of exercise are easily covered. But the effects of pollution, stress, your past health history, your genetic legacy, and, of course, the nutrients (and anti-nutrients) supplied in your diet are not so straightforward to work out. But all these details and more must be taken into account. There are four basic ways to go about it:

- diet analysis
- biochemical analysis
- symptom analysis
- lifestyle analysis

DIET ANALYSIS

This may seem the obvious place to start: finding out what goes in should reveal what is missing. But unfortunately a breakdown of foods eaten over, say, a week, cannot take into account the variations in nutrient content in the food, your individual needs, nor how well the nutrient is used when, and if, it is absorbed. I have seen many people who had superficially "perfect" diets, but still showed signs of vitamin deficiency. For a high proportion of them the problem was poor absorption. These variables make some diet analysis carried out on a computer less useful than might be expected.

Where diet analysis comes in useful is in assessing foods that are known to affect our nutrient needs, such as sugar, salt, coffee, tea, alcohol, food additives, and preservatives. Other factors, such as intake of fats, carbohydrates, protein, and calories, can also be determined from an analysis of your diet.

BIOCHEMICAL ANALYSIS

Tests such as hair mineral analysis or vitamin blood tests give indisputable information about your biochemical status and help a nutrition consultant to know the actual nutritional state of your body. But not all these tests provide useful information to help you build up your nutrition program.

To be accurate, any vitamin or mineral test must reflect the ability of the nutrient to function in the body. For example, iron is a vital constituent of red blood cells; it helps to carry oxygen throughout the body. By measuring the iron status in your cells it is possible to get a good measure of your iron needs. On the other hand, vitamin B6 has no similar direct function to perform in the blood—it is used in other chemical reactions, for example, the production of the brain chemical serotonin, which helps us go to sleep.

So a measure of the B6 level in your blood would tell you nothing. In fact, if B6 is not being used properly in other parts of the body blood levels may be high even though a state of deficiency exists elsewhere. So for vitamin B6 a clever method called a functional enzyme test has been devised. Tryptophan, a constituent of protein, is acted upon by enzymes, which turn it into nicotinic acid (vitamin B3) in the body. One of these enzymes is dependent on vitamin B6. So if you do not have enough B6, instead of making B3 you end up with a by-product, xanthurenic acid, which is excreted in the urine. By measuring the amount of xanthurenic acid excreted, it is possible to gauge whether you are getting enough B6 and if it is being used properly. This is just one of a number of tests now being used to determine vitamin B6 status.

Because each nutrient has a different function in the body, we cannot say that blood tests are better than urine tests, or that analysis of mineral levels in the hair provides more accurate information than blood levels. For each nutrient there are different test, depending on what we want to find out. For instance, for zinc deficiency there are over a dozen tests which involve blood, urine, hair, sweat, and even taste.

To make an extensive series of tests would be expensive. My number one value-for-money test is hair mineral analysis, which reveals a person's mineral status. From a small sample of hair the levels of calcium, magnesium, zinc, chromium, selenium, and manganese can be discovered, although the results need careful interpretation. Hair mineral analysis also provides useful information about lead, cadmium, arsenic, aluminum, and copper, all of which are toxic in excess. Hair mineral analysis can sometimes pinpoint problems of absorption, or reasons for high blood pressure or frequent infections.

To find out vitamin status I use a series of functional enzyme tests, which are more expensive than hair mineral analysis. However, the results of these enzyme tests usually confirm findings already made from deficiency symptom analysis. I mainly use these for fine-tuning, or when there is some doubt about the results of a previous test.

SYMPTOM ANALYSIS

Deficiency symptom analysis is the most underestimated method of working out nutritional needs. It is based on over two hundred signs and symptoms that have been found in cases of slight vitamin or mineral deficiency. For example, mouth ulcers are associated with vitamin A deficiency, muscle cramps with magnesium deficiency. For many of these symptoms, the mechanism is understood. For example, magnesium is required for muscles to relax. Symptoms such as these can be early warning signs of deficiency which show us that our bodies are not working perfectly. However, while deficiency in vitamins C, B3, or B5 would all result in reduced energy because they are involved in the energy production, being low in energy does not necessarily mean that you are deficient. Perhaps you are just working too hard or sleeping badly. However, if you have a cluster of symptoms, all associated with B3 deficiency, you are much more likely to be in need of more vitamin B3 to reach optimum health.

The advantage of deficiency symptom analysis is that health is being measured directly. Results are not dependent on whether you eat oranges that are high in vitamin C, or whether you absorb and utilize food well, as dietary analysis is. Some people have criticized this method because it relies on subjective information from the person concerned—yet the large majority of medical diagnoses are based on subjective information from the patient. If you want to find out how someone feels, isn't it obvious to ask? I always ask my clients why *they* think they are ill. More often than not they are right.

Lifestyle analysis

These three methods of analysis, if properly applied, should define what you need right now to be optimally nourished. But it is good to check that your needs for your particular lifestyle are adequately covered. For example, if you smoke and drink alcohol frequently your nutritional needs will be higher. If you are pregnant, if you live in a city, if you have a high-stress occupation, if you suffer from allergies—all of these factors may alter your ideal needs.

Lifestyle analysis is the fourth piece of the jigsaw puzzle that helps a nutritionist know what you need. The next two chapters tell you how to analyze your diet, your symptoms of deficiency, and your lifestyle in order to work out your own Personal Health Program.

37

YOUR OPTIMUM DIET

Before foods can give us vitality, hundreds of chemical reactions must take place involving twenty-eight vitamins and minerals. These micro-nutrients are the real keys that unlock the potential energy in our food.

Your vitality depends upon a careful balance of at least fifty nutrients. They include sources of energy or calories which may come from carbohydrates, fats, or proteins; thirteen known vitamins, fifteen minerals, twenty-four amino acids (which we get when proteins are digested), and two essential fatty acids. Even though the requirement for some minerals, like selenium, is less than a millionth of our requirement for protein, it is no less important. In fact, one-third of *all* chemical reactions in our bodies are dependent on tiny quantities of minerals, and even more on vitamins. Without any one of these nutrients, vitality, energy, and ideal weight are just not possible.

Fortunately, deficiency in protein, fat, or carbohydrate is very rare. Unfortunately, deficiency in vitamins, minerals, and essential fats is not, despite popular belief. Many nutritionists believe that as few as one in ten people receive sufficient vitamins, minerals, and essential fats from their diet for optimum health.

As much as two-thirds of the average calorie intake consists of fat, sugar, and refined flours. The calories in sugar are called "empty" because they provide no nutrients, and they are often hidden in processed foods and snacks. If a quarter of your diet by weight, and two-thirds by calories, consists of such dismembered foods, there is little room left to get the levels you need of all the essential nutrients.

Wheat has twenty-five nutrients removed in the refining process that turns it into white flour, yet only four (iron and vitamins B1, B2, and B3) are replaced. On average, 87 percent of the vital minerals zinc, chromium, and manganese are lost. Processed meats like hamburgers and sausages are no better: the use of inferior meat high in fat lowers the nutrient content. Eggs, fish, and chicken are nutrient-rich sources of protein, but protein deficiency is rarely a problem.

Vegetables, fruits, nuts, seeds, beans, and grains are full of vitality, being whole foods. Many are "seed" foods, so they have to contain everything that the plant needs to grow, including zinc. Broccoli, carrots, peas, and sweet potatoes are rich in antioxidants. Peppers, broccoli, and fruit are rich in vitamin C and other phytonutrients. Seeds and nuts are rich in essential fats. Beans and grains provide both protein and complex carbohydrate. Foods such as these should make up at least half, if not all, of your diet.

CHECK OUT YOUR DIET

Many people would like to believe that as long as they take their vitamin supplements they can keep eating all the "bad" foods that they love. But you cannot rely on diet, supplements, or exercise alone to keep you healthy. All three are essential.

DIET CHECK QUESTIONNAIRE

Score one point for each "yes" answer. The maximum score is 20 and the minimum score is 0.

- [ ] Do you add sugar to food or drink almost every day?
- [ ] Do you eat foods with added sugar almost every day (read the labels carefully)?
- [ ] Do you use salt in your food?
- [ ] Do you drink more than one cup of coffee most days?
- [ ] Do you drink more than three cups of tea most days?
- [ ] Do you smoke more than five cigarettes a week?
- [ ] Do you take recreational drugs such as marijuana?
- [ ] Do you drink more than 1 ounce of alcohol (one glass of wine, one beer, or one measure of spirits) a day?
- [ ] Do you eat fried food (e.g., bacon and eggs, fish and chips) more than twice a week?
- [ ] Do you eat processed "fast food" more than twice a week?
- [ ] Do you eat red meat more than twice a week?
- [ ] Do you often eat foods containing additives and preservatives?
- [ ] Do you eat chocolate or sweets more than twice a week?
- [ ] Does less than a third of your diet consist of raw fruit and vegetables?

☐ Do you drink less than 8 ounces of plain water each day?

☐ Do you normally eat white rice, flour, or bread rather than whole grain?

☐ Do you drink more than 6 cups of milk a week?

☐ Do you eat more than three slices of bread a day, on average?

☐ Are there some foods you feel "addicted" to?

0–4 *you are obviously a health-conscious individual and your minor indiscretions are unlikely to affect your health. Provided you supplement your diet with the right vitamins and minerals you can look forward to a long and healthy life.*

5–9 *you are on the right track, but must be a little stricter with yourself. Rather than giving up your bad habits, set yourself easy experiments. For instance, for one month go without two or three of the foods or drinks you know are not good for you. See how you feel. Some you may decide to have occasionally, while others you may find you go off. But be strict for one month—your cravings will only be short-term withdrawal symptoms. Aim to have your score below 5 within three months.*

10–14 *your diet is not good and you will need to make some changes to be able to reach optimum health. But take it a step at a time. You should aim to have your score down to 5 within six months. Start by following the advice in this chapter, backed up by the advice in Part Two. You will find that some of your bad dietary habits will change for the better as you discover tasty alternatives. The bad habits that remain should be dealt with one at a time. Remember that sugar, salt, coffee, and chocolate are all addictive foods. Your cravings for them will dramatically decrease or go away altogether after one month without them.*

15–20 *there is no way you can continue to eat like this and remain in good health. You are consuming far too great a quantity of fat, refined foods, and artificial stimulants. Follow the advice in Part Two very carefully and make gradual and permanent changes to your lifestyle. For instance, take two questions to which you answered "yes" and make changes so that one month later you could answer "no" (one example would be to stop eating sugar and drinking coffee in the first month). Keep doing this until your score is 5 or less. You may feel worse for the first two weeks, but within a month you will begin to feel the positive effects of healthy eating.*

EATING FOR VITALITY

One secret of longer and healthier life is to eat foods high in vitamin and mineral vitality. But this is not the only criterion for judging a food. Good food should also be low in fat, salt, and fast-releasing sugars, high in fiber, and alkaline-forming. Non-animal sources of protein are desirable. Such a diet will also be low in calories, but then you will not have to count them because your body will become increasingly efficient and not crave extra food. A craving for food when you have already eaten enough calories is often a craving for more nutrients, so foods providing "empty" calories are strictly to be avoided.

The golden rules for a healthy diet are:

- Avoid sugar

- Avoid refined carbohydrates: white bread, rolls, cakes, refined foods, etc.

- Eat more beans, lentils, and whole grains

- Eat more vegetables, raw or lightly cooked

- Eat three pieces of fresh fruit a day

- Avoid coffee, tea, and cigarettes

- Limit alcohol

Good and Bad Foods for a Long and Healthy Life

Good	Bad
Alkaline-forming Foods: all fresh fruit and vegetables; millet; almonds; brazil nuts; herb teas; yogurt; bean sprouts	*Acid-forming Foods*: beans; all meat and fish; grains; most nuts; seeds; milk produce; tea; coffee; chocolate; sugar; fats
Low-fat Foods: seafood; low-fat yogurt and cheese; skimmed milk; soy milk; tofu; beans; vegetables; fruit	*High-fat Foods*: meat; dairy products, including butter, cheese, and ice cream; margarine; vegetable oils
Non-meat Protein Foods: milk; cheese; yogurt; eggs; beans; rice; lentils; nuts; seeds; tofu	*Meat Protein Foods*: all meat, e.g., beef, pork, lamb; also chicken and fish
Slow-releasing Sugars: fresh fruit; unprocessed whole grains, e.g., muesli; brown rice; lentils, beans	*Fast-Releasing Sugars*: white, brown, and raw sugar; molasses; maple syrup; glucose, malt, honey, and most forms of syrups
High-potassium Foods: fruit, including pineapple, grapes, and bananas; vegetables; dandelion coffee; chicory coffee	*High-sodium Foods*: salt, including sea salt; yeast extracts; all smoked fish; some cheeses; crisps; salted nuts; most canned foods; soy sauce.
Unrefined Foods: nuts, seeds; whole grains; wholemeal flour and bread; lentils; beans; brown rice	*Refined Foods*: white flour; white, brown, and raw sugar; white rice; processed and most packaged foods

Make sure your diet is rich in the foods in the left-hand column, and follow the guidelines given at the end of each chapter in Part 2.

38

Your Optimum Supplement Program

Your personal nutritional needs can be calculated by looking at your lifestyle and identifying signs and symptoms associated with various deficiencies. In the sections that follow, answer the questions as best you can, then work out your score for each nutrient out of ten. If you score five or more the chances are that you do not have the optimal intake of that nutrient, given your current needs. The second part of this chapter shows you how to turn these scores into your optimum supplement program.

OPTIMUM NUTRITION QUESTIONNAIRE

Symptom Analysis

*For each symptom that you experience often, score **1** point. Many symptoms occur more than once, because they can be the result of many nutrient deficiencies. If you experience any of the symptoms in **bold** type, score **2** points. The maximum score for each nutrient is 10 points. **Put your score for each nutrient in the box.***

Vitamin Profile

VITAMIN A

____ **Mouth ulcers**

____ Poor night vision

____ Acne

____ **Frequent colds or infections**

____ Dry flaky skin

____ Dandruff

____ Thrush or cystitis

____ Diarrhea

☐ **YOUR SCORE**

VITAMIN D

____ **Arthritis or osteoporosis**

____ Backache

____ Tooth decay

____ Hair loss

____ **Muscle twitching or spasms**

____ **Joint pain or stiffness**

____ Weak bones

☐ **YOUR SCORE**

VITAMIN E

____ Lack of sex drive
____ **Exhaustion after light exercise**
____ **Easy bruising**
____ Slow wound healing
____ Varicose veins
____ Poor skin elasticity
____ Loss of muscle tone
____ Infertility

[ ] **YOUR SCORE**

VITAMIN C

____ **Frequent colds**
____ Lack of energy
____ **Frequent infections**
____ Bleeding or tender gums
____ Easy bruising
____ Nose bleeds
____ Slow wound healing
____ Red pimples on skin

[ ] **YOUR SCORE**

VITAMIN B1

____ Tender muscles
____ Eye pains
____ Irritability
____ Poor concentration
____ "Prickly" legs
____ Poor memory
____ Stomach pains
____ Constipation
____ Tingling hands
____ Rapid heartbeat

[ ] **YOUR SCORE**

VITAMIN B2

____ **Bloodshot, burning, or gritty eyes**
____ **Sensitivity to bright lights**
____ Sore tongue
____ Cataracts
____ Dull or oily hair
____ Eczema or dermatitis
____ Split nails
____ Cracked lips

[ ] **YOUR SCORE**

VITAMIN B3 (NIACIN)

____ Lack of energy
____ Diarrhea
____ Insomnia
____ Headaches or migraines
____ Poor memory
____ Anxiety or tension
____ Depression
____ Irritability
____ Bleeding or tender gums
____ Acne

[ ] **YOUR SCORE**

VITAMIN B5

____ Muscle tremors, cramps, or spasms
____ Apathy
____ Poor concentration
____ **Burning feet or tender heels**
____ Nausea or vomiting
____ Lack of energy
____ Exhaustion after light exercise
____ Anxiety or tension
____ Teeth grinding

[ ] **YOUR SCORE**

VITAMIN B6

____ **Infrequent dream recall**

____ **Water retention**

____ Tingling hands

____ Depression or nervousness

____ Irritability

____ Muscle tremors, cramps, or spasms

____ **Lack of energy**

☐ YOUR SCORE

VITAMIN B12

____ Poor hair condition

____ Eczema or dermatitis

____ Mouth over-sensitive to hot or cold

____ Irritability

____ Anxiety or tension

____ **Lack of energy**

____ Constipation

____ Tender or sore muscles

____ Pale skin

☐ YOUR SCORE

FOLIC ACID

____ Eczema

____ Cracked lips

____ Prematurely graying hair

____ Anxiety or tension

____ Poor memory

____ **Lack of energy**

____ Depression

____ Poor appetite

____ Stomach pains

☐ YOUR SCORE

BIOTIN

____ **Dermatitis or dry skin**

____ **Poor hair condition**

____ **Prematurely graying hair**

____ **Tender or sore muscles**

____ **Poor appetite or nausea**

☐ YOUR SCORE

Mineral Profile

CALCIUM

____ **Muscle cramps, tremors, or spasms**

____ **Insomnia or nervousness**

____ **Joint pain or arthritis**

____ **Tooth decay**

____ **High blood pressure**

☐ YOUR SCORE

IRON

____ **Pale skin**

____ **Sore tongue**

____ **Fatigue or listlessness**

____ **Loss of appetite or nausea**

____ **Heavy periods or blood loss**

☐ YOUR SCORE

MAGNESIUM

____ **Muscle cramps, tremors, or spasms**

____ Muscle weakness

____ Insomnia, nervousness, or hyperactivity

____ High blood pressure

____ Irregular or rapid heartbeat

____ Constipation

____ Fits or convulsions

____ Breast tenderness or water retention

____ Depression or confusion

☐ YOUR SCORE

ZINC

____ **Decline in sense of taste or smell**

____ **White marks on more than two finger nails**

____ **Frequent infections**

____ **Stretch marks**

____ **Acne or greasy skin**

☐ YOUR SCORE

MANGANESE

____ **Muscle twitches**

____ **Childhood "growing pains"**

____ **Dizziness or poor sense of balance**

____ **Fits or convulsions**

____ **Sore knees**

☐ YOUR SCORE

SELENIUM

____ **Family history of cancer**

____ **Signs of premature aging**

____ **Cataracts**

____ **High blood pressure**

☐ YOUR SCORE

CHROMIUM

____ **Excessive or cold sweats**

____ **Dizziness or irritability after six hours without food**

____ **Need for frequent meals**

____ **Cold hands**

____ **Need for excessive sleep or drowsiness during the day**

☐ YOUR SCORE

Essential Fatty Acid Profile

OMEGA 3 OMEGA 6

____ **Dry skin, eczema, or dry eyes**

____ Dry hair or dandruff

____ Inflammatory health problems, e.g., arthritis

____ Excessive thirst or sweating

____ PMS or breast pain

____ Water retention

____ Frequent infections

____ Poor memory or learning difficulties

____ High blood pressure or high blood lipids

☐ **YOUR SCORE**

Now put all your individual scores into appropriate spaces in the second column (headed Symptom Score) of the chart on p. 244.

Lifestyle Analysis

*The following checks allow you to adjust your nutrient needs according to aspects of your health and lifestyle. Again, answer the questions as best you can and work out your score. In most checks the maximum score is 10, scoring **1** point for each "yes" answer unless otherwise specified. **If you score 5 or more in any category, you will need to add the points shown in the chart on p. 244 to your individual nutrient scores.** The easiest way to do this is to circle all the numbers in the corresponding columns on p. 244. For example, if you scored more than 5 on the Energy check, you would circle all the numbers in the energy column on p. 244.*

*Some checks are either "**yes**" or "**no**." If you answer "yes," circle the numbers in the relevant columns on p. 244.*

Energy Check

____ Do you need more than eight hours' sleep a night?

____ Are you rarely wide awake and raring to go within twenty minutes of rising?

____ Do you need something to get you going in the morning, like a cup of tea or coffee or a cigarette?

____ Do you have tea, coffee, sugar-containing foods or drinks, or smoke cigarettes, at regular intervals during the day?

____ Do you often feel drowsy or sleepy during the day, or after meals?

____ Do you get dizzy or irritable if you have not eaten for six hours?

____ Do you avoid exercise because you do not have the energy?

____ Do you sweat a lot during the night or day or get excessively thirsty?

____ Do you sometimes lose concentration or does your mind go blank?

____ Is your energy less now than it used to be?

YOUR SCORE

Stress Check

____ Do you feel guilty when relaxing?

____ Do you have a persistent need for recognition or achievement?

____ Are you unclear about your goals in life?

____ Are you especially competitive?

____ Do you work harder than most people?

____ Do you easily get angry?

____ Do you often do two or three tasks simultaneously?

____ Do you get impatient if people or things hold you up?

____ Do you have difficulty getting to sleep, sleep restlessly, or wake up with your mind racing?

☐ **YOUR SCORE**

Exercise Check

Score 2 points for each "yes" answer

____ Do you take exercise that noticeably raises your heartbeat for at least twenty minutes more than three times a week?

____ Does your job involve lots of walking, lifting, or any other vigorous activity?

____ Do you regularly play a sport? (football, basketball, etc.)?

____ Do you have any physically tiring hobbies? (gardening, carpentry, etc.)?

____ Are you in serious training for an athletic event?

____ Do you consider yourself fit?

☐ **YOUR SCORE**

Immune Check

____ Do you get more than three colds a year?

____ Do you find it hard to shake an infection (cold or otherwise)?

____ Are you prone to thrush or cystitis?

____ Do you generally take antibiotics twice or more each year?

____ Have you had a major personal loss in the last year?

____ Is there any history of cancer in your family?

____ Have you ever had any growths or lumps removed or biopsied?

____ Do you have an inflammatory disease such as eczema, asthma, or arthritis?

____ Do you suffer from hay fever?

____ Do you suffer from allergy problems?

☐ **YOUR SCORE**

Pollution Check

____ Do you live in a city or by a busy road?

____ Do you spend more than two hours a week in heavy traffic?

____ Do you exercise (do your job, cycle, play sports) by busy roads?

____ Do you smoke more than five cigarettes a day?

____ Do you live or work in a smoky atmosphere?

____ Do you buy foods exposed to exhaust fumes from busy roads?

____ Do you generally eat non-organic produce?

____ Do you drink more than 1 unit of alcohol a day (one glass of wine, one beer, or one measure of spirits)?

____ Do you spend a considerable amount of time in front of a TV or computer screen?

____ Do you usually drink unfiltered tap water?

YOUR SCORE

Cardiovascular Check

____ Is your blood pressure above 140/90?

____ Is your pulse rate after fifteen minutes' rest above 75?

____ Are you more than 14 pounds over your ideal weight?

____ Do you smoke more than five cigarettes a day?

____ Do you do less than two hours of vigorous exercise (one hour if you are over fifty) a week?

____ Do you eat more than one tablespoon of sugar each day?

____ Do you eat meat more than five times a week?

____ Do you usually add salt to your food?

____ Do you have more than two alcoholic drinks a day?

____ Is there a history of heart disease or diabetes in your family?

YOUR SCORE

Female Health Check

Do you regularly suffer from premenstrual syndrome?   YES / NO

Are you pregnant or trying to get pregnant?   YES / NO

Are you breast-feeding?   YES / NO

Do you have menopausal symptoms or are you post-menopausal?   YES / NO

Age Check

Are you under 11?   YES / NO

Are you 11–16?   YES / NO

Are you over 50?   YES / NO

HOW TO WORK OUT YOUR OPTIMUM NUTRIENT NEEDS

From the Symptom Analysis Section of the Optimum Nutrition Question-naire you will have arrived at your basic score for each nutrient, which then needs to be adjusted depending on your answers to the Lifestyle Analysis questions. To do this, add all the numbers you have circled to your symptom score. Do this for each row, entering each total in Your Total Score column on p. 245. The higher your score for any given nutrient, the greater your need for that nutrient.

Once you have arrived at your score for each nutrient you can work out your supplement needs by comparing your score with those in the chart on p. 245. For example, if your vitamin C score was 6, your estimated ideal supplementary intake of this vitamin is 2000 mg per day. Now work out your own supplemental levels for each nutrient.

If you score 0–4 on any nutrient I still recommend you to supplement it on a basic level, which can easily be achieved with good daily multivitamin supplement. Remember: these levels are your supplementary needs, not your overall needs including diet. I have assumed that you have improved your diet—or will do so—so that it provides a basic intake of these nutrients. You will not get the same results from adding supplements to a poor diet.

For example, the ideal daily intake of calcium is 800–1,200 mg (if needs are high, as pregnant women or elderly people). The average intake is around 500 mg. A reasonable intake, having adjusted your diet, is 650 mg. So, if you have no symptoms or lifestyle factors that increase your need, your supplemental requirement in 800–650 = 150 mg. If, on the other hand, you are pregnant, your supplemental requirement is 1,200–650 = 550 mg. This is why the range given for supplementation on p. 245 goes from 150 up to 600 mg.

Levels of minerals other than those in the chart are generally sufficient in most people's diets and can be increased through diet changes. Potassium, which balances sodium (salt), is best supplied by eating plenty of raw fruit and vegetables. Phosphorus deficiency is exceedingly rare, and the mineral is contained in almost all supplements as calcium phosphate. Iodine deficiency is also extremely rare. Copper is frequently over-supplied in our diets and can be toxic. A whole food diet almost always contains enough copper.

SCORES FOR CHILDREN

For children under the age of fourteen, there is a simple method for adjusting the nutrient need figures (which are based on adult requirements). Take the weight of the child in pounds and divide by 100. Now multiply their (adult) supplemental levels by the number you have worked out to give the child's actual supplemental level. For example, if a child weights 50 pounds, and we divide that by 100, we get 0.5. If the child scored 6 for vitamin C, giving a supplemental level of 2,000 mg, we would multiply by 0.5 and get 1,000 mg. This is the child's approximate optimal intake of vitamin C.

Alternatively, use the guide to optimal supplement intakes for children up to the age of thirteen on p. 216. From fourteen onwards, adult levels can be given.

PLANNING YOUR IDEAL SUPPLEMENT PROGRAM

In case you are wondering, it is not necessary to take thirty different supplements every day! Your needs can be compressed into four or five different supplements, each combining the nutrients above. The most common combinations are a multivitamin (containing vitamins A, B, C, D, and E) and a multimineral for all the minerals. Vitamin C is usually taken separately, since the basic optimum requirement of 1,000 mg makes quite a large tablet without adding any more nutrients.

Choosing the right formula is an art in itself. Chapter 39 will help you through the maze by showing you how to decipher the small print and read between the lines, while Chapter 40 explains how to devise a simple daily routine of vitamin supplements. Alternatively you can walk into your local health food store, show the product adviser your calculations of your personal requirements, and ask him or her to suggest a supplement program that meets your needs.

OPTIMUM NUTRITION QUESTIONNAIRE: HOW DO YOU SCORE?

NUTRIENTS	SYMPTOM SCORE	ENERGY	STRESS	EXERCISE	IMMUNE	POLLUTION	CARDIOVASCULAR	PREGNANT / FEEDING	PMS	MENOPAUSE	AGE 14–16	AGE OVER 50
A (beta-carotene)						2	1				1	
D								1		1	1	1
E					1	1	1	1		1		
C		1	2	1	1	2	1					
B1		1	2	1								
B2		1	2	1								
B3		2	2	1			1					
B5		1	2	1								
B6		1	2	1	1			1	2	1		
B12								2				
Folic Acid								2				
Biotin								1			1	
Ω3/Ω6 Fats								2	2	1		1
Calcium			1		1	1	2		2	1	1	1
Magnesium		1	1	1	1				2			1
Iron					1			1				
Zinc			1	1		2	2		2	2	1	1
Manganese												1
Selenium					1	1	1					1
Chromium		2	1									1

YOUR TOTAL SCORE		SCORE				WHAT YOU NEED
		0–4	5–6	7–8	9 or more	
	A	7500	10000	15000	20000	ius
	D	200	400	600	800	ius
	E	100	300	500	1000	ius
	C	1000	2000	3000	4000	mg
	B1	25	50	75	100	mg
	B2	25	50	75	100	mg
	B3	50	75	100	150	mg
	B5	50	100	200	300	mg
	B6	50	100	200	250	mg
	B12	5	10	50	100	mcg
	F A	50	100	200	400	mcg
	Biotin	50	100	150	200	mcg
	GLAΩ6	–	150	225	300	mg
	EPA/Ω3	–	800	1600	2400	mg
	Cal	150	300	450	600	mg
	Mag	75	150	225	300	mg
	Iron	10	15	20	25	mg
	Zinc	10	15	20	25	mg
	Man	2.5	5	10	15	mg
	Sel	25	50	75	100	mcg
	Chro	20	50	100	200	mcg

39

Everything You Need to Know about Supplements

Not all supplements are the same. Analysis of a wide variety of multivitamin tablets to find out how much it would cost to get the basic optimum vitamin requirements produced a range between 45¢ and over $7.50 a day! And with so many supplements available, all promising perfect health, it is easy to get confused. For instance, if you are looking for a simple multivitamin preparation to meet the basic optimum requirements, you have at least twenty products to choose from. This chapter explains what to look for in a good supplement.

Reading the label

Labeling laws vary from country to country, but many of the principles are the same. However, since the laws keep changing many manufacturers are as confused as the public. Below is a typical label with advice on how to interpret the small print.

On this label the dosages are easy to understand, the chemical names for the different vitamins are given, and the fillers (e.g., calcium phosphate) are listed. Directions for when and how to take the tablets are given. These are the things to go for when you are buying supplements: do not be misled by an attractive-looking label or a very cheap price, but do not pay too much either!

Unfortunately, however, not all supplements are true to their labels, so it is not always best to buy the cheapest. Reputable vitamin companies should give you a list of all the ingredients on the label.

Vitamin names and their amounts

For most supplements the ingredients have to be listed in order of weight, starting with the ingredient present in the greatest quantity. This is often confusing, since included in this list are the non-nutrient additives needed to

This product is free of corn, yeast, wheat, soy and dairy products and is formulated without the use of preservatives, artificial flavors or colors.

To assure freshness and potency, store in a cool, dry place, away from heat, light and moisture. Keep out of reach of children.

EXTRA POTENCY
MULTIPLE VITAMINS
WITH AMINO ACID CHELATED MINERALS

360 TABLETS
SUITABLE FOR VEGETARIANS
SUGAR, SALT AND STARCH FREE

This form is well absorbed

This formula is hypoallergenic

The ideal vitamin C intake is 1000 mg - 3000 mg. You will not find much more than 300 mg in a multi due to size.

Most nutrients are supplied in levels much higher than RDAs.

This is natural vitamin E.

Provides additional nutrients not classified as vitamins.

These are elemental mineral levels, so what you see is what you get.

The trace elements are in highly absorbable forms.

Provides the total of vitamin A activity.

SUGGESTED DOSE: As a dietary supplement for adults, one (1) tablet daily, preferably at mealtime, or as directed by a healthcare practitioner.

Each tablet provides:		%US RDA*
Vitamin C (l-ascorbic acid)	250 mg	417
Vitamin E (d-alpha tocopheryl succinate)	150 IU	500
Total Vitamin A Activity	15000 IU	300
from: vitamin A (palmitate)	7500 IU	
Natural Beta Carotene/ Carotenoid Mix (D. Salina)	7500 IU	
providing (typical analysis)		
beta carotene	5.4 mg	
cryptoxanthin	41 mcg	
alpha carotene	171 mcg	
zeaxanthin	34 mcg	
lutein	26 mcg	
Vitamin D (cholecalciferol)	400 IU	100
Vitamin B1 (thiamine mononitrate)	75 mg	5000
Vitamin B2 (riboflavin)	75 mg	4412
Vitamin B6 (pyridoxine HCl)	75 mg	3750
Vitamin B12 (cobalamin)	75 mcg	1250
Niacinamide	75 mg	375
Inositol	75 mg	**
PABA (para aminobenzoic acid)	75 mg	**
Pantothenic Acid (d-Ca pantothenate)	75 mg	750
Biotin	75 mcg	25
Folic Acid	400 mcg	100
Choline (bitartrate)	31 mg	**
Rutin	25 mg	**
Citrus Bioflavonoid Complex	25 mg	**
Hesperidin	5 mg	**
Betaine HCl	25 mg	**
Iodine (kelp)	150 mcg	100
Calcium (buffered amino acid chelate)	20 mg	2
Potassium (amino acid complex)	1.8 mg	**
Iron (bisglycinate)	1.3 mg	7.2
Magnesium (buffered amino acid chelate)	10 mg	2.5
Manganese (amino acid chelate)	1 mg	**
Zinc (buffered amino acid chelate)	10 mg	67
Selenium (L-selenomethionine)	25 mcg	**
Chromium (niacin amino acid chelate)	25 mcg	**
Copper (buffered amino acid chelate)	1 mg	50
Boron (amino acid complex)	5 mg	**
Molybednum (amino acid chelate)	25 mcg	**

* U.S. RDA = U.S. Recommended Daily Allowance
** No U.S. RDA established

WARNING: Accidental overdose of iron-containing products is a leading cause of fatal poisoning in children under 6. Keep this product out of reach of children. In case of accidental overdose, call a doctor or poison control center immediately.

Reading the supplement label

make the tablet. Often the chemical name of the nutrient is used instead of the common vitamin code (for example, ergocalciferol for vitamin D).

Vitamin	Chemical Name(s)
A	retinol, retinyl palmitate, or beta-carotene
B1	thiamine, thiamine hydrochloride, thiamine mononitrate
B2	riboflavin
B3	niacin, niacinamide
B5	pantothenic acid, calcium pantothenate
B6	pyridoxine, pyridoxal-5-phosphate, pyridoxine hydrochloride
B12	cyanocobalamine
C	ascorbic acid, calcium ascorbate, magnesium ascorbate, sodium ascorbate
D	ergocalciferol, cholecalciferol
E	d(l) alpha tocopherol, tocopheryl acetate, tocopheryl succinate
Biotin	biotin
Folic acid	folate

When you have identified which nutrient is which, look at the amount provided by each daily dose. Some supplements state this in terms of two tablets ('Each two tablets provide . . ., since the supplement is designed to be taken twice a day. The amount supplied will be given in milligrams (mg) or micrograms (mcg or µg). Most countries are now switching to "µg" as the symbol for micrograms, which are a thousandth of a milligram.

Vitamin A measurements are a little tricky. This is because beta-carotene is not actually vitamin A but can be turned into vitamin A by the body. So, to indicate the equivalent effect of a certain amount of beta-carotene compared to vitamin A (retinol), a unit called a "µgRE" is used. This stands for "micrograms of Retinol Equivalent." What it is saying is that this amount of beta-carotene has the equivalent effect of so many µg of retinol. In fact, 6 mcg of beta-carotene is equivalent in potency to 1 mcg of retinol, and is therefore written as 1 mcgRE of beta-carotene. If a supplement contains both vitamin A and beta-carotene, add the two amounts of µgRE to arrive at the total vitamin A dose provided.

ELEMENTAL MINERALS

Minerals in multivitamin and mineral tablets often omit the "elemental" value of the compound, stating only the amount of the mineral compound. For instance, 100 mg of zinc amino acid chelate will provide only 10 mg of zinc and 90 mg of the amino acid to which it is chelated (attached). What you want to know is the amount of the actual mineral, in this example, 10 mg. This is called the "elemental value." Most reputable manufacturers make your life easy by stating something like "zinc amino acid chelate (providing 5 mg zinc) 50mg" or "zinc (as amino acid chelate) 5 mg," both of which mean you are getting 5mg of elemental or actual zinc. Otherwise you may have to contact the manufacturer for more detailed information. Most good companies declare this information either on the label or in literature that comes with the product.

Supplement labels are also required to show the percentage of the RDA that is met by the product. But for the purposes of achieving optimum nutrition this is largely irrelevant, since the amounts needed are often many times higher than the RDA.

FILLERS, BINDERS, LUBRICANTS, AND COATINGS

Supplements often contain other ingredients that are necessary in their manufacture. While capsules do not really need to have anything added, tablets usually do to enable the ingredients to stick together to form a tablet. Tablets start off as powders, and to get the bulk right "fillers" are added. "Binders" are added to give the mixture the right consistency, and lubricants are also used. Only when this is done can the mixture be turned into small, uneven granules, which are then pressed into tablets under considerable force. Granulating allows the mixture to lock together, forming a solid mass. The tablet may then be covered with a "protein coating" to protect it from deterioration and make it easier to swallow.

Unfortunately, many tablets also have artificial coloring and flavoring added, as well as a sugar coating. For instance, many vitamin C tablets are colored orange and made to taste sweet, since we associate vitamin C with oranges! Vitamin C is naturally almost white and certainly is not sweet—nor should your supplement be. As a rule of thumb, only buy supplements that declare their fillers and binders (sometimes also called "excipients"). Companies with integrity are usually only too happy to display this information. The following fillers and binders are perfectly acceptable, and some even add further nutritious properties to the tablet:

Dicalcium phosphate   A natural filler providing calcium and phosphate
Cellulose   A natural binder consisting of plant fiber
Alginic acid/sodium alginate   A natural binder from seaweed
Gum acacia/gum arabic   A natural vegetable gum
Calcium stearate or magnesium stearate   A natural lubricant (usually from animal source)
Silica   A natural lubricant
Zein   A corn protein for coating the tablet
Brazil wax   A natural coating derived from palm trees

Stearate, which is the chemical name for saturated fat, is used as a lubricant. The cheapest comes from animal sources, although non-animal stearates are available. If you are a strict vegan or vegetarian you may want to check this with the supplement company. If a product is labeled "suitable for vegans" it cannot legally contain any animal source ingredients.

Most large tablets are coated. This makes them shiny, smooth, and easier to swallow. It is not so necessary with small tablets. If a tablet is chalky or rough on the outside, it is not coated. Coating, depending on the substance used, can also protect the ingredients, increasing their shelf-life. Avoid sugar-coated, artificially colored supplements. Natural colors, for example from berry extracts, are fine.

Very occasionally a manufacturer over-coats a batch of tablets and, particularly for people with a shortage of stomach acid, this can inhibit the tablet's disintegration. Most reliable companies check the disintegration time of each batch to rule out this possibility, so it is a rare problem.

FREE FROM SUGAR, GLUTEN, ANIMAL PRODUCTS, ETC.

Many of the better supplements will also declare that the product is free from sugar and gluten. If you are allergic to milk or yeast, do check that the tablets are also free from lactose (milk sugar) and yeast. B vitamins can be derived from yeast, so you need to be careful. If in doubt, contact the company and ask for an independent "assay" of the ingredients: good companies will supply this information. Sometimes glucose, fructose, or dextrose are used to sweeten a tablet and yet the packaging still declares "no sugar." These are best avoided. A small amount of fructose is the least evil if you are having difficulty enticing a child to take vitamins. Any other preservatives or flavoring agents should be avoided unless they are natural. Pineapple essence, for instance, is a natural additive.

If you are vegan or vegetarian, choose supplements that state this. Retinol (vitamin A) can be derived from an animal source, synthesized, or derived from a vegetable source such as retinyl palmitate. Vitamin D can be synthesized, derived from sheep wool or from a vegetable source. Companies do not have to state the source of the nutrients, just their chemical form.

40

BUILDING YOUR OWN SUPPLEMENT PROGRAM

So now you know how to read the labels and find out if a particular supplement contains what you need. Here's how to turn your nutrient needs into a supplement program.

Theoretically, at one extreme you could take a mega-mega-multi that contains everything you could possibly need. The trouble is that it would be enormous, impossible to swallow, and no doubt give you a lot more than you need of some nutrients. The other extreme is to take one supplement for each vitamin, exactly matching your requirements—but you would end up with handfuls of pills.

Instead, nutritionists use "formulas," combinations of nutrients that, when combined appropriately, get close to your needs. In a typical supplement program you may end up with four or five supplements to take—think of them as building blocks that, when put together, form a complete structure.

IDEAL FORMULAS

Every nutritionist has different ideas about the "best" blend of vitamins and minerals in supplements, which is reflected in the ever-growing range. The ideal formulation ultimately depends on your personal needs, but there are certain basic ones that act as good building blocks for your personal health program:

Multivitamin

A good multivitamin should contain at least 7500 IUs of A, 400 IUs of D, 100 IUs of E, 250 mg of C, 50 mg each of B1, B2, B3, B5, and B6, 10 mcg of B12, and 50 mcg each of folic acid and biotin. Calcium, magnesium, iron, zinc, and manganese may well be included as they are frequently deficient.

Multimineral
This should provide at least 150 mg of calcium, 75 mg of magnesium, 10 mg of iron, 10 mg of zinc, 2.5 mg of manganese, 20 mcg of chromium and 25 mcg of selenium, plus some molybdenum.

Multivitamin and mineral
You simply cannot fit all the above vitamins and minerals into one tablet. So good combined multivitamin and mineral formulas recommend two or more tablets a day to meet these kind of levels. The bulkiest nutrients are vitamin C, calcium and magnesium, which are often inadequately supplied in multivitamin and mineral formulas and may need to be taken separately. With the exception of these three nutrients, a good multivitamin and mineral formula should meet all the "0–4" nutrient levels in the chart on p. 245, and provide the foundation for your supplement program.

Vitamin C
This is worth taking separately, because the amount you need will not fit in a multi. The supplement should provide 1,000 mg of vitamin C with at least 25 mg of bioflavonoids or other synergistic factors such as rosehip or berry extracts.

B complex
If you scored high in the energy or stress categories of the Optimum Nutrition Questionnaire you may need more B vitamins. An easy way to meet your needs is to add a B complex supplement to your program until your scores and symptoms reduce.

Antioxidant complex
If you scored high in the exercise, immune, or pollution categories, or simply want to maximize your life span, you can add an antioxidant complex to your supplement program. This should contain reasonable amounts of the following antioxidants: vitamins A, C, and E, beta-carotene, zinc, selenium, possibly iron, copper, manganese, and the amino acids glutathione and cysteine, plus phytonutrient antioxidants like bilberry extract, pycnogenol, or grape seed extract.

Essential fats
There are two ways of meeting your essential fat requirements: one is to consume one or two tablespoons of a cold-pressed organic blend of seed oils providing both Omega 3 (flax and pumpkin) and Omega 6 (sesame, sunflower, borage, and evening primrose); the other is to supplement concentrated oils. For Omega 3 this means either flax seed oil capsules or the more concentrated fish oil capsules providing EPA and DHA. For Omega 6 this means taking a

supplement of a source of GLA such as evening primrose oil or borage oil. Check the supplement gives you the amount of GLA and EPA/DHA that you have calculated you require. If you scored 0–4 and already eat fatty fish and/or plenty of seeds, these may already cover your needs.

Bone mineral complexes

If the above formulas still leave you short on calcium and magnesium, or if you are pregnant, breast-feeding, post-menopausal, or elderly, you may meet your needs by adding a complex of minerals including calcium, magnesium, vitamin D, boron, and a little zinc, vitamin C, or silica. These help to build healthy bones.

Individual nutrients

Sometimes even the above formulas may still leave you short on specific nutrients. Shortfalls commonly found in vitamin B3 (niacin), vitamin B5 (pantothenate), vitamin B6 (pyridoxine), zinc, and chromium. If you need both vitamin B3 and chromium, take chromium polynicotinate which is a complex of the two. If you need extra B3, remember that ordinary niacin makes you blush, so look for niacinamide or "no-flush niacin." If you need vitamin B6 and zinc you can often find them in one tablet.

A list of recommended supplement companies whose products meet these levels of vitamin and mineral intake is given on p. 341.

HOW TO TURN YOUR NUTRIENT NEEDS INTO A SIMPLE SUPPLEMENT PROGRAM

From your scores in the questionnaire on p. 245 you will have worked out your optimum daily nutrient needs. If you scored less than 5 on each vitamin and mineral your needs will be easily covered by this program:

Supplement	Daily Dose (Tablets)
Multivitamin	1
Multimineral	1
Vitamin C 1,000 mg	1

If you scored 5 or more for vitamins A, D, or E, you will probably need to double the multivitamin. A score of 7 or more on vitamin E will warrant a separate vitamin E supplement. If you scored 7 or more on at least two B vitamins your best bet is to take two B complex tablets per day. However, if you only scored high on B6, for example, adding a B6 supplement of the desired strength will be more practical. The same applies to vitamin C. If your optimum level is 2,000 mg, take two vitamin C tablets a day.

If you scored 5 or more for at least two minerals, you will probably meet your needs by doubling your multimineral intake. However, if only calcium and magnesium were deficient, these can be provided together in a "bone formula." If you are particularly in need of chromium you may also require extra vitamin B3; some manufacturers combine the two. The same is true for zinc and B6, so look out for these combined nutrients since they will save you money and decrease the number of tablets you need to take. If you have a weak immune system or are exposed to a lot of pollution you may need more vitamins A, C and E, zinc, and selenium. These are all antioxidant nutrients which protect the immune system and help you deal with the effects of pollution. They are often combined in one supplement.

Supplements—when to take them

Now that you have worked out what to take, you will want to know when to take them. This depends not only on what is technically best, but also on your lifestyle. If taking supplements twice a day means that you would forget the second lot, you are probably best advised to take them all at once! After all, nature supplies them all in one go, with a meal. Here are the "ten commandments" of supplement-taking:

1   Take vitamins and minerals fifteen minutes before or after a meal, or during it.
2   Take most of your supplements with your first meal of the day.
3   Don't take B vitamins late at night if you have difficulty sleeping.
4   Take extra minerals, especially calcium and magnesium, in the evening—they help you sleep.
5   If you are taking two or more B complex or vitamin C tablets, take one at each meal.
6   Do not take individual B vitamins unless you are also taking a general B complex, perhaps in a multivitamin.
7   Do not take individual minerals unless you are also taking a general multimineral.
8   If you are anemic (iron-deficient) take extra iron with vitamin C.
9   Always take at least ten times as much zinc as copper. If you know you are copper-deficient, take copper only with ten times as much zinc, e.g., 0.5 mg copper to 5 mg zinc.
10 Always take your supplements. Irregular supplementation doesn't work.

There are two supplement-taking strategies which I have found to work for most people. Take most in the morning and a few in the evening, so you do not have to take any to work. Or, if your supplement program consists of say, three multivitamins, three vitamin Cs and three antioxidants, put all three in one jar and take one of each with each meal.

ARE THERE ANY SIDE EFFECTS?

The side effects of optimum nutrition are increased energy, mental alertness, and a greater resistance to disease. In fact, a survey of supplement-takers found that 79 percent noticed a definite improvement in energy, 66 percent felt more emotionally balanced, 60 percent had better memory and mental alertness, skin condition had improved in 55 percent of people, and, overall, 61 percent had noticed a definite improvement in their well-being. As long as you stick to the levels given in this book and do not take toxic levels (explained in Chapter 42), the only side effects are beneficial.

A small number of people do, however, experience slight symptoms on starting a supplement program. This may be because they take too many supplements with too little food, or perhaps because a supplement contains something that does not agree with them, for example yeast. These problems are usually solved by stopping the supplements, then taking one only for four days, then adding another for the next four days, and so on until all supplements are taken. This will usually reveal whether a supplement is causing a problem. More often than not, the problem simply goes away.

Sometimes people feel worse before they feel better. Imagine your body coping with the onslaught of pollution, poor diet, toxins, and stimulants, and then suddenly getting a wonderful diet and all the supplements it needs. This can lead to the process called detoxification, in which the body cleanses itself. This is not a bad thing, and usually subsides within a month. However, if you have inexplicable symptoms see a nutrition consultant.

WHAT HEALTH IMPROVEMENTS TO EXPECT

Vitamins and minerals are not drugs, so you should not expect an overnight improvement in your health. Most people experience a definite improvement to their health within three months—the shortest length of time that you should experiment with a supplement program. The earliest noticeable changes are increased energy, mental alertness and emotional stability, and better skin condition. Your health will continue to improve as long as you are following the right program. If you do not experience any improvement in three months, it is best to see a nutrition consultant.

WHEN SHOULD YOU REASSESS YOUR NEEDS?

Certainly at the beginning your needs will change, and a reassessment every three months is sensible. Your nutrient needs should decrease as you get healthier. Remember, you need optimum nutrition most when you are stressed. So when emergencies arise, or you are working especially hard, make doubly sure that you eat well and take your supplements every day.

41

CHOOSING THE BEST SUPPLEMENTS

While the golden rule of any supplement program is to work out the right doses and take them regularly, there are many other issues to consider when choosing supplements. Is it better to have natural rather than synthetic nutrients? Are capsules better than tablets? Are certain forms of minerals better absorbed? Are there good and bad combinations? What if you are on medication – are there any situations when you should not take supplements?

CAPSULES VERSUS TABLETS

Capsules used to always be made of gelatin, which is an animal product and therefore not suitable for vegetarians. However, thanks to technological advances vegetable cellulose can now be substituted, although not yet for the "soft-gel" capsules used for oils like vitamin E. The advantage of tablets is that, through compression, you can get more nutrients into them. The disadvantage is the need for fillers and binders. Some people think capsules allow for better nutrient absorption; however, provided the tablet is properly made there is little difference even if you have poor digestion. Most vitamins including the oil-based ones, can be provided in tablet form. For instance, natural vitamin E comes in two forms: d-alpha tocopherol acetate (oil) and d-alpha tocopherol succinate (powder). They are equally potent.

NATURAL VERSUS SYNTHETIC

A great deal of nonsense has been said and written about the advantages of natural vitamins. First of all, many products which claim to be natural are simply not. By law, a certain percentage of a product must be natural before the product can be declared "natural" on its label. The percentage varies from country to country. Through careful wording some supplements are made to sound natural when they are not. For instance, "vitamin C with rosehips" invariably means synthetic vitamin C with added rosehips, although it is often confused with vitamin C *from* rosehips. So which is better?

By definition, a synthetic vitamin must contain *all* the properties of the vitamin found in nature. If it does not, the chemists have not done their job properly. This is the case with vitamin E. Natural d-alpha tocopherol succinate is 36 percent more potent than the synthetic vitamin E called dl-alpha tocopherol (in this case the "L" dictates the chemical difference). So natural vitamin E, usually derived from wheat germ or soybean oil, is better.

However, synthetic vitamin C (ascorbic acid) has the same biological potency as the natural substance, according to Dr. Linus Pauling, although advanced scientific techniques have shown visible differences between the two. No one has yet shown that natural vitamin C is more potent or beneficial to take. Indeed, most vitamin C is synthesized from a "natural" sugar such as dextrose; two chemical reactions later you have ascorbic acid. This is little different from the chemical reactions that take place in animals which convert sugar to vitamin C. Vitamin C derived from, say, acerola cherries—the most concentrated source—is also considerably bulkier and more expensive. Acerola is only 20 percent vitamin C, so a 1,000 mg tablet would be five times as large as a normal tablet and would cost you ten times as much!

It is true that vitamins derived from natural sources may contain unknown elements that increase their potency. Vitamin E or d-alpha tocopherol is found with beta, gamma, and delta tocopherol, and the inclusion of these with a measured amount of d-alpha tocopherol may be of benefit. Vitamin C is found in nature together with the bioflavonoids, active nutrients that appear to increase its potency, particularly its capacity for strengthening tiny blood vessels. Good sources of bioflavonoids are berries and citrus fruit, so the addition of citrus bioflavonoids or berry extracts to vitamin C tablets is one step closer to nature.

It is possible that yeast and rice bran, which are excellent sources of B vitamins, also contain unknown beneficial ingredients, so these vitamins are best supplied with yeast or rice bran. Brewer's yeast tablets or powder are far less efficient ways of taking B vitamins than B complex vitamin supplements with a little added yeast—one would have to eat pounds of yeast tablets to get optimum levels of B vitamins. However, some people are allergic to yeast, and if you react badly to any supplements it could be yeast that is the problem. For this reason many supplements are yeast-free.

There are many other potentially helpful substances that may be provided with nutrients in a complex. Included here are substances called co-enzymes, which help to convert the nutrient into its active form. Vitamin B6 needs to be converted from pyridoxine to pyridoxal-5-phosphate before it becomes active in the body. This process requires zinc, which is now included in a number of B6 supplements. Supplements of pyridoxal-5-phosphate are also available, and should, theoretically, be more usable. Time will tell how much of an advantage these innovations will prove. But the key point is to make sure you get enough of each of the essential nutrients.

VITAMIN AND MINERAL ABSORPTION

Vitamins and particularly minerals come in different forms which affect their absorption and availability. Apart from the form of the nutrient, there are dietary and lifestyle factors that help or hinder their availability to the body.

Water Soluble Nutrients

Vitamin or mineral	Best form	When best to take	What helps absorption	What hinders absorption
B1	thiamine	alone or with meals	B complex, manganese	alcohol, stress, antibiotics
B2	riboflavin	alone or with meals	B complex	alcohol, tobacco, stress, antibiotics
B3	nicotinic acid, nicotinamide	alone or with meals	B complex	alcohol, stress, antibiotics
B5	calcium pantothenate	alone or with meals	biotin, folic acid, B complex	antibiotics, stress
B6	pyridoxine hydrochloride phosphate	alone or with meals	zinc, magnesium, B complex	alcohol, antibiotics, stress
B12	cyanocobalamin	alone or with meals	calcium, B complex	alcohol, intestinal parasites, stress, antibiotics
C	ascorbic acid, calcium ascorbate	away from meals	hydrochloric acid in stomach	heavy meals
Folic Acid		alone or with meals	C, B complex	alcohol, stress, antibiotics
Biotin		alone or with meals	B complex	avidin (in raw egg whites), stress, antibiotics

Fat Soluble Vitamins

A	retinol, beta-carotene	take with foods containing fats or oils	zinc, E, C	lack of bile
E	D-alpha tocopherol	take with foods containing fats or oils	selenium, C	lack of bile, ferric forms of iron, oxidized fats
D	ergocalciferol, Cholecalciferol	take with foods containing fats or oils	calcium, phosphorous, E, C	lack of bile

Minerals

Vitamin or mineral	When best to take	What helps absorption	What hinders absorption
Calcium – Ca	with protein food	magnesium, D, hydrochloric acid in stomach	Tea, coffee, smoking
Magnesium – Mg	with protein food	calcium, B6, D, hydrochloric acid in stomach	Alcohol, tea, coffee, smoking
Iron – Fe	with food	C, hydrochloric acid in stomach	oxalic acid, tea, coffee, smoking
Zinc – Zn	on an empty stomach, p.m.	B6, C, hydrochloric acid in stomach	phytic acid, lead, copper, calcium, tea, coffee
Manganese – Mn	with protein food	C, hydrochloric acid in stomach	high dosage zinc, tea, coffee, smoking
Selenium – Se	on an empty stomach	E, hydrochloric acid in stomach	coffee, mercury, tea, smoking
Chromium – Cr	with protein food	B3, hydrochloric acid in stomach	tea, coffee, smoking

MINERAL BIOAVAILABILITY

Most of the minerals essential for health are supplied from food to the body as a compound bound to a larger (food) molecule. This binding is known as chelation, from the Greek word *chela,* meaning a claw. Some form of chelation is important, since most essential minerals in their "raw" state have a slight electrical positive charge. The stomach wall is slightly negatively charged, so once separated from food through the process of digestion these unbound minerals would become loosely bound to the stomach wall. Instead of being absorbed, these minerals would easily become bound to undesirable substances like the phytic acid in bran, the tannic acid in tea, oxalic acid, and so on—these acids remove the mineral from the body.

Bioavailability of a mineral, which is defined as the proportion that can be utilized, depends on many factors, including the amount of "enhancers" and "inhibitors" present, such as phytates, other minerals and vitamins, as well as the acidity of the digestive environment. Most minerals are absorbed in the duodenum, the first part of the small intestine, assisted by the presence of stomach acid.

Minerals are bound, or chelated, to different compounds to help their absorption. Amino acid-chelated minerals are bound to amino acids, examples of which are chromium picolinate, and selenocysteine or zinc amino acid chelate. These are well absorbed, as are other "organic" compounds including citrates, gluconates, and aspartates. Inorganic compounds such as carbonates, sulphates, and oxides are less well absorbed.

For some minerals the extra cost of amino acid-chelated minerals outweighs the advantage. For example, magnesium amino acid chelate is only twice as well absorbed as magnesium carbonate, an inexpensive source of magnesium. Iron amino acid chelate, on the other hand, is four times better absorbed, making the price differential worth it. Generally speaking, the following forms are most readily available to the body, listed in decreasing order of their bioavailability.

Calcium	Amino acid chelate, ascorbate, citrate, gluconate, carbonate
Magnesium	Amino acid chelate, ascorbate, citrate, gluconate, carbonate
Iron	Amino acid chelate, ascorbate, citrate, gluconate, sulphate, oxide
Zinc	Picolinate, amino acid chelate, ascorbate, citrate, gluconate, sulphate
Manganese	Amino acid chelate, ascorbate, citrate, gluconate
Selenium	Selenocysteine or selenomethionine, sodium selenite
Chromium	Picolinate, polynicotinate, ascorbate, gluconate

What about sustained release?

Some vitamins are called prolonged, sustained, or time-released, implying that the ingredients are not all made available for absorption in one go. This can be useful when taking large amounts of water-soluble vitamins such as B complex or vitamin C. However, absorption depends also on the person and the dosage. Some people are able to absorb and use 1000 mg of vitamin C taken in one dose; taking it in sustained release form would provide little benefit. However, if you take three 1,000 mg tablets a day, sustained release would allow you to take them all in one go. Since sustained-release vitamins are more expensive, you have to weigh up the pros and cons. And there is no point in having a sustained-release fat-soluble vitamin, such a A, D, or E, as these can be stored in the body.

The best sustained-release products are capsules containing tiny "beads," each containing the desired nutrients, which dissolve at different rates and so release the nutrients over time. This method, however, consumes a lot of space, so the dose is not usually very high, making the necessity for sustained release less relevant.

GOOD AND BAD COMBINATIONS

The general rule is to take supplements with food. This is primarily because the presence of stomach acid helps many minerals to be absorbed, and because the fat-soluble vitamins are carried by the fats or oils present in most meals. Nutrients do, however, compete for absorption. For example, if you want to absorb a large amount of a specific amino acid such as lysine (good for the arteries and for preventing herpes) more will be absorbed if you take it on an empty stomach or with non-protein foods such as a piece of fruit. Similarly, a tiny mineral like selenium will be absorbed better on its own than as part of a multimineral.

However, no one wants to end up taking each supplement separately. So unless you have a specific need or deficiency and want to maximize absorption by taking the nutrient on its own, spread your nutrients out through the day and take them with meals as nature intended.

There is, however, always one exception. If you want to take the alkaline-forming "ascorbate" type of vitamin C in quite large doses (3 grams or more a day), take it away from meals to avoid neutralizing the acidity in your stomach. If you ever experience a burning sensation after taking vitamin C as ascorbic acid (a weak acid), you may have some gastro-intestinal irritation or even an ulcer. See your doctor and have this possibility checked out. While vitamin C helps to heal wounds, the acid form can irritate an existing problem and should be avoided.

DRUG–NUTRIENT INTERACTIONS: DIFFICULTIES AND DANGERS

There are very few dangerous drug–nutrient interactions. However, there are many drugs which interfere with the action of nutrients, increasing your need.

- Aspirin increases the need for vitamin C

- The birth control pill and HRT increase the need for B6, B12, folic acid, and zinc

- Antibiotics increase the need for B vitamins and beneficial bacteria

- Paracetamol increases the need for antioxidants

Here are details of some potentially dangerous combinations which must be avoided:

- Warfarin (a blood-thinning drug), aspirin, vitamin E, and high EPA/DHA fish oils all thin the blood, and the combined effect would be too much.

It is better to reduce the drugs and increase the nutrients, but first check with your doctor. Warafin also thins the blood by interfering with vitamin K metabolism so don't supplement a multivitamin containing vitamin K if you are on this medication.

- Taking MAOI anti-depressants (such as Nardil or Parstelin) means you must avoid yeast (including supplements), alcohol, and certain specific foods.

- Some anti-convulsants are anti-folate, creating an increased need for folic acid, yet supplementation can impair the action of the drug. Specialist advice from your doctor and nutrition consultant is recommended. Epileptics should be careful about supplementing the brain nutrient DMAE or high-dose essential fatty acids such as evening primrose oil.

- In cases of B12 deficiency, supplementing folic acid can reduce the symptoms while the underlying deficiency gets worse. Therefore it is best to supplement both nutrients, preferably as part of a B complex.

DO'S AND DON'TS OF SUPPLEMENT-TAKING

Very few problems can or do occur with vitamin supplements, but it is sensible to be aware of the following:

- Vitamin A (retinol) in doses in excess of 10,000 IUs (3,000 mcg) should not be taken by pregnant women or women trying to conceive. Check that the total provided by all your supplements (e.g., a multivitamin, antioxidant complex, etc.) does not exceed this level.

- Beta-carotene in excess makes your skin go excessively yellow. If you have excessively yellowing skin check your beta-carotene intake from food and supplements. This is quite different from jaundice or hepatitis, in which the whites of your eyes go yellow.

- Vitamin B2 (riboflavin) makes your urine bright yellow. This is normal.

- Vitamin B3 in the form of niacin, usually in doses of 100 mg or more, can make you flush and get red, hot, and itchy for up to thirty minutes. This is normal and is not an allergy. While the nutrient is beneficial, if you do not like the side effect take less or else take half the dose twice a day. Your flushing potential will reduce with regular supplementation. (Alternatively, buy the "no flush" type of niacin.)

- Vitamin C has a laxative effect in very high doses, normally above 5 grams a day. A small number of people are very sensitive even at 1 gram a day, while others can tolerate 10 grams a day. The ideal level is the "bowel tolerance" level, so adjust your intake accordingly.

- Copper is an essential mineral but toxic. Do not take supplements containing copper unless they contain at least ten to fifteen times as much zinc. So, for example, if there is 1 mg of copper, make sure there is 10–15 mg of zinc. This will prevent copper accumulation.

VALUE FOR MONEY

For a supplement to be good value it must be well made, well formulated, and well priced. The quality of manufacture is hard to assess unless you have an advanced chemistry laboratory in your back room! However, there are four simple tests you can do:

1. Are the stated number of tablets actually in the bottle? (When we tested one manufacturer's product at ION we found an average of 95 tablets instead of 100.)
2. Is the tablet coated all around and therefore easy to swallow? (Uncoated or badly coated tablets can break up or taste unpleasant.)
3. Does the label tell you everything you need to know? (The better the company, the more information it will want to give you.)
4. Does the company emphasize its quality control and, if asked, can it supply you with independent analysis on its products?

42

VITAMINS AND MINERALS—HOW MUCH IS SAFE?

Just how safe are supplements? What happens if you take more vitamins or minerals than you need? How much is too much? These are common concerns, fueled by media reports linking vitamin C with kidney stones and warnings against vitamin A in pregnancy. How much is fact and how much is fiction?

The optimal intake of a nutrient varies considerably for each individual, depending on their age, sex, health, and numerous other factors. It is therefore to be expected that the level that would induce signs of toxicity also varies considerably. When certain illnesses are present, a person's need for a vitamin can increase dramatically: vitamin C is the prime example, when you are fighting an infection. In this chapter I have erred on the side of caution by listing the levels of nutrients that may induce toxicity in a small percentage of people, both if taken over a short period (up to one month), and over a long period (three months to three years), indicating which symptoms persist and which go away once the high level is reduced.

It is important to realize that just about everything is toxic if the dose is high enough. In 1990 a man died of drinking 10 quarts of water in two hours. So the critical question is: how much more of the substance than is normally consumed do you need to consume to reach toxic levels? In other words, what is the safety margin?

THE SAFETY OF VITAMINS

The general conclusion from a survey of the results of over one hundred research papers in scientific journals is that for the majority of vitamins, with the exception of A and D, levels one hundred times greater than the U.S. RDA are likely to be safe for long-term ingestion.[96] In practical terms, this means that the chances of having a toxic reaction to even the higher-dose supplements available in health food shops is extremely unlikely unless you take considerably more tablets than recommended. This is broadly consistent with the public health record of deaths attributed to nutritional supplements. For example, a survey of Local Poison Control Centers in the U.S. between the years 1983 and 1987 listed 1182 fatalities resulting from pharmaceutical drugs, but not one resulting from a vitamin supplement. In Britain, I have been unable to find details of any death attributable to vitamin supplementation, whereas approximately 15,000 deaths per year are attributable to pharmaceutical drugs. Death, however, is a rather severe yardstick. What about toxicity or adverse effects? These too are extremely uncommon as a result of nutritional supplements. In nearly twenty years of practice, teaching, and writing I have yet to come across a single case of actual toxicity.

Vitamin A

Vitamin A comes in two forms: the animal form, retinol, which stores in the body; and the vegetable form, beta-carotene, which is converted into retinol unless body levels are already high. Beta-carotene is therefore not considered toxic, with the exception that excessive intake can cause a reversible yellowing of the skin.

There are a number of incidences of adverse reactions to retinol, usually from intakes of 500,000 IUs of more over a considerable length of time. The symptoms include peeling and redness of the skin, disturbed hair growth, lack of appetite, and vomiting. According to Dr. John Marks, medical director at Girton College, Cambridge, "toxic reactions have been extremely rare below 30,000 IUs...daily administration in adults up to about 50,000 ius would appear to be safe." This is consistent with estimates of the intake of 40,000 IUs of vitamin A that our ancestors would have eaten in a more tropical environment, although a large part of this would have come from beta-carotene.

A number of cases of toxicity and birth defects have been reported for a synthetic relative of vitamin A, isotretinoin, sold as the drug Roaccutane. These effects have been wrongly extended to natural vitamin A. Five cases of birth defects have been reported in babies born to women taking large amounts of retinol (25,000–500,000 IUs per day); however no clear cause-and-effect relationship has ever been established in any of these cases. Other studies have shown that women who supplement their diet with multivitamins including vitamin A, usually at a level of 7500–25,000 IUs, have a lower incidence of defects in their babies. One study published in 1995 found a possible association in a group of 22,747 women, of whom 121 gave birth to children with the kind of defect associated with, among other things, vitamin A toxicity. Of these 121, two of the cases could have been attributable to supplementing in excess of 10,000 IUs of vitamin A in the form of retinol. In view of the possibility that large amounts of retinol could induce birth defects, it is wise for women of child-bearing age to take no more than 10,000 IUs of retinol in supplemental form. The same caution does not apply to beta-carotene.

Vitamin D

Of all the vitamins, D is the most likely to cause toxic reactions. It encourages calcium absorption, and excessive intake can lead to calcification of soft tissue. However, the levels that create this effect are certainly in excess of 10,000 IUs and probably more like 50,000 IUs. A daily intake not exceeding 2,000 IUs for adults and 1,000 IUs for children is generally considered safe. The Food and Nutrition Board's Upper Reference Level is 50 mcg which is 2,000 IUs.

Vitamin E

Vitamin E has been well researched for toxicity. A review of 216 trials of high-dose vitamin E in ten thousand patients showed that daily doses of 3,000 IUs for up to eleven years and 55,000 IUs for a few months had no detrimental effect. However, adverse reactions have occasionally been reported at lower levels of 2,000 IUs, especially in children, possibly due to an allergic reaction to the source of the vitamin E. Vitamin E appears to increase the anti-clotting effects of the drug Warfarin, and therefore high levels are not recommended for those on Warfarin. High levels are also best avoided by people suffering from rheumatic fever. Some old reports that vitamin E should not be taken in supplement form by women with breast cancer are inaccurate: it is highly beneficial to do so. A daily intake of up to 1,500 IUs is considered safe.

Vitamin C

Vitamin C is water-soluble and therefore excess is readily excreted from the body. RDAs vary considerably from country to country. A general consensus based on up-to-date research is that 100 mg a day represents a good basic intake; the optimal intake is probably between 1,000 and 3,000 mg a day. A number of studies have investigated the effects of vitamin C on specific diseases, using over 10,000 mg a day. The recommendation of these high levels has attracted controversy and allegations that vitamin C can cause kidney stone formation, interferes with B12 absorption, and causes a "rebound scurvy" when supplementation is stopped. All these allegations have been shown to be without substance. The only drawback to taking large amounts of vitamin C is that it can have a laxative effect. Generally, supplementing up to 5,000 mg of vitamin C can be considered safe.

Vitamin B

The B vitamins are water-soluble and excess is readily excreted from the body in the urine, so they are generally of very low toxicity. Thiamin (B1), riboflavin (B2), pantothenic acid (B5), B12, and biotin show no sign of toxicity at levels of at least 100 times the U.S. RDA. Vitamin B3 in the form of niacin causes blushing at levels of 75 mg or more; this is part of its natural action and therefore is not generally considered to be a toxic effect. According to Dr. John Marks at Girton College, Cambridge, "doses of 200 mg to 10 g daily have been used therapeutically to lower blood cholesterol levels under medical control for periods of up to ten years or more, and though some reactions have occurred at these very high dosages, they have rapidly responded to cessation of therapy, and have often cleared even when therapy has been continued." Levels of up to 2,000 mg per day on a continuous basis are considered safe. The Food and Nutrition Board's Upper Reference Level for vitamin B6 is 100 mg which is overly conservative.

Vitamin B6 has been extensively tested for toxicity by a number of research groups including the US government Food and Drug Administration, which concluded that "in man, side effects were not encountered with daily administration of 50–200 mg over periods of months." Most of the unfounded reports of low-dose B6 causing nerve damage appear to be based on one well-documented case of a woman who increased her B6 intake from supplements of 500 mg to 5,000 mg over a period of two years, and developed muscle weakness and pain which were attributed to nerve damage. One researcher, investigating seven cases of people taking 2,000–5,000 mg of B6 a day for considerable lengths of time, said that "substantial improvement occurred in all cases in the months after withdrawal of pyridoxine, usually with improvement in gait and less discomfort in the extremities, but in some patients, residual neurological discomfort remained." In rats, daily injected doses of 600 mg/kg, equivalent to 38,000 mg a day in a 140-pound person, caused "peripheral neuropathy," with tingling and numbing of the hands and feet.

Deficiency of vitamin B6 induces the same symptoms. The likely explanation is that, in order to become active in the body where it helps enzymes to work, pyridoxine must be converted to pyridoxal phosphate. If the body is saturated with excessive pyridoxine this conversion does not take place: enzymes become saturated with simple pyridoxine and so do not work properly. So B6 excess may, in fact, induce what are effectively B6 deficiency symptoms. Since zinc is required for the conversion of pyridoxine to pyridoxal phosphate, taking B6 with zinc is likely to reduce its toxicity. In any event, a daily intake of up to 200 mg on a continuous basis is generally considered safe.

THE SAFETY OF MINERALS

The safety of minerals depends on three factors: the amount, the form, and the balance with other minerals in the diet. First, all minerals show toxicity at exceedingly high doses. Where form is concerned, trivalent chromium, for example, is essential, while hexavalent chromium (found in neither foods nor supplements) is very toxic. And as for balance, iron supplementation can exacerbate zinc deficiency since it is a zinc antagonist. The reason for this antagonism is that the shape of the atoms of many minerals is very similar. They are really just different sizes of cogs, so if you lack one mineral but take in an excess of a similar-shaped one it can slot into the wrong enzyme, speeding it up, slowing it down, or simply stopping it from working altogether.

In view of these factors, the levels given in the following pages as safe for long-term consumption presuppose that other essential minerals are also adequately supplied. Larger amounts than those stated may also be safe for short-term use, particularly for people with certain illnesses which result in an extra requirements for a mineral. Selenium requirement, for example, is thought to increase in certain types of cancer.

Calcium

The best-absorbed of calcium's many forms include calcium ascorbate, amino acid chelate, gluconate, orotate, and carbonate. In normal, healthy people there is little danger of toxicity since the body excretes excessive amounts. In some cultures people consume in excess of 2 g a day from their diet alone, so this amount is certainly considered safe. The U.S. Food and Nutrition Board has set an Upper Reference level for calcium at 2.5 g a day and advise not to exceed this. Calcium deficiency disorders are sometimes treated with 3.5 g per day, but these levels should only be used under exceptional circumstances. Problems of excessive calcium arise from other factors such as excessive vitamin D intake (above 25,000 IUs per day), parathyroid, or kidney disorders. Calcium interacts with magnesium and phosphorus, so calcium supplementation should only be given to people with adequate magnesium and phosphorus intake, or supplementing these elements. Phosphorus is rarely deficient, while magnesium deficiency is quite common. The ideal calcium: phosphorus ratio is probably 1:1. Less than 1:2 is not desirable. The ideal calcium: magnesium ratio is probably 3:2.

Magnesium

The best-absorbed of magnesium's many forms include magnesium aspartate, ascorbate, amino acid chelate, gluconate, orotate, and carbonate.

Toxic effects include flushing of the skin, thirst, low blood pressure, loss of reflexes, and respiratory depression. Toxicity is only likely to occur in people with kidney disease who are taking magnesium supplements. For normal, healthy adults a daily intake of up to 1000 mg is considered safe. Magnesium interacts with calcium, so magnesium supplements should only be given to people with adequate calcium intake, or supplementing calcium. The ideal magnesium:calcium ratio is probably 2:3, and in cases of magnesium deficiency 1:1. The Upper Reference Level for magnesium is set at 350 mg a day, but this is because certain magnesium compounds at very high doses can be irritating to the stomach. This does not occur with amino acid chelates, ascorbates, citrate, gluconate, or aspartates, all of which are well absorbed.

Iron

This is one of the most frequently deficient minerals. According to the Health & Nutrition Examination Survey, nine out of ten women were obtaining insufficient iron in their diet. Iron comes in many different forms, the best-absorbed of which include ferrous aspartate, amino acid chelate, succinate, lactate, and gluconate (ferric forms are less well absorbed). Ferrous sulphate is less toxic than ferric forms of iron. Even so, 3g of ferrous sulphate can cause death in an infant, compared to 12 g for an adult. Supplements containing a significant amount of iron should be kept in a child-proof container. Iron stores in the body and therefore toxicity can result from chronic over-intake, producing hemosiderosis, a generalized deposition of iron within body tissue, or hemochromatosis, normally a hereditary condition resulting in cirrhosis of the liver, bronze pigmentation of the skin, diabetes, arthritis, and heart abnormalities. Both conditions are extremely rare as a result of dietary intake; 50 mg a day as a supplement is generally considered safe.

Iron is antagonistic to many other trace minerals including zinc, which is often deficient especially among pregnant and lactating women. Therefore extra iron should not be supplemented without ensuring adequate zinc status or supplementing it. The normal requirement for zinc and iron is approximately equal.

Zinc

This is one of the most thoroughly researched and commonly deficient minerals. About a thousand papers are published each year indicating its value for a variety of conditions. The best-absorbed forms of zinc include zinc picolinate, amino acid chelate, citrate, and gluconate. Zinc supplementation is relatively non-toxic. In doses of 2,000 mg symptoms of nausea, vomiting, fever, and severe anemia have been reported. Small amounts of zinc, particularly in the form of zinc sulphate, can act as an irritant in the digestive tract when taken on an empty stomach. There is also some evidence that, at levels of 300 mg per day, zinc may impair rather than improve immune function. It is generally considered safe to supplement up to 50 mg per day.

Zinc is an iron, manganese, and copper antagonist, therefore an adequate intake of these minerals is advisable if large amounts of zinc are taken over a long period. Manganese is very poorly absorbed, so it is generally advisable to supplement half as much manganese as zinc if more than 20 mg of zinc a day is supplemented. The normal requirement for zinc is about ten times that of copper. Since the average intake of copper for people on a healthy diet is in the order of 2 mg, those supplementing more than 20 mg of zinc may be advised to add 1 mg of copper for each additional 10 mg of zinc. It is also best to ensure that at least 12 mg of iron is supplemented when you are taking more than 20 mg of zinc.

Copper

Deficiency of this mineral is quite rare, probably because we get it from drinking water as well as from unrefined foods. The best-absorbed forms of copper include copper amino acid chelate and gluconate. Requirements are low (2 mg per day), and only 5 mg a day is required to correct deficiency. Toxicity does occur, mainly due to excessive intake from water that flows through copper pipes. Copper is also a strong antagonist of zinc, and for this reason it is advisable not to supplement more than 2 mg or a tenth of one's intake of zinc. Copper also depletes manganese.

Manganese

No more than 2–5 percent of dietary manganese is absorbed, so increasing your intake from food only has a slight effect on overall body levels. The better forms for absorption include amino acid chelates, gluconates, and orotates. There is some evidence that vitamin C may help the absorption of manganese. In animals it is one of the least toxic of all trace elements. Toxicity has never been reported in man. A daily intake of up to 50 mg is considered safe. Excessive zinc or copper intake interferes with manganese uptake.

Selenium

This trace element is required in very small amounts of 25–200 mcg per day. It comes in two forms: organic, such as selenomethionine or selenocystine, sometimes in the form of selenium yeast; and inorganic, as sodium selenite.

The inorganic form is more toxic, with toxicity occurring at levels of 1,000 mcg or more. The organic forms show toxicity above 2,000 mcg. No toxicity has been reported with either form at intakes of 750 mcg. An intake of up to 500 mcg for an adult is generally considered safe. In view of the relatively small difference between beneficial and detrimental intake, selenium should be kept out of reach of children.

Chromium

Of the two forms of chromium found in nature, hexavalent and trivalent, hexavalent is much more toxic. However, it is found neither in food nor in supplements, so contamination can only occur from occupational exposure. The better-absorbed forms of chromium are picolinate and amino acid chelate. Trivalent chromium has a very low toxicity, partly because so little is absorbed. An intake of up to 500 mcg is certainly considered safe.

While there is no substitute for individual assessment of nutrient needs, the following nutritional advice is helpful for people suffering from particular health problems. For the more serious conditions it is best to follow these programs under the supervision of your doctor or nutrition consultant. The supplements recommended are for adults and are based on the formulas given in Chapter 39. Since dosage is crucial, it is best to get supplements close to these formulas. When individual amounts of a nutrient are given, these are the total required. Check that you are not "doubling up" by receiving, for example, vitamin A in a multivitamin, an antioxidant, and a separate supplement. For further guidance on supplement doses stay within the ranges given in Chapter 42, using the higher amounts for conditions that are specifically helped by these nutrients, or when symptoms of deficiency are present.

The recommendations given are aimed at helping to restore health in these conditions. They do not replace medical advice, nor should they be continued on an ongoing basis once the condition is corrected.

ACNE

This condition is most prevalent among teenagers, and the hormonal changes that take place at this age are certainly at the root of many skin problems. These changes cause the sebaceous glands to produce too much sebum, which blocks up the skin pores and makes them more likely to get infected. A diet high in saturated fat or fried food also makes pores more likely to get blocked. Vitamin A deficiency produces skin congestion through over-keratinization of skin cells. Vitamin A and zinc deficiency leads to lowered ability to fight infection, as does lack of beneficial bacteria (through over-use of antibiotics). Optimum nutrition helps by balancing hormones as well as reducing the risk of infection. The most important nutrients are vitamins A, B complex (especially B6), C, and E, zinc, niacin for skin flushing, and vitamin E for wound healing. Good diet and cleanliness are essential. Be careful of supplements with added iodine, which can make acne worse.

Diet advice
Follow an optimum diet and drink plenty of water. Sulphur-rich foods such as eggs, onions, and garlic are also helpful. Avoid sugar, cigarettes, fried, and high-fat foods. Eat plenty of fresh fruit and vegetables (high water content foods).

Supplements

- Multivitamin and multimineral
- Antioxidant complex
- 2 × vitamin C 1,000 mg
- Vitamin B6 100 mg
- Zinc 15 mg
- Vitamin E 500 IUs (helps heal the skin)
- Niacin (B3) 100 mg for thirty days (for flushing and cleansing the skin)

Also read Chapter 22.

ALCOHOLISM

Particularly prevalent among histadelic (high-histamine) people (see p. 200), alcoholism may in part be a way of coping with the excess energy that such individuals produce. B vitamins, especially B1, B2, B3, and B6, are destroyed by alcohol, which primarily affects the liver and nervous system. Vitamins A and C help protect the liver. A very alkaline diet reduces the craving for alcohol. Emotional problems almost always underlie alcoholism, and these, as well as the addiction—which usually also exists for sugar, must be solved.

Diet advice

Follow the recommended diet and eat plenty of whole grains, beans, and lentils. Drink plenty of water. Often, sugar addiction is substituted for alcohol, which is just another form of sugar, so sugar and stimulants are also best avoided. Eat frequent meals containing some protein foods such as nuts, seeds, fish, chicken, eggs, or milk products.

Supplements

- Multivitamin and multimineral
- Antioxidant complex
- 3 × vitamin C 1,000 mg
- Vitamin B6 100mg + zinc 10 mg
- Bone mineral complex (providing 500 mg calcium and 300 mg magnesium)

Also read Chapter 31.

ALLERGIES

"Allergy" is a word that often invokes connotations beyond its original meaning. An allergy is an intolerance to a particular substance. We have an intolerance to coffee, for example, if large amounts produce symptoms. Some people have more pronounced symptoms, even to simple foods like wheat or milk. Since an allergy is like an addiction, it is often the foods that one is most "addicted" to that are suspect. If you feel that you might have allergies but do not know what they are, it is best to see a nutrition consultant or an allergy specialist who can test you and solve any underlying digestive imbalances that provoke allergies. Optimum nutrition will greatly reduce or clear up allergic reactions in most cases. Vitamin C, calcium, and magnesium help to reduce the severity of allergic reactions. L-glutamine heals the stomach and supports the immune system, reducing allergic potential.

Diet advice

Follow a general healthy diet. Avoid suspect foods, dairy products, and grains (the most common allergens), especially wheat. After two months you may be able to reintroduce suspect foods every fourth day without having a reaction. Eventually you may be able to tolerate your allergens in small amounts on a daily basis.

Supplements

- Multivitamin and multimineral
- Antioxidant complex
- 4 × vitamin C 1,000 mg
- Calcium/magnesium complex (providing 500 mg and 300 mg respectively)
- L-glutamine powder, 3 g a day

ANGINA AND ATHEROSCLEROSIS

Atherosclerosis is a narrowing of the arteries due to fatty deposits. When the condition becomes more pronounced, blood pressure begins to increase. If a pronounced block occurs in the arteries that supply the heart with oxygen, then angina, experienced as chest pain on exertion, may result. Optimum nutrition is the primary method for preventing both of these conditions. Antioxidant nutrients help prevent the cellular damage that may underlie these problems. Vitamin C and lysine help to reverse atherosclerosis. Vitamin B3 (niacin) raises HDL, the cholesterol remover. Fish oils, rich in EPA and DHA, thin the blood and reduce cholesterol.

Diet advice
Follow the dietary advice in this book strictly, avoiding sugar, salt, foods high in saturated fat, coffee, and excess alcohol. Ensure there are sufficient essential fats in diet by eating seeds. Get plenty of exercise within your capacity.

Supplements

- Multivitamin and multimineral (with at least 300 mg magnesium)
- 2 × antioxidant complex
- 4 × vitamin C 1,000 mg
- 2 × lysine 1,000 mg
- Vitamin E 500 IU
- "No-flush" niacin 500 mg
- 2 × EPA fish oil 1,200 mg

Also read Chapter 18.

ARTHRITIS

There are two major forms of arthritis and many different causes for both. Osteoarthritis, more common in the elderly, describes a condition in which the cartilage in the joints wears away, inducing pain and stiffness mainly in weight-bearing joints. Rheumatoid arthritis affects the whole body, not just certain joints. Antioxidant nutrients, essential fats, and vitamin B5 reduce inflammation. B vitamins and vitamin C support the endocrine system, which controls calcium balance. Vitamin D, calcium, magnesium, and boron support bone health.

Diet advice
Follow the perfect diet in this book and be sure to avoid adrenal stimulants such as tea, coffee, sugar, refined carbohydrates. Drink plenty of water and herb teas. Check for allergies, and have a hair mineral analysis done to check your mineral levels.

Supplements

- Multivitamin and multimineral
- Antioxidant complex
- 2 × vitamin C 1,000 mg
- Vitamin B5 (pantothenic acid) 500 mg
- GLA 150–300 mg
- EPA 1,200 mg
- Bone mineral complex

Also read Chapter 21.

Asthma

This inflammatory condition affects the lungs and respiration and is characterized by difficulty in breathing and frequent coughing. Often attacks are brought on by underlying allergies, stressful events, or changes in environmental conditions like the weather. Vitamin A helps protect the lining of the lungs, while vitamin C helps to deal with environmental toxins. Antioxidant nutrients and essential fats are anti-inflammatory.

Diet advice

Follow the perfect diet in this book, ensuring an adequate intake of essential oils, and see a nutrition consultant if you suspect you have allergies.

Supplements

- Multivitamin and multimineral
- Antioxidant complex
- 2 × vitamin C 1,000 mg
- 2 × GLA 150 mg from evening primrose or borage oil

Breast cancer

Most breast cancers are hormonally related, linked to estrogen dominance and progesterone deficiency. Stress, excessive use of stimulants, and exposure to pesticides all disrupt hormone balance. Some forms of breast cancer, however, are linked more to carcinogens. Antioxidant nutrients have been shown to decrease risk and increase survival. Use of natural progesterone has been shown to reverse the proliferation of tumor cells. See your doctor or nutrition consultant to get your hormone levels tested and consider natural progesterone cream (see Useful Addresses on p. 339).

Diet advice

Follow the diet in this book, with an emphasis on foods high in antioxidants, avoiding milk and meat due to their hormone content and eating organic as much as possible. Keep saturated fat very low and ensure you have adequate essential fats from seeds and their cold-pressed oils.

Supplements

- Multivitamin and multimineral
- 2 × antioxidant complex
- 4 × vitamin C 1,000 mg
- GLA 150 mg

Also read Chapters 20 and 27.

Bronchitis

In this condition the tissues of the lung get inflamed. Optimum nutrition can help prevent it by strengthening the immune system and helping to maintain healthy lung tissue. Vitamins A, B complex, C, and E, and the minerals selenium and zinc, all strengthen the immune system. Vitamins A and C protect lung tissue.

Diet advice

Follow the diet in this book and do not smoke. You may also find some relief from following a diet low in mucus-forming foods, such as milk and milk products. Keep saturated fat very low and ensure you have adequate essential fats from seeds and their cold-pressed oils.

Supplements

- Multivitamin and multimineral
- Antioxidant complex
- 2 × vitamin C 1,000 mg
- 2 × GLA 150 mg from evening primrose or borage oil
- vitamin E 400 IUs

Also read Chapter 28.

Burns, cuts and bruises

All these conditions require skin to heal, which depends on a good supply of vitamins A, C, and E, zinc and bioflavonoids. These reduce bruising, speed up healing, and minimize scar tissue. Vitamin E oil can be rubbed around, but not on, cuts and burns by piercing a vitamin E capsule. Also useful are creams rich in vitamin A, C, or E in a form that can penetrate the skin, such as retinyl, ascorbyl, or tocopheryl palmitate.

Diet advice

Follow the diet recommended in this book. Drink plenty of water. Ensure you have adequate essential fats from seeds and their cold-pressed oils.

Supplements

- Multivitamin and multimineral with 7,500 IUs (2,270mcg) of both vitamin A and beta-carotene
- Antioxidant complex
- 2 × vitamin C complex 1,000 mg with at least 150 mg of bioflavonoids
- 2 × GLA 150 mg from evening primrose or borage oil
- Vitamin E 500 IUs
- Zinc 15 mg

CANCER

There are many different kinds of cancer, with different causes. Most cancers are associated with exposure or ingestion of cancer-causing agents, coupled with immune insufficiency. Often there is an association with free radical damage of cells, which then become cancerous. Depending on the type of cancer, the first step is to eliminate cancer-stimulating agents—smoking, a high-fat diet, HRT, excessive exposure to sunlight or pesticides, a high meat diet, alcohol, etc. The next step is to build up the strength of the immune system with diet and supplements and to increase your intake of antioxidant nutrients.

Diet advice

Stick strictly to the diet advice in this book. Increase the amount of high antioxidant foods you eat (see p. 84). Cut out red meat and alcohol, and reduce all sources of saturated fat. A vegan-type diet is best. Also, drink plenty of water and herb tea, especially cat's claw which is a potent immune-booster.

Supplements

- Multivitamin and multimineral
- 2 × antioxidant complex
- 4 × vitamin C 1,000 mg (up to 10 g a day)
- 2 × GLA 150 mg from evening primrose or borage oil
- Vitamin A 10,000 IUs (3,000 mcg) a day (check what is in the antioxidant and multi)
- Vitamin E 600 IUs a day (check what is in the antioxidant and multi)
- Selenium 200 mcg a day (check what is in the antioxidant and multi)

Also read Chapters 19 and 27.

CANDIDIASIS

The overgrowth of candida albicans, a yeast-like fungus, can occur anywhere in the body, most commonly in the digestive tract or vagina, and causes thrush or yeast infection. Mild overgrowth can be eliminated by a four-point plan: anti-fungal agents such as caprylic acid and grapefruit seed extract; supplementation of beneficial bacteria; an immune-boosting diet and supplements; and an "anti-candida" diet (see below). It is usually best to work with a nutrition consultant, who can confirm the extent of the infection with proper tests.

Diet advice

Avoid all sources of sugar and especially fast-releasing sugars (including fruit for the first month). Also stay away from yeast-containing foods, mushrooms, and fermented foods such as alcohol and vinegar. Wheat is often best reduced since it irritates the stomach. So that means living off vegetables, grains, beans, lentils, nuts, and seeds. It is worth getting a good anti-candida recipe book!

Supplements

- Multivitamin and multimineral
- Antioxidant complex
- 2 × vitamin C 1,000 mg
- Caprylic acid 700 mg twice a day
- Grapefruit seed extract 15 drops twice a day
- A probiotic supplement such as lactobacillus acidophilus/bifidus (take separately from caprylic acid and grapefruit seed extract, perhaps before bed)

Also read Chapters 19 and 28.

COLDS AND FLU

Exposure to viruses is unavoidable, unless you live like a hermit. However, whether you succumb to a virus depends on the strength of your immune system at the time of infection. Studies have repeatedly shown that taking a daily supplement of 1 gram of vitamin C or more reduces the incidence, severity, and duration of colds. However, optimum nutrition, together with immune-boosting nutrients during cold epidemics, can produce even better results.

Diet advice

Avoid all dairy products, eggs, and excessive meat or soybean consumption, since these foods are mucus-forming. This is a great time to give your body a high-energy pure food diet packed with fresh fruit and vegetables and their juices. Drink cat's claw tea three times a day to boost the immune system.

Supplements

- Multivitamin and multimineral
- Antioxidant complex
- 2 × vitamin C 1,000 mg (4 g every four hours only when infected)
- Elderberry extract (1 dessertspoon four times a day only when infected)
- Echinacea drops (10 drops, two or three times a day)

Also read Chapter 28.

COLITIS

In this condition part of the large intestine is inflamed. It is often stress-induced; however, it can also be due to poor diet, poor elimination, an allergy, or sub-optimum nutrition. Since there is inflammation, the first step is to reduce any aggravating foods including alcohol, coffee, and wheat. These can be replaced by foods and drinks which pass easily through the digestive tract, such as steamed vegetables, rice, fish, and fruit, plus digestive enzyme supplements. Essential fats rich in GLA are powerful anti-inflammatory agents. Antioxidants also help to reduce inflammation.

Diet advice

While the diet recommended in this book is a good one, the high fiber content can act as an irritant in this condition. So a diet of lightly steamed vegetables, fish, and cooked grains is often preferable, with easy-to-digest fruit as snacks. Avoid all digestive irritants, which can include any food you are allergic to, wheat, alcohol, coffee, and spices.

Supplements

- Multivitamin and multimineral
- Antioxidant complex
- 2 × GLA 150 mg
- Vitamin C 500 mg (up to 2,000 mg as ascorbate, because ascorbic acid can irritate an already inflamed bowel)
- digestive enzyme formula with each main meal

Also read Chapter 17

CONSTIPATION

Contrary to popular belief, we should empty our bowels not once but two or three times a day. A healthy stool should break up easily and be no strain to pass. By these criteria, a large majority of people suffer from constipation. A high-fiber diet will help, as will a reduction in meat and milk products. Exercise is crucial, as it strengthens the abdominal muscles. Vitamins B1 and E help, while vitamin C may loosen the bowels. A non-irritant laxative, fructo oligosaccharides powder, helps relieve severe constipation.

Diet advice

Follow the diet advice in this book, in particular eating high-fiber foods. Drink at least a quart of water a day, preferably between meals. Reduce your consumption of meat and milk products. Include oats and prunes in your diet and linseeds, which can be ground and sprinkled on food.

Supplements

- Multivitamin and multimineral
- 3 × vitamin C 1,000 mg
- Vitamin E 500 IUs

  Also read Chapter 17.

CHRONIC FATIGUE

There are many causes of chronic fatigue, the most common of which is sub-optimum nutrition. Nutrients needed in energy production include vitamins C and B complex, iron, and magnesium. However, more pronounced symptoms, sometimes called ME, can include extreme tiredness on exertion. These can result from the body's ability to detoxify being overloaded. Any generation of energy (exercise) or digestion (eating) produces toxins for the body to deal with. If symptoms occur after eating or exercise, see a nutrition consultant who can test your liver detoxification potential.

Diet advice

Eat little and often, choosing from slow-releasing carbohydrates and snacking on fruit. Avoid sugar and stimulants such as tea, coffee, chocolate, and alcohol. In general, follow the dietary recommendations in this book.

Supplements

- Multivitamin and multimineral
- 3 × vitamin C 1,000 mg
- B complex
- Antioxidant complex

  Also read Chapter 24.

CYSTITIS

This is an inflammation and infection of the bladder, which causes frequent and painful urination. Vitamins C and A protect you from such infections, and vitamin C can be particularly helpful at clearing it up. So too can grapefruit seed extract. The following recommendations only apply to clear up a bout of cystitis and should not be followed on a regular basis.

Diet advice

Follow the diet in this book. Avoid all sugar. Drink about 2 quarts of water a day.

Supplements

- Multivitamin and multimineral
- Calcium ascorbate powder 10 grams in water/juice a day until clear
- 2 × vitamin A 7500 IUs (2,270 mcg)
- Grapefruit seed extract 10 drops three times a day

Also read Chapter 28.

DEPRESSION

There are many nutritionally related causes of depression, the most common being sub-optimum nutrition resulting in poor mental and physical energy. Disturbed blood sugar balance can result in periods of depression. People who produce excessive amounts of histamine are also prone to it. Adrenal exhaustion, usually brought on by stress and over-use of stimulants, can have this effect. Allergies too can bring on depression. A nutrition consultant can help identify any factor that can be corrected by nutrition.

Diet advice

Cut out or avoid sugar and refined foods. Cut down on stimulants—tea, coffee, chocolate, cola drinks, cigarettes, and alcohol. Follow the diet in this book. Experiment for two weeks without wheat or dairy products.

Supplements

- Multivitamin
- Multimineral with at least zinc 10 mg, magnesium 200 mg, manganese 5 mg and chromium 100 mcg
- 2 × vitamin C 1,000 mg
- Pantothenic acid 500 mg

Also read Chapter 31.

DERMATITIS

This condition literally means "skin inflammation," and is similar to eczema. Usually the term "dermatitis" is used when the primary cause appears to be a contact allergy. Go through all possibilities such as metals in jewelry and watches, perfumes, cosmetics, detergents, soaps, and shampoos. Where there is a contact allergy there is often a food allergy too: common culprits are dairy products and wheat. Sometimes a combination of eating an allergy-provoking food and contact with an external allergen is needed in order for symptoms to develop. Another frequently encountered factor is a lack of essential fatty acids from seeds and their oils, which in the body turn into anti-inflammatory prostaglandins. Their formation is also blocked by too much saturated fat or fried food, or a lack of certain key vitamins and minerals. The skin is also a route which the body can use to get rid of toxins. A certain kind of dermatitis, called acrodermatitis, responds exceptionally well to zinc supplementation and is primarily caused by zinc deficiency.

Diet advice

Generally a vegan-type diet, low in saturated fat but with enough essential fats from seeds, is best. If you suspect an allergy to dairy products or wheat, test for this by avoiding these foods.

Supplements

- Multivitamin and multimineral (with magnesium 300 mg and zinc 15 mg)
- 2 × vitamin C 1,000 mg
- Antioxidant complex
- GLA 300 mg
- Vitamin E 500 IU

Also read Chapter 22.

DIABETES

Both insulin-dependent diabetes (which occurs most commonly in children and is known as Type 1) and non-insulin dependent diabetes (which occurs more commonly in adults, known as Type 2) are conditions caused by too high blood sugar. Insulin dependent diabetes may develop through a cross-reaction between a protein in milk and beef and a protein in the pancreas. This can occur if genetically susceptible infants are fed dairy products or beef in their first few months, before their digestive tract and immune system are fully matured. Non-insulin dependent diabetes is usually a consequence of poor eating habits (too much sugar and stimulants), often preceded by hypoglycaemia or low blood sugar. Ensuring that adrenal hormones, insulin, and glucose tolerance factor are properly produced by the liver is fundamental in dealing with all forms of glucose intolerance and diabetes. Particularly important are vitamins C, B3, B5, and B6, zinc, and chromium. It is best to discuss any proposed changes in your diet with your doctor.

Diet advice

The key to a diabetic diet is to keep your blood sugar level even. This is achieved best by eating little and often, choosing foods which contain slow-releasing carbohydrates plus some protein. This means eating some nuts with fruit, "seed" vegetables like corn, peas, green beans, or whole grains, beans, or lentils, which contain both slow-releasing carbohydrate and protein. Avoid all sugar and forms of concentrated sweetness, such as concentrated fruit juice, and even excesses of faster-releasing fruits such as dates and bananas, or of dried fruit. Also avoid too many adrenal stimulants such as tea, coffee, alcohol, cigarettes, and salt.

Supplements

- Multivitamin and multimineral
- 2 × vitamin C 1,000 mg
- B complex
- Zinc 20 mg
- Chromium 200 mcg

Also read Chapter 10.

DIVERTICULITIS

This is a condition of the small and large intestine, in which pockets in the intestinal wall become distended and are then more likely to get infected and inflamed. The condition, probably the result of not enough fiber and exercise, is rarely seen in primitive cultures. A general vitamin program is recommended to support the muscle tone surrounding the intestines and to maintain a strong infection-fighting system. Increased soluble fiber and regular exercise such as swimming are the key treatments.

Diet advice

Follow the recommended diet in this book, with particular reference to the high-fiber foods (see Part 9). However, if the inflammation is severe it is best to eat lightly steamed vegetables, oats (which contain soluble fiber) and ground seeds or nuts, and to stay away from added "hard" fibers like wheat bran. It is best to soak grains like oats so as to maximize their water content; these foods provide fiber without irritating the inflamed area. Also have a cold-pressed oil blend rich in Omega 3 and Omega 6 fatty acids, as these help to calm down inflammation.

Supplements

- Multivitamin and multimineral
- Vitamin E 500 IUs
- Vitamin C 1,000 mg

Also read Chapter 17.

EAR INFECTIONS

Infections of this kind are most frequently the result of an underlying allergy. An allergic reaction induces inflammation which blocks the thin tube that runs from the sinuses to the ears. Once this swells and blocks, the inner ear chamber becomes a favorite site for infection. Treatment with antibiotics quadruples the risk of another infection. This may be because antibiotics irritate the stomach wall, making it more leaky, which exacerbates underlying allergies.

Diet advice

Follow the diet recommended in this book. Eat and drink plenty of fruit, vegetables, and their juices. Drink plenty of water, herb teas, and three cups of cat's claw tea a day. Stay away from mucus-forming foods—dairy products, meat, and eggs. Dairy allergy is the single most common cause of ear infections.

Supplements

- Multivitamin and multimineral
- Antioxidant complex
- 3 × vitamin C 1,000 mg
- Echinacea 10 drops twice a day
- Aloe vera a measure a day as instructed on the bottle (get the best, since the concentration of active ingredient varies a lot)
- Grapefruit seed extract 10 drops twice a day

Scale these amounts down, according to weight, for children. Give a child weighing 60 pounds (half an average adult), for instance, 5 drops of both echinacea and grapefruit seed extract, 500 mg of vitamin C three times a day (1,500 mg in total) and a children's multivitamin and multimineral and antioxidant complex.

Also read Chapter 28.

ECZEMA

In this unpleasant condition the skin becomes scaly and itchy; it can crack and be very sore. Dermatitis is very similar in nature and probably also in cause. The possibility of allergy must be strongly considered. Although the mechanism is unknown, optimum nutrition does usually help this condition. Vitamins A and C strengthen the skin, while vitamin E and zinc improve healing. When there is no open wound, vitamin E oil can help to heal the skin. Essential fats also help to reduce inflammation.

Diet advice

Generally a vegan-type diet, low in saturated fat and with sufficient essential fats from seeds, is best. If you suspect an allergy to dairy products or wheat, test for it avoiding these foods.

Supplements

- Multivitamin and multimineral (with magnesium 300 mg and zinc 15 mg)
- 2 × vitamin C 1,000 mg
- Antioxidant complex
- GLA 300 mg
- Vitamin E 500 IUs

Also read Chapter 22.

GALLSTONES

These are accumulations of calcium or cholesterol in the duct running from the liver to the gall bladder, which stores bile used for digesting fats. If this duct is blocked, fats cannot be properly absorbed and jaundice occurs. It is not excesses of calcium or cholesterol in the diet that are to blame, but rather how these substances are dealt with in the body. Often, gallstone victims have inherited very narrow bile ducts, increasing their risk of this condition. Lecithin helps to emulsify cholesterol, and optimum nutrition in general should help prevent such abnormalities occurring. Digestive enzyme supplements contain lipase to help digest fat.

Diet advice

Follow the diet recommended in this book, avoiding saturated fat and keeping your essential fat intake regular, perhaps with seeds for breakfast and a dessertspoon of cold-pressed oil rich in Omega 3 and Omega 6 at lunch and dinner. Avoid meals containing large amounts of fat.

Supplements

- Multivitamin and multimineral
- Antioxidant complex
- Vitamin C 1,000 mg
- 1 dessertspoon lecithin granules or a lecithin capsule, with each meal
- 1 × digestive enzyme (containing lipase) with each meal

Also read Chapter 17.

GOUT

This is caused by improper metabolism of proteins, resulting in uric acid crystals being deposited in fingers, toes, and joints and causing inflammation. Diets low in fat and moderate in protein help this condition, as does exercise. However, the many nutrients involved in protein metabolism, especially B6 and zinc, are also an essential part of a nutritional program for preventing gout.

Diet advice
Follow the diet in this book, avoiding red meat and alcohol. Be sure to drink at least 1 quart of water a day.

Supplements

- Multivitamin and multimineral
- 3 × vitamin C 1,000 mg
- Vitamin B6 100 mg
- Zinc 15 mg
- Bone mineral complex (rich in alkaline-forming calcium and magnesium)

HAIR PROBLEMS

There are many different kinds of hair problems, from dry or oily hair to premature hair loss, but most are linked to what you eat. Oily hair can occur with vitamin B deficiency. Dry or brittle hair is often a sign of essential fat deficiency. Poor hair growth, or loss of color, is a sign of zinc deficiency. Hair loss is connected with general nutritional deficiency, especially a lack of iron, vitamin B1, vitamin C, or lysine (an amino acid). Some hair supplements contain all these. Massaging the scalp also helps, as does hanging upside down which improves circulation to the scalp. The combination of optimum nutrition, stimulating scalp circulation, and correcting underlying hormonal imbalances (see Chapter 20) has proved the most effective answer for hair loss. Unfortunately there is no answer yet for gray hair, nor any apparent connection with nutrition.

Diet advice
Follow the diet recommended in this book. Make sure you do not go short of essential fats and water. Avoid sugar and stimulants like tea, coffee, and chocolate.

Supplements

- Multivitamin and multimineral (with 15 mg iron and 15 mg zinc)
- B complex
- Vitamin C 1,000 mg
- Lysine 1,000 mg (for hair loss only)

HANGOVERS

The symptoms of excess alcohol are half dehydration and half intoxication. Once the liver's ability to detoxify alcohol is exceeded the body produces a toxic substance and it is this that brings about a headache. The advice below, if followed before drinking, will reduce any "morning after" symptoms. So does drinking masses of liquid, which dilutes the alcohol. Needless to say, drinking large amounts of alcohol is not optimum nutrition!

Diet advice
Follow the recommendations in this book. Eat pure foods that will not add to the body's toxic burden. Fruit and vegetable juices, high in antioxidants, are very beneficial, as is lots of water—about 2 quarts in a day. Also drink cat's claw tea.

Supplements

- Multivitamin and multimineral (preferably with molybdenum)
- 6 × vitamin C 1,000 mg (1 every two hours)
- 3 × antioxidant complex

HAY FEVER

Even though allergic reactions to pollen are the identified cause of hay fever, other factors make one person more likely to sneeze than another. The incidence of hay fever has risen dramatically in cities compared to rural areas, which led to the discovery that pollutants such as exhaust fumes prime the immune system to react. During the summer the air in polluted areas contains more free radicals due to the action of sunlight on oxygen molecules, so city-dwellers breathe in more pollutants. Taking a good all-round antioxidant supplement containing vitamins A, C, and E, beta-carotene, selenium, and zinc, plus the amino acids cysteine, cysteine or glutathione, helps increase your resistance (the most effective form of these amino acids is N-Acetyl Cysteine, sometimes called NAC, and "reduced" glutathione). The amino acid methionine, in combination with calcium, is an effective anti-histamine. You need to take 500 mg of l-methionine with 400 mg of calcium twice a day. Vitamin C helps to control excessive histamine levels. Vitamin B6 and zinc have a role to play in balancing histamine levels and strengthening the immune system. Vitamin B5 helps reduce symptoms.

The three most common substances reacted to are pollen, wheat, and milk. Although there is no proven connection, it is interesting to note that all these are originally grass products. It may be that some hay fever sufferers become sensitized to proteins that are common to grains, grasses, and possibly milk. In any event, dairy products encourage mucus production. Similarly, modern strains of wheat are high in gluten, which irritates the digestive tract and stimulates mucus production.

Diet advice

Avoid or at least limit wheat, dairy products, and alcohol. Eat plenty of antioxidant-rich fruit and vegetables, plus seeds rich in selenium and zinc. Where possible, avoid exposure to pollen and traffic fumes.

Supplements

- Multivitamin and multimineral (providing B6 100 mg and zinc 15 mg)
- Antioxidant complex
- 3 × vitamin C 1,000 mg

If you are really suffering try . . .

- L-methionine 500 mg twice a day
- Calcium 400 mg twice a day
- Pantothenic acid 500 mg twice a day

Headaches and migraines

There are many causes of headaches and migraines, ranging from blood sugar drops, dehydration, and allergy to stress and tension, or a critical combination. Peaks and troughs in adrenalin and blood sugar can bring on a headache. Often they go away with optimum nutrition. If they persist, look carefully at the possibility of allergy. See if you can notice any correlation between the foods you eat and the incidence of headaches.

For migraine-sufferers, instead of taking an aspirin, or migraine drugs which constrict the blood vessels, try taking 100–200 mg of vitamin B3 in the niacin form, which is a vasodilator. Start with the smaller dose: this will often stop or reduce a migraine in the early stages. It is best to do this at home in a relaxed environment, so the customary warm blushing sensation will probably not bother you.

Diet advice
Eat little and often and avoid long periods without food, especially if you are stressed or tense. Also make sure you drink regularly. Avoid sugar and stimulants like tea, coffee, and chocolate.

Supplements

- Multivitamin and multimineral
- B complex
- Vitamin C 1,000 mg
- B3 niacin 100 mg

High blood pressure

Hypertension or high blood pressure can be caused by atherosclerosis (a narrowing and thickening of the arteries), arterial tension, or thicker blood. Arterial tension is controlled by the balance of calcium, magnesium, and potassium in relation to sodium (salt). Stress also plays a part. Correcting this balance can lower blood pressure in thirty days. Vitamins C and E and fish oils high in EPA and DHA help to keep the blood thin. To reverse atherosclerosis see p. 274.

Diet advice
Follow the diet recommended in this book. Avoid salt and foods with added salt. Increase fruit (eat at least three pieces a day) and vegetables, which are rich in potassium. Take a tablespoon of ground seeds as a source of extra calcium and magnesium. Unless you are vegetarian, eat poached, grilled, or baked tuna, salmon, herring, or mackerel twice a week.

Supplements

- Multivitamin and multimineral
- Antioxidant
- 2 × vitamin C 1,000 mg
- Vitamin E 500 IUs
- Bone mineral complex (providing 500 mg calcium and 300 mg magnesium)
- EPA/DHA fish oils 1,200–2,400 mg or eat oily fish

Also read Chapter 18.

INDIGESTION

This unpleasant state can be caused by many different factors including too much or too little hydrochloric acid production in the stomach. Excessive stomach acid or a hiatus hernia usually cause heartburn. Insufficient hydrochloric acid or digestive enzyme deficiency usually cause a feeling of indigestion and reduced well-being after a meal. A bacterial imbalance or fungal infection in the stomach can also result in these symptoms, plus bloating after a meal because undesirable organisms multiply on feeding. Nutrition consultants can test these possibilities and identify the cause. The following advice is, however, a good starting-point.

Diet advice

Follow the recommended diet in this book. Balance your diet for acid- and alkaline-forming foods (see Part 9). Avoid stomach irritants such as alcohol, coffee, and chili, concentrated proteins, and any foods which you suspect you are intolerant to.

Supplements

- Multivitamin and multimineral
- Vitamin C 1,000 mg
- Probiotics such as lactobacillus acidophilus/bifidus
- Digestive enzyme (without betaine hydrochloride if heartburn is present) with each main meal

Also read Chapter 17.

INFECTIONS

When the immune system is run down, infections occur. Many nutrients and phytonutrients help to enhance immune function. These include vitamin C, all antioxidants, and the plants echinacea, cat's claw, and aloe vera.

There are also many natural infection fighters including probiotics (for bacterial infection), caprylic acid (for fungal infection), elderberry extract (for viral infection), and grapefruit seed extract for all three. Read Chapters 19 and 28 to find out which remedies are most helpful, depending on the infection. Below is a general infection-fighting program.

Diet advice

Follow the diet recommended in this book. Eat and drink plenty of fruit, vegetables, and their juices. Drink plenty of water, herb teas, and three cups a day of cat's claw tea. Stay away from mucus-forming foods—dairy products, meat, and eggs.

Supplements

- Multivitamin and multimineral
- Antioxidant complex
- 3 × vitamin C 1,000 mg
- Echinacea 10 drops twice a day
- Aloe vera a measure a day, as instructed on the bottle (get the best since the concentration of active ingredient varies a lot)
- Grapefruit seed extract 10 drops twice a day

Also read Chapters 19 and 28.

INFERTILITY

This unfortunate condition is more common in women than in men, although in 30 percent of couples who have difficulty conceiving the problem is due to the man. Vitamins E and B6, selenium, and zinc are important for both sexes, and vitamin C is important for men. Also important are essential fatty acids. There are, however, many causes other than nutritional deficiency, perhaps the most common being hormonal imbalances, particularly in women. These can be checked by a nutrition consultant or your doctor, from saliva samples taken at intervals over a month.

Diet advice

Follow the diet in this book. Essential fatty acids are found in cold-pressed vegetable oils, so make sure your daily diet includes a tablespoon of an oil blend to provide Omega 3 and Omega 6 fatty acids, or a heaped tablespoon of ground seeds.

Supplements

- Multivitamin and multimineral (to include zinc 15 mg and selenium 100 mcg)
- Vitamin E 500 IUs
- 2 × vitamin C 1,000 mg
- GLA 150 mg

Also read Chapter 32.

INFLAMMATION

Many health problems, including all those ending in "itis," are inflammatory. This means that a part of the body such as a muscle or joint, the stomach or respiratory tract, is inflamed. This is a sign that the body is reacting, or over-reacting, to something. A tendency to over-react can arise if a person is deficient in essential fats and their supportive nutrients, vitamins B3, and B6, biotin, vitamin C, zinc, and magnesium. Pantothenic acid (vitamin B5) is also needed to make cortisol, the body's anti-inflammatory hormone. Boswellic acid, found in the plant frankincense, is a natural anti-inflammatory agent which is available in the form of a cream for inflamed joints and muscles. L-glutamine helps to calm stomach inflammation. Anti-oxidant nutrients are also intimately involved in inflammatory responses. However, there is little point in calming down an inflammation if the source of irritation remains. This may be a food allergy or irritating substance such as alcohol.

Diet advice
Avoid immune-suppressing or potentially irritating substances such as coffee, alcohol, and strong spices. Avoid suspect foods such as wheat and dairy products for ten days to gauge your reaction to them. Otherwise, just follow the diet guidelines in this book.

Supplements

- Multivitamin and multimineral (with 300 mg magnesium and 15 mg zinc)
- Antioxidant complex
- 2 × vitamin C 1,000 mg
- 1 × pantothenic acid 500 mg
- L-glutamine powder 3 grams a day
- GLA 300 mg
- EPA/DHA fish oil 1,200 mg a day
- Boswellic acid capsules or cream (optional)

IRRITABLE BOWEL SYNDROME

This term is used to describe intermittent diarrhea or constipation, urgency to defecate, abdominal pain, or indigestion. There are many possible contributory causes to one or more of these symptoms. They include food allergy, stomach inflammation, over-excitation of the stomach muscles, stress, infection, and toxic overload. It is therefore best to see a nutrition consultant who can determine which factors are relevant. Essential fats and the amino acid glutamine calm stomach inflammation, antioxidants help the body to detoxify, and the right mineral balance helps the muscles of the stomach to work properly.

Diet advice

Pursue a simple, pure diet of lightly cooked vegetables, fish, non-gluten grains (rice, millet, corn, quinoa), lentils, and beans, plus ground seeds for essential fats. Avoid any suspect allergens, including wheat and dairy products, coffee, alcohol, and spices, for ten days to see if this makes a difference.

Supplements

- Multivitamin and multimineral
- Antioxidant complex
- 2 × vitamin C 500 mg
- L-glutamine powder 3 grams a day
- GLA 300 mg
- Digestive enzymes with each main meal (if indigestion is a symptom)

  Also read Chapter 17.

MENOPAUSAL SYMPTOMS

These include fatigue, depression, weight gain, osteoporosis, reduced sex drive, vaginal dryness, and hot flashes. While optimum nutrition often helps relieve these, many women respond to small amounts of natural progesterone used as a cream. This is available on prescription from your doctor (see also Useful Addresses on p. 339). Supplementing vitamin C with vitamin E and bioflavonoids may help reduce hot flashes. Also important for this and other symptoms, including vaginal dryness, is sufficient essential fatty acids, which make the prostaglandins that help to balance hormone levels. For prostaglandins to work, sufficient vitamin B6, zinc, and magnesium are required.

Diet advice

Follow the diet recommended in this book, being careful to cut down sources of sugar and stimulants. Have a tablespoon of a cold-pressed oil blend or a heaped tablespoon of ground seeds for essential fats, magnesium, and zinc.

Supplements

- Multivitamin and multimineral
- 2 × vitamin C 1,000 mg with 500 mg of bioflavonoids
- Vitamin E 500 IUs
- Bone mineral complex (including extra magnesium and zinc)
- GLA 300 mg

Also read Chapters 20 and 34.

MUSCLE ACHES AND CRAMPS

Cramps are most commonly due to calcium/magnesium imbalances and are corrected by supplementing 500 mg of calcium and 300 mg of magnesium. Despite popular belief, the condition is very rarely due to a lack of salt. In fact it is best to avoid added salt and to keep fluid intake high. Fruit is naturally rich in potassium and water, and contains sufficient sodium for the body's needs. Muscle aches can occur for the same reason, or when muscle cells are not able to make energy efficiently from glucose. Magnesium, particularly in the form of magnesium malate, helps here too, as do B vitamins. Aches can also occur due to inflammation (see p. 293).

Diet advice

Follow the diet recommended in this book. Avoid salt and increase your intake of fruit (rich in potassium) and seeds (rich in calcium and magnesium). Drink plenty of water.

Supplements

- Multivitamin and multimineral
- Vitamin C 1,000 mg
- B complex
- Bone mineral complex (to provide 500 mg calcium and 300 mg magnesium) or magnesium malate plus calcium

OBESITY

As well as eating no more than you need, choosing foods that keep the blood sugar even, backed up by an optimal intake of nutrients that help stabilize blood sugar, will assist you to lose weight by stabilizing your appetite and burning fat. These nutrients include vitamins B3, B6, and C, zinc, and chromium. Konjac fiber, a source of glucomannan, also helps to stabilize blood sugar levels. Also helpful is HCA, which slows down the ability of the body to turn excess fuel into body fat. In some people, food allergies cause water retention which contributes to obesity. If you suspect any foods, the most common being wheat and dairy products, eliminate them for ten days to test whether they are associated with weight gain. Thyroid problems can also be a factor in obesity. If all else fails, ask your doctor to check your thyroid.

Diet advice
Follow the diet in this book, emphasizing high water-content foods such as fresh fruit and vegetables and slow-releasing carbohydrates (see Part 9). Avoid all sources of fast-releasing sugars. Experiment with fasting one day a week, or sticking to fruit only. Make aerobic exercise a regular part of your day.

Supplements

- Multivitamin and multimineral
- Vitamin B6 100 mg with zinc 10 mg
- Chromium 200 mcg and HCA 750 mg
- Vitamin C 1,000 mg
- 3 g Glucomannan/konjac fiber (optional)

Also read Chapter 29.

OSTEOPOROSIS

In this condition the density of the bones decreases, increasing the risk of fracture and compression of the spinal vertebrae. From a nutritional perspective there are three main contributors. These are excessive protein consumption, leading to leaching of calcium from the bone to neutralize excess blood acidity; relative dominance of estrogen to progesterone, the latter being a major trigger for bone growth; and deficiency of bone-building nutrients which include calcium, magnesium, vitamin D, vitamin C, zinc, silica, phosphorus, and boron. The use of natural progesterone cream, prescribable by your doctor, has proven four times more effective than synthetic estrogen HRT in restoring bone density.

Diet advice
Follow the diet in this book, keeping all sources of saturated fat to a minimum due to their estrogenic effects. Have a heaped tablespoon of ground seeds each day as a source of calcium, magnesium, and zinc.

Supplement advice

- Multivitamin and multimineral
- Vitamin C 1,000 mg
- Bone mineral complex

Also read Chapter 21.

PMS

Pre-menstrual syndrome describes the occurrence of a cluster of symptoms including bloatedness, tiredness, irritability, depression, breast tenderness, and headaches, occurring most commonly in the week leading up to menstruation. There are three main causes: estrogen dominance and relative progesterone deficiency—corrected by natural progesterone and avoiding sources of estrogen; glucose intolerance, marked by a craving for sweet foods and stimulants; and deficiency in essential fatty acids and vitamin B6, zinc, and magnesium, which together create prostaglandins which help to balance hormone levels. While the need for these is greater just before the period is due, it is wise to take the supplements throughout the month. If dietary and supplementary intervention do not result in significant improvement, consider seeing a nutrition consultant and having your hormone balance checked.

Diet advice
Follow the diet in this book. Eat little and often prior to menstruation, snacking on fruit but avoiding sugar, sweets, and stimulants. Ensure that your daily diet contains one tablespoon of cold-pressed vegetable oil rich in both Omega 3 and Omega 6 fatty acids.

Supplements

- Multivitamin and multimineral
- 2 × vitamin B6 100 mg with zinc 10 mg
- Vitamin C 1,000 mg
- Magnesium 300 mg
- GLA 300 mg

Also read Chapter 34.

PROSTATE PROBLEMS

The most common prostate problem is prostatitis or benign prostatic hyperplasia, in which the prostate gland enlarges, interfering with the flow of urine. This is thought to be due to hormonal imbalances, possibly testosterone deficiency and estrogen dominance, affecting prostaglandins, which have an anti-inflammatory effect. Reversal can be achieved through supplementing essential fatty acids and testosterone. Also important is zinc and a herb called saw palmetto. The prostate gland is also a common site of cancer, most likely triggered by hormonal imbalances.

Diet advice
Follow the diet in this book, with an emphasis on foods high in antioxidants, avoiding milk and meat due to their hormone content and eating organic as much as possible. Keep saturated fat very low and ensure that you have adequate essential fats from seeds and their cold-pressed oils.

Supplements

- Multivitamin and multimineral
- Antioxidant complex (double for prostate cancer)
- 2 × vitamin C 1,000 mg (double for prostate cancer)
- GLA 300 mg
- Saw palmetto 300 mg (for enlarged prostate only)

Also read Chapter 27.

PSORIASIS

This is a completely different kind of skin condition from eczema or dermatitis and does not generally respond as well to nutritional intervention. It can occur when the body is "toxic," perhaps due to an overgrowth of the organism candida albicans, digestive problems leading to intoxication, or to poor liver detoxification. Otherwise consider the factors discussed for eczema and dermatitis (pp. 286 and 283).

Diet advice
Follow the diet recommended in this book, with an emphasis on low levels of meat and dairy products (to keep you low in saturated fat) and plenty of seeds and their oils for essential fats. If you suspect allergy to dairy products or wheat, test by avoiding these foods.

Supplements

- Multivitamin and multimineral
- Antioxidant complex
- Vitamin C 1,000 mg
- GLA 300 mg
- Fish oils or flax seed oil daily

SCHIZOPHRENIA

This severe form of mental health problem is suffered by one in a hundred people. There are many causes, the majority of which can be alleviated by nutrition. It is strongly advised that you see a nutrition consultant who can run tests to determine whether biochemical imbalances may underlie this condition. Nutrients that can help include folic acid, essential fatty acids, and megadoses of niacin (B3). These do not help all sufferers, and can make certain types worse—hence the need for testing. Often there is an underlying glucose imbalance and allergies.

Diet advice
Cut out or at least avoid sugar and refined foods. Cut down on stimulants—tea, coffee, chocolate, cola drinks, cigarettes, and alcohol. Follow the diet recommended in this book. Experiment for two weeks without wheat or dairy products.

Supplements

- Multivitamin
- 2 × vitamin C 1,000 mg
- Multimineral with zinc, magnesium, manganese, and chromium
- Extra folic acid, niacin, or essential fatty acids are best tried only under supervision

Also read Chapter 31.

SENILITY

This condition is primarily characterized by a loss of memory, but the precise cause is not known. Contributors are poor circulation, a lack of antioxidants resulting in poor oxygen utilization, a decrease in the brain chemical acetylcholine and an excess accumulation of toxic elements such as aluminum. A hair mineral analysis should be carried out to determine if any toxic levels of metals are present, especially aluminum. "Smart" nutrients such as choline, pantothenic acid, DMAE, and pyroglutamate may enhance memory. Antioxidants may also help. Senility may prove to be another degenerative condition that results from years of sub-optimal nutrition. Reversal is rare, although improvement is often achieved.

Diet advice
Follow the diet in this book, and be sure to drink plenty of water. Fish, especially sardines, are a good source of brain nutrients. Avoid fried food, stimulants, and alcohol.

Supplements

- Multivitamin
- Multimineral (with at least 10 mg zinc)
- Smart nutrient complex (with choline, pantothenic acid, DMAE, pyroglutamate)
- 2 × antioxidant complex
- 2 × vitamin C 1,000 mg
- Also worth trying is the herb ginkgo biloba 100–200 mg two to three times a day

Also read Chapters 23 and 35.

SINUSITIS

An inflammation of the sinus and nasal passages, sinusitis often leads to sinus infections. Contributory factors are nasal irritants such as exhaust fumes, cigarettes, smoky places, dust, and pollen; allergies, often to dairy products and wheat, which are mucus-forming; plus a weakened immune system. Too much alcohol, fried food, or stress, or a lack of sleep or over-eating, all weaken the immune system. Vitamins A, C, and zinc, among other nutrients, help boost immunity. Essential fats are also needed to control inflammation.

Diet advice

Eat lightly, but do eat—lots of vital foods such as the best organic fruit and vegetables (baby vegetables, just sprouted), plus seeds. You do need protein (quinoa, seeds, nuts, fish, tofu, quorn, etc.) but avoid mucus-forming foods such as milk, eggs, and meat.

Also inhale tea tree oil or olbas oil, in the bath or by holding it under your nose (be careful not to irritate the skin too much), to stop your nasal passages from blocking. Tiger balm is good on the chest. Drink home-made ginger and cinnamon tea (five slices of fresh ginger root and one stick of cinnamon in a thermos with 1 cup of boiling water) or cat's claw tea to boost the immune system.

Supplements

- Multivitamin and multimineral
- Antioxidant complex
- 2 × vitamin C 1,000 mg (3 g every four hours only when infected)
- 2 × vitamin A 7,500 IUs (2,270 mcg) when infected, or a glass of carrot juice
- 2 × zinc 15 mg
- Echinacea 15 drops in water three times a day

Also read Chapters 19 and 28.

SLEEPING PROBLEMS

For some sufferers the major problem of insomnia is waking up in the middle of the night; for others it is not getting to sleep in the first place. Both can be the effect on the nervous system of poor nutrition or too much stress and anxiety. Calcium and magnesium have a tranquilizing effect, as does vitamin B6. Tryptophan, a constituent of protein, has the strongest tranquilizing effect and, if taken in doses of 1,000–3,000 mg, it is highly effective for insomnia. It takes about an hour to work and remains effective for up to four hours. While tryptophan is non-addictive and has no known side effects, its regular use in not recommended—it is better to adjust your lifestyle so that no tranquilizing agents are needed.

Diet advice

Follow the diet recommended in this book, avoiding all stimulants. Do not eat sugar or drink tea or coffee in the evening. Also, do not eat late. Eat seeds, nuts, root and green leafy vegetables, which are high in calcium and magnesium.

Supplements

- Multivitamin and multimineral
- Vitamin B6 100mg with zinc 10mg
- Calcium 600mg and magnesium 400mg
- Vitamin C 1,000 mg
- 2 × L-Tryptophan 1,000 mg (only if absolutely necessary)

THYROID PROBLEMS

The thyroid gland, situated at the base of the throat, controls our rate of metabolism. In hyperthyroidism or over-active thyroid, symptoms such as over-activity, loss of weight, and nervousness are common; in hypo-thyroidism or under-active thyroid, the symptoms are lack of energy, overweight, and goiter, in which the throat region swells. Over-stimulation of the endocrine system through living off stress and stimulants, and estrogen dominance, are common causes for an underactive thyroid later in life. This can also be caused by a lack of iodine, although this is rare, and taking iodine in kelp is advised to help the condition. Since the thyroid gland is controlled by the pituitary and adrenal glands, the nutrients involved in hormone production and regulation for all three glands are particularly important. These are vitamins C and B complex (especially B3 and B5), manganese, and zinc. Selenium also appears to have a role to play in thyroid health, as does the amino acid tyrosine from which thyroxine is made. Often, a low dose of thyroxine is required to correct this condition.

Diet advice
Avoid all stimulants and follow the diet in this book.

Supplements

- Multivitamin and multimineral
- B complex
- Vitamin C 1,000 mg
- Manganese 10 mg
- For hypothyroidism only: kelp with iodine and tyrosine 1,000 mg

Also read Chapter 20.

ULCERS

These can occur in the stomach and duodenum—the first section of the small intestine, which is not so well protected as the rest of the intestines against the acid secretions of the stomach. In prolonged stress the stomach can over-secrete acid, so stress can be a cause. Also, diets that are too acid-forming are to be avoided. Vitamin A is the primary nutrient needed to protect the lining of the duodenum. While vitamin C does help people with duodenal ulcers, not more than 500 mg should be taken as it can cause irritation. If a burning sensation is experienced after taking vitamin C, the dose is too high. The most common cause of ulcers is infection with helicobacter pylori. This should be tested by your doctor and treated with a specific anti-bacterial agent.

Diet advice
Follow the diet recommended in this book, keeping mainly to alkaline-forming foods as listed in Part 9.

Supplements

- Multivitamin and multimineral
- 2 × vitamin A 7,500 IUs (2270 mcg retinol) short-term only and not if pregnant
- Vitamin C 500 mg (as calcium ascorbate)
- Beneficial bacteria, such as lactobacillus acidophilus/bifidus after antibiotics if treated for helicobacter infection

VARICOSE VEINS

Veins carry blood returning to the heart. A varicose vein is one which has become enlarged and swollen; the condition usually occurs in the legs, where circulation is most difficult. It is unlikely that optimum nutrition can do much for veins that are already varicose; however, adequate vitamins C and E as well as other antioxidants can help to prevent further occurrences. Also, there is some evidence that a high-fiber diet can help to prevent varicose veins.

Diet advice
Follow the diet recommended in this book. Regular exercise, especially swimming, will improve the circulation. Putting your feet up and gentle leg massages are all helpful. Application of vitamin E cream is beneficial.

Supplements

- Multivitamin and multimineral
- Antioxidant complex
- Vitamin E 500 IUs
- 2 × vitamin C 1,000 mg plus bioflavonoids

VITAMINS

■ A (retinol and beta-carotene)

What it does Needed for healthy skin, inside and out, protecting against infections. Antioxidant and immune system booster. Protects against many forms of cancer. Essential for night vision.

Deficiency signs Mouth ulcers, poor night vision, acne, frequent colds or infections, dry flaky skin, dandruff, thrush or cystitis, diarrhea.

How much?
RDA *Children* 700 ug   *Male Adults* 1,000 ug   *Female Adults* 800 ug
SONA *Children* 800–1000 mcgRE   *Adults* 2,000 mcgRE (6,000 IUs)
THERAPEUTIC RANGE 2,250–6,000 mcg retinol (if pregnant or trying to conceive do not exceed 3,000 mcg retinol (10,000 IUs); 3,000–30,000 mcg beta-carotene per day
(Note: RE = retinol equivalent. 1 mcgRE = 3.3 IUs)
TOXICITY May occur above
Children 4,000–20,000 mcg per day or 25,000 mcg single dose of retinol
Adults 8,000–30,000 mcg per day long term or 300,000 mcg single dose of retinol

Best food source Beef liver (35,778 IUs), veal liver (26,562 IUs), carrots (28,125 IUs), watercress (4,700 IUs), cabbage (3,000 IUs), squash (7,000 IUs), sweet potatoes (17,055 IUs), melon (3,224 IUs), pumpkin (1,600 IUs), mangoes (3,894 IUs), tomatoes (1,133 IUs), broccoli (1,541 IUs), apricots, papayas (2,014 IUs), tangerines (920 IUs), and asparagus (829 IUs).

Best supplement Retinol (animal source), natural beta-carotene and retinyl palmitate (vegetable source).

Helpers Works with zinc. Vitamin C and E help protect it. Best taken within a multi or antioxidant formula with food.

Robbers Heat, light, alcohol, coffee, and smoking.

▪ B1 (thiamine)

What it does Essential for energy production, brain function, and digestion. Helps the body make use of protein.

Deficiency signs Tender muscles, eye pains, irritability, poor concentration, "prickly" legs, poor memory, stomach pains, constipation, tingling hands, rapid heartbeat.

How much?
RDA *Children* 1.0 mg   *Male Adults* 1.5 mg   *Female Adults* 1.1 mg
SONA *Children* 3.1–3.3 mg   *Adults* 3.5–9.2 mg
THERAPEUTIC RANGE *Children* 12.5–50 mg   *Adults* 25–100 mg
TOXICITY Not a concern.

Best food source Watercress (0.1 mg), squash (0.05 mg), zucchini, lamb (0.12 mg), asparagus (0.11 mg), mushrooms (0.1 mg), peas (0.32 mg), lettuce (0.07 mg), peppers (0.07 mg), cauliflower (0.10 mg), cabbage (0.06 mg), tomatoes (0.06 mg), brussels sprouts (0.10 mg), beans (0.55 mg).

Best supplement Thiamine.

Helpers Works with other B vitamins, magnesium and manganese. Best supplemented as part of a B complex with food.

Robbers Antibiotics, tea, coffee, stress, birth control pills, alcohol, alkaline agents, e.g., baking powder, sulphur dioxide (preservative), cooking, and food refining/processing.

▪ B2 (riboflavin)

What it does Helps turn fats, sugars, and protein into energy. Needed to repair and maintain healthy skin, inside and out. Helps to regulate body acidity. Important for hair, nails, and eyes.

Deficiency signs Burning or gritty eyes, sensitivity to bright lights, sore tongue, cataracts, dull or oily hair, eczema or dermatitis, split nails, cracked lips.

How much?
RDA *Children* 1.2 mg   *Male Adults* 1.7 mg   *Female Adults* 1.3 mg
SONA *Children* 1.8–2 mg   *Adults* 1.8–2.5 mg
THERAPEUTIC RANGE *Children* 12.5–50 mg   *Adults* 25–100 mg
TOXICITY No known toxicity. Loss or excess results in bright yellow-green urine.

Best food source Mushrooms (0.4 mg), watercress (0.1 mg), cabbage (0.05 mg), asparagus (0.12 mg), broccoli (0.3 mg), pumpkin (0.04 mg), bean sprouts (0.03 mg), mackerel (0.3 mg), milk (0.19 mg), bamboo shoots, tomatoes (0.04 mg), wheat germ (0.25 mg).

Best supplement Riboflavin.

Helpers Works with other B vitamins and selenium. Best supplemented as part of B complex with food.

Robbers Alcohol, birth control pills, tea, coffee, alkaline agents, e.g., baking powder, sulphur dioxide (preservative), cooking, and food refining/processing.

■ B3 (niacin)

What it does Essential for energy production, brain function, and the skin. Helps balance blood sugar and lower cholesterol levels. Also involved in inflammation and digestion.

Deficiency signs Lack of energy, diarrhea, insomnia, headaches or migraines, poor memory, anxiety or tension, depression, irritability, bleeding or tender gums, acne, eczema/dermatitis.

How much?
RDA *Children* 13 mg *Male Adults* 19 mg *Female Adults* 15 mg
SONA *Children* 25 mg *Adults* 25–30 mg
THERAPEUTIC RANGE *Children* 25–50 mg *Adults* 50–150 mg
TOXICITY None known below 3,000 mg.

Best food source Mushrooms (4 mg), tuna (12.9 mg), chicken (8.2 mg), salmon (7.0 mg), asparagus (1.11 mg), cabbage (0.3 mg), lamb (4.18 mg), mackerel (8.0 mg), turkey (8.5 mg), tomatoes (0.7 mg), zucchini and squash (0.54 mg), cauliflower (0.6 mg) and whole wheat (4.33 mg).

Best supplement Niacin (may cause flushing) and niacinamide.

Helpers Works with other B complex vitamins and chromium. Best taken with food.

Robbers Antibiotics, tea, coffee, birth control pills, and alcohol.

■ B5 (pantothenic acid)

What it does Involved in energy production, controls fat metabolism. Essential for brain and nerves. Helps make anti-stress hormones (steroids). Maintains healthy skin and hair.

Deficiency signs Muscle tremors or cramps, apathy, poor concentration, burning feet or tender heels, nausea or vomiting, lack of energy, exhaustion after light exercise, anxiety or tension, teeth grinding.

How much?
RDA *Children and adults 3–7 mg*
SONA *Children* 10 mg *Adults* 25 mg
THERAPEUTIC RANGE *Children* 25–150 mg *Adults* 50–300 mg
TOXICITY None known below 100 times RDA level.

Best food source Mushrooms (2 mg), watercress (0.10 mg), broccoli (0.10 mg), alfalfa sprouts (0.56 mg), peas (0.75 mg), lentils (1.36 mg), tomatoes (0.33 mg), cabbage (0.21 mg), celery (0.40 mg), strawberries (0.34 mg), eggs (1.8 mg), squash (0.16 mg), avocados (1.07 mg), whole wheat (1.1 mg).

Best supplement Pantothenic acid.

Helpers Works with other B complex vitamins. Biotin and folic acid aid absorption. Best taken with food.

Robbers Stress, alcohol, tea, coffee. Destroyed by heat and food processing.

■ B6 (pyridoxine)

What it does Essential for protein digestion and utilization, brain function, hormone production. Helps balance sex hormones, hence use in PMS and menopause. Natural anti-depressant and diuretic. Helps control allergic reactions.

Deficiency signs Infrequent dream recall, water retention, tingling hands, depression or nervousness, irritability, muscle tremors or cramps, lack of energy, flaky skin.

How much?
RDA *Children* 1.4 mg *Male Adults* 2.0 mg *Female Adults* 1.6 mg
SONA *Children* 2–5 mg *Adults* 10–25 mg
THERAPEUTIC RANGE *Children* 25–125 mg *Adults* 50–250 mg
TOXICITY Cases of pyridoxine toxicity reported with dosages above 1,000 mg—unaccompanied by a B complex to help balance the intake.

Best food source Watercress (0.13 mg), cauliflower (0.20 mg), cabbage (0.16 mg), peppers (0.17 mg), bananas (0.51 mg), squash (0.14 mg), broccoli (0.21 mg), asparagus (0.15 mg), lentils (0.11 mg), red kidney beans (0.44 mg), brussels sprouts (0.28 mg), onions (0.10 mg), seeds and nuts (varies).

Best supplement Pyridoxine, pyridoxal-5-phosphate only if "enterically" coated (as stated on the label).

Helpers Works with other B complex vitamins, as well as zinc and magnesium. Best supplemented with food and zinc.

Robbers Alcohol, smoking, birth control pills, high protein intake, processed foods.

▪ B12 (cyanocobalamin)

What it does Needed for making use of protein. Helps the blood carry oxygen, hence essential for energy. Needed for synthesis of DNA. Essential for nerves. Deals with tobacco smoke and other toxins.

Deficiency signs Poor hair condition, eczema, or dermatitis, mouth over-sensitive to heat or cold, irritability, anxiety or tension, lack of energy, constipation, tender or sore muscles, pale skin.

How much?
RDA *Children* 1.4 ug *Adults* 2.4 ug
SONA *Children* 2 mcg *Adults* 2–3 mcg
THERAPEUTIC RANGE *Children* 2.5–25 mcg *Adults* 5–100 mcg
TOXICITY None reported with oral dose. Very rarely, an allergic reaction to injection occurs.

Best food source Oysters (15 mcg), sardines (28 mcg), tuna (5 mcg), lamb (trace), eggs (1.7 mcg), shrimp (1 mcg), cottage cheese (5 mcg), milk (0.3 mcg), turkey and chicken (2 mcg), cheese (1.5 mcg).

Best supplement Cyanocobalamin.

Helpers Works with folic acid. Best taken as B complex with food.

Robbers Alcohol, smoking, lack of stomach acid.

▪ Biotin

What it does Particularly important in childhood. Helps your body use essential fats, assisting in promoting healthy skin, hair, and nerves.

Deficiency signs Dry skin, poor hair condition, premature graying hair, tender or sore muscles, poor appetite or nausea, eczema or dermatitis.

How much?
RDA *Male Adults* 30 mcg *Female Adults* 20 mcg

SONA *Children and adults* 50–200 mcg
THERAPEUTIC RANGE *Children* 25–100 mcg   *Adults* 50–200 mcg
TOXICITY None reported.

Best food source Cauliflower (1.5 mcg), lettuce (0.7 mcg), peas (0.5 mcg), tomatoes (1.5 mcg), oysters (10 mcg), grapefruit (1.0 mcg), watermelon (4.0 mcg), sweet corn (6.0 mcg), cabbage (1.1 mcg), cauliflower (17.0 mcg), almonds (20 mcg), cherries (0.4 mcg), herrings (10.0 mcg), milk (2.0 mcg), eggs (25 mcg).

Best supplement Biotin.

Helpers Works with other B vitamins, magnesium, and manganese. Best supplemented as part of a B complex with food.

Robbers Raw egg white contains avidin (but not significant in cooked egg whites), fried food.

■ C (ascorbic acid)

What it does Strengthens immune system—fights infections. Makes collagen, keeping bones, skin, and joints firm and strong. Antioxidant, detoxifying pollutants and protecting against cancer and heart disease. Helps make anti-stress hormones, and turns food into energy.

Deficiency signs Frequent colds, lack of energy, frequent infections, bleeding or tender gums, easy bruising, nose bleeds, slow wound healing, red pimples on skin.

How much?
RDA *Children* 45 mg   *Adults* 60 mg
SONA *Children* 150 mg   *Adults* 400–1,000 mg
THERAPEUTIC RANGE *Children* 150–1,000 mg   *Adults* 1,000–10,000 mg
TOXICITY May cause bowel looseness in excess, but this is not a sign of toxicity and stops rapidly when dose is reduced.

Best food source Peppers (100 mg), watercress (60 mg), cabbage (60 mg), broccoli (110 mg), cauliflower (60 mg), strawberries (60 mg), lemons (80 mg), kiwi fruit (85 mg), peas (25 mg), melons (25 mg), oranges (50 mg), grapefruit (40 mg), limes (29 mg), tomatoes (60 mg).

Best supplement Vitamin C is ascorbic acid. This is mildly acidic in the digestive tract and in large doses (5 g plus) does not suit everyone. The ascorbate form (e.g., calcium ascorbate, magnesium ascorbate) is mildly alkaline and more easily tolerated. However, if you take large amounts during a meal you may neutralize stomach acidity necessary for protein digestion. The ascorbate form is good if you also want to supplement the mineral it is bound to. Vitamin C works with bioflavonoids. Best supplements include these. Ester C is also a good form to take.

Helpers Bioflavonoids in fruit and vegetables increases its effect. Works with B vitamins to produce energy. Works with vitamin E as an antioxidant.

Robbers Smoking, alcohol, pollution, stress, fried food.

■ D (ergocalciferol, cholecalciferol)

What it does Helps maintain strong and healthy bones by retaining calcium.

Deficiency signs Joint pain or stiffness, backache, tooth decay, muscle cramps, hair loss.

How much?
RDA *Children* 10 ug *Adults* 5 ug
SONA *Children and adults* 10–20 mcg
THERAPEUTIC RANGE *Children* 5–12 mcg *Adults* 10–25 mcg (400–1,000 IUs)
TOXICITY 1,250 mcg is potentially toxic.

Best food source Herrings (22.5 mcg), mackerel (17.5 mcg), salmon (12.5 mcg), oysters (3 mcg), cottage cheese (2 mcg), eggs (1.75 mcg).

Best supplement Cholecalciferol (animal origin), ergocalciferol (yeast origin).

Helpers Sufficient exposure to sunlight, as vitamin D is made in the skin. Under these conditions dietary vitamin D may not be necessary. Vitamins A, C, and E protect D.

Robbers Lack of sunlight, fried foods.

■ E (d-alpha tocopherol)

What it does Antioxidant, protecting cells from damage, including against cancer. Helps body use oxygen, preventing blood clots, thrombosis, atherosclerosis. Improves wound healing and fertility. Good for the skin.

Deficiency signs Lack of sex drive, exhaustion after light exercise, easy bruising, slow wound healing, varicose veins, loss of muscle tone, infertility.

How much?
RDA *Children* 7 mg   *Male Adults* 10 mg   *Female Adults* 8 mg
SONA *Children* 70 mg   *Adults* 100–1,000 mg
THERAPEUTIC RANGE *Children* 70–100 mg   *Adults* 100–1,000 mg
TOXICITY None reported below 2,000 mg d-alpha tocopherol long-term use and 35,000 mg short-term use.

Best food source Unrefined corn oils (83 mg), sunflower seeds (52.6 mg), peanuts (11.8 mg), sesame seeds (22.7 mg), other "seed" foods, e.g., beans (7.7 mg), peas (2.3 mg), wheat germ (27.5 mg), tuna (6.3 mg), sardines (2.0 mg), salmon (1.8 mg), sweet potatoes (4.0 mg).

Best supplement D-alpha tocopherol (not synthetic dl-alpha tocopherol).

Helpers Works with vitamin C and selenium.

Robbers High-temperature cooking, especially frying. Air pollution, birth control pills, excessive intake of refined or processed fats and oils.

■ Folic acid

What it does Critical during pregnancy for development of brain and nerves. Always essential for brain and nerve function. Needed for utilizing protein and red blood cell formation.

Deficiency signs Anemia, eczema, cracked lips, prematurely graying hair, anxiety or tension, poor memory, lack of energy, poor appetite, stomach pains, depression.

How much?
RDA *Children* 300 ug   *Adults* 400 ug
SONA *Children* 300 mcg   *Adults* 400–1,000 mcg
THERAPEUTIC RANGE *Children* 25–300 mcg   *Adults* 400–1,000 mcg
TOXICITY Seldom reported, but gastro-intestinal and sleep problems have occurred above 15 mg.

Best food source Wheat germ (325 mcg), spinach (140 mcg), peanuts (110 mcg), sprouts (110 mcg), asparagus (98 mcg), sesame seeds (97 mcg), hazelnuts (72 mcg), broccoli (130 mcg), cashew nuts (69 mcg), cauliflower (39 mcg), walnuts (66 mcg), avocados (66 mcg).

Best supplement Folic acid.

Helpers Works with other B complex vitamins, especially B12. Best supplemented as part of B complex with food.

Robbers High temperature, light, food processing and birth control pills.

■ K (phylloquinone)

What it does Controls blood clotting.

Deficiency signs Hemorrhage (easy bleeding).

How much?
RDA *Children* 30 ug   *Male Adults* 80 ug   *Female Adults* 65 ug
SONA *Children* 45 mcg   *Adults* 55–80 mcg
THERAPEUTIC RANGE Not necessary to supplement.
TOXICITY Not a concern.

Best food source mcg per 100 grams. Cauliflower (3,600 mcg), brussels sprouts (1,888 mcg), lettuce (135 mcg), cabbage (125 mcg), beans (290 mcg), broccoli (200 mcg), peas (260 mcg), watercress (56 mcg), asparagus (57 mcg), potatoes (80 mcg), corn oil (50 mcg), tomatoes (5 mcg), milk (1 mcg).

Best supplement Not necessary to supplement.

Helpers Healthy intestinal bacteria—then no need for dietary source.

Robbers Antibiotics. In babies, lack of breast-feeding. Some anti-coagulant drugs act by interfering with vitamin K metabolism and they become less effective if you are supplementing vitamin K. These include Warfarin, Nicoumalone, and Phenidione. Therefore, beware of supplementing a multivitamin that contains vitamin K if you are currently taking any of these medications.

MINERALS

■ Calcium

What it does Promotes a healthy heart, clots blood, promotes healthy nerves, contracts muscles, improves skin, bone and teeth health, relieves aching muscles and bones, maintains the correct acid-alkaline balance, reduces menstrual cramps and tremors.

Deficiency signs Muscle cramps or tremors, insomnia or nervousness, joint pain or arthritis, tooth decay, high blood pressure.

How much?

RDA *Children* 800 mg   *Adults* 800 mg

SONA *Children* 600–800 mg   *Adults* 800–1200 mg

THERAPEUTIC RANGE *Children* 600–800 mg   *Adults* 800–1200 mg

TOXICITY Problems of excessive calcium arise from other factors such as excessive vitamin D intake (above 25,000 IUs per day). Excess will interfere with absorption of other minerals, especially if their intake is slightly low. May lead to calcification of kidneys, heart, and other soft tissue, e.g., kidney stones.

Best food source Swiss cheese (925 mg), Cheddar cheese (750 mg), almonds (234 mg), brewer's yeast (210 mg), parsley (203 mg), corn tortillas (200 mg), globe artichokes (51 mg), prunes (51 mg), pumpkin seeds (51 mg), cooked dried beans (50 mg), cabbage (4 mg), winter wheat (46 mg).

Best supplement Calcium is reasonably well absorbed in any form. The best forms of calcium to supplement are calcium amino acid chelate or citrate, which are approximately twice as well absorbed as calcium carbonate.

Helpers Works well in ratios of 3.2 calcium:magnesium and 2:1 calcium:phosphorous. Vitamin D and boron. Exercise.

Robbers Hormone imbalances, alcohol, lack of exercise, caffeine, tea. Lack of hydrochloric acid and excess fat or phosphorus hinders absorption. Stress causes increased excretion.

▪ Chromium

What it does Forms part of glucose tolerance factor (GTF) to balance blood sugar, helps to normalize hunger and reduce cravings, improves life span, helps protect DNA and RNA, essential for heart function.

Deficiency signs Excessive or cold sweats, dizziness or irritability after six hours without food, need for frequent meals, cold hands, need for excessive sleep or drowsiness during the day, excessive thirst, addicted to sweet foods.

How much?

RDA *Children* None   *Adults* None

SONA *Children* 35–50 mcg   *Adults* 100 mcg

THERAPEUTIC RANGE *Children* 35–50 mcg   *Adults* 20–200 mcg

TOXICITY There is a wide range of safety between the helpful and harmful doses of chromium. Toxicity only occurs above 1,000 mg, which is ten thousand times the top therapeutic level.

Best food source Brewer's yeast (112 mcg), wholemeal bread (42 mcg), rye bread (30 mcg), oysters (26 mcg), potatoes (24 mcg), wheat germ (23 mcg), green peppers (19 mcg), eggs (16 mcg), chicken (15 mcg), apples (14 mcg), butter (13 mcg), parsnips (13 mcg), cornmeal (12 mcg), lamb (12 mcg), Swiss cheese (11 mcg).

Best supplement Chromium polynicotinate/picolinate, brewer's yeast.

Helpers Vitamin B3 and three amino acids—glycine, glutamic acid, and cystine—combine to form glucose tolerance factor (GTF). Improved diet and exercise.

Robbers High intake of refined sugars and flours, obesity, additives, pesticides, petroleum products, processed foods, toxic metals.

■ Iron

What it does As a component of hemoglobin, iron transports oxygen and carbon dioxide to and from cells. Component of enzymes, vital for energy production.

Deficiency signs Anemia, e.g., pale skin, sore tongue, fatigue, listlessness, loss of appetite, nausea, sensitivity to cold.

How much?
RDA *Children* 10 mg *Adults* 10–15 mg
SONA *Children* 7–10 mg *Adults* 15 mg
THERAPEUTIC RANGE *Children* 7–10 mg *Adults* 15–25 mg
TOXICITY None below 1,000 mg.

Best food source Pumpkin seeds (11.2 mg), parsley (6.2 mg), almonds (4.7 mg), prunes (3.9 mg), cashew nuts (3.6 mg), raisins (3.5 mg), brazil nuts (3.4 mg), walnuts (3.1 mg), dates (3.0 mg), pork (2.9 mg), cooked dried beans (2.7 mg), sesame seeds (2.4 mg), pecan nuts (2.4 mg).

Best supplement Amino acid chelated iron is three times more absorbable than iron sulphate or oxide.

Helpers Vitamin C (increases iron absorption), vitamin E, calcium but not in excess, folic acid, phosphorus, stomach acid.

Robbers Oxalates (spinach and rhubarb), tannic acid (tea), phytates (wheat bran), phosphates (soft fizzy drinks, food additives), antacids, high zinc intake.

■ Magnesium

What it does Strengthens bones and teeth, promotes healthy muscles by helping them to relax so important for PMS, important for heart muscles and nervous system. Essential for energy production. Involved as a co-factor in many enzymes in the body.

Deficiency signs Muscle tremors or spasms, muscle weakness, insomnia or nervousness, high blood pressure, irregular heartbeat, constipation, fits or convulsions, hyperactivity, depression, confusion, lack of appetite, calcium deposited in soft tissue, e.g., kidney stones.

How much?
RDA *Children* 170 mg   *Male Adults* 350 mg   *Female Adults* 280 mg
SONA *Children* 200–375 mg   *Adults* 375–500 mg
THERAPEUTIC RANGE *Children* 400–800 mg   *Adults* 400–800 mg
TOXICITY None below 1,000 mg.

Best food source Wheat germ (490 mg), almonds (270 mg), cashew nuts (267 mg), brewer's yeast (231 mg), buckwheat flour (229 mg), brazil nuts (225 mg), peanuts (175 mg), pecan nuts (142 mg), cooked beans (37 mg), garlic (36 mg), raisins (35 mg), green peas (35 mg), potato skin (34 mg), crab (34 mg).

Best supplement Amino acid chelate and citrate are twice as well absorbed as magnesium carbonate or sulphate.

Helpers Vitamins B1, B6, C, and D, zinc, calcium, phosphorus.

Robbers Large amounts of calcium in milk products, proteins, fats, oxalates (spinach, rhubarb), phytate (wheat bran, bread).

■ Manganese

What it does Helps to form healthy bones, cartilage, tissues, and nerves, activates more than twenty enzymes including an antioxidant enzyme system, stabilizes blood sugar, promotes healthy DNA and RNA, essential for reproduction and red blood cell synthesis, important for insulin production, reduces cell damage, required for brain function.

Deficiency signs Muscle twitches, childhood growing pains, dizziness or poor sense of balance, fits, convulsions, sore knees, joint pain.

How much?
RDA *Children* 2.5 mg   *Adults* 3.5 mg

SONA *Children* 2.5 mg *Adults* 5 mg
THERAPEUTIC RANGE *Children* 2.5–5 mg *Adults* 2.5–15 mg
TOXICITY Not a concern.

Best food source Watercress (0.5 mg), pineapple (1.7 mg), okra (0.9 mg), endive (0.4 mg), blackberries (1.3 mg), raspberries (1.1 mg), lettuce (0.15 mg), grapes (0.7 mg), lima beans (1.3 mg), strawberries (0.3 mg), oats (0.6 mg), beet (0.3 mg), celery (0.14 mg).

Best supplement Amino acid chelate, manganese citrate, or gluconate.

Helpers Zinc, vitamins E, B1, C, K.

Robbers Antibiotics, alcohol, refined foods, calcium, phosphorus.

■ Molybdenum

What it does Helps rid the body of the protein breakdown products, e.g., uric acid, strengthens teeth and may help reduce the risk of dental decay, detoxifies the body from free radicals, petrochemicals, and sulphites.

Deficiency signs Deficiency signs are not known unless excess copper or sulphate interferes with its utilization. Animals show signs of breathing difficulties and neurological disorders.

How much?
RDA None
SONA None
THERAPEUTIC RANGE *Children.* Not known *Adults* 100–1,000 mcg (1 mg)
TOXICITY Intakes of 10–15 mg/day cause a high incidence of gout-like symptoms associated with high uric acid.

Best food source Tomatoes, wheat germ, pork, lamb, lentils, beans.

Best supplement Supplements of extra molybdenum are not recommended.

Helpers Protein including sulphur-containing amino acids, carbohydrates, fats.

Robbers Copper, sulphates.

■ Phosphorus

What it does Forms and maintains bone and teeth, needed for milk secretion, builds muscle tissue, is a component of DNA and RNA, helps maintain pH of the body, aids metabolism and energy production.

Deficiency signs Dietary deficiencies are unlikely since it is present in almost all foods. May occur with long-term antacid use or with stresses such as bone fracture. Signs include general muscle weakness, loss of appetite and bone pain, rickets, osteomalacia.

How much?
RDA *Children* 800 mg   *Adults* 800 mg
SONA None established
THERAPEUTIC RANGE Not necessary to supplement
TOXICITY No known cases; however, it may result in deficiency of calcium, increased neuroexcitability, and convulsions.

Best food source Present in almost all foods.

Best supplement Calcium phosphate, lecithin, monosodium phosphate.

Helpers Correct calcium: phosphorus ratio, lactose, vitamin D.

Robbers Too much iron, magnesium, aluminum.

■ Potassium

What it does Enables nutrients to move into and waste products to move out of cells, promotes healthy nerves and muscles, maintains fluid balance in the body, relaxes muscles, helps secretion of insulin for blood sugar control to produce constant energy, involved in metabolism, maintains heart functioning, stimulates stomach movements to encourage proper elimination.

Deficiency signs Rapid irregular heartbeat, muscle weakness, pins and needles, irritability, nausea, vomiting, diarrhea, swollen abdomen, cellulite, low blood pressure resulting from an imbalance of potassium: sodium ratio, confusion, mental apathy.

How much?
RDA *Children* 1,600 mg   *Adults* 2,000 mg
SONA *Children* 1,600 mg   *Adults* 2,000 mg
THERAPEUTIC RANGE *Children* 200–1,600 mg   *Adults* 200–3,500 mg
TOXICITY Around 18,000 mg cardiac arrest may occur.

Best food source Watercress (329 mg), endive (316 mg), cabbage (251 mg), celery (285 mg), parsley (540 mg), zucchini (248 mg), radishes (231 mg), cauliflower (355 mg), mushrooms (371 mg), pumpkin (339 mg), molasses (2925 mg).

Best supplement Potassium gluconate/chloride, slow-releasing potassium, seaweed, brewer's yeast.

Helpers Magnesium helps to hold potassium in cells.

Robbers Excess sodium from salt, alcohol, sugar, diuretics, laxatives, corticosteroid drugs, stress.

▪ Selenium

What it does Antioxidant properties help to protect against free radicals and carcinogens, reduces inflammation, stimulates immune system to fight infections, promotes a healthy heart, and helps vitamin E's action, required for male reproductive system, needed for metabolism.

Deficiency signs Family history of cancer, signs of premature aging, cataracts, high blood pressure, frequent infections.

How much?
RDA   *Children* 30 ug   *Male Adults* 70 ug   *Female Adults* 55 ug
SONA   *Children* 50 mcg   *Adults* 100 mcg
THERAPEUTIC RANGE   *Children* 30–50 mcg   *Adults* 25–100 mcg
TOXICITY   None below 750 mcg, when interferes with normal structure and functions of proteins in hair, nails, and skin, "garlic breath" may occur.

Best food source Tuna (0.116 mg), oyster (0.65 mg), molasses (0.13 mg), mushrooms (0.13 mg), herrings (0.61 mg), cottage cheese (0.023 mg), cabbage (0.003 mg), beef liver (0.049 mg), zucchini (0.003 mg), cod (0.029 mg), chicken (0.027 mg).

Best supplement Selenomethionine, selenocysteine.

Helpers Vitamins E, A, and C.

Robbers Refined food, modern farming techniques.

▪ Sodium

What it does Maintains body's water balance, preventing dehydration, helps nerve functioning, used in muscle contraction including heart muscle, utilized in energy production, helps move nutrients into cells.

Deficiency signs Dizziness, heat exhaustion, low blood pressure, rapid pulse, mental apathy, loss of appetite, muscle cramps, nausea, vomiting, reduced body weight, headache.

How much?

RDA *Children* 1,900 mg   *Adults* 2,400 mg

SONA *Children* 1,900 mg   *Adults* 2,400 mg

THERAPEUTIC DOSE 1,600 mg.

TOXICITY May occur with high intake from processed foods and restricted water intake, edema, high blood pressure, kidney disease.

Best food source Sauerkraut (664 mg), olives (2,020 mg), shrimp (2,300 mg), miso (2,950 mg), beet (282 mg), ham (1,500 mg), celery (875 mg), cabbage (643 mg), crab (369 mg), cottage cheese (405 mg), watercress (45 mg), red kidney beans (327 mg).

Best supplement None needed. Plentiful in food.

Helpers Vitamin D.

Robbers Potassium and chloride counteract sodium, to keep a balance in the body.

▪ Zinc

What it does Component of over two hundred enzymes in the body, component of DNA and RNA, essential for growth, important for healing, controls hormones which are messengers from organs such as testes and ovaries, aids ability to cope with stress effectively, promotes healthy nervous system and brain especially in the growing fetus, aids bones and teeth formation, helps hair to "bloom," essential for constant energy.

Deficiency signs Poor sense of taste or smell, white marks on more than two fingernails, frequent infections, stretch marks, acne or greasy skin, low fertility, pale skin, tendency for depression, loss of appetite.

How much?

RDA *Children* 10 mg   *Male Adults* 15 mg   *Female Adults* 12 mg

SONA *Children* 7 mg   *Adults* 15–20 mg

THERAPEUTIC RANGE *Children* 5–10 mg   *Adults* 15–50 mg

TOXICITY 2 g or more can result in gastro-intestinal irritation, vomiting, anemia, reduced growth, stiffness, depraved appetite, and death. Zinc has been administered to patients in tenfold excess of the dietary allowances for years without adverse reactions, but copper levels should be monitored.

Best food source Oysters (148.7 mg), ginger root (6.8 mg), lamb (5.3 mg), pecan nuts (4.5 mg), dry split peas (4.2 mg), haddock (1.7 mg), green peas (1.6 mg), shrimp (1.5 mg), turnips (1.2 mg), brazil nuts (4.2 mg), egg yolk (3.5 mg), whole-wheat grain (3.2 mg), rye (3.2 mg), oats (3.2 mg), peanuts (3.2 mg), almonds (3.1 mg).

Best supplement Amino acid chelate, zinc citrate, and picolinate are better than zinc sulphate or oxide.

Helpers Stomach acid, vitamins A, E, and B6, magnesium, calcium, phosphorus.

Robbers Phytates (wheat), oxalates (rhubarb and spinach), high calcium intake, copper, low protein intake, excess sugar intake, stress; alcohol prevents uptake.

SEMI-ESSENTIAL NUTRIENTS

▪ Bioflavonoids

What they do Helps vitamin C to work, strengthens capillaries, speeds up healing of wounds, sprains, and muscle injuries, antioxidant.

Deficiency signs Easy bruising, varicose veins, frequent sprains.

How much?
RDA None
SONA None
THERAPEUTIC RANGE 50–1,000 mg.
TOXICITY None known.

Best food source Berries, cherries, citrus fruit.

Best supplement Citrus bioflavonoids, rosehip extract, berry extracts.

Helpers Vitamin C.

Robbers Free radicals.

▪ Choline

What it does Component of lecithin which helps break down fat in liver, facilitates movement of fats into cells and synthesis of cell membranes in nervous system, protects lungs.

Deficiency signs Development abnormalities in newborn babies, high blood cholesterol and fat, fatty liver, nerve degeneration, high blood pressure, atherosclerosis, senile dementia, reduced resistance to infection.

How much?

RDA *Male Adults* 550 mg *Female Adults* 425 mg
SONA None
THERAPEUTIC RANGE *Children* 12.5–75 mg *Adults* 25–150 mg
TOXICITY None known.

Best food source Lecithin, eggs, fish, liver, soybeans, peanuts, whole grains, nuts, legumes, citrus fruits, wheat germ, brewer's yeast.

Best supplement Lecithin.

Helpers Vitamin B5, lithium.

Robbers Alcohol, birth control pills.

■ Co-enzyme Q10

What it does Central role in energy metabolism, improves heart function and other functions, helps to normalize blood pressure, increases exercise tolerance, antioxidant, boosts immunity.

Deficiency signs Lack of energy, heart disease, poor exercise tolerance, poor immune function.

How much?

RDA None
SONA None
THERAPEUTIC RANGE 10–90 mg per day.
TOXICITY None known.

Best food source Sardines (6.4 mg), mackerel (4.3 mg), pork (2.4–4.1 mg), spinach (1.0 mg), soy oil (9.2 mg), peanuts (2.7 mg), sesame seeds (2.3 mg), walnuts (1.9 mg).

Best supplement Co-enzyme Q10 in a lipid base (aids absorption).

Helpers B complex, iron.

Robbers Stimulants, sugar.

■ Inositol

What it does Needed for cell growth, required by brain, spinal cord, and for formation of nerve sheath, mild tranquilizer, maintains healthy hair, reduces blood cholesterol.

Deficiency signs Irritability, insomnia, nervousness, hyper-excitability, reduction in nerve growth and regeneration, low HDL level.

How much?
RDA None
SONA None
THERAPEUTIC RANGE *Children* 12.5–75 mg *Adults* 25–150 mg.
TOXICITY None known.

Best food source Lecithin granules, legumes, soy flour, eggs, fish, liver, citrus fruits, melon, nuts, wheat germ, brewer's yeast.

Best supplement Lecithin granules or capsules.

Helpers Choline.

Robbers Phytates, antibiotics, alcohol, tea, coffee, birth control pills, diuretics.

Recommended Daily Allowance (RDAs) are a set of nutrient standards established by the U.S. Committee on Dietary Allowances last updated in 1989. The Institute of Medicine Food and Nutrition Board are currently revising RDAs. The RDA levels given here are based on those for children aged 7-10 and adults aged 25-50.

WHICH PROTEIN FOODS?

The protein in foods varies in both its quantity and quality. The table opposite shows you how much protein is in the listed foods (percentage of calories as protein), how much of the food you would need to eat to obtain 20 grams of protein, and how "usable" is the protein, which is a measure of its quality in isolation. Less "usable" protein sources may become highly usable when combined with other foods (see p. 38). Most people need no more than 35 grams a day, so two of any of the servings below would suffice. If the quality of the protein is high, one and a half servings may be enough. Pregnant women, people recovering from surgery, athletes and anyone who does heavy manual work may need three servings a day.

Protein Quantity and Quality

Food	Percentage of calories as Protein	Amount required for 20 g of Protein	Quality of Protein
Grains/legumes			
Quinoa	16%	100 g/1 cup dry weight	Excellent
Corn	4%	500 g/3 cups	Reasonable
White rice	8%	338 g/2.5 cups	Reasonable
Brown rice	5%	400 g/3 cups	Excellent
Kidney beans	26%	99 g/0.66 cup	Poor
Chickpeas	22%	109 g/0.66 cup	Reasonable
Soybeans	54%	60 g/1 cup	Reasonable
Tofu	40%	275 g/1 packet	Excellent
Baked beans	18%	430 g/1 large tin	Reasonable
Wheat germ	24%	132 g/2 cups	Reasonable
Lentils	28%	92 g/⅓ cup	Poor
Fish/meat			
Tuna, canned in oil	61%	84 g/1 small tin	Excellent
Cod	60%	35 g/1 small piece	Excellent
Sardines, canned	49%	100 g/1 serving	Excellent
Scallops	15%	133 g/1 serving	Excellent
Oysters	11%	182 g/0.5 cup	Excellent
Lamb chop	24%	110 g/1 small	Reasonable
Beef	52%	80 g/2 slices	Excellent
Chicken	63%	71 g/1 small breast roast	Excellent
Nuts/seeds			
Sunflower seeds	15%	188 g/1 cup	Reasonable
Pumpkin seeds	21%	70 g/0.5 cup	Reasonable
Cashew nuts	12%	112 g/1 cup	Reasonable
Peanuts	17%	90 g/0.5 cup	Reasonable
Almonds	13%	110 g/1 cup	Reasonable
Eggs/dairy			
Eggs	34%	169 g/2 medium	Excellent
Yogurt, natural	22%	440 g/3 small pots	Excellent
Cheddar cheese	25%	84 g/0.33 oz	Excellent
Cottage cheese	49%	120 g/1 small pot	Excellent
Milk, whole	20%	600 ml/2 cups	Excellent
Edam cheese	28%	70 g/2.5oz	Excellent
Camembert cheese	25%	110 g/2 wedges	Excellent
Vegetables			
Peas, frozen	26%	259 g/2 cups	Reasonable
Green beans	20%	200 g/2 cups	Reasonable
Broccoli	50%	600 g/large bag	Reasonable
Spinach	49%	390 g/large bag	Reasonable
Potatoes	11%	950 g/4 large	Reasonable

Which fats and oils?

Foods vary in the quality and quantity of fat they contain. The perfect diet provides no more than 20 per cent of its calories from fat. However, more important is the kind of fat. Polyunsaturated fats, or rather oils as they are always liquid, are essential, while monounsaturated and saturated fats are not. So in an ideal food more of the fat is polyunsaturated. The table opposite shows which fat-containing foods to avoid and which to increase. Those in **bold** type are best avoided, or limited, because they contain few essential fats, are high in saturated fat and have an overall high fat percentage.

There are different families of unsaturated fats. The Omega 6 and Omega 3 families are essential. Ideally your diet should provide roughly equal amounts of these. The Omega 9 family derive from the monounsaturated fat oleic acid, of which olive oil is a good source. These are not essential, but not harmful, except in excess. The table below shows which cold-pressed oils contain which unsaturated fats.

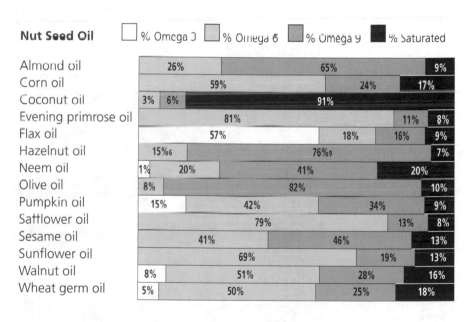

Fats and oils—which omega?

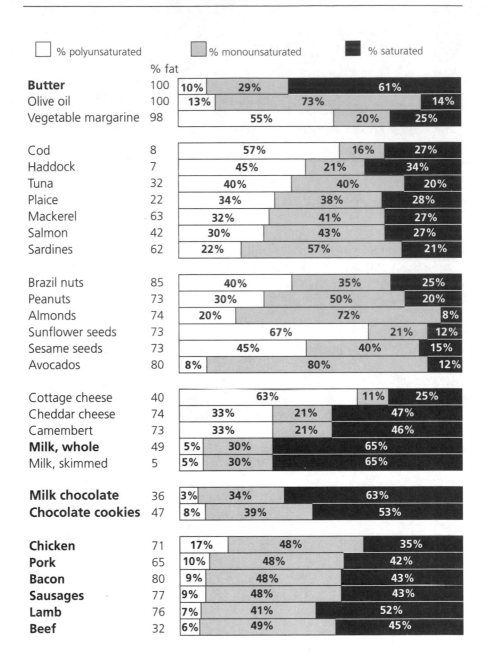

| | % polyunsaturated | % monounsaturated | % saturated |

	% fat			
Butter	100	10%	29%	61%
Olive oil	100	13%	73%	14%
Vegetable margarine	98	55%	20%	25%
Cod	8	57%	16%	27%
Haddock	7	45%	21%	34%
Tuna	32	40%	40%	20%
Plaice	22	34%	38%	28%
Mackerel	63	32%	41%	27%
Salmon	42	30%	43%	27%
Sardines	62	22%	57%	21%
Brazil nuts	85	40%	35%	25%
Peanuts	73	30%	50%	20%
Almonds	74	20%	72%	8%
Sunflower seeds	73	67%	21%	12%
Sesame seeds	73	45%	40%	15%
Avocados	80	8%	80%	12%
Cottage cheese	40	63%	11%	25%
Cheddar cheese	74	33%	21%	47%
Camembert	73	33%	21%	46%
Milk, whole	49	5%	30%	65%
Milk, skimmed	5	5%	30%	65%
Milk chocolate	36	3%	34%	63%
Chocolate cookies	47	8%	39%	53%
Chicken	71	17%	48%	35%
Pork	65	10%	48%	42%
Bacon	80	9%	48%	43%
Sausages	77	9%	48%	43%
Lamb	76	7%	41%	52%
Beef	32	6%	49%	45%

Fat composition of foods

WHICH CARBOHYDRATES?

Carbohydrates should make up the major part of your diet, accounting for two-thirds of the calories you consume. Since there are more calories per gram of both protein and fat this means that, by weight, carbohydrates should make up more than two-thirds of your diet.

The type of carbohydrate is as important as the amount. Carbohydrates are classified as "complex" (starch) or "simple" (sugars). Of the simple carbohydrates most are "fast-releasing," which means that they raise your blood sugar level quickly. However fructose, a sugar predominant in raw fruit, is "slow-releasing." The table below shows which proportion of the foods listed consists of slow-releasing carbohydrates and how much is fast-releasing, plus the overall effect on blood sugar, known as the Glycemic Index.

Generally it is better to eat slow-releasing foods those scoring (below 50), or, when eating small amounts of fast-releasing foods, to combine them with slow-releasing foods.

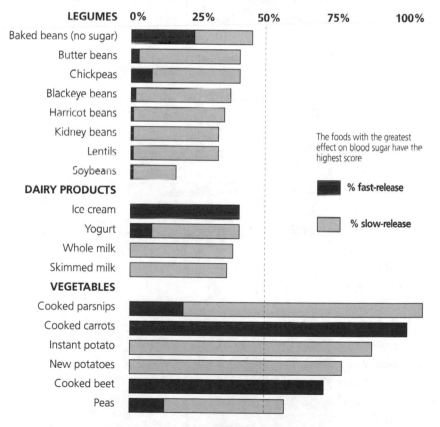

Which foods raise blood sugar levels, and which foods are slow-releasing?

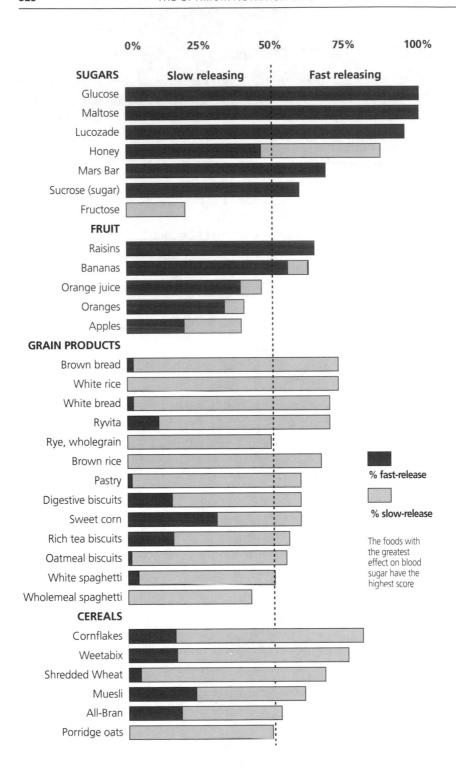

How much fiber?

Foods vary in both the amount of fiber they contain and its quality. One measure of quality is the amount of water that the fiber absorbs, which indicates to what extent it can make fecal matter lighter, bulkier and easier to move through the digestive tract. The ideal intake of fiber is not less than 35 grams a day. The following table shows you how much of given foods provides 10 grams of fiber (or the equivalent effect of 10 grams of grain fiber if the type of fiber is substantially more absorbent and therefore the amount you need in comparison is less). All measures are based on raw or dry foods. Please note that cooking decreases the fiber content of foods. So four servings of any of these foods will provide an ideal intake of fiber. All foods are raw, unless otherwise stated.

Amount of food required to supply 10 g of fiber

Food	Amount (for equivalent of 10 g grain fiber)
Wheatbran	23 g/0.5 cup
All-Bran	37 g/0.5 cup
Apricots, dried	42 g/1 cup
Figs, dried	54 g/0.3 cups
Oats	75 g/1 cup
Peas	83 g/1 cup
Cornflakes	91 g/3.5 cups
Almonds	107 g/0.8 cups
Wholemeal bread	115 g/5 slices
Peanuts	125 g/1 cup
Baked beans	137 g/small can
Prunes	146 g/1 cup
Sunflower seeds	147 g/1 cup
Rye bread	160 g/6 slices
Rice crispies	222 g/8 cups
Oatcakes	250 g/10 biscuits
Lentils, cooked	270 g/2 cups
Carrots	310 g/3 carrots
Broccoli	358 g/1 large head
White bread	370 g/15 slices
Baked potato (skin on)	400 g/1 large
Coleslaw	400 g/1 large serving
Oranges	415 g/3 oranges
Cabbage	466 g/1 medium
Cauliflower	475 g/1 large
Apple	500 g/3–4 apples
New potatoes, boiled	500 g/7 potatoes
Bananas	625 g/3 bananas
Peaches	625 g/6 peaches

BALANCING ACID/ALKALINE

When foods are metabolized by the body, a residue is left which can alter the body's acidity and alkalinity. Depending on the chemical composition of the "ash," the food is called "acid-forming" or "alkaline-forming." This is not to be confused with the immediate acidity of a food. Oranges, for example, are acid due to their citric acid content. However, citric acid is completely metabolized and the net effect of eating an orange is to alkalize the body, hence it is classified as alkaline-forming. Roughly 80 percent of our diet should come from alkaline-forming foods, and 20 percent from acid-forming foods. The table below shows which foods are which.

Which foods are Acid, Alkaline, and Neutral

ACID		NEUTRAL	ALKALINE	
High	*Medium*		*Medium*	*High*
	Brazil nuts		Almonds	
	Walnuts		Coconut	
Edam	Cheddar cheese	Butter	Milk	
Eggs	Stilton cheese	Margarine		
Mayonnaise			Beans	Avocado
		Coffee	Cabbage	Beet
Fish	Herrings	Tea	Celery	Carrots
Shellfish	Mackerel	Sugar	Lentils	Potatoes
		Syrup	Lettuce	Spinach
Bacon	Rye		Mushrooms	
Beef	Oats		Onions	
Chicken	Wheat		Root vegetables	
Liver	Rice		Tomatoes	
Lamb				
Veal	Plums		Apricots	Dried fruit
	Cranberries		Apples	Rhubarb
	Olives		Banana	
			Berries	
			Cherries	
			Figs	
			Grapefruit	
			Grapes	
			Lemon	
			Melon	
			Oranges	
			Peaches	
			Pears	
			Raspberries	
			Tangerines	
			Prunes	

RECOMMENDED READING

The following books and publications will help you to dig deeper into the subjects covered in this book. The numbers in the left column relate to the chapters whose contents these books relate to.

PART 1—What Is Optimum
2. *What Is Optimum?* Dr. Emanuel Cheraskin, ION (1994)
3. *Biochemical Individuality* Professor Roger Williams, Texas University Press (1996)
4. *Nutrition and Evolution* Professor Michael Crawford and David Marsh, Keats (1995)
6. *Our Stolen Future* Colborn, Myers and Dumanoski, Little Brown (1996)
   How to Protect Yourself from Pollution Patrick Holford & Dr. Philip Barlow, ION Press (1990)

PART 2—Defining the Perfect Diet
9. *Fats that Heal, Fats that Kill* Dr. Udo Erasmus, Alive Books (1994)
11. *The Vitamin Controversy* ION (1987)
12. *Elemental Health* Patrick Holford, ION Press (1983)
14. *Living Food—The key to Health and Vitality* Patrick Holford, ION Press (1996)

PART 3—The Wonderful World Within
17. *Improve Your Digestion* Patrick Holford, Piatkus (1999)
18. *Say No to Heart Disease* Patrick Holford, Piatkus (1998)
    Unified Theory on the Cause and Treatment of Cardiovascular Disease Dr. Linus Pauling, (video) ION (1995)
19. *Boost Your Immune System* Jennifer Meek & Patrick Holford, Piatkus (1998)
20. *Balancing Hormones Naturally* Kate Neil & Patrick Holford, Piatkus

(1998) *What Your Doctor Didn't Tell You About Menopause* Dr. John Lee, Warner Books (1996)
22. *Say No to Arthritis* Patrick Holford, Piatkus (1999)

PART 4—The Benefits of Optimum Nutrition
26. *Stopping the Clock* Dr. Ronald Klatz and Dr. Robert Goldman, Keats (1996)
27. *Cancer Prevention and Nutritional Therapies* Dr. Richard Passwater, Keats (1993)
    Say No to Cancer Patrick Holford, Piatkus (1999)
28. *Boost Your Immune System* Jennifer Meek & Patrick Holford, Piatkus (1998)
29. *The 30-Day Fatburner Diet* Patrick Holford, Piatkus (1998)
30&31 *Mental Health and Mental Illness—The Nutrition Connection* Patrick Holford & Dr. Carl Pfeiffer, ION Press (1996)

PART 5—Nutrition for All Ages
32 & 33. *The Better Pregnancy Diet,* Patrick Holford & Liz Lorente, ION Press (1992)
34. *What Your Dr. Didn't Tell You About Menopause* Dr. John Lee, Warner Books (1996)
    The Male Menopause Dr. Malcolm Carruthers, Harper Collins (1996)
35. *The 20 Day Rejuvenation Diet Program* Dr. Jeffrey Bland, Keats (1997)

REFERENCES

The references listed here relate to the main studies referred to, and numbered, in the text. These represent a fraction of the scientific literature used to compile this book. Those readers who wish to dig deeper are advised to access the scientific literature held on file at the Institute for Optimum Nutrition, who can carry out literature and library searches on any topics of interest (see p. 339)

1. Stephens, N. et al. "Randomized controlled trial of vitamin E in patients with coronary disease: Cambridge Heart Antioxidant Study (CHAOS)," *Lancet*, p347, (March 23, 1996).

2. Bergkvist, L. et al., "The risk of breast cancer after estrogen and estrogen-progestin replacement," *N. Engl. J. Med*, vol 32, p293–297 (1989).

3. Rodriguez, C. et al. "Estrogen replacement therapy and fatal ovarian cancer," *Am. J. Epidemiology*, vol 141:9, p828–835, (1995).

4–5. "The Aquatic Ape'" *Nutrition and Health*, vol 9:3, (1993).

6. Cheraskin, E., "The breakfast/lunch/dinner ritual," *J. Orthomolecular Med*, vol 8, p6–10, (1993).

7. Popper, H. and Steigmann, F.J., *Am. Med. Assoc.*, vol 123, p1108–114, (1943).

8. Hoffer, A. & Osmond, H., "Treatment of Schizophrenia with Nicotinic Acid," *Acta. Psych. Scand.* vol 40, p.171–189, (1964) & Hoffer, A. "Chronic Schizophrenic Patients Treated Ten Years or More," *J. Orthomol. Med.*, vol 9:1, p1–37 (1994).

9. Barker, H., MRC Environmental Epidemiology Unit, Southampton, UK.

10. Bryce-Smith, D., "Pre-natal zinc deficiency," *Nursing Times* (1985).

11. Schoenthaler, S. et al., "Controlled trial of vitamin-mineral supplementation on intelligence and brain function," *Person. Individ. Diff.*, vol 12:4, p343–350 (1991). Schoenthaler, S. et al., "Controlled trial of vitamin-mineral supplementation: Effects on intelligence and performance," *Person. Individ. Diff.*, vol 12:4, p351–362 (1991).

12. Losonczy K. et al., *Am. J. Clin. Nutr.*, vol 64(2), p190–196 (1996).

13. Bartus, R. T. et al., "Profound effects of combining choline and piracetam on memory enhancement and cholinergic function in aged rat" *Neurobiology of Aging.*, vol 2, p105–111 (1981).

14. Schectman, G. et al., "Ascorbic acid requirements for smokers: Analysis of a population survey." *Am. J. Clin. Nutr.*, vol 53:6, p1466–1470, (June 1991).

15. Ash, J., "Investigation into the mechanisms of the effects of azo dyes on hyperactive children," Final-year project, School of Biological Sciences, University of Surrey, Guildford, UK. Copy held by Dr. Neil Ward.

16. Dickerson, J.W. T. et al., "Disease patterns in individuals with different eating patterns," *J. of Royal Soc. of Health*, vol 105, p191–194, (1985).

17. Dosch, H.M., "Interview with Hans-Michael Dosch—An update of the Ig-G-mediated cow's milk and insulin-dependant diabetes connection, part 2." *The Immuno. Review*, vol 2:3 (Spring 1994).

18. Davies, S. "The myth of the balanced diet," Power of Prevention Conference 1993. Available from ION —cassette T16—"The Myth of the balanced diet."

19. "A square meal for Britain?" Research by the Bateman Catering Organization (Pub. 1981).

20. *The Vitamin Controversy*, ION (1987).

21. Cheraskin, E. et al., "Establishing a suggested optimum nutrition allowance (SONA)," (1994).

"What is optimum?," *Optimum Nutrition Magazine*, vol 7.2, p46–47, (1994).

22. Hemila, H. et al., "Vitamin C and the common cold: A retrospective analysis of Chalmers' review," *J. Am. College Nutrition*, vol 14:2, p116–123, (1995).

23. Cheraskin, E., "Antioxidants in health and disease: The big picture," *J. Orthomolecular Med.*, 10:2, p89–96.

24. Cheraskin, E. et al., "The ideal daily vitamin C intake," *J. Med Assoc of the State of Alabama*, 46:12, p39–40, (June 1977).

25. Enstrom, J. and Pauling, L., "Mortality among health-conscious elderly Californians," *Proc. Natl. Sci*, vol 79: p6023–6027, (1982).

26. Davies, S., "The myth of the balanced diet." Power of Prevention Conference 1993. Available from ION —cassette T16—"The Myth of the balanced diet."

27. *Reader's Digest*, (Dec. 1995).

28. *Reader's Digest*, (Dec. 1995).

29. Kotulak, R. and Gorner, P. (eds), "Aging On Hold—Secrets of Living Younger Longer," Chapter 5 by R. Walford, 51–73; Tribune Publishing, USA, (1992).

30. Aaman, Z. et al., "Plasma concentrations of vitamins A and E and carotenoids in Alzheimer's Disease," *Age and Aging*, vol 21:2, p91–94, (March 1992).

31. Jacques, P.F., "Relationship of vitamin C status to cholesterol and blood pressure," *Annals of the New York Academy of Sciences*, vol 669, p205–214, (1992).

32. Robertson, J.M. et al., "Vitamin E intake and risk of cataracts in humans," *Annals of the New York Academy of Sciences*, vol 570, p372–382, (1989).

33. Bond, G. et al., "Dietary vitamin A and lung cancer: Results of a case-control study among chemical workers," *Nutrition and Cancer*, vol 9:2,3, p109–121, (1987).

34. Mayne, S. T., "Dietary beta carotene and lung cancer risk in U.S. non-smokers," *J. Nat. Cancer Institute*.

35. Garwal, H.S. et al., "Response of oral leukophakia to beta carotene," *J. of Clin. Oncology*, vol 8, 1715–1720, (1990).

36. Manson, J.E. et al., "A prospective study of antioxidant vitamins and incidence of coronary heart disease in women," *Abstract in Circulation*, vol 84:4, p11–546, (1991).

37. Osilesi, O. et al., "Blood pressure and plasma lipids during ascorbic acid supplementation in borderline

hypertensive and normotensive adults," *Nutrition Research*, vol 11:405–412, (1991).

38. Zhang,Y. et al., "A major inducer of anticarcinogenic protective enzymes from broccoli: Isolation and elucidation of structure," *Proc. Natl. Acad. Sci. USA* 89, p2399–2403, (March 1992).

39. *New Eng. J. Med.*, pp1444–1449 (May 20, 1993).

40. *New Eng. J. Med.*, pp1450–1455 (May 20, 1993).

41. Mullins, K., "The blood pressure project," (1990). Copy held at ION library, London. Tel: 0181 877 9993.

42. As reported in *The New Super-Nutrition* by Richard Passwater, published by Pocket Books, (1991).

43. *Optimum Nutrition* magazine, vol 8.2, p8–9, (Autumn 1995).

44. Cheraskin, E., "If high blood cholesterol is bad — is low good?", *J. Orthomolecular Med.*, vol 1:3, p176–183, (Third quarter, 1986).

45. Colgan, M., "Effects of nutrient supplements on athletic performance," paper given to the U.S. Navy Research and Development Center, San Diego, (April 1983).

46. Saynor, R. et al., "The long-term effect of dietary supplementation with fish lipid concentrate on serum lipids, bleeding time, platelets and angina," *Atherosclerosis*, vol 50, p.3–10, (1984).

47. Pauling, L. and Rath, M., "A unified theory of human cardiovascular disease leading the way to the abolition of this disease as a cause for human mortality," *J. Orthomolecular Med.*, vol 7:1, p5–12, (1992).

48. Harakeh, S., Jariwalla, R. and Pauling, L., "Suppression of human immunodeficiency virus replication by ascorbate in chronically and acutely infected cells," *Proc. Natl. Acad. Sci. USA* 87, p7245–7249, (September 1990).

49. Geoffrey Cannon, *Super Bug*

50. Keicolt-Glaser, J.K. et al., "Modulation of cellular immunity in medical students," *J. Beh. Med.*, vol 9:5, (1986).

51. Chandra, R.K., "Study of mulitivitamin/mineral supplementation in elderly." *Lancet*, (1992).

52. Allen, L.N. et al., "Protein-induced hypercalcuria: A longer term study," *Am. J. Clin. Nutr.*, vol 32:71–749, (1979).

53. Anand, C.R. et al., "Effect of protein intake on calcium balance of young men given 500 mg calcium daily," *J. of Nutrition*, vol 104: 695–700, (1974).

54. Kubula, A.J., *Gen. Psych.*, 96 p343–352, (1960).

55. Schauss A., *J. App. Nutr.*, 35, 1, (1983).

56. Needleman, H.N., *Eng. J. Med.*, 300 p689–695, (1979).

57. Benton, D., "Effect of vitamin and mineral supplementation on intelligence of a sample school children," *Lancet* (Jan 23, 1988).

58. Schoenthaler, S. et al., "Controlled trial of vitamin-mineral supplementation: Effects on intelligence and performance," *Person. Individ. Diff.*, vol 12:4, p351–362, (1991).

59. Harrel, R., *Proc. Nat. Acad. Sci.*, USA, 78:1, p574–578, (1981).

60. Pepeu, G. et al., "Neurochemical actions of 'Nootropic Drugs,'" *Advances in Neurology*, vol. 51: *Alzheimer's Disease*, New York: Raven Press Ltd, (1990).

61. Bartus, R. T. et al., "Profound effects of combining choline and piracetam on memory enhancement and cholinergic function in aged rats," *Neurobiology of Aging*, vol 2, p. 105–111, (1981).

62. Colgan, M., "Effects of nutrient supplements on athletic performance," paper given to the U.S. Navy Research and Development Center, San Diego, (April 1983).

63. Kotulak, R. and Gorner, P., *Aging On Hold—Secrets of Living Younger Longer*, Chapter 5 by R. Walford, p. 51–73. Tribune Publishing, USA, (1992).

64. *Am. J. Clin. Nutr.,* vol 64:190–196, (1996).

65. Huang, L.A. et al., "Treatment of acute promyelocytic leukemia with all-trans retinoic acid: 'a five-year experience,'" *Chin. Med. J.*, vol 106:10, p743–748, (Oct. 1993).

66. Lippman, S.M. et al., "Molecular epidemiology and retinoid chemoprevention of head and neck cancer," *J. Natl. Cancer Inst.*, vol 89:3, p199–211 (Feb. 5 1997). Lippman, S.M. and Hong, W.K., "13-cis-retinoic acid plus interferon-alpha in solid tumors: keeping the cart behind the horse (editorial)," *Ann. Oncol.*, (Netherlands), vol 5:5, p391–393, (May 1994).

67. Hirayama, T., "A large scale cohort study on cancer risks by diet—with special reference to the risk reducing effects of green-yellow vegetable consumption," *Princess Takamatsu Symp.,* (USA), vol 16, p41–53, (1985).

68. Omenn, G. et al., *New Eng. J. Med.* vol 334, p1150–1155, (1996).

69. Cameron, E. and Pauling, L., "Supplemental ascorbate in the supportive treatment of cancer: Prolongation of survival times in terminal human cancer," *Proc. Nat. Academy Sci.*, vol 73:3685–3689, (1976); and Cameron, E. and Pauling, L., "Supplemental ascorbate in the supportive treatment of cancer: A re-evaluation of prolongation of survival times in terminal human cancer," *Proc. Nat. Academy Sci.*, vol 75, p4538–4542, (1978).

70. *Am J. Clin. Nutr.*, vol 64: 190–196, (1996).

71. Salonen, J. T., "Risk of cancer in relation to serum concentrations of selenium and vitamin A and E," *Brit. Med. J.*, vol 209:417–420, (Feb. 9, 1985).

72. Yu, S.Y. et al., "Chemoprevention trial of human hepatitis with selenium supplementation in China." *Biol. Trace Glem. Res.*, Apr–May 20:1–2, p15–22, (1989).

73. Chang, K-J. et al., "Influences of percutaneous administration of estradiol and progesterone on human breast epithelial cell cycle in vivo," *Fertility and Sterility*, vol 63:4, p785, (April 1995).

74. Hirayama, T., "A large scale cohort study on cancer risks by diet—with special reference to the risk reducing effects of green-yellow vegetable consumption," *Princess Takamatsu Symp.*, (USA), vol 16, p41–53, (1985).

75. You, W.C. et al., *J. Natl. cancer Inst.*, vol 81:2, p162–164 (18 Jan. 1989), *J. of the Nat. Med. Assoc.*, vol 80(4), 88, p439–445.

76. Peters, R.K. et al., "Cancer Causes and Control," vol 3, p. 457–473, (1992), and Golkin, B.R. and Gorbach, S.L., J.N.C.L., vol 64, p255–261, (1980).

77. Zakay-Rones, Z. et al., "Inhibition of several strains of influenza virus in vitro and reduction of symptoms by an

elderberry extract (Sambucus nigra L.) during an outbreak of influenza B Panama," *J. Alt. and Comp. Med.*, vol 1:4, 361–369, (1995).

78. Bendle, S., "The effect of konjac fibre on weight loss." (1991), paper held by ION library available from ION, London, Tel: 0181 877 9993.

79. Casper and Prasad, (1980).

80. Safai-Kutti, *Am. J. Clin. Nut.*, vol 44, p581–582, (1986).

81. Katz, et al., *J. Adol. Health Care*, vol 8, p400–406, (1987).

82. Birmingham, et al., *Int. J. Eat Disord.* vol 15:3, p251–255, (1994).

83. Hoffer, A. & Osmond, H., "Treatment of Schizophrenia with Nicotinic Acid," *Acta. Psych. Scand.*, vol 40, 171–189, (1964) and Hoffer, A., "Chronic Schizophrenic Patients Treated Ten Years or More," *J. Orthomol. Med.*, vol 9:1, p1–37, (1994).

84. Wittenborn, J.R. et al., "Niacin in the Long-Term Treatment of Schizophrenia," *Arch. Gen. Psychiatry*, vol 28, (March 1973).

85. Turkel, H. et al., "Intellectual Improvement of a Retarded Patient Treated with the 'U' Series," *J. Orthomol. Psychiatry*, vol 13:4, p272–276, (1984).

86. Libby, A.F. and Stone, I., "The Hypoascorbemia-Kwashiorkor Approach to Drug Addiction Therapy: Pilot Study," *Orthomolecular Psychiatry*, vol 6:4, p300–308, (1977).

87. Godrey, P.S.A., Reynolds, E.H. et al., "Enhancement of recovery from psychiatric illness by methylfolate," *Lancet*, vol 336, p392–395, (1990).

88. Hargreave, T.B. et al., "Randomized trial of mesterolone versus vitamin C for male infertility," *Br. J. Urol.*, vol 56:6, p740–744, (1984) and Abel, B.J. et al., "Randomized trial of clomiphene citrate treatment and vitamin C for male infertility," *Br. J. Urol.*, vol 54:6, p780–784, (1982).

89. Milunsky, A. et al., "Multivitamin/folic acid supplementation in early pregnancy reduces the prevalence of neural tube defects," *JAMA* 262:20, p2847–2852 (Nov. 24, 1989).

90. Brush, M.G., "Nutritional approaches to the treatment of premenstrual syndrome," *Nutrition and Health*, vol 2:3/4, p203–209, (1983).

91. Abraham, G.E. et al., "Effect of vitamin B6 on premenstrual symptomatology in women with premenstrual tension syndromes: a double-blind crossover study," *Infertility* 3, p155–165, (1980).

92. Horrobin, D.F., "Gamma linolenic acid: An intermediate in essential fatty acid metabolism with potential as an ethical pharmaceutical and as a food," *Rev. Contemp. Pharmacother 1*, p1–45, (1990).

93. Flynn, A.M. and Brooks, M., *A Manual of Natural Family Planning*, Thorsons/HarperCollins, London, (1990).

94. Cooper, J., "Vitamin E—Its benefit in menopause," paper held by ION library available from ION, London, Tel: 0181 877 9993.

95. Purdy, C., "The effects of calcium, magnesium, vitamin D and vitamin E on menopausal symptoms," paper held by ION library available from ION, London, Tel: 0181 877 9993.

USEFUL ADDRESSES

Arica Institute
The Arica Institute offers one-day training's in the exercise system Psychocalisthenics, plus other trainings. Arica Institute Inc., 145 Palisade Street, Suite 401, Dobbs Ferry, New York 10522-1617. Tel: (914) 674-4091 Fax: (914)674-4093

Institute for Optimum Nutrition
ION is a U.K. charitable trust whose mission is to help people reach their maximum potential through optimum nutrition. It offers personal consultations with ION qualified nutrition consultants in the U.K. Training courses include Optimum Nutrition Workshops, a Homestudy Course and the three-year Nutrition Consultants Diploma course. ION membership entitles you to the *Optimum Nutrition Magazine,* Nutrition Updates, a Nutrition Resource Center and Information Service which you can access by fax or mail, plus discounts on books and courses. The annual membership fee is $45. To become a member fax your credit card details. For further information write to ION, Blades Court, Deodar Road, London SW15 2NU, England. Tel: 011 44 181 877 9993 Fax: 011 44 181 877 9980, or visit the website at www.optimumnutrition.co.uk

For a list of Patrick Holford's seminars and events in the US visit his website www.lpatrickholford.com

Laboratory Tests
The following laboratories offer tests referred to in this book. These tests are best administered with the guidance and advice of your natural practitioner.

Immuno Laboratories
1620 W. Oaklands Pk Boulevard
Fort Lauderdale, FL 33311
Tel: (954) 486 4500
Fax: (954) 739 6563
www.immunolab.com

Aeron Life Cycles Laboratory
1933 Davis Street, Suite 310
San Leandro, CA 94577
Tel: (800) 631 7900
Fax: (510) 729 0383
www.acron.com

Great Smokies
63 Zillicoa Street
Asheville, NC 28801-1074
Tel: (704) 253 0621
Fax: (704) 252 9303
www.gsdl.com

Diagnostech
6620501 92nd Place J-104
Kent, WA 98022
Tel: (425) 251 0596
Fax: (425) 251 0637
www.diagnostech.com

Nutrition Consultations

One to one nutrition consultations are available in the U.S. through naturopathic physicians, nutritionists and physicians trained in the optimum nutrition approach. The following organizations can help you find a practitioner in your area.

Healthcomm International Inc.
5800 Soundview Drive
Gig Harbour, WA 98335
Tel: (253) 851 3943
Fax: (253) 851 9749

Bastyr Naturopathic University
14500 Juanita Drive North East
Bothell, WA 98011
Tel: (425) 823 1300
Fax: (425) 823 6222

American Association of
Naturopathic Physicians
2366 Eastlake Avenue, Suite 322
Seattle, WA 98102
Tel: (206) 323-7610

American Holistic Medical
Association
4101 Lake Boone Trail, Suite 201
Raleigh, NC 27607
Tel: (919) 787-5146

American College of Alternative
Medicine
P.O. Box 3427
Laguna Hills, CA 92654
Tel: (800) 532-3688

American Preventive Medical
Association, P.O. Box 2111
Tacoma, WA 98401
Tel: (206) 926-0551
Fax: (303) 417-9378

Either for consultations in the U.K. or for postal and telephone consultations with Patrick Holford and his team of clinical nutritionists visit his website www.patrickholford.com which explains the procedure.

DIRECTORY OF SUPPLEMENT COMPANIES

There are many excellent nutritional products available through natural food stores. You are best to seek the guidance of nutritional advisors in these stores who can meet your needs calculated from the Optimum Nutrition Questionnaire, based on recommending high quality products that provide the right amounts of nutrients at the right price. Here are a few companies whose products fulfill these criteria.

Enzymatic Therapy
825 Challenger Drive
Green Bay WI 54311
Tel: (920) 469 1313
Fax: (920) 469 4400
www.enzy.com

Nature's Plus
548 Broad Hollow Road
Melville, NY 11747
Tel: (516) 293 0030
Fax: (516) 293 2934

Solgar Vitamin and
   Herb Company Inc.
500 Willow Tree Road
Leonia NJ 07605
Tel: (201) 944 2311
Fax: (516) 293 2934
www.solgar.com

Source Naturals
23 Janis Way
Scotts Valley, CA 95066
Tel: (831) 461 6334
Fax: (831) 438 2169

Twin Laboratories Inc.
150 Motor Parkway
Hauppauge, NY 11788
Tel: (516) 467 3140
Fax: (516) 467 0145

INDEX

RELATED BOOKS BY THE CROSSING PRESS

Good Food: *The Comprehensive Food & Nutrition Resource*

By Margaret M. Wittenberg

"An exceptionally well-organized, up-to-date, and easily accessible treatise on food and nutrition. Wittenberg delineates a direct connection between food and quality of life."

—Susan Jane Cheney, Food Writer/Columnist

$18.95 • Paper • ISBN 0-89594-746-3

The Herbal Menopause Book: *Herbs, Nutrition, and Other Natural Therapies*

By Amanda McQuade Crawford

This comprehensive volume provides dozens of specific herbal remedies and other natural therapies for women facing the health issues that arise in premenopause, menopause, and post menopause.

$16.95 • Paper • ISBN 0-89594-799-4

The Information Sourcebook of Herbal Medicine

By David Hoffman, B.Sc., M.N.I.M.H.

A comprehensive guide to information on western herbal medicine, offering a bibliography of herbalism and herbal pharmacology, a glossary of herbal and medical terms, computer databases for the herbalist, and Medline citations for commonly used medicinal herbs.

$40.00 • Hardcover • ISBN 0-89594-671-8

The Male Herbal: *Health Care for Men & Boys*

By James Green

This preventive health care guide offers remedies for specific male problems, information on choosing the right herb, and preparation of herbal medicines.

"A wealth of information-recommended for alternative health care collections."

—*Library Journal*

$14.95 • Paper • ISBN 0-89594-458-8

Pocket Herbal Reference Guide
By Debra St. Claire

The medicinal use of plants is our oldest form of healing. This guide describes the appropriate use of herbs in an easily referenced format, including the therapeutic use of over 140 medicinal plants and natural remedies for over 100 common health problems.

$6.95 • Paper • ISBN 0-89594-568-1

Quit Smoking for Good: *A Supportive Program for Permanent Smoking Cessation*
By Andrea Baer

The program emphasizes coping skills, problem solving strategies, stress management, and supportive natural therapies. Relapse prevention is also a dominant part of the program.

$10.95 • Paper • ISBN 0-89594-943-1

Rejuvenate: *A 21-Day Natural Detox Plan for Optimal Health*
By Helene Silver

Rejuvenate will show you how you can create a retreat for yourself in the comfort and privacy of your own home. With step-by-step instructions, Silver's 21-day plan will cleanse your body of toxins and rejuvenate both body and mind.

$16.95 • Paper • ISBN 0-89594-938-5

Vitamins, Minerals & Supplements
By Gayle Skowronski and Beth Petro Roybal

Vitamins, Minerals & Supplements gives general information about the role of supplements in nutrition and how to choose them wisely. It gives details for specific common nutritional supplements and the daily requirements necessary to maintain good health.

$11.95 • Paper • ISBN 0-89594-935-0

To receive a current catalog from The Crossing Press
please call toll-free, 800-777-1048.
Visit our Web site: www. crossingpress.com

Cesar Chavez's Fasting Room, Forty Acres, Delano, California, 2016

In the midst of the Delano Grape Strike of 1968, United Farm Workers' (UFW) organizer César Chavez fasted for twenty-five days in an effort to publicize the farm workers' struggle. He asked consumers across the country to refuse to purchase table grapes until the growers negotiated a suitable contract with the farm workers, some of the poorest working people in the nation. Chavez's fast demonstrated his deep spirituality and his commitment to the principals of nonviolence and peaceful forms of protest on behalf of labor and immigrant rights. The UFW headquarters, "The Forty Acres," where Chavez conducted his fast, is now a National Historic Landmark.

Crazy Horse's Vision, Bear Butte, Sturgis, South Dakota, 2011

Throughout the short life of the Sioux warrior Crazy Horse, Bear Butte, on the northern edge of the Black Hills, remained his place of refuge. It was on this hilltop, jutting sharply out of the Great Plains, that both the Lakota Sioux and Cheyenne believe that the Creator handed down the laws that governed their nations. And it was here that Crazy Horse (like his father before him) would climb in the 1850s to receive his vision, which was to dedicate his life to defending the sacred hunting grounds of his people. Today, Bear Butte State Park is located only a few miles from the biker bars of Sturgis, South Dakota. While the butte is covered in prayer flags left by visitors from the Indian reservations to the east, many Americans are more familiar with the annual Sturgis biker rally just down the road. To listen to the roar of the Harley engines and be served a drink at the Full Throttle Saloon, sitting next to a stuffed bison, is to experience the heavy price of victory.

MAROON FORT

Christina Snyder

Little remains of the fort at Prospect Bluff, but its otherworldly landscape—live oaks and Spanish moss enveloped in mist—is appropriate for a site that was once the staging ground for American dreams. In the early nineteenth century, Prospect Bluff was the largest maroon community in mainland North America and home to Native American refugees and British abolitionists.[1] As the United States pushed south and west, slaveholders carved plantations out of recently ceded Indian land, but those who came together at Prospect Bluff offered an alternative vision of what America was and might be.

Constructed in the spring of 1814, the fort at Prospect Bluff sat at the mouth of the Apalachicola River in Florida's panhandle. The fort was a key component of British strategy late in the War of 1812. Only sixty miles from the U.S. border, the British beckoned runaway slaves and Native Americans to help them defeat the United States. Alexander Cochrane, commander of the

North American Squadron of the Royal Navy, spearheaded the plan, encouraging "all those who may be disposed to emigrate from the United States" to present themselves to British troops: "they will have their choice of either entering into His Majesty's Sea or Land forces or of being sent as FREE settlers to the British possessions in North America or the West Indies where they will meet with all due encouragement."[2] Cochrane, who had employed similar strategies while serving in the Caribbean, believed that this attack on slavery would destabilize Southern society and swell British military ranks. Col. Edward Nicolls, a fiery abolitionist, enthusiastically oversaw implementation of the policy, with the assistance of George Woodbine, a trader who became an honorary captain in the British Navy.

Muscogee Creek leaders Josiah Francis and Peter McQueen pledged their support: "We will get all the Black Men we can to join your Warriors . . . we will do our best to unite all our Red Brethren and form a strong Arm, that will be ready to crush the Wicked and rebellious Americans when they shall dare to insult our Father and his Children."[3] Francis and McQueen came from a Creek faction called the Red Sticks, named for the traditional red war clubs they used in battle. Red Sticks opposed rising American influence in Creek country and, in 1813, sought to purge their nation of Anglo culture. They raided plantations, killed livestock, and intimidated those friendly to the United States. What began as a Creek civil war escalated after the Red Sticks' victory at Fort Mims, when the United States joined the "friendly" Creeks. In March 1814, the Red Sticks' power was broken at the bloody Battle of Horseshoe Bend, where Gen. Andrew Jackson's army of white Americans and U.S.-allied Indians killed eight hundred and took over three hundred captive. Thereafter, Jackson imposed a devastating treaty that punished even his Creek allies, forcing a land cession of over twenty million acres. Many Red Sticks, however, vowed to continue the fight. Over two thousand, including a teenaged Osceola, regrouped at Prospect Bluff.[4]

African Americans, too, saw Florida as a sanctuary. Throughout the colonial era and well into the nineteenth century, freedom-seeking slaves from Georgia and the Carolinas were more likely to run south than north. Taking advantage of imperial rivalries, slaves escaped to Spanish Florida even before 1693, when King Charles II issued a royal proclamation offering freedom to those who fled British North America. Florida remained a contested borderland and, 120 years later, Britain issued a similar proclamation.[5] Word spread throughout the South, and slaves fled Georgia, Mississippi Territory, and even places under Spanish or Indian control, including Florida and the Creek and Seminole nations. Prospect Bluff became home to perhaps four hundred to five hundred black men, but also women and children. Black and Indian soldiers constructed and manned the fort while others built houses and farms along the banks of the Apalachicola.

Although they drilled, the soldiers of Prospect Bluff never saw action during the War of 1812. After learning that the Treaty of Ghent had concluded the war, the British officers, having been recalled, left the fort in the hands of their troops. As supplies dwindled, most Native Americans departed, finding refuge among the Seminoles. By 1815, a large and well-armed African American population controlled Prospect Bluff, a prospect that terrified Southern planters, who feared that the "Maroon Fort" might spearhead a slave uprising that would ignite the entire region. These fears were stoked as escaped slaves continued to flee to Prospect Bluff. On the grounds that Prospect Bluff blocked access to U.S. forts farther inland, the U.S. military planned to destroy it. The maroons successfully repelled ground attacks, but on July 27, 1816, American gunboats attacked from the river. A cannonball hit the powder magazine and the fort exploded.

That didn't end the story, however. In fact, most of Prospect Bluff's inhabitants were not in the fort at the time of explosion; only about forty died. Some of the survivors fell victim to slave-raiding in the ground assault that followed, but several hundred managed to escape. Most went to the Suwannee River, where they sought protection under the powerful Seminole chief Bowlegs. Bowlegs instituted a kind of vassalage system, whereby maroons gave him a share of their agricultural produce in exchange for military support and protection. The maroons enjoyed relative autonomy and some, including former Prospect Bluff resident Abraham, ascended to positions of power within the Seminole Nation. Florida endured as a land of liberty until 1842, the end of the Second Seminole War. Some African Americans went with the Seminoles to Indian Territory (now Oklahoma), while others sought refuge with their old British allies in the Bahamas.[6] The fort at Prospect Bluff was destroyed in a violent conflagration, but its inhabitants and their descendants would carry their dreams of freedom to new places.

CHEVY IN THE HOLE

Kevin Boyle

What exactly is there to commemorate at Chevy in the Hole? Not the twenty-some buildings that once stood there: the warren of parts plants, the two massive assembly lines, the apprenticeship school, the tool-and-die center, the powerhouses, the storage sheds and the loading docks, the whole lot of them tucked into a depression leading down to a bend in the Flint River. From a distance they looked impressive enough. But no one made their maintenance a priority, not even in their heyday, when General Motors was the world's largest industrial corporation. So the plants would be freezing or stifling because the heat never worked as it was supposed to, the air would thicken with dust and grime because there wasn't enough ventilation, the toilets would back up, and after a rain the damp that held in the hollow would seep in through the walls. "Believe me when I say: This was, 'Chevy in the Hole' in more ways than one," wrote a former employee. "It was called the hole because of the valley it was in, but [for] those that worked there [it] had a little bit different meaning. . . ."[1]

Not the work either, though nowadays people like to talk about manufacturing as if there were something mystical about it. The truth is making cars was a tedious, taxing, sometimes debilitating way to earn a living. About 10 percent of Chevy's workers had skills that gave them some control over their days. Most of the rest did the same small jobs over and over—grinding crankshafts, spraying paint, hauling stock, hanging side panels along the assembly line—the pace of their work set by someone over in the administration building on the other side of Chevrolet Avenue or at GM's elegant headquarters down in Detroit. Sometimes the labor required pure muscle power, sometimes nothing more than the ability to endure the repetition. Either way, workers were hardly under the illusion that their bosses saw them as anything more than the bodies they required to keep production moving. In Chevy 4, the engine assembly plant, they liked to say that management hired employees from the neck down.

There's the sit down strike, of course. It was an extraordinarily audacious act, working people with essentially no power occupying two of GM's factories for forty-four days—from December 30, 1936, to February 11, 1937—to demand their right to be represented by the United Automobile Workers, a union so new it had almost no members. The larger of the plants, Fisher Body 1, was on the south side of Flint, two miles from Chevy. The other, Fisher 2, was right next door to the Hole. For a month the strike didn't cross the line. But on February 1, 1937, the union pushed the occupation into the heart of the Hole by seizing Chevy 4. Ten days later the corporation capitulated. From Flint the demand for unionization rolled across industrial America. U.S. Steel, Jones & Laughlin, Chrysler, Packard, Hudson, General Electric, RCA,

Firestone Tire, American Woolens—all were organized within a year and a half of the sit-down, some with similar sit-down strikes, others with more conventional walkouts, one or two simply because their executives realized that the workers' time had come.

Obviously an event of such importance ought to be commemorated. And it is, in print, in archives, in oral histories, on film, on the Web, and in memorials around Flint. The UAW put up a statue of the sit-down strikers behind its regional office down by Fisher 1. The local museum created a small permanent exhibit. And the state erected three historical markers, one for each of the plants the strikers held. But the plants themselves are gone. Fisher 1 was shut in 1987, Fisher 2 three years later. Both were demolished not long after. Chevy 4 lasted until 2004, one of the last buildings in the complex to go.

A lot of people blame the union for the loss. It squeezed too much out of GM, they say, made it uncompetitive, and drove the jobs away. But the jobs didn't disappear for a long time. In 1937 there were 45,000 people working in Flint's auto plants. Forty years later there were almost 74,000, all of them taking home union-won wages and benefits, paid by a corporation that turned a record profit of $3.3 billion. The Chevy plants still grew sodden in the rain. The work was still numbing. And working in the Hole wasn't making anybody rich: in 1980 Flint's median household income was almost exactly the same as the nation's. Still those union wages bought a lot of people homes, cars, TVs, weekends up north, and the occasional college fund, while the benefits gave them a sense of security and stability that would have been unimaginable before the union arrived. Then the changes came: a bewildering mix of economic upheavals at home and abroad, followed by sweeping shifts in corporate strategy, political power, and public policy that a more creative UAW might have tempered but was never going to stop. As it happened, General Motors met the new order with cut after cut. In the 1980s the company eliminated 43,000 auto jobs in the Flint metropolitan area alone; 10,000 more in the 1990s; another 17,000 since then, as the corporation tumbled through bankruptcy.

As GM went, so went Flint. In the last few years the city's population has fallen below 100,000, its lowest number in almost a century. The unemployment rate hovers around 10 percent, more than double the national average. Forty-one percent of its people live in poverty, the second highest rate in the country for a city its size. Eighty-one percent of its schoolchildren qualify for free lunches. And it's still too early to say what damage was done to its kids by the dangerously high levels of lead in its water supply, the consequence of unconscionable decisions made by state-appointed officials who'd been given control of Flint after the Great Recession ravaged its finances. Maybe that's what ought to be commemorated down in the Hole, where the city and a local land bank are slowly building a nature reserve they're calling Chevy Commons. Not a long-gone factory or the work that went on there but the opportunities ordinary people made for themselves in that dank little hollow and the losses they've suffered as those opportunities were stripped away, a memorial to the promise that once flourished in Flint and the fierce injustices of now.

THE ROUGE

Kevin Boyle

They wanted the moment preserved. Otherwise they wouldn't have invited the newspaper photographers; or agreed to go up to the overpass as soon as they arrived, so their photos could make the evening editions; or positioned themselves as perfectly as they did, four union men in their suits and ties, smiling as the Service Department boys walked into the frame, the "Ford Motor Company" sign looming behind them. And when it was over—the blood wiped away, their injuries treated, the images published in the major papers and the most influential magazines—they commemorated it with a heroic name that didn't quite fit because there hadn't been a battle on the overpass. There'd been an assault, endured for the movement's sake, a courageous claiming of the moral high ground.

But a single demonstration of corporate brutality, even an artfully managed one, wasn't enough to unionize the Rouge Plant. Henry Ford had conceived of it in his glory days in the mid-

1910s, when everyone still thought of him as the homespun genius of America's industrial age. Construction started in 1917. It took ten years to complete it: ninety-three buildings on two thousand acres in suburban Dearborn, Michigan, right across the border from Detroit, each component linked to the next in a production process so extensively mechanized, so thoroughly integrated, so staggeringly complex the Rouge immediately became one of the wonders of the modern world. It is "altogether a symphony," wrote one of the many international visitors who came to see it in the 1920s, "an entirely closed whole, a single other-worldly machine. . . ."[1]

It was also a vicious place. Workers had always struggled under Ford's demand for continuous production. At first he'd tried to coax them along with progressive, even radically innovative labor policies. By the time the first Model A rolled off the Rouge's assembly line in 1927, those days were gone. Ford's managers divided the complex's 75,000 workers among a bewildering number of units, each under the control of a foreman whose job depended on maintaining discipline and squeezing out production. Then management looked the other way as the factory floor turned into a patchwork of petty tyrannies. Whatever dissent that arrangement produced was quickly crushed by the Rouge's two thousand–member Service Department, the plant's ruthlessly repressive internal security force. And as Ford made perfectly clear to the department's director Harry Bennett, whom he considered the brutish son he'd never had, there was no worse form of dissent than unionization.

So the Rouge's thugs pummeled the United Automobile Workers organizers posing on the overpass and the thirty-some UAW activists, most of them women, handing out leaflets at the streetcar stop at the bottom of the stairs. Of course there were investigations once the photos were published, the most damning by the newly formed National Labor Relations Board. But the company stonewalled them until the moment's momentum faded away. After that the

SAND CREEK

Ari Kelman

Before dawn on November 29, 1864, approximately seven hundred volunteer soldiers from the 1st and 3rd Colorado regiments crept up to an Arapaho and Cheyenne encampment nestled in a bend of Sand Creek, in southeastern Colorado Territory. The men attacked without warning, driving approximately one thousand Native people, whose leaders believed they had recently made peace with white authorities, up the dry creek bed. The onslaught left perhaps 175 Cheyennes and Arapahos dead, the vast majority of whom were women, children, or the elderly. The troops then disgraced themselves further by combing the field for trophies: scalps, fingers and toes, and genitalia, which they hacked from their victims' dead bodies. After burning what remained of the Native village, the soldiers returned to Denver, where they were greeted as conquering heroes. In the weeks after, the Colorado volunteers exhibited their grim plunder at a downtown theater.

Nearly a century and a half later, on April 28, 2007, the National Park Service cut the ribbon marking the opening of its 391st unit. The Sand Creek Massacre National Historic Site would be the first component of the National Parks System to cast American soldiers as perpetrators rather than heroes or victims. Given that, and given a national cultural and political climate marked by strains of hyper-patriotism, the task of creating the memorial turned out to be, even when placed against the backdrop of recent struggles over the American past, unusually contentious. The site's sponsors—federal employees, representatives of the State of Colorado, descendants of Sand Creek's victims, and local people in Kiowa County— confronted thorny questions about the interplay of politics and violence on the nineteenth-century borderlands. They also had to address questions about the righteousness of expansion into the trans–Mississippi West and the interrelated wars, the Civil War and the so-called Indian Wars, spawned by that bloody process.

The commemorative project ground to a halt before it even got rolling when another, unexpected question stumped the Sand Creek team: where, precisely, had the massacre taken place? It turned out that before Sand Creek could be memorialized, it first had to be found. The search that ensued became contentious when fundamental disagreements over how best to interpret the historical record divided the people looking for the killing field. The Sand Creek descendants typically based their understanding of the episode's history and geography on their traditional tribal methods; on numerous oral histories preserved in the years after the slaughter; and on written records, including stories and maps that a Cheyenne survivor of Sand Creek, a warrior named George Bent, had produced around the turn of the twentieth century. For decades, the Sand Creek descendants had used Bent's maps and writings as a guide, making pilgrimages and performing sacred ceremonies at a spot atop a rise overlooking a sharp bend in the creek. Near what they called the "traditional site," the descendants of the massacre's victims had venerated their ancestors.

The Park Service, by contrast, tried to solve the mystery of the hallowed ground's location by looking to other materials, especially written records produced by the troops who had fought at Sand Creek, and then by consulting a detailed map drawn by a soldier named Samuel Bonsall. Bonsall had visited the site several years after the massacre with William Tecumseh Sherman, then in charge of the U.S. Army's forces in the West. Using Bonsall's map, the Park Service arrived at a hypothesis: the massacre had actually begun less than a mile upstream from the traditional site identified by the Arapahos and Cheyennes. Archeological findings, a huge plume of artifacts unearthed during the latter stages of the site search, seemed to confirm that conjecture. Most of the Park Service employees celebrated this discovery. They believed that they had solved an enduring mystery and that they would soon accurately memorialize one of the bloodiest chapters in the history of the settlement of the West.

Many of the descendants, though, were outraged. In their view, the Park Service had accepted the veracity of sources produced by Sand Creek's white perpetrators rather than those penned by one of the massacre's Native victims. Federal authorities were, it seemed, recapitulating more than a century of arrogance toward indigenous peoples. A Northern Cheyenne chief accused the Park Service of cultural genocide. The descendants again looked to George Bent's maps, drawing their own diagram of the massacre site. Wrong-footed by this dispute over competing cartographies, the Park Service eventually floated a compromise: a site with boundaries capacious enough to encompass many different interpretations of Sand Creek's history. Finally, after a number of additional twists and turns, including a casino corporation stepping in to broker a deal that secured a key piece of property for the memorial, the Park Service opened the historic site. All of which leads back to the creek banks, pictured here.

Andrew's photograph serves as an apt metaphor for how Sand Creek has been remembered and forgotten. The cottonwoods cast shadows, attenuated in some cases, clearer in others, over the creek bottom, suggesting a connection between the past and the present. Throughout the memorialization project, the descendants spoke often of "witness trees," features of the landscape that took root at the time of the massacre and remained extant early in the twenty-first century. Based on their size, the pictured trees are too young to have witnessed the butchery at Sand Creek. But older cottonwoods, in some cases just huge stumps, stand sentinel in the creek bottom, where the worst violence transpired. That part of the national historic site, a federal public space, remains off limits to visitors at the urging of the descendants. These trees, part of a large cottonwood grove, mark the most fertile part of Sand Creek's floodplain, land drenched on November 29, 1864, with the blood of Cheyenne and Arapaho victims of American imperialism.

UNMARKED

Deer Island, Winthrop, Massachusetts, 2011

By the 1670s enough indigenous peoples had converted to Christianity to form dozens of sep-arate "Praying Indian" villages across New England. Chief Metacomet's success in attacking and destroying many of the white settlements of New England during King Philip's War created a panic among the colonists. During the bitterly cold winter of 1675–76, colonists rounded up even those Indians who had converted to Christianity and interned them on Deer Island in Boston Harbor, creating America's first concentration camp. Denied adequate shelter or food, hundreds of "Christian Indians" starved or froze to death on the island. Now connected to the mainland, Deer Island is part of a National Park Service recreation area, though no public marking of its dismal past is visible to those who enjoy its scenic vistas.

Mose Wright's Church, East Money, Mississippi, 2010

In 1955, when Emmett Till's great uncle, Mississippi sharecropper and lay preacher Mose Wright, identified Emmett's two killers in open court, his courageous act could be considered the birth of the civil rights movement. After his testimony, Wright immediately fled to Chicago, knowing that retaliation in Money, Mississippi, would be swift and brutal. To walk in Wright's footsteps in the Delta today is to visit a sparse, depopulated landscape. The hard life of the black laborers who once brought in the cotton crop has been replaced by modern farm machinery, and the churches, shacks, and towns lay abandoned on the edge of every field, ghosts of another time.

Denmark Vesey's Rebellion, Emanuel AME Church, Charleston, South Carolina, 2012

A choir boy prepares for a service at Emanuel AME Church in Charleston, in a sanctuary designed by the son of slave rebel Denmark Vesey. A former slave and skilled artisan who had purchased his own freedom, Vesey organized America's largest slave rebellion. A highly religious man and class leader in the African Methodist Episcopal Church in Charleston, Vesey was driven to rebellion after authorities fearful of African gathering places harassed his church and its members. Inspired by the recently successful slave revolt in Saint Domingue (Haiti), Vesey planned his rebellion to begin on Bastille Day, July 14, 1822, by seizing ships in the Charleston harbor and sailing to that liberated island. Betrayed by two slaves, the revolt was crushed before it could begin and local whites burned the AME church to the ground. They executed thirty-five accused rebels, including Vesey. His son, Robert Vesey, survived, and rebuilt the Emanuel AME Church, which still stands in downtown Charleston today—on a street named after pro-slavery South Carolina Sen. John C. Calhoun.

Three years after this photograph was taken, a young white supremacist, probably aware of the historical significance of this church, joined a bible study and then murdered nine African American parishioners in a shooting spree.

Slave Port, Under the Hill, Natchez, Mississippi, 2010

From the 1820s through the 1860s, Natchez, Mississippi, served as a major hub for the country's internal slave trade. Slaves were transported, either on forced marches over land, or more often by boat on the Mississippi River, from the declining plantations of Virginia to the more extreme conditions in the cotton fields of Louisiana and Mississippi. Slave owners often wielded the threat of being sold to the newer markets of the Deep South to keep their slaves in line, or sold those who appeared rebellious "down the river" as punishment. Just as often, slave masters sold their slaves for the money, creating a breeding program for human beings in the wealthier lands of eastern Virginia, and a new generation of laborers in the cotton and cane fields of the expanding Deep South.

One of America's wealthiest and most successful slave traders was Isaac Franklin, who founded Franklin and Armfield with his nephew, John Armfield. This company specialized in purchasing and collecting slaves in Alexandria, Virginia, across the Potomac from Washington, D.C., and then bringing them to market in Natchez. By the 1830s, the firm sent upwards of one thousand slaves a year southward. With the huge profits Franklin made from his business, he purchased several large plantations in Louisiana, one of which, still named Angola, is now the Louisiana State Penitentiary.

Pequot Massacre, Mystic, Connecticut, 2009

In May 1637, Capt. John Mason led a raid against the Pequot Indians. Guided by scouts from the Narragansett tribe, traditional enemies of the Pequots, Mason and his soldiers made a surprise attack on a Pequot fort that they discovered on a hill in what is now Mystic, Connecticut. The Englishmen brought with them to the New World a style of warfare that emphasized victory over personal valor. They surrounded the fort and burned it down, slaughtering the women and children who tried to flee from the flames. Mason's troops massacred over five hundred Pequots in this raid. As a reward for his success, Connecticut Colony granted Mason an island in the nearby Fishers Island Sound, still named Mason's Island. Today, the area where the fort once stood is a quiet residential neighborhood, only a few blocks away from an Interstate 95 exit and near the popular tourist attraction of Mystic Seaport. For many years, a statue of Capt. John Mason stood in this traffic circle. In 1995 members of the Pequot Tribal Council, owners of the nearby Foxwoods Casino and major taxpayers, landowners, and employers in eastern Connecticut, successfully petitioned to have Mason's statue removed to Windsor, Connecticut, leaving this once-marked historic site unmarked.

Grassy Knoll, Dealey Plaza, Dallas, Texas, 2016

The location of President John F. Kennedy's assassination in downtown Dallas, Texas, is as well-marked a historical site as can be. Every day thousands of tourists from around the world visit the Sixth Floor Museum, formerly the Texas School Book Depository, where assassin Lee Harvey Oswald fired on Kennedy's car below. A large X in the middle of Elm Street marks the spot where the president received a gunshot in the head while riding in his motorcade. Off to the side, amateur historians give their own version of events of what happened on November 22, 1963, attempting to debunk the Warren Commission as a government cover-up. The fence on the infamous Grassy Knoll, where many believe a second sniper was hiding that day, remains unmarked and serves as a perimeter for a parking lot. Even today, over half a century later, there are more questions than answers about Kennedy's murder, and the Grassy Knoll has come to symbolize all that we do not know about America, both marked and unmarked, past and present.

Death of Karen Silkwood, Highway 74, Logan County, Oklahoma, 2016

A worker and union activist at Kerr-McGee's Cimarron, Oklahoma, plutonium plant, Karen Silk-wood died in a mysterious car crash at this highway culvert in November 1974. At the time, she worked tirelessly as a member of the Oil, Atomic, and Chemical Workers' Union to uncover and combat hazardous conditions and the danger of exposure to radiation at the plant. Suffering from radiation poisoning herself, the night she was killed Silkwood was on her way to meet a reporter and was allegedly carrying a folder of documents that would expose corporate malfeasance and ongoing safety violations on the part of Kerr-McGee. Crash investigators never found this whis-tleblower's file, and to this day Silkwood's mysterious death remains unexplained.

Nelson Lynching, North Canadian River Bridge, Okemah, Oklahoma, 2016

In May 1911, the African American Nelson family faced a sheriff's posse investigating a recent stock theft. The Nelsons' teenage son, L. D., fired a shot, killing a deputy sheriff. Although arrested and taken to jail, a few weeks later a mob overpowered the local jailer and removed L. D. Nelson and his mother Laura from the Okemah jail before they could come to trial. The next morning, their bodies were found hanging from a railroad bridge over the Canadian River, six miles outside of town. As was usually the case with such lynchings of blacks by white vigilante mobs, no one was ever brought to justice for this crime. Like thousands of other lynchings, no public acknowledgment of this atrocity marks this location.

Though the Nelson lynching is largely forgotten now, the atrocity was widely known at the time. A photograph of the Nelsons' hanged bodies subsequently circulated as a grisly "souvenir" postcard. Woody Guthrie, whose father witnessed—and perhaps participated in— the lynching, later wrote a song about the Nelsons' murder. There is no way to know if the perpetrators of the Nazi and Klan graffiti now defacing the concrete bridge support near where Laura and L. D. Nelson's bodies dangled are aware of this unacknowledged history.

War on Poverty, Martin County, Kentucky, 2010

When President Lyndon Johnson decided to announce his War on Poverty in 1964, he chose to travel to Martin County, in the heart of impoverished Appalachian coal country. An essential part of Johnson's Great Society, many of the programs established to help America's poorest communities were whittled down or abolished during the political backlash that followed the 1960s. When Johnson visited in 1964, the poverty rate in this corner of Kentucky stood at nearly 60 percent. Government programs have helped, but today Martin County remains one of the poorest counties in America, with few jobs available to those who want to climb out of poverty. Jobless young people continue to leave the area to seek economic opportunities elsewhere.

Detroit Riots, Clairmount Avenue and Rosa Parks Boulevard, Detroit, Michigan, 2016

Early in the morning of Sunday, July 23, 1967, the Detroit police raided an illegal bar on the corner of Clairmount Avenue and 12th Street (now renamed Rosa Parks Boulevard after the civil rights heroine and longtime Detroit resident), and broke up a party held for two black soldiers returning home from Vietnam. They decided to arrest everyone present. Why does one spark light a fire when dozens before it failed to? Thus began five days of rioting, looting, burning, and civil disobedience in Detroit, which resulted in more than forty deaths—many at the hands of the police and National Guard—and $50 million in property damage. In response, President Lyndon Johnson convened the Kerner Commission to investigate racial inequality, police brutality, and the causes of widespread urban violence.

Decades later, the long, slow slide of deindustralization has destroyed what a sudden burst of rioting could not. Once made relatively prosperous by employment in the post–World War Two automobile industry, Near West Side Detroit has been transformed over the years into an unrecognizable ghost town. A once-thriving commercial strip is now filled with empty lots and boarded-up homes as a flourishing and vibrant, if aggrieved, African American community vanished with the jobs.

Harriet Tubman's Raid, Beaufort County, South Carolina, 2012

The ruins of a slave cabin still remain on a former plantation's land along the banks of the Combahee River. During the summer of 1863, fugitive slave, abolitionist, and daring Underground Railroad "conductor" Harriet Tubman returned to the South in the midst of the Civil War. In her boldest raid, she led black Union troops twenty-five miles up the swampy Combahee River, freeing over seven hundred slaves from the surrounding rice plantations, including this one. After the Civil War, black families working the rice fields continued to live in this cabin until the 1970s.

Nat Turner's Rebellion, Cabin Pond, Southampton County, Virginia, 2010

In August 1831 a Virginia slave and preacher named Nat Turner received his final vision that the time had come for him to lead a rebellion to free his people. Turner had carefully planned his revolt in the wooded swamp known then and now as Cabin Pond. After leading forty fellow slaves on a killing spree that left fifty-five whites dead, Turner and his slave rebellion were quickly crushed outside of Jerusalem, Virginia. Turner managed to escape, but searchers discovered him a few months later less than a mile from Cabin Pond, where he had returned to hide and wonder why God had forsaken him and his people. On November 11, 1831, the Commonwealth of Virginia executed Nat Turner by hanging.

Cabin Pond Road, Southampton County, Virginia, 2010

Today, Cabin Pond Road runs past the swampland of Cabin Pond, several miles southwest from the small community of Cross Keys in rural Southampton County. The pond is hidden in undergrowth and by pine trees that line the rural dirt road. There are no historical markers or walking paths or any sign that this is an area of historical importance. Even today, Southampton County remains a place with an intentionally buried past.

Murder of Frank Little, Butte, Montana, 2013

During World War One, the rough, unregulated copper mines of Montana supplied raw materials for the military, with little concern for workers' wages or safety. After the Speculator Mine disaster of 1917 killed 168 miners, Industrial Workers of the World (IWW) union organizer and antiwar agitator Frank Little arrived in Butte to support an ongoing strike for better working conditions in the mines. A fierce opponent of American entry into the war, Little publicly denounced soldiers as "Uncle Sam's scabs in uniform." On August 1, 1917, a group of armed masked men abducted him from his boardinghouse, beat and then dragged him through the streets from the back of a car, and finally hung his lifeless body from this railroad trestle on the southern edge of town. Part of a widespread and state-sanctioned campaign to suppress the IWW, no one was ever charged for Little's murder, which remains unsolved a century later.

Eastland Plantation, Doddsville, Mississippi, 2015

From 1941 until 1978, Sen. James O. Eastland of Mississippi, along with other senior Democratic senators collectively known as the "Dixiecrats," killed in committee, used the filibuster, or otherwise blocked national civil rights legislation, including an anti-lynching law. Elected to consecutive terms because prior to the Voting Rights Act only 5 percent of Mississippi's black population was registered to vote and he only had to appeal to white voters, Eastland and his fellow Southern Democrats gained tremendous power. They used that power to help delay democracy in the Deep South for a century, in open defiance of the Fourteenth and Fifteenth Amendments to the Constitution.

On the Eastland family plantation along the banks of the Sunflower River, just west of the small Mississippi Delta town of Doddsville, the senator's father had once organized the capture and lynching of a sharecropper couple, Luther and Mary Holbert. In 1904, Luther Holbert had shot and killed Eastland's uncle, also named James, in a plantation dispute. After a posse hunted down Holbert and his wife, they were brought back to Doddsville, and in front of a huge crowd gathered near the sharecroppers' black church, tortured and burned to death.

Trail of Tears, Charleston, Tennessee, 2012

The Trail of Tears, in which the Cherokee people of the southeastern United States were stripped of all their property and rights after the passage of the Indian Removal Act of 1830 and compelled to journey under brutal conditions to "Indian Territory" in present-day Oklahoma, has been a dark stain on America's reputation since the mid-nineteenth century. The federal government has recently invested money in preserving the memory of this ethnocidal removal. Key points along the trail, from the mountains of northern Alabama and Georgia to the plains of eastern Oklahoma, are well marked by the National Park Service with road signs and historical information. However, the harshest concentration camps, where Cherokee refugees were forced to camp during the hard winter of 1838 in eastern Tennessee to await transportation further west, remain unmarked. Today, much of this region, where so many indigenous people died from exposure and starvation, consists of silent farmers' fields and new suburban housing developments.

Camp Grant Massacre, Aravaipa Valley, Pinal County, Arizona, 2012

Blaming an outbreak of banditry on a large group of Aravaipa Apache who had been provided refuge by the U.S. Cavalry at a compound adjacent to Camp Grant, not far from Tucson in the Arizona Territory, local citizens decided to take matters into their own hands. In late April 1871, a posse of Anglos, Mexicans, and Papago Indians descended on the Aravaipa refuge, indiscriminately slaughtering eight men and 110 women and children. The raiders kidnapped twenty-eight young Apache and sold them into slavery in Mexico. Although over one hundred of the perpetrators were later brought to trial in Tucson, a jury acquitted them all after less than twenty minutes of deliberation. The exact spot of the massacre in the valley remains in dispute and is unacknowledged by any public marker.

California Water Wars, No Name Canyon, Owens Valley, Inyo County, California, 2012

In 1927, at this exact spot, in a remote canyon in Owens Valley, farmers used dynamite to blow up a section of the recently constructed Los Angeles water aqueduct. William Mulholland, a powerful Los Angeles water official, had been depleting Owens Valley in northern California of its water, sending it to an expanding Los Angeles and the adjacent San Fernando Valley over two hundred miles to the south. There, he and his friends had made real estate investments based on their plans to bring water to arid southern California. This diversion of a precious resource, leaving Valley farmers without sufficient irrigation, sparked the California Water Wars of the 1920s. Today, Los Angeles is an ever-expanding city of four million people, while the orchards and towns of distant Owens Valley have vanished.

Gila River War Relocation Center, Pinal County, Arizona, 2012

The Gila River War Relocation Center was a concentration camp built for interned Japanese Americans located on Indian reservation land during World War Two. Despite strong objections from the tribal authorities, by 1942 this camp housed over thirteen thousand prisoners transported from the West Coast to the dry desert south of Phoenix, making it the fourth largest city in Arizona at the time. Compared to some of the nine other internment camps built during World War Two for Japanese and Japanese Americans, conditions at this site of imprisonment were regarded as a "showcase," with well-organized desert gardens and baseball fields and only a single watchtower. Although there is a nearby memorial on a hillside overlooking the camp, down below in the desert at this abandoned site, only a few rusty nails and concrete pilings remain, disappearing into the sand. Permission from the Gila River Indian Community is needed to visit the site.

Captain Joe Byrd Cemetery, Huntsville, Texas, 2009

Between 1923 and 1973, when the Supreme Court declared the death penalty unconstitutional, the State of Texas sentenced 506 people—more than two-thirds of them black or Hispanic—to death, and sent 361 of them to the electric chair. The machinery of death restarted in 1982; in the thirty-five years since then, Texas has executed well over five hundred additional people, four times more than any other state.

Along with other Texas Department of Corrections and Justice prisoners who pass away in the state prison system and whose families cannot afford funeral costs, Texas inters the executed in the Captain Joe Byrd Cemetery, in the shadow of the "Walls" prison in Huntsville. The cemetery is colloquially known as "Peckerwood Hill." Executed prisoners, like the one buried here, get an X next to their prison number, rather than a name on their cross.

Prisoner #643, executed on August 22, 1986, was Larry Smith, age thirty, an African American laborer from Dallas. Convicted in 1979 of killing a night manager while robbing a 7-Eleven convenience store, Smith received two stays of his execution before exhausting his appeals. His last words were:

> Tell my mother I love her and continue on without me. God bless her. Tell the guys on death row to continue their struggle to get off death row. That's about it.

DENMARK VESEY'S CHURCH

Douglas Egerton

The young congregant, deep in thought before a prayer, or perhaps a hymn, appears to feel the weight of history upon his shoulders. As he well knows—as every black Charlestonian well knows—Charleston's Emanuel African Methodist Episcopal Church, now in its third incarnation, has a long and storied history. Its saga is synonymous with struggle, and for the pensive youth in the photograph, there is no other church in the South quite like it.

Just inside the steps leading to the front door of the church sits a small but unique statue. In the piece, the busts of four black children listen intently to an unseen speaker. They lean upon a stage, one resting his head on his folded arms, another cups his chin on his palm. Like the modern youth in his robe, the ill-dressed children in the monument understand they are listening to something of great moment.

Whether they knew it or not, their city was atypical in the young republic. In no other Southern state did whites constitute a minority until 1855, when Mississippi also earned that particular status. In the years just after the War of 1812, Charleston housed 24,780 people, only 10,653 of whom were white. Free people of color were a tiny percentage, at 623, and most of them were the mixed-race offspring of white fathers and black mothers. One of the few free blacks in the city at that time was a former slave turned carpenter, Denmark Vesey.

Although most black Carolinians attended one of the city's many white-run churches each Sunday, they chafed at the brand of pro-slavery theology they heard from the pulpits. White ministers routinely hectored their black congregants on "their duties and obligations" to their masters and avoided troublesome stories, like the exodus out of Egypt, or Christ's sermons on human brotherhood. When in 1817, 4,376 black Methodists quit their white-controlled church in protest over the elders' decision to construct a hearse house—a garage—over a black cemetery, Vesey, a practicing Presbyterian, joined the protest movement. As a carpenter, he may even have assisted in constructing the first Emanuel Church, which stood not far from the present building.

The African Church, as black Charlestonians called it, promptly attracted the animosity of the authorities. As a lay minister, Vesey, in his off hours, taught congregants to read and write—a violation of the state's ban on black literacy. State and city ordinances allowed for blacks to worship only in daylight hours and only with a majority of white congregants. City authorities raided the church in 1818, arresting and whipping 140 "free Negroes and Slaves," one of them presumably Vesey. In 1819 they again shuttered the church, and in 1820 the city council warned Rev. Morris Brown not to allow his church to become "a school for slaves."

HARRIET TUBMAN'S RAID

Stephen Kantrowitz

Freedom was the first battle.

By the end of May 1863, many people in South Carolina's Combahee River rice district knew—or should have known—that the Union gunboats were coming. The rice planters had been warned, first by insufficiently cryptic reports in Northern newspapers, then by their own government, that a federal raid was imminent. The slaves who toiled in those swampy fields had been alerted as well, almost certainly by the same official warnings but perhaps also by Union scouts and spies. Some slave owners, measuring the risks, drove their slaves inland, away from the river. But most looked at the calendar and thought about the hugely profitable rice crop that would be spoiled or lost. Surely this was another false alarm. At worst they would face a desultory raid by a few companies of federals, something the detachments assigned to defend them should be able to handle. After all, if they could not continue to reap the profits generated by their human property, what was this rebellion worth?

The reckoning came on the morning of June 2, 1863, when two Union troopships steamed up the Combahee.

In the pilot house of the lead vessel stood escaped slave Harriet Tubman. On a dozen or more dangerous journeys during the 1850s, she had shepherded hundreds of other slaves to freedom from her former home on Maryland's eastern shore. On those missions, she carried a sidearm and her indomitable will as her only weapons. But not today. Over the past months she had laid the groundwork for this raid by interviewing recently escaped slaves about conditions in the Confederate rice country. She had also helped nurse and provision the rapidly growing regiments of soldiers recruited from among those escapees. Now she ventured into the heartland of slavery accompanied by three hundred armed and uniformed men, most of them companies of the 2nd Regiment South Carolina Volunteer Infantry (African descent). Even the pilot who stood beside Tubman, guiding the lead vessel upriver, had recently been a slave.

It might only be June, but today was harvest time. The gunboats deposited soldiers at every landing as they ascended the river. There were a few skirmishes, but soon black soldiers put most of the Confederate defenders to flight. They burned plantation buildings. They broke open the sluice gates, flooding and ruining the rice fields. And as they did, more than seven hundred enslaved rice workers pushed past their owners and overseers, streaming down the banks toward the landing craft that waited to receive them. As Tubman watched men and women run for the landings, their children in their arms, she laughed in joy and exultation—"laughed, an' laughed, an' laughed," she later told her biographer. This was sweet victory indeed.

The black laborers of the rice country won some of the next battles as well. By the time the war ended, all of South Carolina's slaves were free. Within a few more years, black men—a large majority of the potential voters in the state, and an even larger majority in the rice country—put the party of Lincoln into power. This was Reconstruction. For almost a decade, until 1876, former slaves helped elect the state's highest officials. Their new government made it easier for former slaves and other poor people to buy land, and harder for employers to cheat or coerce them. Crucially, it allowed African Americans to occupy the positions of local authority—juries and judges, militias and sheriffs—that had historically subjugated them. Former slaves and their allies sowed seeds of democracy and equality in the ruins of the slaveholders' citadel.

This remains an American liberation story for our time. Its heroes are black and white, women and men, self-empowered and determined. It tells a story many of us yearn to hear—that people committed to freedom can band together, call upon the best impulses of their countrymen, and win that prize.

It is a true story, and an important one. Those who do not already know it need to learn it, and those who do know it need to tell it.

But freedom is never won once and for all. Our story cannot end only with Harriet Tubman's laugh, or Reconstruction's promise.

Emancipation and Confederate defeat destroyed the former slaveholders' political and economic hegemony. Although their armies withdrew from the field, these men surrendered neither their expectation of superiority nor their willingness to secure it through violence. Slaveholding had trained them to this. Throughout the decade of Reconstruction they waged a continuing war against black people's autonomy and authority, building alliances with hard-pressed whites and fostering divisions among blacks.

They built a mighty Ku Klux Klan to harass, coerce, and kill their opponents, and to force former slaves into low-paid agricultural labor. After the federal government put that rebellion down, the former slaveholders reorganized as "rifle clubs." Meanwhile, rice workers on the Combahee mounted a strike in the fields, simultaneously demanding higher pay and warning Republican officials that they were not to be taken for granted.

The rice workers lost. In 1876 white supremacist paramilitaries shot and stole their way to political victory, as national Republicans threw up their hands or looked the other way. As soon as white Democrats took control of the state, they set about strangling black political power. By the end of the nineteenth century, most rice workers were politically disempowered tenants or sharecroppers.

The freedom won in the 1860s offered little protection from the hardships and terrors of the new regime, what we call the Jim Crow South. It was not until the world wars created a vast market for labor that the descendants of the rice-field workers could hope for much better. Like their forebears, they fled their cabins for what looked like a better future—not in a boat this time, but in a train or a car. Disenfranchised in South Carolina, they cast votes in Northern states, eventually pushing the Democratic Party to embrace civil rights.

You could say that they won. You could even take a moment, as Harriet Tubman did, to exult in another victory of hope over oppression. And then you could remember that the flight from the tenant cabin led, within a few decades, to the penal gulag—to today's incarceration of African Americans on a scale and in a proportion that may be unique in human history.

Freedom is the first battle. But that battle has to be fought again and again.

CABIN POND

Scot French

If Cabin Pond had a conventional roadside marker, modeled after others erected over the past century by the Virginia Department of Historic Resources, it would probably read like this:

CABIN POND MEETING SITE

NAT TURNER CONSPIRACY

Somewhere in the woods near here, on the evening of August 21–22, 1831, Nat Turner and six other slaves gathered to plan one of the largest and bloodiest slave uprisings in American history. Over a feast of roasted pig and brandy, they plotted to kill the white people of Southampton County, Virginia, and form an army of liberated slaves to fight the forces arrayed against them. The insurrection that followed lasted three days and resulted in massive casualties.

No such sign exists, and one would be hard-pressed to find any direct reference to Cabin

Pond in the memorial landscape of Turner's Rebellion. Finding Cabin Pond requires a deep dive into primary and secondary sources, from *The Confessions of Nat Turner, as told to Thomas R. Gray* (1831), through the most recent works of academic scholarship on the subject. There, in densely footnoted text and latter-day photographic images, lie oblique references to a site that—in truth—no longer exists.

Cabin Pond is perhaps best viewed as a socially constructed space rather than a bounded geographic entity or point on a map. Like the mountain hideouts occupied by the maroons of Latin America, the woods and ponds and swamps of Southside Virginia represent a hidden world of slave life beyond the control of masters and overseers. Nat Turner, a slave preacher and exhorter, knew the terrain well. So, too, did his fellow conspirators, who lived and labored on nearby plantations. For these local slaves turned black revolutionaries, the Cabin Pond meeting site provided a safe haven, free from the surveilling eyes of white masters and black spies/traitors alike. Here they could discourse openly on the violence they had endured at the hands of whites and the sacrifices they would make in pursuit of liberty.

At Cabin Pond, the Southampton slave conspiracy evolved from biblically inspired, apocalyptic visions in Turner's head to a concerted plan of action that necessitated the killing of every white man, woman, and child at every household visited. Here the rebel leaders decided to commence their "work of death" at the home of Turner's master, then proceed methodically from household to household, gathering arms and recruits along the way. It was here, too, after several days at war, that "Gen. Nat" sought to rendezvous with his scattered troops and, finding no one, went into hiding. As an active conspiracy involving (at its peak) an estimated forty to sixty armed slaves and free blacks, Turner's Rebellion ended—remarkably—in the woods near Cabin Pond, almost exactly where it began.

As a site of memory associated with Nat Turner's Rebellion, Cabin Pond remains as curiously unmarked in the historical record as it is on the commemorative landscape. Turner makes no mention of the pond in his so-called *Confessions*, saying only that he and his six coconspirators met "in the woods" on the evening of August 20, 1831, to "concert a plan," as they "had not yet determined on any." Was the location of Cabin Pond an earthly detail of such little significance to Turner that he simply neglected to mention it? Or did he purposefully suppress the location, along with other details of the conspiracy, to shield from suspicion those more innocently associated with the site?

Documentary references to Cabin Pond derive from later sources—most notably historian William Sidney Drewry's 1900 monograph, *The Southampton Insurrection*. A native-born white resident of the county, Drewry interviewed local residents and included details about Cabin Pond—identifying its owner, Giles Reese, and establishing its location relative to other sites— that more recent historians have routinely cited and elaborated upon. Drewry included forty-one illustrations, including photographs of many sites associated with the rebellion, but none of Cabin Pond. More than seventy years passed before Henry Irving Tragle published a small, landscape-view photograph of Cabin Pond in *The Southampton Slave Revolt of 1831: A Compilation of Source Material* (1971).

Significantly, for Turner, it was the "Heavens" that served as the primary locus of action and focus of memory. When asked to give "a history of the motives which induced me to undertake the late insurrection," Turner recalled a series of visions and strange atmospheric conditions that led him to act. Thomas R. Gray, the white Southampton County lawyer who interviewed Turner in his jail cell and recorded his *Confessions* for posterity, took note of the rebel leader's otherworldly orientation. "Clothed with rags and covered with chains; yet daring to raise his manacled hands to heaven, with a spirit soaring above the attributes of man; I looked on him and my blood curdled in my veins." In viewing Cabin Pond, or any historic site associated with Turner's Rebellion, it seems one should look up and not simply around.

TRAIL OF TEARS

Julie Reed

Whose stories get told?

The narrative of Cherokee Removal, also commonly referred to as the Trail of Tears, is often cast as some combination of the following: first, an American tragedy—a failure of the young United States to live up to the promises of democracy—and second, a necessity for American westward expansion. The message that often transcends that merged narrative is that Indian Removal was a tragic but *inevitable* event. The recent efforts to remove President Andrew Jackson, the key proponent of the Indian Removal Act, from the $20 bill suggests we collectively desire to blame a single human villain for the deadly outcome. This enables us to dismiss the complexity of the Long Removal Era, which in fact began when President Thomas Jefferson first suggested voluntary removal by the Cherokee—self-deportation, if you will—in 1803. The shorter timeline of removal offered in public school textbooks, confined to the 1830s, encourages historical blind spots and chronologically short attention spans. We remain ignorant of the real alternatives to forced removal that Cherokee people exercised at the time and the experiences and activities that ripple from the past to the present in Cherokee families today. We should stop to ask: Who gets buried unremembered and whose deeds do we acknowledge today?

The key settings, events, and characters of removal narratives that public history perpetuates center on the political and legal theater that led up to the forced Cherokee removal, which took place between 1838 and 1840. We learn about some Supreme Court decisions and what year they took place. We look at a map with color-coded arrows from east to west to indicate the physical routes Cherokees, and perhaps a few other tribes, traveled. If we learn about specific Cherokee people, we learn about the big men. We meet John Ross, the son of a Scottish trader and a Cherokee mother, elected principal chief after Cherokees in the east adopted their 1827 Constitution. We might be introduced to monolingual Major Ridge, a former Chickamauga warrior and War of 1812 veteran who embraced English education for his sons and daughters. We may also encounter bilingual and bi-literate Elias Boudinot, the nephew of Major Ridge, who became the editor of the bilingual *Cherokee Phoenix*, the first Native American newspaper published in the United States. More often than not, the narrative of removal we learn suggests that these accomplishments were the by-products of the wise civilization policy of the United States aimed at assimilating Native peoples, not the efforts of talented indigenous intellectuals in their own right that occurred in spite of U.S. policy.

In the popular narratives of removal, everyday Cherokee people remain statistics and demographics. Maps and numbers stand in for the land itself and the many people who struggled and died on it during the removal era. Their individual hardships dissolve into the approximately four thousand who lost their lives as a result of Cherokee Removal. The efforts and actions of Cherokee people to hold on to their older matrilineal family systems and clan laws, their homelands, and their sacred spaces vanish. The difficult and diverse decisions people reached in response to the often violent circumstances they faced melt away. These aspects of removal cannot be reduced to a multiple-choice answer on an AP U.S. history exam to the question "What caused Cherokee Removal": (c) the discovery of gold on Cherokee lands in Georgia in 1829.

In this simplistic explanatory narrative we never meet the Cherokee woman and her three children murdered by her husband and their father in 1817. The event took place after Cherokee leaders and U.S. officials signed a treaty in 1817 that gave Cherokee people the option to move west of the Mississippi voluntarily. The man wanted to go, his wife wanted to stay. After killing his family, he put them in a cellar and departed.

We never meet Margaret Morgan, the granddaughter of Cherokee parents Nonnie and George Lowry. In contrast to the outcome of the Treaty of 1817, which cost one Cherokee woman and her three children their lives, the Treaty of 1819 included provisions that enabled Margaret Morgan to remain in what is today east Tennessee. This treaty not only contained provisions to move the border of the Cherokee Nation from the north side of the Hiwassee River to the south side where Charleston, Tennessee, sits today; it also enabled Margaret Morgan to claim 640 acres of ceded Cherokee communal lands as her own property. Her marriage to Gideon Morgan, an elite Tennessee resident, and her own political and economic acumen enabled her to navigate the Long Removal Era without the economic, political, and family losses suffered by the vast majority of her female Cherokee compatriots. Margaret Morgan remained in east Tennessee until 1845, when she left her husband and moved to Indian Territory on her own.[1]

We never meet Poor Bear. Poor Bear faced forced removal westward in 1838. When he arrived in Indian Territory, he filed a claim for his losses in the east. It included a chain and a bear hide. When compared with other people's claims, these two items stand out. In his explanation for the losses,

Poor Bear explained that he had a pet bear, but that a soldier had shot and killed the bear. Poor Bear itemized the material losses, but what losses couldn't be itemized?

And we never meet Young Pig, who lived just south of Charleston in Chatata until 1833. In October of that year, shortly after the Supreme Court's *Worcester v. Georgia* decision and two years before Major Ridge and Elias Boudinot signed the unlawful removal treaty, Young Pig registered with the U.S. agent to the Cherokees to voluntarily move west to Indian Territory. His family included one woman and two female children under the age of ten. Young Pig, later known as Pig Smith, would serve the Cherokee National Council in the years following the Civil War. He also raised a son named Redbird Smith, who became a leader of the Nighthawk Keetoowahs, who peacefully resisted allotment of Cherokee lands before Oklahoma statehood. Redbird faced arrest for his resistance. Young Pig was my great-great-great grandfather and Redbird Smith my great-great grandfather.

Charleston, Tennessee, was not simply Gen. Winfield Scott's headquarters and the central location where U.S. officials incarcerated Cherokee people in stockades before their forced march westward to Indian Territory— although it was that. It was also the site of shifting borders and diverse strategies by Cherokee people to adapt to or resist life with Anglo American neighbors, policies, and intrusions. It was the region my family chose to depart rather than face growing violence, second-class citizenship, and degradation at the hands of emboldened Jacksonian settlers. What acts of intellectual repatriation does learning about removal require? Is it about the discovery of gold? The calculated decisions of elite politicians? Is it the land or the lives of the people who lived on those lands? I know my answer.

REMEMBERED

Prayer for the Ancestors, Rockaway Beach, Queens, New York, 2010

By some estimates, upwards of twelve million Africans were kidnapped and forced onto ships headed to the New World to be sold as slaves. Millions died on the journey. Every September, parishioners from St. Paul's Community Baptist Church in East New York, Brooklyn, remember this holocaust by offering a prayer to their ancestors who died on these slave ships crossing the Atlantic Ocean. Hundreds of worshippers, wearing white, attend a dawn ceremony at the western edge of the Atlantic Ocean in Rockaway Beach, Queens.

Reading of the Emancipation Proclamation, Galveston, Texas, 2010

With the Emancipation Proclamation, President Abraham Lincoln declared slaves in the rebellious Confederate States to be free as of January 1, 1863. This had little effect for the vast majority of America's slaves, who still lived under Confederate control. In the state of Texas, nearly 200,000 enslaved African Americans had to wait until June 19, 1865, for the enforcement of their liberation, when Union Maj. Gen. Gordon Granger finally read the Proclamation from the balcony of a Galveston mansion. By combining the words "June" and "Nineteenth," local black families made the event a festive holiday to celebrate their freedom. Today Juneteenth is the oldest known event commemorating the end of slavery in America. As part of the Juneteenth celebrations, the Emancipation Proclamation is still read to local residents every year from the same location in Galveston, Texas.

"Days of 76" Rodeo Parade, Deadwood, Black Hills, South Dakota, 2011

Of all the broken treaties and land grabs conducted by the United States government, perhaps none was as naked as the conquest of the Black Hills in western South Dakota. The sacred hunting grounds of the Lakota Sioux had been explicitly exempted from white settlement by the Fort Laramie Treaty of 1868. Only six years later, the government sent Gen. George Custer to investigate rumors of gold in the area. The discovery of the precious metal in the area's creek beds led to the founding of gold rush towns like Deadwood, in the heart of the Hills, and the termination of Sioux rights to the land in 1877. Subsequent to the U.S. Supreme Court's 1980 declaration of this land confiscation as unconstitutional, the area has remained in legal limbo. At the demand of the settlers nearly a century before, the U.S. Army had forcibly relocated the Sioux to poverty-stricken reservations far to the east in 1889. Tribal descendants continue to consider the Black Hills their sacred land and have refused economic compensation in exchange for giving up their restored legal ownership.

Every summer the residents of Deadwood still celebrate their "frontier" heritage with a cowboy and rodeo parade through the center of town for the thousands of tourists who have come to visit the natural beauty of the Black Hills.

Wounded Knee Massacre, Pine Ridge Reservation, South Dakota, 2011

Two Lakota women from the Pine Ridge Reservation look on as secret service agents guard the perimeter of the Wounded Knee cemetery during a visit by U.S. Attorney General Eric Holder, who laid a wreath at the mass grave where the victims of the 1890 massacre are buried. The slaughter of 250 Lakota "Ghost Dance" revivalists by the U.S. 7th Cavalry Regiment, on the snow-covered prairie of the Pine Ridge Reservation, marked the end of nearly four centuries of violent conquest of America's indigenous people. In 1973 American Indian Movement activists occupied this symbolic spot for seventy-one days in a "Red Power" protest action that ended in a deadly shootout with the FBI. Today, Pine Ridge remains one of the most impoverished communities in America.

150th Anniversary of John Brown's Raid, Charles Town, West Virginia, 2009

In October 1859, militant abolitionist John Brown led a band of twenty-one followers on a raid of the Harper's Ferry arsenal in western Virginia. Brown intended to arm hundreds of slaves, spark a slave uprising across the South, and bring slavery to an end in a violent cataclysmic revolt. The U.S. military, led by Robert E. Lee, quickly suppressed the raid, and brought Brown to trial in nearby Charles Town. Brown's short-lived rebellion became a potent symbol of the African American struggle for liberty. On the 150th anniversary of the Harper's Ferry Raid, the Jefferson County, West Virginia, NAACP honored the memory of John Brown and the descendants of his fellow abolitionists in a procession from the jailhouse to the site of the gallows, where he was hung for treason.

Black Seminole Scouts Association Reunion, Brackettville, Texas, 2014

Every year in the border town of Brackettville, descendants of the Black Seminole Scouts hold a barbecue reunion in memory of their ancestors. The story of the Black Seminoles is the story of an epic American journey. During the eighteenth and nineteenth centuries, slaves from the plantations of South Carolina and Georgia escaped into the wilds of Spanish Florida and joined the Seminole Indian tribe, becoming full tribal members and valued warriors. This migration posed a major threat to North American slave owners, and the United States prosecuted two wars to conquer the Seminole Territory. Like most of the other southeastern Indian tribes, the Seminoles were finally forced into a brutal trek to Oklahoma in the 1840s, where arid land had been set aside for them. Once there, however, whites raided the reservation to kidnap darker skinned former slaves, and sell them back into slavery. Under the leadership of Black Seminole warrior John Horse, many fled to Mexico, where the Mexican government provided them with land and refuge. After the Civil War, some of the Black Seminole returned to the United States when they were offered jobs as cavalry scouts along the Texas border. From South Carolina to Florida to Oklahoma, to Mexico and back to Texas, these men and women fought and survived across the expanding frontier, redefining what it meant to be African, Indian, and American.

Centenary of the Lynching of Jesse Washington, City Hall, Waco, Texas, 2016

In 1916, a black teenager, Jesse Washington, was accused of murdering a local white farmer's wife. A mob broke into the McLennan County courthouse at the conclusion of Washington's trial—he was found guilty—and marched him to Waco's central square in front of City Hall. There, a crowd of fifteen thousand citizens, including city officials and children, helped to torture and burn him. No members of the vigilante posse or the mob were charged with a crime. Washington's murder remains one of the more infamous spectacle lynchings in America, in part because a local professional photographer documented the entire event from the balcony of the mayor's office, and sold the images as "souvenir" postcards.

Exactly one hundred years later, on May 15, 2016, the mayor of Waco officially apologized to some of Washington's descendants at a ceremony held at a community center. After the ceremony, the family came to visit the scene of the crime. In 2016 the local NAACP filed with the Texas Historical Commission to erect an historical marker on the site. Their application was approved.

Carlisle Indian School Cemetery, United States Army War College, Carlisle, Pennsylvania, 2010

U.S. Cavalry Officer Capt. Richard Pratt first attempted to transform Indians into "white men" through military discipline at Fort Marion in Florida, where as commander of the fort in 1875 he witnessed the horrible effects imprisonment had on his captives. The reform-minded Pratt convinced the War Department to allow him to open a boarding school in Pennsylvania for the children of the recently defeated Native American tribes of the western territories. School policies forced students to abandon their languages, dress in military uniforms, and learn the ways of white society. While the "before and after" photographs that Pratt arranged to have taken at the Carlisle Indian School remain harrowing documents of cultural genocide, these were viewed at the time as illustrative of reform measures designed to assimilate and protect indigenous people—in Pratt's words, to "kill the Indian, and save the man." Unfortunately, though, large numbers of the boarders at Carlisle died from infectious diseases. One hundred eighty lie in a cemetery that remains on the campus of what is now the Army War College, where visiting descendants of the plains tribes leave small mementos by the headstones. Thirty-nine years after its founding, the Carlisle Indian School closed in 1918. In a new era of mythmaking about the recent settlement of the West, the fully assimilated graduates of the school seemed to diminish the virtue of the conquerors.

Manzanar War Relocation Center, Independence, California, 2012

The National Park Service has restored a small section of the Manzanar Japanese internment camp in Owens Valley, California. Every year Japanese Americans organize a pilgrimage to the camp for victims and their families to remember President Roosevelt's wartime Executive Order 9066, which in early 1942 set the stage for the imprisonment of over 110,000 people of Japanese descent, two-thirds of them American citizens. Eleven thousand internees were forced to call the remote camp at Manzanar home. Aiko Morimoto, eighty-three, who lived in the Topaz camp in Utah as a young girl, sits on a cot in a cabin designed to recreate the barracks at Manzanar. "It is good they have built this," she said. "But it is not the same. The dust, the bugs, the heat . . . no one would come visit if it were really the same."

Upper Big Branch Mine Memorial, Whitesville, West Virginia, 2015

Under the leadership of its anti-union CEO, Don Blankenship, Massey Energy operated its West Virginia coal mines more like a criminal enterprise than a federally regulated industrial company. In the drive for profits, and in a relentless effort to extract as much coal from the ground as quickly as possible, Massey routinely flouted environmental and safety regulations. It was only a matter of time before the state would experience another coal mine disaster.

That day came on April 5, 2010, in the heart of West Virginia's Coal River Valley, when Massey's Upper Big Branch Mine, outside of Whitesville, exploded, killing twenty-nine miners. With money provided by the coal operators, a formal memorial was built for the miners in the town of Whitesville. The memorial includes an overview of the history of mining in the region from a company perspective. But for the miners and their community, the real memorial remains an informal one, up on the hill outside of town, by the now closed entrance to the Upper Big Branch Mine. There, local residents and family members of the miners have left flowers and other mementos to honor the dead, victims of an industry that over the years has cost so many miners their health and their lives.

In 2016, almost exactly six years after the Upper Big Branch explosion, Blankenship was convicted in federal court of conspiring to evade federal mine safety laws and sentenced to a year in prison.

The Last Resident of Pigeonroost Hollow, Blair Mountain, Logan County, West Virginia, 2010

In 1921 thousands of armed union coal miners marched into West Virginia's Logan County to help striking miners who were being attacked by company gunmen. On Blair Mountain, sheriff's deputies, armed guards, and soldiers halted the march. The ensuing battle lasted for five days, and the miners left defeated after airplanes bombed their trenches and federal troops arrived to suppress the rebellion. For many years the State of West Virginia, under pressure from the coal industry, refused to list Blair Mountain as an historical site, until recently ordered to do so by a federal court.

James Weekley was the last resident of Pigeonroost Hollow, on Blair Mountain. A former coal miner, he refused to sell his land to coal mining companies, which sought to mine the forested mountain. Instead, he opened his door to journalists and environmental activists documenting the mining destruction occurring on the historical site of the Battle of Blair Mountain. Despite harassment and threats from many of his neighbors, who felt Weekley's activism had cost the impoverished area much-needed new jobs, he refused to sell his land until the bitter end. He died in 2014.

Bloody Sunday Anniversary, Edmund Pettus Bridge, Selma, Alabama, 2013

In March 1965, national television footage of civil rights marchers being attacked by state troopers as they crossed over the Alabama River on the Edmund Pettus Bridge in Selma proved a defining moment in the civil rights era. In response to the violent assault on a peaceful protest by state and local authorities, President Lyndon Johnson moved forward with the 1965 Voting Rights Act, which used federal power to protect black voters in the Southern states from disfranchisement and violence. Every year, local marchers, national politicians, and civil rights activists from around the country commemorate the anniversary of the march, still known as "Bloody Sunday," by walking over the bridge again. Civil rights tourism brings a much-needed boost to the economically depressed Selma area.

Confederate Heritage Rally, Montgomery, Alabama, 2011

To celebrate the 150th anniversary of the inauguration of the president of the Confederacy, Jefferson Davis, the Sons of Confederate Veterans hold a rally in downtown Montgomery, the first capital of the Confederate States of America. At the rally speakers declared Davis "the last true President of the free Republic" and vehemently denied that the Civil War had anything to do with defending slavery.

Rosa Parks and the Bus Boycott, Montgomery, Alabama, 2011

Confederate Civil War reenactors join in the commemorative events in Montgomery on the 150th anniversary of Jefferson Davis's inauguration. Perhaps by coincidence, these three women waiting for the rally to begin sit on the very bench where civil rights activist Rosa Parks boarded the city bus she was arrested on in 1955. The arrest of Mrs. Parks touched off the year-long Montgomery Bus Boycott, resulting in the desegregation of the city's buses.

Remembering Victims of the Triangle Shirtwaist Fire, New York City, New York, 2010

On March 25, 1911, the Triangle Shirtwaist Factory in New York City caught fire. One hundred forty-six garment workers trapped on the upper floors of the building died, many of them leaping to their deaths to the pavement below. The stairway and exit doors had been locked to keep the mostly young, underpaid Jewish and Italian women workers on their sewing machines without a break. Every year, on the anniversary of the fire, a small group of volunteers chalks the names of the victims on city sidewalks in front of the Lower East Side addresses where the women had lived.

Assassination of Martin Luther King Jr., National Civil Rights Museum, Lorraine Motel, Memphis, Tennessee, 2012

On April 4, 1968, Martin Luther King Jr. was assassinated by white supremacist James Earl Ray while standing on the balcony outside his room at the Lorraine Motel in Memphis. King had come to Memphis to support striking black sanitation workers, who worked under dangerous and degrading conditions for extraordinarily low pay. The segregation-era Lorraine has been preserved, and is now the National Civil Rights Museum. Every year on the anniversary of King's murder, a memorial ceremony is held at the museum, and every year the Reverend Jesse Jackson, who was with King the day he died, attends the event. In this photograph Jackson embraces Elmore Nickleberry, one of the original striking sanitation workers, after attending the brief ceremony in King's memory.

Dakota Riders Return to Mankato, Minnesota, 2012

On the morning after Christmas, Dakota Sioux riders enter the town of Mankato, Minnesota, to mark the 150th anniversary of the execution of thirty-eight warriors who were hanged by the U.S. government in the center of town in 1862. The hanging, which remains America's largest mass execution, ended a rebellion by the Dakota, who fought against starvation after the government's promised winter provisions never arrived on their reservations. Minnesota settlers were so disturbed by the uprising that in 1863 the U.S. Congress passed a law permanently expelling all Sioux from the state.

PRAYER FOR THE ANCESTORS

Clarence Taylor

For four centuries, from 1500 to 1900, an estimated 10 to 15 million Africans were kidnapped and brought onto ships bound for Europe and the Americas, where they became victims of one of the worst crimes in history—the so-called "Middle Passage." Those Africans and millions of their descendants were forced into human bondage. While on the slave ships, they were chained and forced into cramped quarters; the area on the ships where Africans were placed was so crowded they had to sleep shoulder to shoulder. The quarters provided for the slaves were unbearably hot, unsanitary, disease infested, and overcrowded. This grueling and inhuman voyage from Africa to the West Indies and the Americas took seven weeks. During that long voyage many captives contracted smallpox, measles, dysentery, scurvy, and other diseases. Historians point out that conditions were so horrendous on the slave vessels that perhaps up to 25 percent of the Africans on board died. It is estimated that at least two million perished during the Middle Passage. It is said that sharks learned to follow the ship routes to feed on the carcasses of those thrown overboard.

Even though the countries that participated and profited from the slave trade have only rarely officially acknowledged their complicity in one of the most savage events in human history, people of African origins in the United State and elsewhere have long commemorated the victims of the Middle Passage. The parishioners of St. Paul Community Baptist Church in East New York, Brooklyn, are a case in point. Thanks to Andrew Lichtenstein's wonderful photo of two members of St. Paul Community Baptist Church conducting a prayer to commemorate those who perished during the Middle Passage, we can gain insight into why remembering the Middle Passage is vital.

When looking at Lichtenstein's photo, I immediately notice the rushing white water drawing closer to the feet of the parishioners. The water recaptures for me the rough seas that kidnapped Africans experienced during the Middle Passage. The two participants in the commemoration for their ancestors are dressed all in white, symbolizing the innocence and righteousness of the slaves who were captured and forced onto slave ships. The worshippers' all-white garments emphasize the humanity of those forced into bondage as well as those murdered during the cruel journey. The participants in the prayer have taken an episode of the black experience where white captors reduced black people to less than human and have reclaimed the humanity of their ancestors. By wearing white and standing in water, they lay claim to their closeness to God and also recognize the sea as a burial ground for the unknown millions who died on the slave ships and were thrown overboard.

What is also quite noticeable about the photo is that the two black parishioners face each other while gently holding hands. One does not see their faces in the photo or know their sex. One can imagine their heads are bowed while they pray for those who faced the horrors of the Middle Passage.

By standing in the water, the two people in the photo perform a paradigmatic act similar to Holy Communion. During Holy Communion, Christians eat bread that symbolizes the body of Jesus and drink wine that symbolizes his blood. The major purpose of Holy Communion is to reenact the Crucifixion so Christians can imagine the experience of Jesus's death. Like those taking part in Communion who imagine the ordeal of the Crucifixion, the major purpose of parishioners commemorating the Middle Passage is to imagine the plight of their ancestors who were forced on this horrendous journey. Even though (as far as we know) no slave ships docked at Rockaway Beach, by reliving the Middle Passage the parishioners of St. Paul Community Baptist Church have made that spot in Rockaway a sacred space. Even though we are more than two hundred years removed from the slave trade, the parishioners' reenactment of the Middle Passage made the time of their commemoration sacred time.

Those taking part in this annual commemoration also remind black people in the United States that they are part of the diaspora, where millions of their ancestors were kidnapped and brought to Europe, the Americas, the Middle East, and elsewhere and forced into slavery. They insist to those who were responsible for the Middle Passage and slavery and who refuse to recognize their complicity that the descendants of kidnapped and enslaved Africans refuse to forget this crime against humanity. The commemoration tells black people that they are obligated to remind the world of what took place and what is still taking place to black people.

The commemoration directly rebuts those who argue that slavery was a long time ago and that black people need to get over it. The remembrance defies those who insist that blacks should stop claiming victimization and advance in society like others who faced hardships. The parishioners of St. Paul Community Baptist Church rightfully claim that the crime of the Middle Passage not only had an adverse impact on the captured Africans, their families, and the continent, but it also has traumatized the millions of their descendants. The commemoration recognizes that some of the social and economic ills that black people continue to face have their origins in slavery.

The photo suggests that the parishioners treated the commemoration as a solemn moment and reminds people that we should never forget the Middle Passage and those who died. Instead we should mourn for our ancestors because they experienced one of the most horrible crimes in world history. For many people of African origin, the Atlantic slave trade stands as their "Holocaust." Praying for the victims of the Middle Passage is more than a religious act. It is also a form of resistance to how black people have been treated throughout their experience in America. Every year, this event drives home the message to those who refuse to officially recognize the crime of the Middle Passage that "Black Lives Matter."

MANZANAR

Gary Y. Okihiro

Spaces are unmarked; places are marked spaces. All life forms inhabit and thereby register spaces. Humans are unexceptional in that regard. The creation of space requires time; time is a feature of space. All life forms are susceptible to the imperatives of space/time. Humans are undistinguished in that regard. Of places and times, topographies emerge and move, locating the whimsical subject-self in an equally indeterminate time/space.

There are places I remember, not from the imagined present to the conjured past but from all spaces and times, which are borderless. There are no divides, no prophecy, no history. I, as place and time, embody continuities, kinships. Desolate deserts, abandoned ruins signal terminations, but they also comprise building blocks for new beginnings. Barren barracks echo with the sounds of silence, while the bare walls and floors record and resound with the voices of their inhabitants. Emptiness is never the sole option; circles never end.

Possibilities and contradictions abound. We bury our dead, even as we resurrect them in our memories. We commemorate events, even as we admit to their arbitrary natures. We memorialize particular sites, even as we neglect other places. Never forget, we hold, even as we believe the past never repeats itself. How then can the past confer meaning to our present and guide our future?

I once made a pilgrimage to Manzanar, the concentration camp that confined my ancestors. Treading upon that hallowed ground, I could make out the concrete slabs that configured the flimsy barracks that rattled in fierce winds and freely admitted sand and dust, I found a garbage heap of broken china and rusted forks and spoons, and I located the barbed wire fence that ringed and restrained its keep. Cattle trucks hauled the people, tagged with numbers not names, to deposit them into animal stalls that reeked of manure in racetracks and county fairgrounds. Humanity was only hinted at in this demonstration of democracy.

Manzanar, a scar on the splendor of California's high desert, faced the Sierra Nevada, that magnificent range of mountains that comprises a portion of the chain of tectonic plate uplifts from Tierra del Fuego at America's southern extremity to the Aleutian islands at the continent's northern reach. Confinement was impossible in that unbounded world. I discovered a tree growing in that arid land. I knew it to be a cherry tree from its delicate, pink blossoms. Someone must have planted this tree, I knew. Someone must have defied the state's attempt to deny the people a future, I thought, because planting a tree requires faith in a future. And at the camp's westernmost edge, caressing the snowcapped mountains, I found the graveyard marked by an obelisk inscribed in Japanese characters, "Soul Consoling Tower," for the living and dead. Humanity saturated this forgotten place.

I recall associations to temper disengagements because even antipodes form unions.

Indian country was the place for concentration camps for Japanese. Dillon S. Myer, the self-proclaimed "Great White Father," was charged with the War Relocation Authority that administered the camps and then the Bureau of Indian Affairs that managed the reservations. The bureaucrat instituted assimilation for Japanese and for Indians, termination, which sought to eradicate Indian nations, thereby seeking the extermination of both as peoples. At times, the U.S. nation-state classified both Indians and Japanese as "aliens" not of the "citizen race." Alienations comprise our common ground on native soil.

Pilgrimages can express devotions. Sweet-smelling incense, cooling water, and gifts of food bridge and thereby cross the imaginary divide between the living and dead, animate and inanimate bodies, indeed, the assigned distinctions and valuations of race, gender, sexuality, class, and nation. Pilgrimages are purposeful movements over space/time, marking the unmarked, revealing profound connections. Transported, thus, our spirits soar, spiraling in circles that link heaven with earth. At the intersections of language and ideology, consciousness and practice we can conceive and imagine ourselves as human.

LORRAINE MOTEL

Michael K. Honey

The murder of Martin Luther King Jr., the prince of peace, on April 4, 1968, remains stuck in my mind as one of the great traumatic events of my life. Our Oakland University campus in Michigan shut down; black students stopped talking to white students; nearby Detroit, which had one of the worst urban rebellions of the 1960s only one year before, went into crisis again. Across the nation in over one hundred cities, windows were smashed, stores were burned, and people died as the federal government called out more troops to suppress domestic rebellion than at any time since the U.S. Civil War. After an initial outburst of burning and looting in Memphis, some forty thousand people walked wordlessly through the streets on April 8. All you could hear was the shuffle of feet and occasional weeping. They came from all over the nation to mourn and to express solidarity with both King and the striking black sanitation workers he had come to Memphis to support. One young African American woman recalled that at first all she wanted to do was kill a white person, but when Coretta King, Martin's widow, put out a call for nonviolent action, she too fell in line with a silent, stoic tribute. The least she could do, she thought, was to honor his belief in not responding to violence with violence. Paraphrasing Gandhi, King had said, "An eye for an eye and a tooth for a tooth leaves everyone toothless and blind."

On April 16, 1968, less than two weeks after King's murder, some thirteen hundred Memphis sanitation workers won their strike. King's sacrifice to them meant union recognition, a contract, checkoff of union dues from their paychecks—essential to the survival of a poor person's union—and steps toward better pay, safer working conditions, a place to change their clothes and shower, and most importantly, recognition of the idea of dignity they emblazoned on their picket signs: "I *Am* a Man." On every April 4 since then, sanitation workers and community supporters have honored their families, themselves, King, and Local 1733 of the American Federation of State, County, and Municipal Employees (AFSCME) by retracing the peaceful April 8 march.

Yet people have to fight to remember. The city first wanted to tear down the site of King's assassination, but union and civil rights advocates pressured governments, raised money, and turned the Lorraine Motel into the National Civil Rights Museum. King's room 306 became a shrine to his memory, the place where the Poor People's Campaign began its journey to the nation's capital after his death, and the spot at which people still stand and remember the prince of peace. The last time I looked out of King's room in the museum onto the courtyard below, I saw a young white man glance up to the balcony, put his hands over his eyes, and then hang his head to cry. I still cry whenever I am there.

In 2012, Rev. Jesse Jackson, one of King's associates who had stood in the courtyard below King when he was shot through the head, made his annual trek to Memphis. After a brief ceremony of remembrance and rededication, he affectionately hugged Elmore Nicklebury, an elderly man who had gone on strike in 1968. But these many years later, the trauma remained raw. Like many elderly workers who did not have adequate retirement benefits, Nicklebury was still working hard to survive. Draconian budget cuts, mechanization, and layoffs had reduced employment of Memphis sanitation workers by more than half. Republican governors across the country continued their efforts to destroy unions in the public sector, the bulwark of African American union membership in the United States. These workers have seen their voting rights attacked, their benefits eroded, their jobs disappear, and the lion's share of wealth funneled to the top 1 percent of the wealthy. Meanwhile the working poor struggle harder than ever to get access to King's dream of— as he put it in Memphis—"economic equality," in which all people would have good jobs or adequate incomes, decent housing, health care, education, and dignity on the job and in society. Every year on April 4 I wonder: Will we remember not only King, but the many people who died so that we can live free? Will we take up the cause of the working poor? Will we ever be privileged to find that moment to embrace and to feel the joy in the struggle, as experienced by Reverend Jackson and Mr. Nicklebury? With struggle comes hope, with hope comes strength, with strength comes peace. How should we remember Martin Luther King?

MANKATO MEMORIAL RIDE

Stephen Kantrowitz

On a brutally cold morning, the day after Christmas, the riders entered downtown Mankato, Minnesota, the shoes of their horses clattering over blacktop toward the crowd that awaited them on a small patch of grass. Exactly 150 years before, the scene would have been quite different. The riders would have seen a vast assemblage of settlers and soldiers surrounding an enormous gallows. They would have watched as uniformed men led thirty-eight Dakota Indians—a handful of those who had just mounted a fierce rebellion against U.S. settlement of their homeland— to thirty-eight dangling nooses. A moment later, they would have witnessed the largest mass execution in United States history. In the months that followed they would have seen the state's remaining Dakota population, as well as many other Indians, banished to barren western reservations.

That was 1862. Now it was 2012, and they were back: Dakotas on horseback, joined by non-Dakotas who heard the call. Over the past weeks they had ridden east across the wintry plains, their faces set toward Mankato's Reconciliation Park, where the gallows once stood. But they did not come to protest or demand. Instead, they came to forgive, and to heal, and perhaps even to knit fractured memory into a common history.

When the United States was born, the bands that comprised the Dakota people ranged across a vast swath of North America that they called Mni Sota Makoce, "the land where the waters reflect the clouds," most of what is today southern Minnesota as well as much of Wisconsin, Iowa, and South Dakota. At first, the fur trade forged durable ties between Dakotas and non-Dakotas. But in 1805 the United States began its conquest of the Dakota homeland with a transparently fraudulent treaty, signed by a total of two Dakotas, and in the decades to come the government demanded many further cessions. Settlers streamed in, until in the 1850s they became a flood. By the time Minnesota became a state in 1858, the remaining Dakota were confined to a narrow strip of land along the Minnesota River.

In exchange for the fertile hunting and growing land they surrendered, the Dakota were to receive annuity payments. But the treaties assigned pitifully small values to this vast acreage, and the promised payments frequently came late. Decades of deception and dispossession reached a crisis in the second year of the American Civil War, when annuity payments did not arrive. Traders would provide neither food nor credit, and hunger began to wrack Dakota communities. Bonds of trade and marriage had once softened these conflicts; now a trader sneered, "Let them eat grass."

In August 1862 the Dakota went to war. Attacking farms and towns, Dakota warriors killed nearly five hundred settlers, most of them noncombatants, and put thousands more to flight, virtually emptying western Minnesota of white settlers.

Their victory was brief. Within six weeks, state and federal troops crushed the rebellion and imprisoned thousands of Dakotas. Hasty military tribunals sentenced nearly four hundred Dakota men to death. President Lincoln reviewed and commuted most of the death sentences, but the ones he let stand were carried out that December. The thirty-eight were not the last casualties of the Dakota war: 120 more of those originally condemned perished in an internment camp before the survivors received pardons in 1866, and hundreds of Dakota women and children also died under internment that first winter. Still more expired during the forced removals that followed.

This was to be the beginning of a new order in Minnesota. The Dakota, declared Gov. Alexander Ramsey, "must be exterminated or driven forever beyond the borders of the state." His government put bounties on those who remained, offering $25 or more for each Dakota scalp. In the generations that followed, the roots of the conflict were forgotten or ignored, and the U.S.-Dakota War lingered in settlers' memories only as evidence of Indians' essential savagery. By the twentieth century, if non-Indians knew about the conflict at all, they remembered it mainly as several of Laura Ingalls Wilder's characters did in *Little House on the Prairie*—as proof that "the only good Indian was a dead Indian."

But for Dakotas the legacy of conquest never faded. Ensuing generations of U.S. Indian policy chipped away at their lands, outlawed their traditions, and sought to replace their native tongue with English. Traumatized and impoverished, isolated on barren reservations, the Dakota struggled to maintain their sense of themselves as a people.

It was in this struggle that the ride began, when a Dakota man named Jim Miller reached to the past to salve history's wounds. He bore the scars of a childhood in the notorious Indian boarding schools, where Native students were punished for speaking their own languages. He battled with himself, with alcohol, and with the memory of those he killed as a soldier in the Vietnam War. He did not know the history of the U.S.-Dakota War. But one night in a dream he found himself riding east until he reached the banks of a river. There, just before he awoke, he saw his ancestors hanged. Miller's quest to understand this dream led him to learn its history, and to make it real. In December 2008, he led the first ride from South Dakota to Mankato.

It was to be a journey of reconciliation. "We're going to be the first ones to forgive," Miller said. "Forgive everyone everything" emerged among the riders as a motto and a creed. Every two years since 2008, the riders, supporters, and observers have converged on December 26 at the site of the hanging, in what is now called Reconciliation Park.

But reconciliation entails more than forgiveness, especially if it means reconciling Dakota and settler versions of the past. That remains hard work. In 1862, most settlers had occupied Minnesota for a bare handful of years. All they could see was an incomprehensible and murderous uprising. From the governor's office in 2012, Mark Dayton repudiated his predecessor Alexander Ramsey's call for murderous violence. But Dayton described the war through settlers' eyes, as if it began, out of the blue, in August 1862. Seen this way, the land was there for the taking, the settlers' innocence was a given, and the Dakotas' attack was simply murder.

But the Dakotas did not kill for the sake of killing, and a full history of the U.S.-Dakota War must include a longer view: the Dakotas' countless generations of residence before U.S.

settlement; the trail of brazen and broken treaties that cleared a path for conquest; and the retribution and banishment that followed their rebellion in 1862.

That longer view is faintly perceptible from Reconciliation Park. When Mankato Mayor John Brady welcomed the first riders in 2008, his proclamation noted the Dakotas' loss of land and their forcible relocations as precursors to the war of 1862. The new monument in the park similarly looks the pain of that history in the face: it is a plaque made to look like buckskin, the names of the thirty-eight hanged men inscribed upon it.

It's a start. But if reconciliation is to go deeper than wishful expression, it must confront history's unpaid debts. The Dakota have already been forced to give up so much—land, language, a way of life. Perhaps reconciliation means that non-Dakotas must give something up as well.

That something may be the heroic story of manifest destiny and its sturdy pioneers, the bounty of Mni Sota Makoce theirs for the taking. It may be the silent assumption that settlers' lives and aspirations were more precious than those of the people their settlement dispossessed. Or perhaps the thing that must be forsworn is the victors' privilege of forgetting— the belief that as long as one is ignorant of the past, one is also innocent.

Memorial for Mike Brown, Ferguson, Missouri, 2014

ACKNOWLEDGMENTS

There are so many people to thank for their generous support with this project over the last seven years. I would have to begin with all the old friends, new ones, acquaintances, and strangers alike, who offered me a couch in my travels across America. This work would never have been more than an idea without Sara Terry and the Aftermath Project. A grant from Leica Cameras allowed me to explore the high plains in search of Crazy Horse's burial site; Molly Roberts and *Smithsonian Magazine* helped to fund a trip along the Combahee River; while Stokes Young at MSNBC provided crucial support when the creditors were calling. A personal grant from Yunghi Kim made it possible to explore the haunting legacy of lynching. Fran Sterling, Leah Bendavid-Val, Cara Sutherland, Lucian Perkins, Sue Johnson, Stephen Kantrowitz, and Jamie Wellford all believed in the project when there was very little to show for it, and their support carried me through some hard times. My brother Alex's vital bridge to academia, Regina Monfort's incredible editing and sequencing skills, and Gareth Smit's patience with my luddite tendencies on the scanner all played vital roles in bringing this work to completion. Justin King and LTI Lightside processed all the film I never found the time to get to. Support from Indiana University's Center for Documentary Research and Practice allowed me to present this work in an academic setting, and thus garner support for the project in the lofty precincts of the ivory tower; a Grant-in-Aid from the Indiana University Office of the Vice-Provost for Research, secured by my brother, helped defray some of the costs of production. To all the local people on the back roads across America who pointed me in the right direction and helped me find what I was looking for, thank you. Finally, to Linda, Adrian, and Jade, who accepted my extended absences as a fact of life, this work, like all things, could not have been done without you.

NOTES

FOREWORD

1. Robert A. Orsi, *History and Presence* (Cambridge, Mass.: Harvard University Press, 2016), 251, 29; Patricia Limerick, *Something in the Soil: Legacies and Reckonings in the New West* (New York: W. W. Norton & Company, 200), 33.

2. Judith Richardson, *Possessions: The History and Uses of Haunting in the Hudson Valley* (Cambridge, Mass.: Harvard University Press, 2003), 3.

3. For more on the significance of the store, see Edward T. Linenthal, "Epilogue: Reflections," in *Slavery and Public History: The Tough Stuff of American Memory*, ed. James Oliver Horton and Lois E. Horton (New York: The New Press, 2006), 221–23.

INTRODUCTION

1. Erika Doss, *Memorial Mania: Public Feelings in America* (Chicago: University of Chicago Press, 2010); David Lowenthal, *The Heritage Crusade and the Spoils of History* (New York: Free Press, 1997).

2. Jacqueline Trescott, "Descendants of Nat Turner's Family Donate Bible to Museum," *Washington Post*, February 16, 2012, http://americanhistory.si.edu/changing-america-emancipation-proclamation-1863-and-march-washington-1963/1863/resistance.

3. David Glassberg, *A Sense of History: The Place of the Past in American Life* (Amherst, Mass.: University of Massachusetts Press, 2001), 18–21.

4. Chip Colwell-Chanthaphonh, *Massacre at Camp Grant: Forgetting and Remembering Apache History* (Tucson: University of Arizona Press, 2007), 5.

5. Leah Bendavid-Val, *Facing Change: Documenting America* (New York: Prestel, 2015); Andrew Lichtenstein, "The Aftermath Project: American Memory," http://theaftermathproject.org/.

6. "Unresolved History," in "The Photographer Discloses," October 29, 2013, https://thephotographerdiscloses.com/2013/10/.

7. Kenneth Foote, *Shadowed Ground: America's Landscapes of Violence and Tragedy* (Austin, Texas: University of Texas Press, 1997), 7, 33.

8. Cedric Nunn, *Unsettled: The 100 Year War of Resistance by Xhosa against Boer and British* (Brooklyn: Archipelago Books, 2015), ix.

9. Kate Brown, *Dispatches from Dystopia: Histories of Places Not Yet Forgotten* (Chicago: University of Chicago Press, 2015), 5–6.

10. Colwell-Chanthaphonh, *Massacre at Camp Grant*, 8, 41, 46; Ari Kelman, *A Misplaced Massacre: Struggling Over the Memory of Sand Creek* (Cambridge, Mass.: Harvard University Press, 2013)

11. Marita Sturken, *Tourists of History. Memory, Kitsch, and Consumerism from Oklahoma City to Ground Zero* (Durham, N.C.: Duke University Press, 2007), 4, 7.

12. "Unresolved History."

13. For the first view, see Robert Harriman and John Lucaites, *No Caption Needed: Iconic Photographs, Public Culture, and Liberal Democracy* (Chicago: University of Chicago Press, 2007), 10–18; Sturken is more inclined to the latter view, emphasizing commodification.

14. "Unresolved History."

15. Foote, *Shadowed Ground*, 294. On shame, see Doss, *Memorial Mania*, chap. 5.

16. Brown, *Dispatches from Dystopia*, 37, describes the "reverse archive" found in a Seattle hotel basement, a one-time repository for the belongings of interned Japanese Americans.

17. John Bodnar, *Remaking America: Public Memory, Commemoration, and Patriotism in the Twentieth Century* (Princeton: Princeton University Press, 1992), 15, 19–20; Glassberg, *A Sense of History*, 12–13.

18. Glassberg, *Sense of History*, 207–8.

19. Foote, *Shadowed Ground*, 214–15, is also attentive to the protean nature of memorial landscapes.

20. Brown, *Dispatches from Dystopia*, 35.

21. Lichtenstein, "The Aftermath Project: American Memory."

MAROON FORT

1. On population size, see Nathaniel Millett, *The Maroons of Prospect Bluff and Their Quest for Freedom in the Atlantic World* (Gainesville: University Press of Florida, 2013), 142–46. Millett's book is the most comprehensive study of the Maroon Fort.

2. Proclamation of Alexander Cochrane, April 2, 1814, Papers of Vincente Sebastian Pintado, reel 3, P. K. Yonge Library of Florida History, University of Florida, Gainesville.

3. Talk of Josiah Francis and Peter McQueen to Alexander Cochrane, September 1, 1814, Joseph Byrne Lockey Collection of Documents Related to the History of Florida, box 21, P. K. Yonge Library.

4. Claudio Saunt, *A New Order of Things: Power, Property, and the Transformation of the Creek Indians, 1733–1816* (New York: Cambridge University Press, 1999), chaps. 11–12; Brent Richards Weisman, *Unconquered People: Florida's Seminole and Miccosukee Indians* (Gainesville: University Press of Florida, 1999), 48.

5. Jane Landers, *Black Society in Spanish Florida* (Urbana: University of Illinois Press, 1999).

6. Christina Snyder, *Slavery in Indian Country: The Changing Face of Captivity in Early America* (Cambridge, Mass.: Harvard University Press, 2010), chap. 8.

CHEVY IN THE HOLE

1. Gerry Godin posting, February 11, 2012, "Flint Expatriates: A Blog for the Long-Lost Residents of the Vehicle City," http://www.flintexpats.com/2012/02/chevy-in-hole.html.

THE ROUGE

1. Mary Nolan, *Visions of Modernity: American Business and the Modernization of Germany* (New York: Oxford University Press, 1994), 37, quoting the German engineer Franz Westermann.

TRAIL OF TEARS

1. I owe a debt of gratitude to all of the students enrolled in my Fall 2015 "Cherokee History" course. Students researched individuals living in the area around Charleston, Tennessee, during the Long Removal Era. For the biographical information on Margaret Morgan, I am citing one of the papers that emerged from the course. Eric Schweickart, "The Walker Women: The Biography of a Family on the Early 19th Century Cherokee-American Frontier" ("Cherokee History," Fall 2015, University of Tennessee, 2015).

CONTRIBUTORS

Kevin Boyle teaches history at Northwestern University. His books include *The UAW and the Heyday of American Liberalism, 1945–1968* and *Arc of Justice: A Saga of Race, Civil Rights, and Murder in the Jazz Age.*

Douglas Egerton teaches at Le Moyne College in Syracuse and has held visiting appointments at Colgate, Cornell, and the University College Dublin. His books include *Thunder at the Gates: The Black Civil War Regiments That Redeemed America* and *The Wars of Reconstruction: The Brief, Violent History of America's Most Progressive Era.*

Scot French is an associate professor of history and director of public history at the University of Central Florida. He is the author of *The Rebellious Slave: Nat Turner in American Memory*, and he has contributed essays on race, slavery, and American memory to several edited volumes.

Michael K. Honey, a Guggenheim fellow, has won numerous awards for his books on Southern labor and civil rights history, including *Going Down Jericho Road: The Memphis Strike, Martin Luther King's Last Campaign.* He teaches at the University of Washington Tacoma as the Haley Professor of Humanities, and formerly was a civil liberties organizer in Memphis and the South.

Stephen Kantrowitz has taught history at the University of Wisconsin–Madison since 1995. He is the author of *Ben Tillman and the Reconstruction of White Supremacy* and *More Than Freedom: Fighting for Black Citizenship in a White Republic, 1829–1889.*

Ari Kelman teaches history at the University of California–Davis. He is the author of *A Misplaced Massacre: Struggling Over the Memory of Sand Creek.*

Alex Lichtenstein is a professor of history at Indiana University, where he serves as editor of the *American Historical Review*. His most recent book, with Rick Halpern, is *Margaret Bourke-White and the Dawn of Apartheid.*

Andrew Lichtenstein is an independent photojournalist based in Brooklyn, New York, a contributor to *Facing Change*, and the author of *Never Coming Home*.

Edward T. Linenthal is professor of history at Indiana University Bloomington. He is most recently the coeditor of *The Landscapes of 9/11: A Photographer's Journey*.

Gary Y. Okihiro is a professor at Columbia University's School of International and Public Affairs. He is the author of *American History Unbound: Asians and Pacific Islanders* and, with Linda Gordon, *Impounded: Dorothea Lange and the Censored Images of Japanese American Internment*.

Julie Reed is a citizen of the Cherokee Nation, author of *Serving the Nation: Cherokee Sovereignty and Social Welfare, 1800–1907*, and an assistant professor of history at the University of Tennessee.

Christina Snyder is the McCabe Greer Professor of History at Pennsylvania State University. Her research explores colonialism, race, and slavery, with a focus on North America from the precontact era through the nineteenth century. She is the author of *Slavery in Indian Country: The Changing Face of Captivity in Early America* and *Great Crossings: Indians, Settlers, and Slaves in the Age of Jackson*.

Clarence Taylor is professor of history at Baruch College and the Graduate Center, CUNY. He is the author of *Reds At the Blackboard: Communism, Civil Rights, and the New York City Teachers Union*.